Veterinary Cooperative Care

Enhancing Animal Health Through Collaboration with Veterinarians, Pet Owners, and Animal Trainers

Compiled by

Pat Miller, CBCC-KA, CPDT-KA
and
Dr. Leslie Sinn, CPDT-KA, DVM, DACVB

Dogwise Publishing

Wenatchee, Washington U.S.A.

Veterinary Cooperative Care
Enhancing Animal Health Through Collaboration with Veterinarians, Pet Owners, and Animal Trainers
Pat Miller, CBCC-KA, CPDT-KA and Dr. Leslie Sinn, CPDT-KA, DVM, DACVB

Dogwise Publishing
A Division of Direct Book Service, Inc.
403 South Mission Street, Wenatchee, Washington 98801
1-509-663-9115, 1-800-776-2665
www.dogwisepublishing.com / info@dogwisepublishing.com
© 2024 Pat Miller and Leslie Sinn

Interior: Lindsay Davisson
Cover design: Erika Austin

Library of Congress Cataloging-in-Publication Data
Names: Miller, Pat, 1951 October 14- compiler. | Sinn, Leslie, 1959- compiler.
Title: Veterinary cooperative care : enhancing animal health through collaboration with veterinarians, pet owners, and animal trainers / compiled by Pat Miller and Leslie Sinn.
Description: Wenatchee, Washington, U.S.A. : Dogwise Publishing, a Division of Direct Book Service, Inc., [2023] | Includes bibliographical references and index. | Summary: "Veterinary cooperative care is a guidebook to the future of animal handling in the veterinary profession. In recent years, "cooperative care" has increasingly become the buzzword in professional animal care circles. So what is cooperative care? It is simply an approach to working with patients using handling methods and protocols that encourage them to be calm, happy, willing participants in their treatment programs rather than having them struggle (sometimes violently) against the forcible restraint techniques often used to get them to submit to necessary procedures. Your patients and human clients will benefit from cooperative care and of course you and your staff will all benefit from a happier relationship with the animals you care for and about every day"-- Provided by publisher.
Identifiers: LCCN 2023000086 (print) | LCCN 2023000087 (ebook) | ISBN 9781617813344 (paperback) | ISBN 9781617813351 (ebook)
Subjects: LCSH: Animal handling. | Cooperative care (Hospital care) | Veterinary medicine.
Classification: LCC SF760.A54 V48 2023 (print) | LCC SF760.A54 (ebook) | DDC 636.08/32--dc23/eng/20230210
LC record available at https://lccn.loc.gov/2023000086
LC ebook record available at https://lccn.loc.gov/2023000087

ISBN: 9781617813344   Printed in the U.S.A.

Table of Contents

More Praise

Cooperative Care is the most important modern veterinary care buzzword. This amazing group of expert authors has captured the importance of recognizing and preventing fear, anxiety and stress, and they provide great examples of body language, facial expression, and communication signals that can help a clinician identify how a pet is feeling. This book offers valuable advice to relieve patient stress throughout their entire experience, from arrival to the clinic, examination and returning home; with tips for future visits and how to create a calm experience during end of life protocols. It is a must-read for every veterinary professional so we can finally standardize the respect and care that our animal family members need.

Amy Learn VND, DACVB, Animal Behavior Wellness Center

If you are a veterinary professional, a behavior consultant/trainer, or a pet parent who wants to ensure pets get the best health care possible, this book is for you! Whether you want to learn how to teach pets to cooperate in their care, how to communicate with them and understand what they are trying to tell us, or how to treat their emotional health, this book has it all.

Amy L. Pike, DVM, DACVB, IAABC-CDBC

What an amazing book! This work is packed full of useful and important information about cooperative care. In addition, it pulls together the sometimes diverse communities of veterinary professionals, animal trainers, and owners in an inclusive way. There's so much we can do to make physical care easier and more comfortable for our companion animals, and this book is a fantastic resource. As someone who cares deeply about the experiences of our animals during both necessary and routine care, I highly recommend this work. This one definitely needs to be in every animal lover's library!

Deborah Jones, Ph.D.

Preface by Pat Miller

You are holding in your hands a guidebook to the future of animal handling in the veterinary profession. In recent years, "cooperative care" has increasingly become the buzzword in professional animal care circles. So what is cooperative care? It is simply an approach to working with patients using handling methods and protocols that encourage them to be calm, happy, willing participants in their treatment programs rather than having them struggle (sometimes violently) against the forcible restraint techniques often used to get them to submit to necessary procedures.

You probably entered the veterinary profession because you care about animals. You may have had childhood visions of loving greetings between you and your furred, feathered and scaled patients as they entered your exam room (or you entered their pastures or enclosures) with wagging tails, happy purrs and chirps, or warm whinnies. Perhaps you have come to realize that all too often the cheerful, wriggly puppy you first met a few years ago now must be muzzled and carried into the waiting room, even for that routine annual well-pet checkup. Despite your laudable efforts to be gentle and friendly with your patients, rather than being their friend, you are perceived by far too many of your patients as a threat to be feared and avoided.

What happened?

Simply this: In a culture that perceived our animal companions as "subjects," veterinary patients were often subjected to a "put up with it or else" approach – standard practice in the industry. Each time that puppy came in for a visit he was poked and prodded (and he stayed that one time to get neutered – that was really scary!), and as a result he formed an increasingly negative association with going to see the doctor. The more he resisted, the more restraint was necessary, and the more things just went from bad to worse with each subsequent visit.

Fortunately, as the dog training and behavior world began a quantum shift toward force-free training methods in the late 1990s, pioneers in the veterinary community began to do the same. The late Dr. Sophia Yin provided a wealth of information for her colleagues, and her book, *Low Stress Handling, Restraint and Behavior Modification of Dogs & Cats - Techniques for Developing Patients Who Love Their Visits,* published in 2009, remains an invaluable resource to this day, as do many of her other works (Yin, 2009). In 2016, Dr. Marty Becker founded The Fear-Free® Initiative – Taking the "Pet" Out of Petrified – and published *From Fearful to Fear Free* in 2017 with Dr. Lisa Radosta (Becker, 2017). Fear-Free now offers certifications for veterinarians, veterinary staff and clinics, trainers, groomers and pet sitters, with more than 64,000 professionals certified to date. Deb Jones, a psychologist who turned dog trainer/behavior professional some 25 years ago, added to our body of knowledge in this arena with the publication in 2018 of her excellent book *Cooperative Care, Seven Steps to Stress-Free Husbandry* (Jones, 2018). Also in 2018, *Cooperative Veterinary Care* was published, written by RVT Alicea Howell and LVT Monique Feyrecilde (Howell and Feyrecilde, 2018).

And now, after a bit of a pause in the release of cooperative care resources, this book which was originally the brainchild of The American Animal Hospital Association (AAHA). I was approached by AAHA staff at a North American Veterinary Conference a few years ago and asked if I would consider being the editor for a very worthwhile project: the compilation of written works by veterinary professionals who were committed to utilizing patient-friendly handing techniques in their practices. My job would be to solicit appropriate authors for the various chapters, facilitate communications with AAHA, compile the material and ensure that we all met the various publishing jobs (a task, I soon came to realize, akin to herding cats...). As I am a dog behavior and training professional, not a veterinarian, we brought Dr. Leslie Sinn on board as co-editor. Dr. Sinn is a highly respected veterinary behaviorist, well-versed in the benefits of cooperative care, and her perspective has been invaluable to this effort.

The rights to the near-completed manuscript were transferred to Dr. Sinn and me when AAHA downsized their publishing department and dropped this project. We were at a bit of a loss as to how to proceed, when our wonderful friends at Dogwise came to our rescue. Their response when we inquired if they might be interested in taking on the project was a resounding "YES!!"

So here you have it – the thoughts and perspectives from more than a dozen highly esteemed veterinarians and animal training professionals who are all committed to seeing that the animals in their care have as positive an experience as humanly possible. Thank you and kudos to you for your interest in cooperative care. Your patients will benefit, your human clients will benefit and of course you and your staff will all benefit from a happier and safer relationship with the animals you care for and about every day.

Introduction
by Dr. Lynn Honeckman, DVM

It has become an essential part of the standard of care for the veterinary professional to understand and respond appropriately to the presence of fear, anxiety, and pain in the veterinary patient. Animals who are stressed or afraid may be more challenging to handle and diagnose, may not respond to treatment plans, and may hurt themselves or those who are trying to help them. A patient's fear can also directly affect the veterinary staff, as those without a thorough understanding of fear and anxiety may be reluctant or unsure how to approach a stressed patient. A patient who exhibits aggression as a result of anxiety may not get the respect and care necessary for diagnosis and treatment. A patient who becomes withdrawn or frozen in a hospital setting may make it difficult to assess clinical signs of pain or discomfort and may also not get the necessary care.

This book will equip the whole practice team with the tools and knowledge to enhance the patient experience during the hospital visit. Clients' role in preparing their pet for the hospital visit will also be thoroughly discussed, including the teaching of cooperative care protocols. Patients who are anxious will have a more positive veterinary experience if they are able to predict what will happen to them. Patients of all species can benefit greatly from learning how to be active participants in their own care. Above all other behavior management techniques, teaching consent can change the course of all future visits.

Behavioral techniques for reducing fear and anxiety will be drawn from evidence-based research and focus on positive reinforcement. The interactions between the humans and the patients in the veterinary setting can establish the tone for the patient's entire experience. When the emotional needs of everyone are met, clients will be more inclined to seek medical care for their pets, and the veterinary team will experience greater job satisfaction and are less likely to experience patient-related injuries such as scratches, lacerations and bites. With a thorough understanding of behavior, all team members will recognize signs of fear and will be empowered to implement protocols designed to reduce stress and anxiety in the veterinary setting in both humans and patients.

Each chapter will offer practical guidance that can be immediately implemented by the entire team. Suggestions will be made throughout the book on how to evaluate potential triggers within the hospital environment. Special attention will be paid to visual and auditory stimuli, as well as olfactory and tactile triggers. Portions of this book will be devoted to the many steps that can be taken to reduce the potential for stress and anxiety due to the sights and sounds of the hospital.

Chapter 3 on adding behavioral expertise to the hospital describes the various pathways a dedicated member of the practice team can travel to attain a level of proficiency in animal behavior. The chapter also describes how to identify and partner with capable, experienced, and qualified force-free behavior consultants in the community who can offer hands-on training and help the veterinary team successfully design and implement a behavior program.

Chapter 11 is devoted to behavior in emergency and critical care contexts and provides tools for minimizing stress for the most urgent cases, which can lead to valuable time saved and improved recovery outcomes for patients. Psychotropic medications and products that can be used in conjunction with a behavioral modification program will also be addressed.

This book will focus primarily on the behavior of dogs and cats but will also include a dedicated chapter (Chapter 12) on exotic companion animals, including rabbits, guinea pigs, ferrets, birds, and ectotherms. The growing popularity and incredible diversity of these animals merit special attention.

The final chapter (Chapter 13) will explore palliative care and the special considerations surrounding euthanasia. Working with clients to reduce fear and stress in their animal companions during their most trying time and ensuring appropriate behavioral protocols are met by the entire veterinary team will be covered in depth.

You may see patients as part of a general practice or a specialty practice, as a member of a critical care team at an emergency clinic, in a shelter setting, or as a member of academia in a university setting. All of these roles require a complete understanding of the patient's needs. The entire veterinary staff must be proficient in handling techniques that can help manage anxiety in the veterinary setting. Everyone needs to be aware that an animal's stress levels will directly affect their response to the situation, and your veterinary team must be capable of solving problems as they arise and making accommodations for particular patients.

The interactions between the humans and the patients in the veterinary hospital can set the tone for the patient's entire experience. When the emotional needs of everyone are met, the client and patient will continue to seek medical care, and the veterinary team will report greater confidence in their ability to offer the highest quality medical services to every patient. With a thorough understanding of behavior, all team members will recognize signs of fear, stress and anxiety and will be empowered to implement protocols designed to reduce anxiety in the veterinary setting. Clients will continue building their relationships with their animal companions and will be more inclined to seek further veterinary care.

Here are a couple of my cases as examples, with our treatment plan described.

Case Example #1
Maxwell: 6-year-old M/N Retriever/Staffordshire mix, 39 lbs

- Rescued along with 65 other dogs from a hoarding case.

- At the hoarder's property, Maxwell was locked in a crate and hidden in the hoarder's shed. There was little to no daylight in the shed and poor ventilation. Initial reports indicated that Maxwell was let outside every couple of days.

- Bite events with handling, especially veterinary or grooming care.

- Behavior assessment revealed visible shaking, withdrawal, head and gaze averted, hyper-vigilance, crouched and cowering body, yawning, lip-licking, and increased respiratory rate throughout a two-hour consultation.

Behavior Diagnosis: Severe global fear of people and new environments.

Treatment Plan
Management: Provide a structured and predictable environment

Behavior modification:

1. DS/CC to entering/exiting the car
2. DS/CC to bathing and nail trims
3. DS/CC to physical examinations and treatments

Medication:

1. Daily SSRI (Sertraline) to decrease fear and facilitate learning
2. Daily adjunctive anti-anxiety medications (clonidine)
3. Event-specific medications for car rides and vet visits

Case Example #2
Bailey: 2-year-old F/S Beagle mix; 45 lbs

- Found as a stray and brought to the shelter; no previous history.

- Initial visits to the veterinary hospital went well, but then Bailey tried to withdraw when the vet and technician entered the room. She became extremely resistant to any restraint and bit the owner when he tried to put a muzzle on her. A blanket was used to cover her head while vaccinations were given, but this only helped minimally as Bailey continued to growl, snap, and try to escape.

Behavior diagnosis: Fear aggression at veterinary visits.

Treatment plan
Management: Worked with family and veterinary team to understand body language and signs of stress

Behavior modification:

1. Begin building a positive relationship with the veterinary staff with fun vet visits and treats starting in the parking lot and building up to the waiting room and exam rooms

2. Offer Bailey options for her veterinary care including staying on the floor rather than picked up onto an exam table, and having blood drawn from a rear leg with lidocaine gel and minimal restraint

3. Counterconditioning to a basket muzzle to help vet and staff feel safer during office visits

4. Teach Bailey to offer body parts for examination and blood draw, in addition to stationing exercises such as a chin rest behavior

Medication:

Event-specific medications given the night before and the morning of veterinary visits

These two dogs and countless other animal patients have been successfully treated in my practice, in large part thanks to using the cooperative care methods described in the following pages. It is our hope that after reading this book, every veterinary team member will feel more comfortable with the behavior issues of their patients. Focusing on the behavior and emotional needs of the patients will touch every other aspect of the veterinary hospital and enable you to achieve the highest possible standard of care. Thank you for caring.

Chapter 1
The Basics of Behavior
by Pat Miller, CBCC-KA, CPDT-KA

Introduction

Welcome to the world of behavior! Unless you are a recent graduate from your courses of study, there's a very good likelihood that you didn't take many (or any!) classes in animal behavior. The good news is that this is changing, as the veterinary profession has come to realize the critical role that an understanding of behavior plays in successful treatment, as well as client and patient satisfaction and comfort. It is our fervent hope and expectation that in the future, veterinarians, technicians and other animal care professionals will graduate with an in-depth understanding of how animals think and learn, and how best to apply that information in their practices.

Meanwhile, it's never too late to learn. This chapter will lay out for you the foundations of classical (respondent) and operant (instrumental) conditioning, as well as some of the recent advances that have been made in the realm of animal cognition. These concepts will inform the chapters that follow, and better enable you to understand and put into practice the information and protocols that will be introduced. We fully anticipate that you will be motivated to make changes as a result, and that you, your clients, your patients, your staff and your practice will all benefit from the modernization of your animal handling practices. You are about to embark on an exciting journey into the future of veterinary care!

Let's start with classical conditioning.

Classical conditioning

Does the name Pavlov ring a bell?

Also referred to as respondent conditioning, the concept of classical conditioning was developed by Ivan Petrovich Pavlov, a Russian physiologist who was born in 1849 and died in 1936. Although most widely known for his work with classical conditioning, much of Pavlov's work focused on digestion – in fact he won a Nobel prize in 1904 in recognition of his work on the physiology of digestion.

His interest in classical conditioning occurred serendipitously to his study of canine digestion and saliva. Food was presented to his laboratory subjects (dogs) in order to induce them to salivate. The saliva was then collected for study. Quite coincidentally, Pavlov observed that his subject dogs were salivating prior to the presentation of food, when they heard the sound of the buzzer that signaled the arrival of the food.

(Contrary to popular folklore, it is currently believed that Pavlov never actually used a bell – the "bell" belief is now attributed to a mistranslation from the Russian documents.) Pavlov went on to formulate and develop the idea of the conditioned reflex, for which he is lauded to this day.

So, what is classical conditioning, and why is it so important? Classical conditioning is defined as: a learning process that occurs when two stimuli are repeatedly paired; a physiological/emotional response which is at first elicited by the second stimulus is eventually elicited by the first stimulus alone. In simpler terms, it is the process of creating associations. It looks like this:

Classical conditioning

Unconditioned Stimulus (US) (i.e.: food) → Unconditioned Response (UR) (salivation)

Neutral Stimulus (NS) (buzzer) → Unconditioned Stimulus (US) (food) → Unconditioned Response (UR) (salivation)

Conditioned Stimulus (CS) (buzzer) → Conditioned Response (CR) (salivation)

Note that the neutral stimulus must occur immediately prior to the unconditioned stimulus in order for the most effective classical conditioning to occur.

This process – and our understanding of it – is important because it is happening all the time, whether we are thinking about it, or executing it deliberately, or not. It explains why the happy puppy who joyfully licks your face on his first visit for a well-puppy check and first vaccinations, is often cowering under a chair and has to be muzzled on the exam table by the time he is two years old (if not sooner). Repeated exposure to fear-or-pain-causing stimuli creates a negative association with the veterinary clinic and everyone/everything associated with it. Here's how it happens:

Creating a negative association

US (restraint/vaccination) → UR (pain/fear)

NS (visit to vet clinic, person in white coat, etc.) → US (restraint/vaccination) → UR (pain/fear)

CS (visit to vet clinic, person in white coat, etc.) → CR (pain/fear)

This happens, not just once, but several times during puppyhood for a puppy's series of vaccinations. The icing on the cake is often the very scary overnight stay for spay/neuter surgery, and the considerable discomfort associated with that procedure.

Classical conditioning also underlies the success of good puppy socialization programs, giving the pup a positive association with new things before he learns to be afraid of them:

Creating a positive association

US (yummy treats) → UR (salivation/yay!)

NS (person, exam table, nail clippers, etc.) → US (yummy treats) → UR (salivation/yay!)

CS (person, exam table, nail clippers, etc.) → CR (salivation/yay!)

A well-socialized puppy has developed a very positive classical association with hundreds of stimuli, and as a result becomes an optimist – he assumes that new things are good unless proven otherwise. He is also more likely to be resilient enough to recover from the inevitable unpleasant incident that occurs from time to time in any dog's life. An under-socialized or unsocialized pup is a pessimist – because he has developed a negative association with new things he assumes, for survival reasons, that new things are bad unless proven otherwise (and it takes a lot to convince him!), and any unpleasant incidents that occur just reaffirm his pessimistic world view.

Counterconditioning and Desensitization

Counterconditioning (also called reverse conditioning) is a subset of classical conditioning. While classical conditioning creates associations with a neutral stimulus, counter conditioning changes already-existing associations with a stimulus. The "desensitization" part refers to starting at a low intensity of stimulus (could be distance, volume, duration, number, amount of pressure, location of touch, amount of movement…), then gradually increasing intensity of stimulus as the animal habituates. You can do desensitization without counterconditioning, but it is generally more effective if you actively work to change the association rather than just waiting for habituation.

We most commonly want to change a negative association to a positive one. We do sometimes want to change a very enthusiastic positive association to a calmer, less positive one, and occasionally perhaps someone may want to change a positive to a negative (such as using taste-aversives with predators to deter sheep or cattle killing, or a shock collar association with snakes for snake aversion training with dogs. (This is not recommended for this or any other training or behavior modification purpose, due to the potential for significant negative behavioral fallout, including but not limited to aggression, and the potential for creating a strong negative association to the wrong stimulus.). For counterconditioning to change a negative response to a positive one, the conditioned stimulus (negative association) is presented first, followed immediately by the unconditioned stimulus (often food, but not always) to change the conditioned response (fear) to a new, happier response. The easiest way to give most dogs a positive association is with very high value (really yummy) treats. I like to use chicken – baked, boiled, or thawed out frozen strips – since most dogs love chicken, it's healthy, and it's a low-fat, low-calorie food. Toys and play can also effectively help to change associations.

Here's an example of how counterconditioning works:

Counterconditioning in action

CS (person in white coat) → CR (fear/growl – from past fear/pain causing experiences at the clinic)

CS (person in white coat) → US (food) → UR (salivation/yay!)

CS (person in white coat) → New CR (salivation/yay!)

It looks pretty simple but of course it takes many repetitions to change an existing CR, especially when trying to change a negative to a positive. It makes sense, for survival reasons, for an organism to cling to a negative response to something that it believes can cause it harm.

In order to do successful counterconditioning, you need to start with the aversive stimulus just below threshold – where the dog, cat or other animal is aware of it but not stressed or reacting. Present the aversive, then feed a high value treat, and remove the stimulus. If, for example, a dog is afraid of nail clippers, you start with clippers in one hand, treats in the other, with both hands behind your back. Show him the clippers at least a couple of feet away from him, pause briefly, feed the treat with clippers still in view, and then treat-hand and clippers go out of sight behind your back again. (If he moves away from the clippers at this distance, you are too close; on the next try present the clippers farther away.) Repeat this without bringing the clippers any closer, until every time you present the clippers, he happily looks toward your other hand in anticipation of the treat. We call this "Yay, where's the treat?" response the CER look (short for Conditioned Emotional Response). In reality, it is the physical manifestation of the CER – we can't actually see the internal emotional change, just the outward expression of it. Now you can present the clippers an inch or two closer to the dog, and continue the process. With nail trimming, it's likely that you will also need to do a separate counter conditioning process for paw touch and paw holding, since many dogs also have a very negative association with that restraint. When the dog has a new, positive association with the clippers and paw touch/restraint separately, then you can combine paw holding and clipper presentation in a third conditioning procedure.

It does take time and patience. I tell my clients "If you think you're going too slow… slow down." Then I add a phrase I've borrowed from trainer/friend Laura Glaser-Harrington of Pets in Motion in Wayne, Pennsylvania, "Think crockpot, not microwave." I like it – and it resonates with clients.

Here's a complete, step-by-step counterconditioning and desensitization process for a dog who is sensitive to paw touching and restraint, and nail clipping:

Step 1. Determine the location of touch your dog can be aware of and handle without reacting fearfully or aggressively. Perhaps it's her shoulder, perhaps her elbow, or maybe her knee. She should be a little worried, but not growl or try to move away. This is just below threshold.

Step 2. With your dog on leash, touch her briefly and gently at just sub-threshold. The instant your dog notices the touch, start feeding bits of chicken, non-stop.

Step 3. After a second or two, remove the touch, and stop feeding chicken.

Step 4. Keep repeating Steps 1 to 3 until touching at that location for 1 to 2 seconds consistently causes your dog to look at you with a happy smile and a "Yay! Where's my chicken?" expression. This is the conditioned emotional response (CER) – your dog's association with the brief touch at that location is now positive instead of negative.

Step 5. Now you need to increase the intensity of the stimulus by increasing the length of time you touch her at that same location, a few seconds at a time, obtaining a new CER at each new time period before increasing the time again. For example, several repetitions at 2 to 4 seconds, until you get consistent "Yay!" looks, then several repetitions at 4 to 8 seconds, then several at 8 to 12 seconds, etc., working for that consistent CER at each new duration of your touch.

Step 6. When you can touch her at that spot for any length of time with her in "Yay" mode, begin to increase the intensity of stimulus again, this time by moving your hand to a new location, 1 to 2 inches lower than your initial threshold. I suggest starting at your initial touch location and sliding your hand to the new spot, rather than just touching the new spot. Continue with repetitions until you get consistent CERs at the new location.

Step 7. Continue gradually working your way down to your dog's paw, an inch or two at a time, getting solid CERs at each spot before you move closer to the paw.

Step 8. When you get below the knee, also add a gentle grasp and a little pressure to the procedure – each separate steps in the CC&D process. Be sure to get the "Yay!" response with touch before you add the grasp, and with grasp, before you add pressure. Continue working down the leg, all the way to the paw.

Step 9. When you can touch, grasp, and put pressure on the paw, add lifting the paw.

Step 10. If your goal is happy nail trimming, start the process over, this time with the nail clipper in your hand. Show her the clippers, feed a treat, until the appearance of the clippers elicits a "Yay!" response. Then do CC&D with the clipper action – squeezing the clippers to make the sound and motion it would make if you were actually clipping nails. Go through the whole touch sequence again, this time with the clippers in your hand, also touching her with the clippers, then again while you squeeze the clippers. Remember that you are still feeding yummy treats and obtaining CERs along the way, throughout the whole process. When you can hold her paw and make the clipper action right next to her nail with a happy response, clip one nail, feed lots of treats, and stop. Do a nail a day until she's happy with that, then advance to two nails at a time, then three, until you can clip all her nails in one setting.

The more complex/intense the stimulus, the more successful the dog's avoidance or aggressive strategies have been, the longer the dog has been practicing the successful strategy and the more intense the response, the more challenging the behavior is likely to be to modify. Whatever the aversive, you can help your client figure out how to break the process down into small enough steps to make the procedure successful.

Using counterconditioning to change a dog's negative association with another dog.

Using counterconditioning to change a dog's negative association for touching/ reaching for a collar.

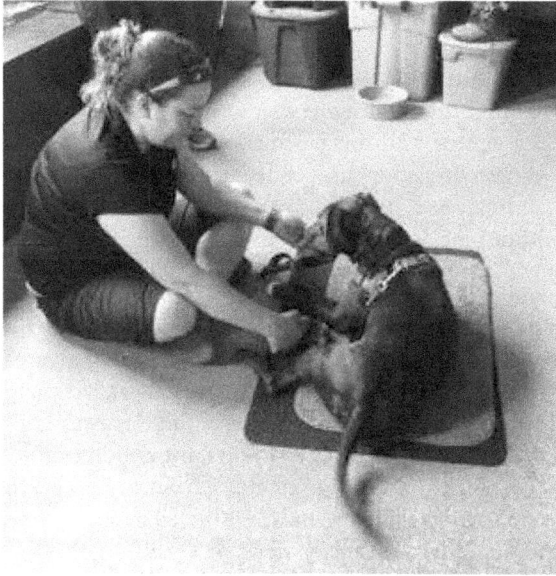

Using counterconditioning to change a dog's negative association with nail clippers to a positive association.

Using counterconditioning and desensitization to help a dog learn to accept paw handling, and eventually nail trimming.

Operant conditioning

Does Skinner push your buttons?

Burrhus Frederic Skinner (no wonder he went by BF!) was an American psychologist, behaviorist, author, inventor, and social philosopher. He lived from 1904 to 1990, and is the behaviorist most commonly associated with operant conditioning – although there are certainly others who have contributed significantly to this body of knowledge (operant conditioning was first extensively studied by Edward L. Thorndike, 1874–1949).

Operant conditioning (also called instrumental conditioning) is a learning process through which the strength of a behavior is increased or decreased by reinforcement or punishment. There are four principles (often called quadrants) of operant conditioning, and they can be confusing because the terms are not used the way the words are used in common language – i.e.: in operant conditioning, "positive" doesn't always mean a good thing, and "negative" doesn't always mean bad. Understanding the definitions of the words can help you keep the four operant principles straight in your head. Here are the individual terms defined:

- **Positive**: Something is added
- **Negative**: Something is taken away
- **Reinforcement**: Behavior increases
- **Punishment**: Behavior decreases

When you combine those terms in their various permutations, you get the four principles of operant conditioning as follows:

The 4 principles of operant conditioning

1. Positive Reinforcement: The subject's behavior causes a good thing to happen (something desirable is added), and as a result the strength of the behavior increases, because we all want good stuff to happen more. Example: The cat goes into her carrier and gets a tasty treat. The behavior of going into the carrier made a good thing (treat!) happen, and the cat is more likely to go into her carrier again, possibly faster. (Note: Positive reinforcement is likely to be the most successful operant principle, is the one most often used in force-free training programs and is the least likely to have negative fallout.)

2. Negative Punishment: The subject's behavior causes a good thing to go away (something desirable is taken away), and as a result the strength of the behavior decreases, because we all want to keep our good stuff! Example: The horse pushes his nose into the trainer's chest to try to get a bit of apple. The trainer turns his back on the horse and steps away. The behavior of mugging the trainer for a treat made the treat go away, and the horse is more likely to wait for the trainer to offer the apple next time. (Note: most force-free training programs also make some use of negative punishment. Negative punishment is considered more effective if it is immediately followed by positive reinforcement for a desirable behavior.)

3. Negative Reinforcement: The subject's behavior causes a bad thing to go away (something is aversive is taken away), and as a result the strength of the behavior increases, because we all want bad stuff to go away. Example: The feral BLM burro tenses and raises her head when the trainer steps into the stall door opening. The trainer stands and waits until the burro finally relaxes and lowers her head, then the trainer steps away from the stall door. The burro's behavior of relaxing made the bad thing (scary trainer) go away, and the burro is more likely to relax sooner the next time. Over time, the trainer can move closer and closer, and eventually interact with the burro. (Note: negative reinforcement can be used successfully and benignly as in the above-described example, if carefully applied. It can also be used very aversively, such as the dog-training forced-retrieve "ear-pinch" in which a dog's ear is pinched painfully over the chain collar until he grabs the dumbbell, at which point the ear is released. The dog learns to grab the dumbbell quickly in order to avoid having his ear hurt. The aversive use of negative reinforcement is not recommended!)

4. Positive Punishment: The subject's behavior causes a bad thing to happen (something is added), and as a result the strength of the behavior decreases, because none of us wants bad stuff to happen. Example: The dog approaches and jumps up on a person, and person knees her in the chest. The dog is less likely to jump up the next time – unless of course the dog thinks a knee in the chest is an invitation to a rousing and fun game of body slam, in which case the dog just got reinforced for the behavior and is now *more* likely to jump up. It is important to remember that the subject (the dog, cat, etc.) decides what is aversive or reinforcing, not the human doing the training or handling. (Note: The knee in the chest method is not recommended! The dog may also become fearful of humans, and may be less likely to approach, or develop other fear-related behaviors. Force-free training programs do not use positive punishment due to the high likelihood of undesirable side effects, including aggression.)

It is important to acknowledge here that force-based/coercive training and handling methods *can* work to suppress behaviors and otherwise intimidate dogs into shutting down and submitting to restraint and handling in the veterinary practice. And there are always undesirable side-effects, even though they may not always be apparent in the moment. These include but are not limited to a negative association (ranging from mild to very strong) with the human delivering the aversive and possibly a generalized negative association to many or all humans, which can manifest as fear and/or aggression.

Operant conditioning in action

- Positive reinforcement can be used to teach a dog to rest his paws on a block so nails are easily accessible and nail trimming can be done without paw restraint. Positive reinforcement can be used to teach a cat to open her mouth and keep it open so you can do a dental exam without restraint.

- Positive reinforcement can be used to teach a miniature horse prone to laminitis to lie down so that her hooves can be trimmed and treated without having to bear weight on three very painful feet while the fourth is lifted.

- Negative reinforcement can be used to teach a fearful pot-bellied pig that calm, relaxed behavior, rather than lunging and charging, makes scary people go away. In learning to offer calm, relaxed behavior the pig eventually becomes calm and relaxed and no longer feels the need to make people go away.

- Negative punishment can be used to teach a softer bite to a mouthy puppy – hard teeth on skin causes treats to be hidden in the closed fist – followed by positive reinforcement for soft mouth – the hand opens and treats are delivered.

The opportunities for the application of operant protocols in your practice and in your patients' lives are virtually endless. Any good, modern, science-based force-free trainer can help you identify many more.

Using operant conditioning to teach a dog to file his front nails.

Using operant conditioning to teach a dog to file her back nails.

The cognitive canine

The idea that dogs and other non-human animals are capable of cognitive thought and action is a relatively new (dare I say revolutionary?) concept in the world of behavior science. As we entered the 21st century, you would have rarely heard "canine" and "cognition" in the same sentence. Today there are canine cognition labs all over the world, and we are also exploring (and being astounded by) the cognitive capabilities of many other species. Notables such as Adam Miklosi (full professor and the head of the Ethology Department at the Eötvös Loránd University in Budapest, Hungary, founder of The Family Dog Project), Brian Hare (professor of evolutionary anthropology at Duke University in Durham, North Carolina, founder and co-director of the Duke Canine Cognition Center and the Dognition project), and Alexandra Horowitz (senior research fellow, adjunct associate professor and head of the Horowitz Dog Cognition Lab at Barnard College, Manhattan, New York), are just a few of the brilliant scholars investigating the cognitive potential of canines and other species.

So – what is cognition? The simple answer is "thinking," but it includes processes such as applying logic, problem solving, grasping concepts, imitation, theory of mind, and more. Of course, the whole evolution of our appreciation of other species' ability to think and feel goes way back.

Early philosophers and scientists asserted that animals didn't feel pain – and of course we know now how very wrong they were. Still, some people are surprised by recent studies that suggest that not only do fish feel pain (of course they do!) but even insects feel pain. Today the use of analgesics is common practice in much of veterinary medicine. It wasn't always so.

Then we were told that only humans, with our special brains, could make and use tools. Once again, we learned we were wrong when Dr. Jane Goodall reported observing chimpanzees making and using tools. We now know that there are species of crows that are notorious for tool construction and usage, and we appreciate that our domesticated animals can be pretty handy at using tools, even if they don't make them. A quick online search on "Animals, Tools" finds multiple intriguing articles and videos about a multitude of various animals that make and use tools, including insects, birds, mammals, and more. So much for our superior brains….

Next, we were warned that if we attributed 'human' emotions to non-human animals we were engaging in (horrors!) – anthropomorphism, defined as "the attribution of human traits, emotions, and intentions to non-human entities." It's now widely accepted that many other animals, including dogs, share essentially the same range of emotions that we do, and in fact that it's pretty arrogant of us to claim them as human emotions. Think about it. Can a dog, a cat, a rabbit, a horse, be happy? Sad? Frightened? Worried? Yes, They can. Those are emotions. Not human emotions – just emotions.

Finally, we were long assured that dogs and other non-human animals were pretty weak in the cognition department. Once again, we now accept that many animals are much deeper thinkers than we have given them credit for in the past. We now see dogs learning through imitation, demonstrating an ability to read and count, exhibiting "theory of mind" behaviors, and performing cognitive tasks such as object, shape and color discrimination (within their somewhat limited ability to see color), match-to-sample, and more.

So, what does all this mean for the veterinary profession? The knowledge gained and shared by canine cognition researchers has inspired forward-thinking dog training and behavior professionals to introduce new and interesting activities in their dog training programs. These, in turn, can be utilized in your cooperative care programs.

One example of applying cognition concepts in your practice involves giving your patients choices. Dr. Susan Friedman is a psychology professor at Utah State University who has pioneered the application of Applied Behavior Analysis (ABA) to captive and companion animals. Dr. Friedman says, "The power to control one's own outcomes is essential to behavioral health." Simply implementing meaningful choice options in an animal's world can have a surprisingly positive impact on behavior.

For example, the chin rest – or alternatively the Bucket Game, gives the patient the choice – or not – to have a procedure continue. Rather than tensing, snapping or growling, a dog can merely lift his chin off the chin rest surface (i.e.: a towel on a chair), or look away from the bucket. When the dog looks at the bucket again, or rests his chin, he is choosing to allow you to continue. Because he has control over the procedure, it is no longer stressful for him, and he is much more likely to calmly allow you to examine body parts, take his temperature, and more, with no tension whatsoever. Here's a protocol for teaching the Bucket Game that you can share with clients. They teach it at home, and your job becomes easier – and safer:

The Bucket Game – The game of choice

This fun and easy dog training protocol is designed to empower the learner, by creating an environment where animals have choice and can communicate their willingness to participate. The Bucket Game gives your patients the ability to tell you:

- When they are ready to start
- When they need to take a break
- When they want to stop
- When you need to slow down

The Bucket Game was designed and brought to the world by Chirag Patel – a training and behavior expert at Domesticated Manners, in London, England. Patel encourages conversations between animals and people. The Bucket Game can be used in many instances, not only for husbandry training and caregiving behaviors, but also as a confidence builder, phobia reducer and for fun – hence also useful in giving your patients a more positive association with your clinic, and your procedures. This protocol uses shaping, targeting, stationing and other behavioral principles in a way that makes it fun for both the animal and the human.

What your client will need:

- A bucket (size appropriate for your learner)
- Rewards (high value food or toys)
- A bed/mat or safe place
- Access to water

Step 1: Teaching manners and impulse control around the bucket (put treats in the bucket)

1. Start by holding the bucket out to the side. Reward for looking at the bucket but maintaining some distance from it (2 to 4 feet).

2. Then put the bucket on the ground/chair and reward the dog for looking at it but not jumping in it. It doesn't matter what position the dog is in (sit/down/stand). He is rewarded for engagement with the bucket.

3. Start reinforcing when the dog maintains eye contact with the bucket for longer durations. Don't increase criteria too soon or too quickly as this may cause the behavior to extinguish. The dog is allowed to look around between focusing on the bucket – remember this is a game of choice and a conversation between human and dog. No need to call them, shake the bucket, tug on lead, etc.

4. Let the dog make the choice to engage, to participate in the training program. Allow access to a bed/mat and water. This will give the dog confidence that he can take a break as needed.

Step 2: Choose what you want to teach the dog to do – for this example – allowing his mouth to be examined.

1. Wait until the dog is able to focus on the bucket (remember it doesn't matter what position the dog is in – it could be a sit/down/stand). When he is focused on the bucket and able to hold his focus for at least 5 to 10 seconds, start moving a hand an inch or two toward his face (not touching him).

2. At this point he can choose to continue to look at the bucket – and if he does, he will be rewarded. If he looks at the hand or otherwise looks away from the bucket, he has communicated that he was uncomfortable. Stop. Remember this is a game of choice.

3. When he re-engages with the bucket, the game begins again. This time don't move the hand so fast or far. If he is able to maintain focus on the bucket – reward.

4. Very gradually increase the hand movement until the entire mouth examination procedure is replicated. You want to set your subject up to succeed. If he is looking away from the bucket frequently, or moves away entirely, you are going too fast. Think crockpot, not microwave.

5. This continues until the dog is calm and relaxed about having his mouth examined.

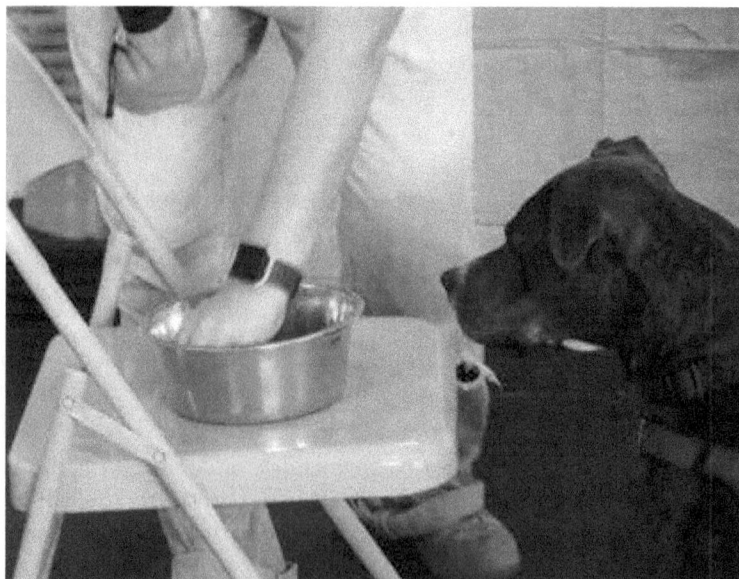

Introducing the Bucket Game

Implementing the Bucket Game to help the author's dog, Bonnie, be more comfortable with brushing.

Using the Bucket Game to give the dog a choice about participating in grooming activities.

Remember that this game of choice will only work if you allow the subject to communicate that he wishes to begin, break and stop the game. You must honor his communications, or the game fails. If the dog looks away from the bucket, the game breaks/stops. When he re-engages with the bucket, the game continues. The value? Immeasurable! How many of your clients don't continue administering medications or procedures when you send your patients home because it's too hard, the dog or cat hates it and won't let them, and in fact bites them when they try? Just imagine the improvement in home care and outcomes when your clients can actually do what you need them to do.

This is just one example of how cognition can serve your clients, your patients and your practice. There are others…. If your patient has learned imitation, he can walk on the scale just by seeing his human do it. And "brain games" as we call them, are fantastic for enrichment, and for exercise for animals on restricted activity – mental exercise is surprisingly tiring and can keep a patient on restriction from damaging sutures and repaired body parts that need cage rest.

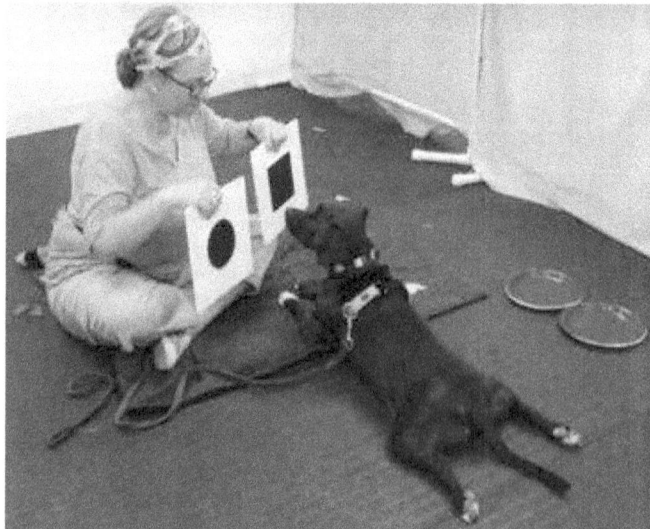

Cognition – dogs can learn to read, count, discriminate between shapes, and much more!

They all work together

It is critically important to recognize that operant, classical and cognitive functions are happening together all the time. When a patient lies down on the table and your client feeds her a treat to reward her for lying down (positive reinforcement to increase a lying down behavior), the dog is also getting a positive classical association with the table – "Yay, treats happen here!" When you forcibly restrain a dog (positive punishment to decrease the struggling behavior), the dog is also getting a negative classical association with the clinic and anyone involved in the restraint and procedure – "Bad things happen here, and these people do it!" And now that we are aware of their cognitive abilities, we know that those are going on all the time also – dogs are observing and figuring out what we are thinking, grasping concepts, drawing conclusions – all of which feeds their future behaviors.

You will read more in the chapters to come about how to take full advantage of operant, classical and cognitive procedures in order to provide the best quality of care to your patients and cultivate the most satisfied human clients. Enjoy the journey!

Chapter 2
Understanding Body Language

By Dr. Deb Bryant, DVM, DACVB and Dr. Fiia Jokela, DVM, DABVP

Introduction

At the heart of striving to reduce stress and promote behavioral well-being in our animal patients is the ability to assess their emotional state. The very purpose of assessing their emotional state is to mitigate situations, interactions and environments to reduce potential fear, anxiety and stress, and beyond that, to promote a positive emotional state. In this chapter we will explore the phenotypic expressions of complex neurobiological processes when a possible threat is perceived by a dog or cat.

Fear, anxiety, and stress

There are three terms (fear, anxiety, and stress) often used interchangeably to denote suboptimal emotional states, but with differences between them. It is important to know the classical definitions, although for our purposes the terms may be used interchangeably within this chapter.

Fear

Fear is an adaptive state in which the organism employs physiologic mechanisms to avoid a perceived threat. In an acute phase, there is arousal of the sympathetic nervous system with release of norepinephrine and epinephrine, activation of the hypothalamic-pituitary-adrenal (HPA) axis with release of cortisol and anti-diuretic hormone (ADH), mobilization of the immune system, and other mechanisms, all geared toward readiness for survival. This physiologic response allows for the classic 'flight' or 'fight' behavioral manifestations. Our animal patients, given a choice, would most likely flee, although they are most often approached or restrained, leading to defensive (fight) responses of increased struggling to get away, or of aggression (Doring et al., 2009). Generally, when in the flight mode the animal attempts to increase distance from the perceived threat by moving away from it, but when in the fight mode the animal acts to increase distance by causing the perceived threat to move farther away.

Anxiety

Anxiety involves fear, but with apprehension about a threat that may not yet be readily apparent. Physiologic and behavioral manifestations of anxiety may be similar to those of fear, often also with increased vigilance and scanning of their surroundings. According to the DSM library, the difference between fear and anxiety can be summarized as: "Fear is the emotional response to real or perceived imminent threat, whereas anxiety is anticipation of future threat."

Stress

The concept of stress, also often used interchangeably with the terms "fear" and "anxiety," is not well defined in literature relating to animal welfare. Stress has been described as affecting an organism's physiologic homeostasis or psychologic well-being (Beerda et al., 2000). A network of physiologic or behavioral mechanisms, as described above, are activated toward a return to a normal, adaptive state. The term "distress" has been used to describe a state in which an animal is no longer able to adapt and successfully cope with its environment leading to compromised physical and emotional well-being. Distress can be brought on by prolonged adjustments to stressors over time, or result from short, but intense, stressors, both of which lead to compromised welfare. Chronic fear, anxiety, stress or distress leads to sustained elevation of cortisol and suppression of the immune system, potentially leading to physical illness.

The following set of photos show what stress looks like in a dog if you know what to look for:

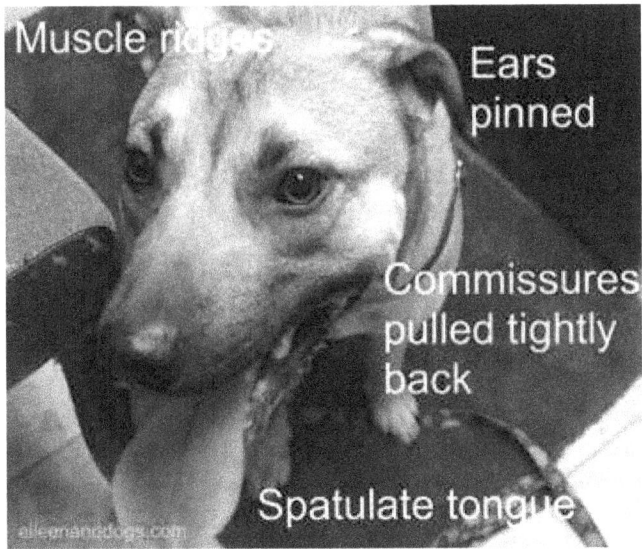

Muscle ridges
Ears pinned
Commissures pulled tightly back
Spatulate tongue
aileenanddogs.com

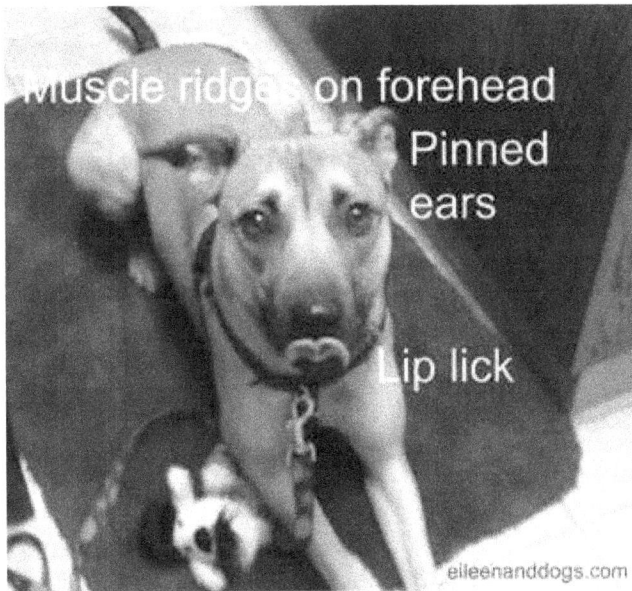

Muscle ridges on forehead
Pinned ears
Lip lick
eileenanddogs.com

Fear conditioning

The formation of memories of fear can occur quickly and are long-lasting through a process of synaptic plasticity. Brain pathways of acute perceived fear bypass cognitive areas with signals more directly to the amygdala and hippocampus, two primary brain regions involved in fear memory formation. A rapid cascade of alterations to proteins, neurochemicals and neural receptors occurs with resultant change in gene expression. Fear conditioning is a form of associational learning, primarily involving the amygdala and hippocampus (Overall, 2013). Variations in inherent coping mechanisms affect responses to stress by individual animals. Past experiences contribute to lasting memories of fear, affecting how an animal will respond to a current situation through associational learning. Such memory 'priming' may lead to more rapid escalation of responses in subsequent similar anticipated events, including ones of aggressive defense, even before the perceived threat is apparent.

Features of communication

Sending and receiving

Information gleaned from situations and environments that animals find themselves in is a compilation of sensory systems including visual, auditory, olfactory, tactile and taste. The information they perceive has the potential to signal to them whether the situation is a safe one to be in or holds risks to their safety. To effectively reduce the risk of an animal experiencing fear, we must be concerned with how animals communicate their emotional state to us, as well as what we may communicate to them. Communication of any form is a two-way street that depends on a sender and a receiver.

The sender must be able to convey a signal that is clear and accurate. The receiver must first be able to perceive the signal and second to recognize what the signal means. Perception of a signal depends on its clarity, and subsequently its interpretation, potentially leading to some type of action or change in behavior. Animals often signal primarily through non-vocal body language, and also through vocalizations. These visual and auditory cues to emotional state are the subject of this chapter. The clinician must have the ability to assess many features of physical health through a learned skillset for accurate diagnosis and treatment of medical issues.

Certain behaviors are also often associated with pain and illness. As part of a holistic approach, proficient behavioral evaluation of emotional state in animal patients should also be part of total clinical assessment. Knowledge to recognize species-specific signals is the responsibility of the clinic team, and requires a skill set that should evolve along with other clinical proficiencies. In fact, learning to recognize the role that stress may play in changing physiologic parameters is essential for accurate medical diagnoses (Shepherd, 2009). Essentially, this means learning different species-specific languages. Signals range from the overt and easily recognized, to other signals that are far more subtle. Our intent to more closely evaluate the patient, or to initiate treatment, may send signals that are interpreted differently by the patient, resulting in fear instead of intent to lend aid. Even our intent to engage in friendly interactions may cause the animal to feel threatened. The patient's perception is their reality. In addition to signals from humans, features of the clinic environment also send signals to our patients, as is discussed elsewhere in this book.

There are many possible physiologic and behavioral manifestations of fear, anxiety and/or distress in dogs and cats. Many of these signs are easily recognizable as stemming directly from sympathetic nervous system arousal (mydriasis, urination, defecation, salivation, attempt to flee) (Overall, 2013), although other behavior patterns often referred to as "displacement behaviors" can be appear less directly related. Such patterns can be highly variable and unique to an individual, such as yawning, paw lifting, head tossing, impulsive licking/grooming, sniffing, and others, can occur in direct response to an acute or long-term stressful situation. Examining the context in which the behaviors occur is imperative to lend meaning to their display.

Recognizing fear

Fear occurs beyond anxiety. It happens when a perceived fear-inducing stimulus is present, and is manifested by one or more of the following:

- Lowering body, crouching, tucking of neck, head, tail and limbs
- Hunched back
- Trembling
- Panting
- Salivation
- Licking lips
- Turning away
- Hiding, averting eyes
- Shutting down, freezing, or curling up
- Urination and defecation in extreme cases
- Release of anal glands
- Increased dander, shedding coat, sweaty paws
- Refusal of even high value food treats
- Vocalization

(Overall, 2003)

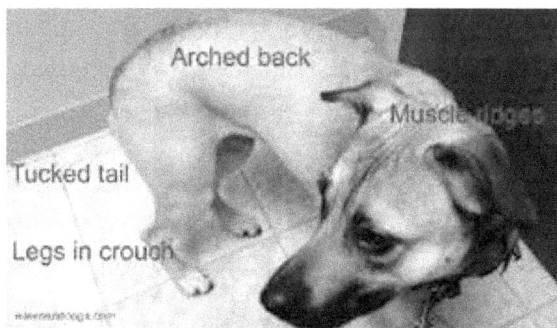

Some of the common signs of fear in a dog.

Recognizing pain

Pain can compound anxiety and fear at the veterinary hospital. Signs of pain can be very similar to the body language of anxiety and fear. It is important to remember to consider pain in your overall assessment of the patient.

Assessing gait can often give clues of pain. A stilted gait or reluctance to walk or stand on a slick surface, may indicate pain or discomfort. Sometimes just the memory of pain that occurred in the past at the veterinary hospital or the anticipation of pain can change a dog's body language and behavior. For example, a dog who normally is comfortable and friendly during exams may react with aggression if he has an ear infection and the veterinarian tries to examine the dog's ears.

Signs of possible pain include:

- Changes in usual behavior - unusually quiet, reluctance to move, decreased appetite, reluctance to interact, increased agitation
- Crying out or yelping
- Sensitivity to touch
- Limping, stiffness of gait
- Panting, increased respiratory rate
- Irritation, snapping
- Avoidance

Recognizing anxiety

Anxiety is the anticipation of threat or danger. It can be displayed in dogs by:

- Constant monitoring of the social and physical environment, manifested by increased locomotion, attentiveness, and vigilance.
- Difficulty focusing and concentrating, being easily distractible by the environment.
- Hyper-reactivity involving a lower threshold for reactions, reacting out of context, and difficulty recovering from episodes of reactivity.
- Physical and physiological changes which can include dilated pupils, elevated heart rate, increased respiratory rate, piloerection (raising of the hackles or hair along the spine).
- Specific behavioral responses and reactions can include pacing, whining, barking, growling, lunging, snapping, and biting.
- Decreased interest in food.

(Overall, 2013).

When do the signals of stress actually start?

Our patients may express signs of emotional discomfort long before the actual entry to the clinic. This may be particularly true of cats who rarely leave the house. Signs of fear, stress, and anxiety may be exhibited by patients upon entering the clinic building and/or before the point of interactions and handling by staff. Dogs have been observed to be more willing to play and eat treats outside the clinic than when inside the clinic. Also, dogs who are stressed are less likely to willingly engage in social interaction with someone unfamiliar to them. Dogs show multiple signs of stress in the waiting area and as they are moved from there to an exam room (Hernander, 2009). Dogs have been shown to exhibit stress throughout the veterinary experience, particularly while on the exam table and often when removed from their human caretakers. Such concerns about signs of stress in feline patients has also been studied in the veterinary clinic, with cats showing signs of fear and stress in all phases of a veterinary visit, beginning during transport to the clinic, the visit itself, and sustained stress after returning home. Concern by owners for the welfare of their cats and their perception of the veterinarian's poor handling of their cats was given as a reason to change veterinarians. Signaling of fear and emotional discomfort in young animals should not be discounted assuming they will simply 'grow out of it.' An important pilot study showed that eight-week-old puppies who displayed fear during a routine physical exam also showed signs of fear at 18 months of age (Overall, 2013).

Stressed in the lobby: Panting and commissure drawn back.

Types of signals and what they mean

Vocalizations can range from sounds of distress, typically with a higher pitch (whining, plaintive barking or meowing, howling), to more aggressive sounds (growling, snarling, hissing, screaming, aggressive sounding barking). Not only is vocalization a potential sign of emotional distress (attention-seeking at the least), but sounds emitted from the vocalizing animal have the potential to impact other animals (Yeon, 2007; Schwartz, 2003). Obviously, sounds can be detected without direct visual observation of the patient, and for many humans it may be the first indication of an animal's poor emotional state. However, depending on the situation, vocalizations are often farther down the line of expressions of emotional discomfort, and earlier and more subtle visual cues are not noticed. An animal may have already started up the Ladder of Aggression with early signs that were not heeded, either because the observer was not aware of the meaning of such signs or simply wasn't paying attention.

Visual signals given by animals are often fleeting and easily missed. Such signaling by animal patients is not static, with potential for fluid moment-to-moment changes. Assessment of an animal's emotional condition should be continually reassessed throughout their time spent in the clinic setting. Examples of assessment tools are given in a separate section. When the clinician is focused on features of illness or injury, participation by at least one other trained clinic team member offers another set of eyes, essential for more complete observation of emotional discomfort.

Many expressions of fear, anxiety and stress are recognized in dogs and cats, although due to the complexity of living creatures, conformation and individual traits, there is no one set of behaviors or even a single behavior that is uniformly expressed by all within a species. Many animals may appear to show minimal behavioral signs of stress. They may be more still and appear compliant but are really merely tolerating an unpleasant circumstance. One should always ask if the animal is "fine," as they may truly not be. A goal should be toward physical and emotional comfort, as opposed to mere tolerance. Animals who show aggression in the veterinary clinic most often do so because of a direct response to, or anticipation of, fear and/or pain.

Aggressive behavior falls along a continuum extending beyond efforts at appeasement, toward behaviors ranging from vocal and visual signals (growling, hissing, lip lift, teeth bared as examples) to actual bites with variable bite pressure that may or may not cause injury. Dogs and cats who become aggressive in the veterinary setting should not be regarded as 'naughty' or 'difficult,' but rather with realization of their perception that they are defending against harm to themselves. If an animal escalates to aggressive behavior, veterinary staff must assess how the situation progressed to that point and make a plan toward rehabilitation to prevent a reoccurrence, bearing in mind the power of traumatic memory instilled in the animal from that single incident. Allowing a situation to progress to the point of aggression has obvious consequences for risk to clinic staff, emphasizing the need to heed early warning signaling from the patient.

In addition, there is much variation in the ability of pet owners to accurately assess signs of stress in their own animals. The majority of the time there is a lack of recognition of such signs (Reisner, 2009; Simpson, 1997). It is the responsibility of the veterinary team to educate owners on the language of stress signals in their own animal.

It can be invaluable to have a systematic method to note behavioral observations as part of the patient record, as well as to track progress, in either direction, throughout a visit and from one visit or hospital stay to the next. Unfortunately, although several have been proposed, there are no standardized and validated uniform stress scales or scoring systems for dogs and cats. Development of such a scale within the individual practice can be accomplished, taking care to define the criteria for each tier of the scoring system.

Human body language and interactions

There are many features on the human/veterinary setting side of the equation that send signals to the animal. The presence of humans and how they conduct themselves within that environment is a primary component of the patient's total experience. The set-up of the environment and amount of space can also have a dramatic effect on an animal's sense of safety and emotional state. The specific importance of the clinic environment and its impact, including ways to make helpful changes to the environment, is covered elsewhere in this book.

It must be clearly stated that aversive tools, rough handling, and physical and verbal 'corrections' have no place in interactions with animals. Nowhere is this concept more important than in the veterinary clinic, in which the patient may already be afraid and stressed. Associational learning involving fear can form quickly and be compounded by unkind interactions. There is also danger that aversive interactions cause suppression of subtle warnings of impending aggression, leading to an eruption of more dangerous aggressive behavior. There must be a complete mindset and practical shift away from such confrontational and oppressive techniques, rather toward a more compassionate and gentle approach.

Veterinary professionals need to see themselves from the dog's point of view. Our patients are reading us from the top of our heads to the tip of our toes through every moment of the exam. How we present our bodies will say more to our patients than any words we speak. As part of a two-way communication system, members of the veterinary team must learn awareness of their own postures, actions and gestures to minimize patient fear and stress. As stated in the introduction to this chapter, the very purpose of learning to read body language signals is to adjust human behavior and interactions accordingly. Development of a sensitivity for non-verbal communication is essential. One study suggested that dogs are affected, showing signs of uncertainty, in interactions with humans with a lower level of non-verbal sensitivity. Many well-meaning humans send threatening signals to dogs through habit and lack of under-standing. For example, humans are taught that eye contact is polite and appropriate during human introductions and conversations. To a dog, this type of approach can be very threatening. When meeting a dog, simply averting direct gaze is an effective way to say, "I mean you no harm."

The subtlest of our motions and postures can greatly impact how an animal responds to us, as can the order of practice procedures. Efforts toward appropriate signaling from humans may be reactive in response to the animal's communication, but ideally will be proactive, thus avoiding inappropriate and potentially threatening signals to begin with. Every species has a 'bubble' of personal space, into which humans or animals may be allowed with increased familiarity and acceptance. Remember, this is about the patients' perceptions, even when we don't intend to send harmful messages.

Don'ts and Do's

Here are some common interactive mistakes humans make when first interacting with an animal, especially in the veterinary hospital setting – these are the DON'Ts:

DON'T suddenly enter a room and surprise the animal.

DON'T walk directly toward the animal, bend at the waist and reach directly to allow the animal to smell your hand to 'make friends.'

Direct approach

DON'T look directly at the animal, especially with intensity and a look of concern.

DON'T speak in a loud voice.

DON'T move toward an animal to restrain him when he is in a corner or against the wall or under a chair or table.

DON'T lift the animal off the floor and onto a cold slippery surface for examination that may begin with insertion of a thermometer directly into his rectum.

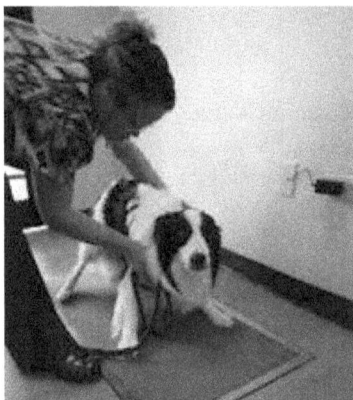

Avoid removing the patient from her owner if possible.

DON'T remove the patient from the owner, his secure base, for routine procedures.

When first encountering an animal patient, and throughout a visit, as much as possible – these are the DOs:

DO enter the exam room together with the patient and client.

DO take time to talk to the client in a pleasant voice before attempting any interactions with the patient – history taking and discussions while also peripherally observing the animal give the staff members and veterinarian time to assess the level of stress and allow the animal time to assess the humans as well. Do not reach over or toward the patient to shake hands or otherwise directly greet the owner.

DO smile! (Coren, n.d.)

DO position your body obliquely to the patient and/or stand facing the same direction as the animal (vs. facing head-on).

DO wear a treat pouch and toss food on the floor – this serves as a gauge to partly determine stress level, as stressed animals may not be willing to take food. (Avoid reaching your hand with food toward the animal initially, both as a safety precaution and to not provoke fear.)

DO speak in a soft and upbeat tone.

DO avoid direct eye contact, especially staring.

DO ideally, allow the animal to make the choice to come to you. If you must approach, do so slowly; avoid moving quickly toward the animal, and avoid trapping the animal in corners.

Use treats to lure the dog to encourage her to move forward toward you.

DO keep your upper torso straight as much as possible, whether standing or sitting/ kneeling on the floor.

DO keep your arms close to your body and bend them at the elbows.

DO extend your hands palms up, and avoid reaching directly for the collar, face or top of the head.

DO place your hands on the animal gently and maintain gentle and fluid contact to avoid startle with on/off/on/off touching of the body.

DO allow the animal to stay with the client, coaching the client on helpful things they can do. Attachment of pets to their owners also plays a significant role in the level of anxiety they may experience. Dogs have been found to show increased signs of anxiety when separated from their owners, indicating that owners provide a secure base for increased comfort (Mariti et al., 2015).

The power of food!

Another key 'signal' to assessing emotional state in animals is their willingness to eat food when offered. Food is often used to aid in creating positive associations with situations and stimuli. In addition, food can serve as a gauge to an animal's emotional state as many animals are not able to eat food (aside from satiety and/or a medical reason for decreased appetite) when they are stressed. Reluctance to eat food can indicate when an animal has gone over its individual threshold toward a more fearful or stressed state and should prompt adjustments to mitigate stressors. Food 'value' – in terms of taste and preference – can also help to determine stress level, as many animals who are mildly stressed may not eat low value food (such as dry kibble), but may accept higher value options (more aromatic, moist treats, for example). This is a matter of what the animal values in the appeal of the food and does not refer to nutritional value.

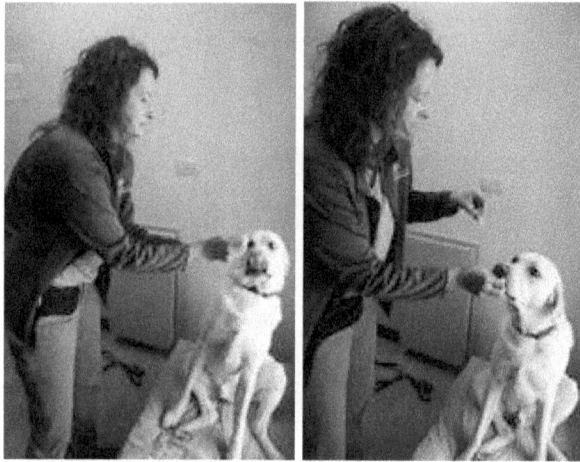

Eye drops without treat *Eye drops with treats*

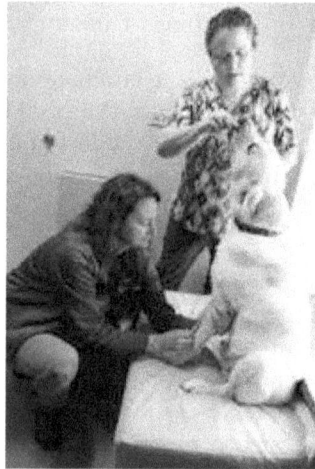

Injection with treats

At least 60 percent of dogs who visit their veterinarian for routine physical examinations show submissive or fearful behaviors (Beaver, 1999; Döring, 2009). For most dogs who have been to the veterinary hospital more than once, just entering the building predicts that unpleasant or painful experiences are about to happen. This fear can lead to resistance or aggression, which restricts our ability to provide preventive care, diagnostic testing, and treatment for our patients. Each visit will become more difficult unless efforts are made to prevent and alleviate the stress and fear of veterinary visits (Simpson, 1997). Preventing and reducing stress and fear are crucial roles for the entire veterinary team.

Behavior descriptions

Behavior is not a trait of an individual, nor does it exist in a vacuum. The environment always sets the stage. Context must always be considered, contexts will change, and behavior changes will follow. Behavior and body language exist on a continuum.

Descriptions of behavior need to be objective descriptions rather than subjective conclusions. Avoid attaching labels such as "the dog is angry or mad," "the dog is dominant or mean," or "the dog is fine." Objective and fluid descriptions are important, such as "the pupils are dilated, the brow is furrowed and the dog is growling with cheek teeth exposed," or "the dog's eyes are squinting, and the tail is swishing softly side to side."

Dogs communicate with humans for many reasons. One of the most important reasons is their desire to get along with us without conflict and to avoid harm. Dogs are constantly evaluating if they are safe or not safe. The veterinary hospital is full of scary sights, sounds, and smells. There are many ways veterinary patients use their body language to ask for peace between us, to slow down, and to give them space. Veterinary professionals need to recognize and respond appropriately to these signals from our patients. If we don't, we will create anxiety and conflict, resulting in attempts to escape or the emergence of aggressive behavior. When excessive force or restraint prevents escape, aggression may become the only option left for the dog. This results in unnecessary danger to the veterinary staff, the client, and to the patient. Aggressive behavior also limits the amount and quality of veterinary care the patient receives (Reisner, 2013).

Using a Hansel and Gretel treat trail to coax dog onto a scale.

Dogs communicate with us in several ways:

- Through posture and movement involving their body from nose to tail.
- By facial expressions involving their facial muscles, eyes, ears, and mouth.
- Through vocalizations such as whining, barking, growling, howling (Reisner, 2013).

Lost in translation between dog and humans

The language of dogs and humans can get lost in translation from both sides. For example, yawning is frequently seen during veterinary examinations. This is often misinterpreted as the dog being bored or tired. It is important to consider the context of the behavior. Most dogs in the veterinary setting are experiencing some level of emotional stress. In the context of the exam room, yawning is most likely a sign of stress, as well as the dog's attempt to relieve its stress.

Canine body language experts have identified a variety of factors that come into play when humans and dogs are interacting, many of which are relevant to veterinary examinations:

- Mixed signals and misinterpreted signals leading to an inability to read the dog's body language.
- A lack of understanding a dog's displacement and submissive behaviors.
- A lack of understanding a dog's avoidance strategies which can lead to aggressive behaviors.

Mixed and misinterpreted signals

It is critically important to look at the whole picture. Interpretation of a particular body language signalment must be considered in conjunction with the rest of the body and what the dog's other body parts may be signaling. Interpretation can become difficult when a discrepancy exists between body language signals. These mixed signals can mean mixed emotions, just as humans can experience mixed emotions. This indicates that the dog's emotions may be in flux as it evaluates the situation, and that emotion and behavior may rapidly change.

For example, a shy dog may be lured or coerced to approach an unfamiliar person with a treat. The dog's approach may seem to indicate a willingness to interact, however the dog's tail may be down, his ears are pulled back and his posture is shifted backward. An unfortunate sequela of this emotional conflict is often that the shy dog grabs the treat and then bites the hand.

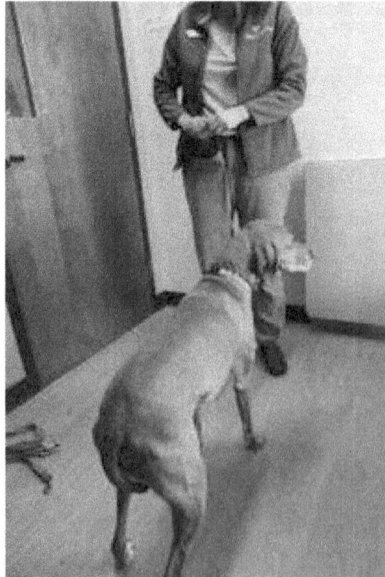

Standing directly in front of the dog may make her uncomfortable - note the tucked tail and looking away.

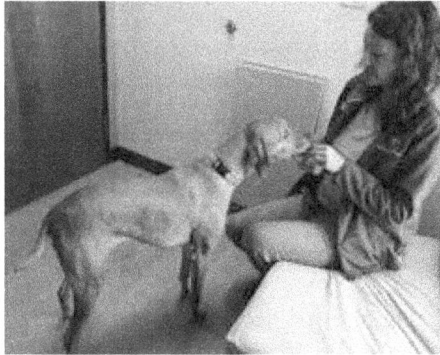

Sitting and providing treats may allow the dog to relax when first meeting the vet.

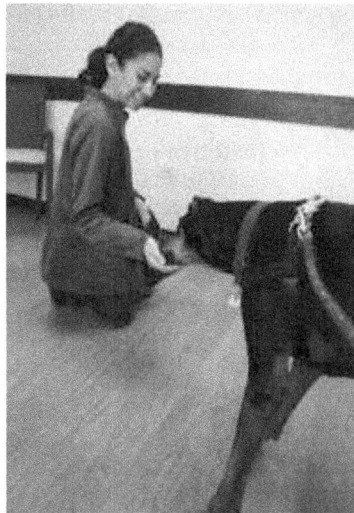

Proper positioning helps encourage the dog to "meet and greet."

A dog rolling over and exposing her belly is another frequently misinterpreted signal. This behavior is usually an appeasement signal asking for a peaceful end to the interaction. It is all-too-frequently misread by people as a request for closer interaction and a belly rub, which can result in a defensive bite. Some dogs do enjoy having their belly rubbed, but this is usually a learned behavior, and may only apply to interactions with a trusted person. A dog may invite such an interaction with a familiar person by rolling onto her back, keeping her body loose, with legs held wide and face soft and relaxed. If a person has initiated an interaction that is painful or unpleasant, such as trying to trim the dog's nails and their approach results in the dog rolling onto her back, exposing her belly, with legs tightly tucked, the dog is communicating that she is afraid and asking for space. If the person reaches for the belly or continues to force the interaction, the dog will likely interpret an escalating threat and may feel the need to defend herself.

Averting eyes, blinking, and lowering or turning the head are communications often offered by dogs being reprimanded or punished. Humans tend to misinterpret these responses as admissions of guilt. In reality, these signals are offered to appease the human and to communicate that the dog intends no harm to the person and wishes no conflict. If the person does not back off, the dog will perceive an escalating threat. In turn, the dog is likely to intensify to exaggerated signals of fear such as lifting a foreleg, sitting or lying down, lowering or turning the body, urinating, or becoming defensively aggressive (Reisner, 2013).

If mixed signals are noted, caution is advised. This is good time to stop and change the interaction with the dog to relieve the concern, then closely observe the dog's next signals. Is the change in approach de-escalating the fear or it still rising? Observe, evaluate, and modify your own behavior accordingly.

Fortunately, canine communication frequently provides redundancy to clarify the message. For example, yawns due to stress typically do not include the extension of the tongue. A stressed dog may yawn but may also be averting his gaze and lifting a paw into the air to enunciate the message of stress. A tired dog makes a wide yawn, and the tongue usually extrudes. To clarify the message, tired yawns are usually accompanied by supporting signs such as stretching of the limbs (Reisner, 2013).

Displacement and submissive displays in reaction to human behaviors
Canine mouth signals. Submissive displays associated with the canine mouth are often misinterpreted by humans. The submissive/appeasement grin is offered with the lips are pulled back horizontally. This can result in exposing the front teeth, which may be confused with a lip-lift of a dog offering an aggressive snarl. For a submissive/appeasing dog, in addition to the submissive grin, the muzzle is lifted, eyes are squinty, the ears are back, and the front lip is not lifted upward (Simpson, 1997). If the warning signal is ignored, the dog may react as shown in the photo below. This dog is threatening, its front lip is retracted upward exposing the front teeth. In addition, the pupils are dilated, eyes are wide giving a hard stare and the commissure is pulled forward. The ears are tense and back, the brow is furrowed.

Dogs licking. There probably is no other canine behavior that is more misinterpreted than licking. This is not the same as a kiss. Frequent lip-licking and lip-smacking are commonly used stress signals. Licking of human faces may be a ritualized social gesture derived from food soliciting, as puppies do when soliciting mother dogs to regurgitate food for them (Simpson, 1997). It may also signal appeasement or submission. In some contexts, it may be a request for space and distance. Jennifer Shryock, founder of the Family the Paws Parent Education Program, has labelled this as "a kiss to dismiss." She suggests, "Consider your response when your dog licks your face. Most likely you turn away and certainly you look away. This increases the distance and comfort for the dog when things are too intense. Or it manipulates you to move a bit." This is an especially important concept to share with clients who have children.

Displacement behaviors. These are normal behaviors that are done out of normal context. Dogs display these behaviors toward other dogs when they become uncomfortable, and they usually are mutually understood. People have to learn what these signals are because they indicate the dog is attempting to defuse stress and deflect attention in a setting such as a veterinary clinic. Examples of displacement behaviors are:

- Shaking off as if wet
- Scratching
- Licking and grooming
- Sniffing
- Sneezing

Shaking can be a displacement behavior of a dog who is not wet.

Avoidance strategies

Dogs use four strategies to maintain their safety when they perceive danger. An ability to recognize the signals that accompany these strategies can lead to avoiding aggressive behaviors on the part of the dog. These four are:

Flight: Most dogs wish to avoid confrontation as that could put them at risk. If a flight option is available to them, they will choose to escape or hide.

Fight: Dogs often choose aggressive behavior if no flight option is available. Some dogs, especially those with a learning history in which aggression has been a successful behavior strategy, may go directly to aggression to drive a perceived threat away. A dog who chooses aggression does not necessarily mean to cause harm. Dogs use aggression to drive perceived threats away. Escalating to a bite occurs when other lower level signaling is not effective.

Freeze: Some dogs will freeze when they feel trapped and helpless and see no escape. It is common for dogs to freeze when placed on an exam table, and these dogs are often perceived as being "fine." They are not. As veterinary professionals trying to offer quality care, we tend to capitalize on this behavior, as it helps us get our jobs done. Although the dog seems cooperative, it is important to realize that the frozen dog is extremely stressed.

Displacement behaviors: As discussed above.

Reading a dog to evaluate his emotional state

Below are examples of the progression of body language as a dog's emotional state transitions from relaxed to stressed; and fearful to aggressive. Many of the clues involved facial expressions.

- **Ears:** height, position and distance apart
- **Brow Ridge:** controlled by muscle contraction
- **Head Posture:** in relation to the neck
- **Lips:** position and movement
- **Eyes:** open wide, muscles tight, squinting, blinking, pupil size, gaze direction
- **Jaw:** taught, loose, rigid or in motion
- **Nose and nostrils:** changing shape as the dog evaluates the environment, dry or dripping

Body posture

Relaxed:
- Weight balanced on all four limbs
- Muscles relaxed throughout the body, loose and wiggly
- Curves in the body posture
- Play bow may be offered

Stressed and fearful:
- Holding up one paw
- Muscles tight, weight shifted back
- Body posture has fewer curves, becoming stiff and straight
- Lowering or turning the head
- Back may be hunched with head down
- Body may be lowered, crouched, with or without urination

- Rolling over to expose belly, with legs held tightly, with or without urination
- Displacement posturing such as shaking off (as if wet) or hind-end checking

Extremely fearful, or preparing for an aggressive response:
- Muscles are tense and hard, movement is stiff
- Body is straight
- Hackles raised along spine
- Shutting down, freezing
- Curling into the ground
- Sudden release of urine, feces, or anal glands
- May display attempts to escape such as climbing walls, flipping when handled (gator roll)

Tail

Relaxed:
- Relaxed, neutral position, not high or low (may vary with breed conformation)
- Loose, wide swishing tail

Stressed and fearful:
- Stiff tail held down or tucked
- May have a low wag which can be fast or slow, with shorter strokes

Extremely fearful, may be close to an aggressive response:
- Tail held high above the back
- Tail moving in a stiff manner
- May be rapidly moving back and forth

Eyes

Relaxed:
- Relaxed gaze, may squint or blink lids slowly
- Pupils normal size for the light level of environment
- Eyebrows and eyelids are soft and neutral, and may be partially closed

Stressed and fearful:
- Alert, pupils dilated, scanning
- Eyelids full open, may show large areas of the sclera (white of the eyes)
- Eyebrows furrowed and shifting; may be averting gaze to avoid eye contact

Extremely fearful, may be close to an aggressive response:
- Hard stare
- Eyelids held wide open without blinking
- Pupils fully dilated

Ears

Relaxed:
- Soft and loose, neutral without being pressed or flattened back, will vary depending on conformation and breed
- May be facing different directions without alerting anything specific

Stressed and fearful:
- Pulled to the side or back, tight
- Floppy ears may be pinched and tense

Extremely fearful, may be close to an aggressive response:
- Held tightly back or flattened
- Little movement
- Held erect and hard forward

Mouth

Relaxed:
- Long, loose lips
- Mouth may be open but relaxed with tongue relaxed and lolling
- Mouth may be closed with the lips relaxed and covering the teeth

Stressed and fearful:
- Lips pulled back into a "V" to expose cheek teeth, or tensely held over teeth
- Oral displacement behaviors; excessive or harsh panting, lip licking, chewing, yawning, grooming

Ready for aggression:
- Top lip pulled forward into C shape, exposing front teeth only

Vocalization

Relaxed:
- Typically, none
- Groan, moan, or happy grumble

Stressed or fearful:
- Excessive whining or whimpering
- Low growl

Fearful, may be close to an aggressive response:
- Barking, growling, snarling, snapping (Herron and Shreyer, 2014).

Other types of signaling used by dogs

Olfactory signaling (scent) is constantly used in dog-to-dog communication. For example, urine marking leaves information about the marker dog's identity, sex, health, stress level, how long ago the dog was there, familiarity, and social relationships. Dogs are likely also sensing and interpreting many olfactory signals from humans that we are generally unaware of. We humans are generally unable to understand or translate the olfactory signals of dogs, and for the most part we don't know how our involuntary olfactory signals may translate to them.

Tactile signaling (touch) frequently occurs between dogs and humans. Animal guardians often pet their dog with quick, short strokes on their face, head, and shoulders. These short choppy strokes may signal the person's own anxiety that often occurs when watching their dog be examined or subjected to a procedure such as venipuncture. Dogs seem to sense human anxiety, and if the veterinary staff or the client are anxious it can also trigger stress in the dog and raise his level of anxiety. Long, slow strokes, or deep muscle massage, are better choices to help relax the dog. When guardians use these calmer methods to soothe their dogs, it will encourage their dogs to look to their humans for guidance and reassurance when there is uncertainty or fear in a situation.

Dogs also will press against their humans for comfort or will lay their head or paw on their person's arm, legs, or lap. Pressure or touching can be very soothing. This close contact also serves to alert the dog if something is about to change or happen (Overall, 2013).

Dogs reading humans

It is also challenging for dogs to translate human body language. Any behaviors that do not occur naturally among dogs can be misinterpreted as a direct threat from a human, even behaviors offered with the best of intentions. We frequently offer human signs of affection toward unfamiliar dogs that at best bewilder them, and at worst are misinterpreted as threats. As veterinary professionals, we need to see ourselves from the dog's point of view. Our patients are reading us from the top of our heads to the tip of our toes, through every moment of the exam. How we present our bodies says more to our patients than any words we speak.

Eye contact. For example, making and holding direct eye contact is something humans do when speaking to each other. Humans are taught that eye contact is polite and appropriate during human introductions and conversations. To a dog, this type of approach can be very threatening. When meeting a shy dog, simply turning our head away and averting gaze is an effective way to say, "I mean you no harm."

Turning away and averting your gaze can help a dog relax during an intial meeting.

Direct approaches. A direct or swift posture approach toward a dog also can appear threatening to dogs, who prefer to meet in curves. Turning your body to the side or trying to look smaller by crouching or sitting down can help a patient to relax.

Bending and reaching. Humans frequently bend or reach toward or over a dog's head to offer a friendly greeting. People almost instinctively extend their hands toward an unfamiliar dog for a sniff. These human greetings can look very scary to shy or nervous dogs and can result in defensive responses such as growls or bites. It is less threatening – and more polite from the dog's perspective – to keep your hands at your sides and wait for the dog to approach and offer affiliative behavior.

Touching and petting. When a dog does approach to sniff an unfamiliar person, the person often mistakes this as an invitation to touch or pet the dog. This is often exactly what the dog does not want. Dogs communicate via their noses and have a need to get close to smell, investigate and identify who the stranger is. The dog is information-seeking, not inviting interaction. Once he investigates, he often walks away. If he stays close and offers friendly, affiliative body language, then he is inviting interaction.

People almost universally assume that all dogs find touching and petting desirable. It is difficult for many humans to understand that it can be a trigger for fear and aggression. Dogs can learn to enjoy and solicit touch from people they know and trust. However, dogs can find touch from a stranger to be very intimidating. For our veterinary patients, our touch is often associated with past painful procedures, and thus can be even scarier.

Hugging and kissing. Hugging is not a natural behavior for dogs nor one they share with each other. It can be confusing as well as threatening to dogs. Hugging can eliminate a chance for escape, makes the dog feel trapped, and creates close face-to-face contact, which is especially dangerous for children. Kissing and attempting to show a dog affection with face-to-face contact can send the exact opposite of the intended message. Puppies and submissive dogs do express affiliative behavior by licking the mouths of other dogs. When they do this, they usually approach with lowered body posture from underneath the other dog's jaw. When humans kiss dogs, we tend to bend over and come straight down to the dog's head. This can be interpreted by the dog as a threat rather than a sign of affection.

Feline body language and vocal signals

Cats communicate instinctively, both involuntarily and intentionally, to send information, or as a request to another (animal or human) to try to change the other's behavior (Overall, 2013). Cats in the veterinary setting communicate in different ways to indicate a willingness to interact, or to protect themselves from perceived threats and interactions. Communication is facilitated through visual, tactile, auditory and olfactory means as well as through physiological changes (Overall, 2013; Beaver, 1999).

Visual signals
Cats communicate visually with body posture; eye, ear, head and tail position; and a cat's willingness to make eye contact.

Tactile signals. Cats communicate positive signals with touch through rubbing (bunting) against others (including humans); grooming; and nose-touching during greeting, and with negative signals such as swatting and biting.

Auditory communication. These are transmitted by purring, trills (chirrups), mews, and meow vocalizations which are used as greeting or distance decreasing sounds. Cats also utilize distance increasing auditory signals such as growling, hissing, spitting, yowling and shrieking.

Olfactory communication. Olfactory signaling is possible because cats have a keen sense of smell. Felines communicate using scent through facial, scratching, urine and fecal marking. Cats living closely together share a group scent that is used to identify members of the group.

Physiological changes. Rapid, deep breathing, or panting can be due to either stress or disease, which can sometimes make differentiating stress and fear from cardiac or respiratory conditions a challenge. Extreme acute stress responses may lead to diarrhea, or evacuation of the bladder, bowel, or anal glands. Anxious or fearful cats may produce increased sweat from their paws (Berger, 2014).

How cats alleviate stress and fear

When faced with a stressor, cats will evaluate the danger and utilize survival mechanisms to help protect themselves or to cope better with the situation (Ellis et al., 2015; Ryan, 2018). These mechanisms include the following avoidance strategies:

Flight: The goal of flight is to create distance between the cat and the stressor. Cat carriers, cages, and the physical restraint used in the veterinary setting limit a cat's ability to utilize this strategy. Thwarting the flight strategy increases stress.

Hiding: Cats may respond to stress and confrontation by hiding in the back of the crate, under bedding, or under a chair. Allowing cats to feel hidden while they are at the veterinary practice, using items such as towels or carriers, may reduce stress and facilitate handling (Rodan et al., 2011).

Feigning sleep: Hospitalized cats may appear to be sleeping but actually remain hypervigilant and stressed as they observe the environment around them. By feigning sleep, they deflect attention away from themselves. This behavior is often mistaken for the cat being calm and relaxed.

When avoidance is not possible

Cats may utilize a variety of other behavioral strategies when avoidance is not possible. These include:

Freeze (inhibition): Cats may freeze while waiting/hoping for the situation to pass. The cat adopts a crouched body position with arched back and lowered head, tail close to the body, and all four feet planted underneath. Veterinary staff must realize that silence and/or lack of movement do not indicate lack of pain or lack of anxiety. A cat that 'freezes' is signaling that she is anxious or uncomfortable (Ryan, 2018).

Fiddling (displacement or appeasement behavior): A stressed cat may start grooming or try to look preoccupied by sniffing to deflect interest and attention away from herself. Well socialized cats who find a medical procedure such as an injection unpleasant but are not in a high state of fear, may show some additional fiddling behaviors such as a head shake, a tongue flick, skin twitching or rippling, exaggerated swallowing, short sharp grooming bursts, or a quick scratch behind the ears (Ryan, 2018).

Fight (repulsion of the trigger): Feline aggression often occurs if freeze or fiddle strategies do not reduce the feelings of fear or eliminate the stressor. If aggression successfully removes the stressor, the cat will have learned to use fighting as a successful strategy. She may well choose aggression first in similar situations. She may no longer give warning hisses or growls and instead is likely to go directly to swiping, scratching, or biting in the future (Ryan, 2018).

Stressed and fearful cats who have learned that their best defense is a good offense may develop more offensive postures, even though they remain fearful. Conflicted body posture is also common in these cats. Some of their body posture may appear defensive (e.g., pupil dilation, muscle tension), while at the same time, some of their posture may look more confident, with their bodyweight carried forward instead of back, with whiskers and ears facing forward instead of back, and attempting to look taller with front legs extended. The tail, instead of being tucked as in fear, may be extended or carried partially up with piloerection of the tail fur (Ellis, 2015).

Veterinary and other animal care professionals must learn to recognize flight, freeze, fiddle (displacement) and fight behaviors. They should also monitor for body postures that are withdrawn, defensive, offensive, and conflicted. It is important to understand that cats may demonstrate their stress differently due to differing temperaments and experiences, and responses may rapidly change for a given cat depending on varying stressors and contexts (Ellis, 2015).

Continuum of feline behavior

Feline behavior can escalate and de-escalate depending on what is happening in the environment moment to moment. During the examination, veterinary professionals need to evaluate the patient's body language from the tip of the nose to the tip of the tail and re-assess it frequently to determine how the patient is handling the experience. With this information, the veterinary team can adjust their approach and make changes to their plan to minimize distress for the cat's future evaluation and treatment. Evaluate these various body parts to reach a conclusion about the cat's response to the clinic situation:

Ear position
- Forward and up – alert and aware
- Swiveling in different directions, scanning for sounds – concerned
- Held sideways and flat (airplane ears) – stressed
- Drawn back – more stressed
- Held back and flattened against head – very stressed

Eyes
- Pupil size and shape – slit (calm), round (alert, worried), dilated (stressed)
- Eyelids – squinting (relaxed), fixed (alert, concerned), blinking (worried), or wide open (stressed)
- Gaze averted (relaxed – or avoidance), scanning (alert, concerned), forward gazing (alert, concerned), wide eyed (worried, stressed), staring (stressed)

Facial expression
- Whisker position – downward (calm, relaxed), forward (alert, concerned), backward (stressed)
- Mouth – closed (relaxed), open (alert, concerned), open and tight with teeth showing (stressed); wide open with hissing or spitting (very stressed); panting (very stressed)
- Gaping or flehmen response with head lifted, mouth open slightly, tongue is flicking, lips curled back slightly, eyes squinting; usually in response to a strange odor, or response to a pheromone chemical communication signa – investigating

Body posture
- Lying semi-recumbent or curled – relaxed
- Lying with legs tucked under body – relaxed
- Crouched or hunched – worried, frightened, stressed
- Stiff-legged, body forward – anxious, stressed
- Legs extended and back arched – very stressed

Tail posture and movement
- Low (relaxed), horizontal (interested), high (friendly), high and vibrating (excited) (all not-fluffed)
- Low and fluffed (fearful/worried), horizontal and fluffed (worried/stressed), high and fluffed – very stressed
- Tucked or curled around body – relaxed or worried
- Tip of tail moving side to side – predatory, or slightly annoyed
- Full tail swishing slowly – stressed
- Full tail swishing vigorously – very stressed

Behavior changes and responses
All of these body language signals may also be on a continuum, and can escalate and de-escalate depending on what is going on in the environment:

- Flight: hiding, fleeing, escaping
- Freezing: immobile, feigning (faking) sleep
- Fiddle (displacement behavior): sniffing, scratching, frantic grooming
- Fight (aggression): swatting, scratching, hissing, biting, attacking

Feline body language illustrations

This first illustration shows a cat who is giving signals that it is safe to approach and interact with. The following pages contain illustrations of feline body language to help you interpret what you may see in a veterinary clinic environment (ASPCApro. org, n.d.).

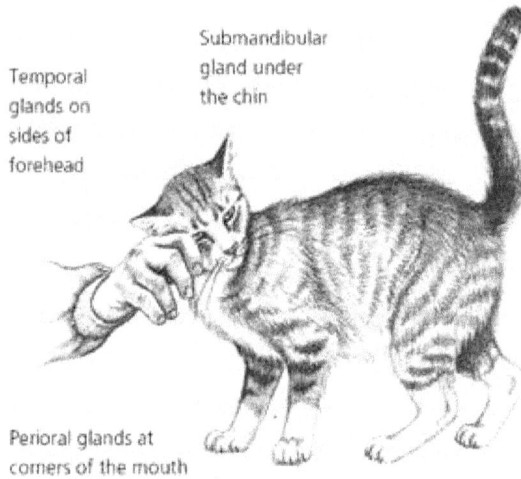

Temporal glands on sides of forehead

Submandibular gland under the chin

Perioral glands at corners of the mouth

- Eyes may be partially closed, and pupils are normal
- Ears relaxed and forward
- Rubbing face and chin on person
- Whiskers forward or straight
- Tail may be up but mostly still
- Muscles relaxed, may be sitting or lying down
- May be purring

This illustration presents a relaxed and confident cat seeking interaction.

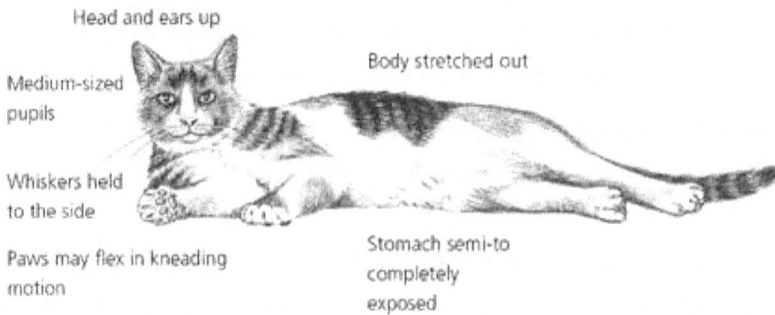

Head and ears up

Body stretched out

Medium-sized pupils

Whiskers held to the side

Paws may flex in kneading motion

Stomach semi-to completely exposed

This illustration presents a cat that is not to approach to reach out or touch the cat.

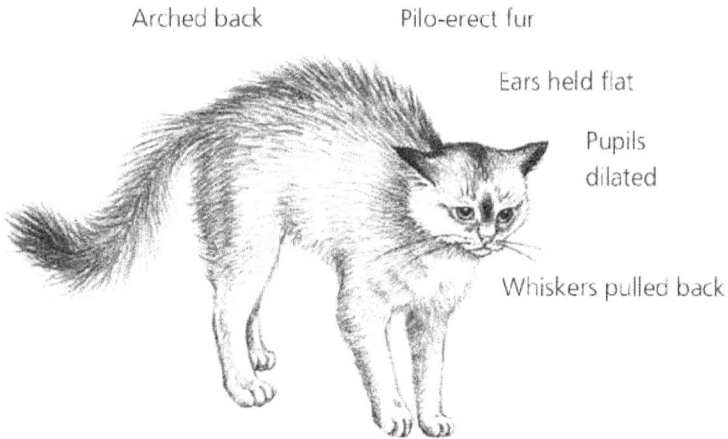

Arched back   Pilo-erect fur

Ears held flat

Pupils
dilated

Whiskers pulled back

- Turning head away
- Averting gaze, pupils dilating
- Ears turning back
- Tail swishing or twitching
- Growling or hissing
- Standing tall and arching back to look larger
- Lifting front leg, ready to swat or scratch if necessary
- Putting teeth on the person as a warning to stop

This illlustration shows an anxious cat who is nervous, insecure or fearful.

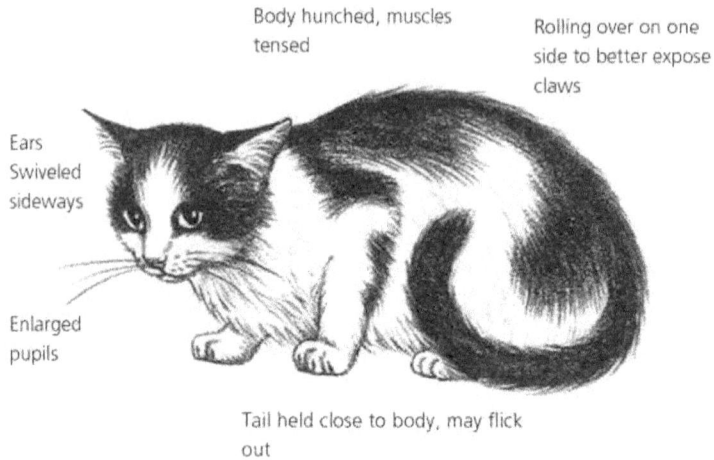

Body hunched, muscles tensed

Rolling over on one side to better expose claws

Ears Swiveled sideways

Enlarged pupils

Tail held close to body, may flick out

- Pupils are dilated
- Ears sideways or back, or swiveling independently
- Respiratory rate may be increased
- Tail is low or tucked between legs or wrapped around body
- Muscles are tense
- Body posture is lowered and crouched to appear small
- Head down and pulled into neck
- All four paws are on the ground ready for escape
- The cat may be looking to turn away, hide, or moving away
- May have a plaintive meow, yowling, growling, or quiet

This illustration shows a cat that is startled or frightened and should be assumed to be defensively aggressive.

Ears pulled flat and back against the head

Pupils dilated

Facial muscles tensed, displaying teeth

Paw ready to swat with claws exposed

- Ears back or flattened against head
- Whiskers are back
- Piloerection of the hair on the spine
- Head may be lowered
- Cat's back may be arched
- Piloerection of hair along spine/tail may be noted
- Tail can be erect or low
- May growl, yowl, hiss, or spit in some cases
- Dilated pupils
- Ears flattened back
- May be showing teeth

The effect of pain on feline communication and body language

The most accurate method for evaluating pain as well as anxiety, stress, and fear in animals is by observing behavior. It may not be easy to distinguish behaviors associated with fear and anxiety from those associated with pain. Every cat exhibiting problem behavior must be assessed for current signs of pain and the possible fear/anticipation of pain. (Ellis, 2013).

Observe for the presence of the subtle behaviors listed below:

- The cat is laying down and quiet but moving its tail.
- The cat contracts and extends its pelvic limbs and/or contracts its abdominal muscles (flank).
- The cat's eyes are partially closed (eyes half closed).

Facial expressions have been shown to be different between painful and non-painful cats (Steagall and Monteiro, 2015). The development of a Feline Grimace Scale by Paulo Steagall at the University of Montreal has revealed further differences between painful and non-painful cats. Five 'action units' were identified. These included ear position, orbital tightening, muzzle tension, whiskers and head position. Very recently this Feline Grimace Scale has been shown to be a valid tool for acute pain assessment. It has displayed good inter- and excellent intra-rater reliability, and successfully discriminates painful from non-painful cats. Current studies are investigating its responsiveness and the cut-off for analgesic administration. You can get more information on the Feline Grimace Scale at felinegrimacescale.com where information can be downloaded and now there is even a phone app available.

Here's how to open communication with the cat and appear less threatening:

- Avert your gaze and avoid direct eye contact.
- Slowly blink your eyes, which signals your intent to do no harm.
- Move slowly and deliberately.
- Minimize your movement and hand gestures.
- Allow the cat to choose where she wants to interact, in the bottom half of the carrier if she prefers to stay there.
- Try to be at the cat's chosen level: sit next to the exam table, have the cat sit on your lap or next to you on a bench, or sit on the floor if the cat prefers being on the ground.
- Invite the cat to approach on her own if possible.
- If you must approach, do so from the side; avoid a rapid direct approach to the front of the cat.
- Avoid looming or bending over the cat.
- Minimize words, speak slowly with a calm and quiet voice, or whisper.
- Avoid animated discussions with the client during the exam.
- If the cat is anxious, allow her to find refuge back inside the carrier before discussing your findings and recommendations with the client. Cover the carrier to help the cat relax.
- Keep your body relaxed and be aware that the emotional states of veterinary team members can influence the cat's emotional state and behavior (Carney, 2012).

All patient communication signals need to be viewed in context (remember that context and signals change rapidly). If we "listen" with the desire to make things better for our patients and we respond appropriately by adjusting the situation or environment, a reciprocating conversation can develop to change the patient's emotional state and behavior for the better (Overall, 2013). Behavior is always in a continuum that is affected by the environment around it. The veterinary team has an opportunity to create changes in that environment to lower the patient's anxiety and stress.

Conclusions

Miscommunicated signals, either on the sender or the receiver end, can have dire consequences for welfare and safety, both for humans and animals. Sustained stress in animals has been demonstrated to lead to physical ailments (Beerda et al., 2000). There is no question that fear, anxiety or stress in our animal patients – at any level – in the veterinary setting causes both short- and long-term compromise to patient welfare (Lloyd, 2017).

Chapter 3
Working with Behavior and Training Professionals
by Jessica Hekman, DVM, PhD

Understanding and modifying animal behavior is an exciting and rewarding challenge, best approached with respect for both the vast existing body of knowledge and the depth of expertise attained by many animal behavior experts. Designing and implementing a clinic behavior program is a significant commitment, including educating veterinary clinic staff about animal behavior and changing clinic protocols to accommodate the needs of their patients. Such a program will entail that at least one member of the clinic team becomes very well-educated in animal behavior. This team member will need to immerse themselves in both the theory and the practice of animal behavior and welfare, including acquiring training techniques and learning to interpret the body language of different species. This expertise cannot be acquired entirely from a book but includes hands-on skills that must be learned from a mentor and practiced on real animals. While this team member need not commit an entire full-time position to behavior, they do need to feel a passion for it as a primary part of their practice and be eager to champion the changes that this book lays out. Without such a knowledgeable trailblazer, the path described in this book will be rocky and difficult to complete.

Models for working with your behavior expert

Behavioral expertise in the clinic can come from a current staff member who has an interest in companion animal behavior and undertakes an education program to increase their knowledge and skillset. On the one hand, this approach provides the clinic with a behavior expert who is already well known to clinic staff and who in turn is very comfortable with the clinic's current approaches to animal care. On the other hand, bringing in outside expertise can be helpful, as someone looking at old protocols with fresh eyes may notice animal welfare issues that someone more familiar with "how we've always done it" may miss. If a current staff member chooses to go this route, they should consider getting certification from a reputable organization (see Behavior Certifications below). Working through an established program provides structure and mentorship, both critical pieces of this kind of education.

Having a behavior expert work with both staff and human patients promotes one of the goals of cooperative care which is to have the pet's owner involved to minimize stress as shown in the photos below:

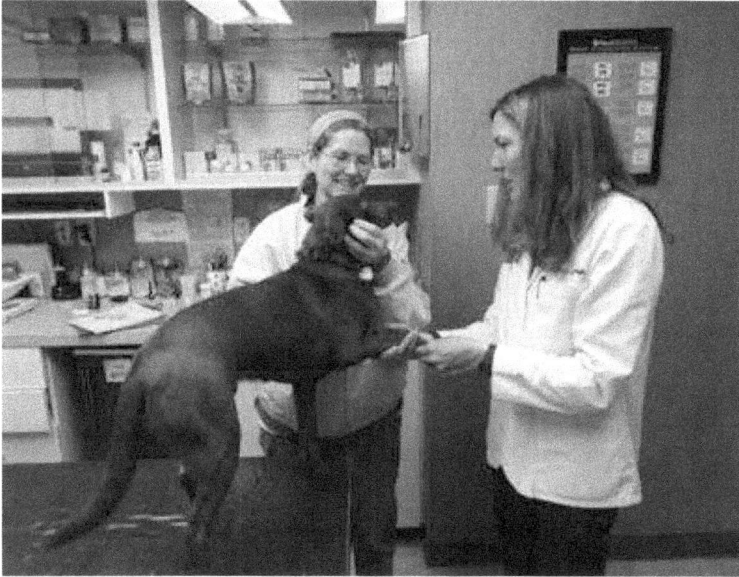

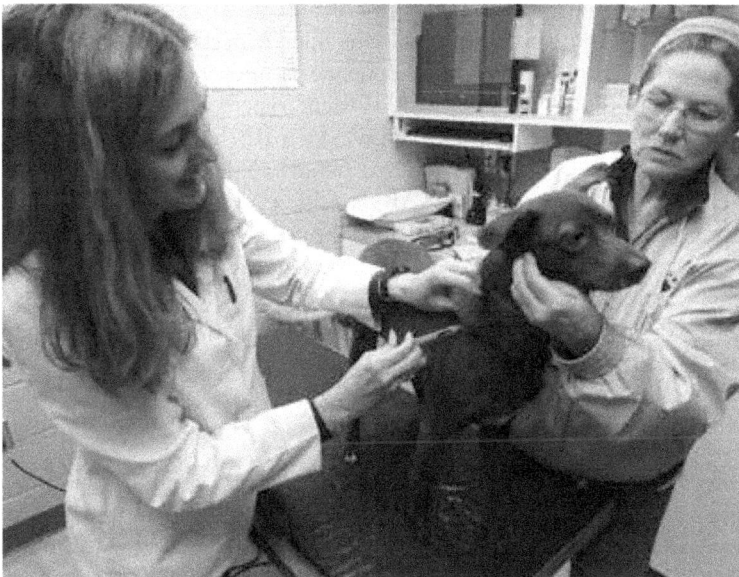

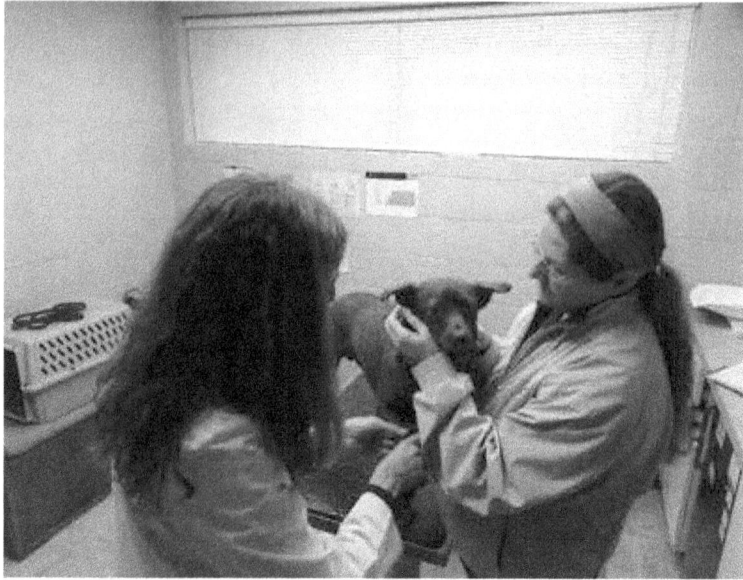

Cooperative care in action with the dog's person holding and calming the dog using minimal restraint.

Alternatively, clinic leadership may choose to hire a new full or part time staff member to guide the new clinic behavior program. Depending on the clinic's needs, this new staff member may be a veterinary technician with behavioral expertise, a veterinarian who specializes in behavior, or a behavior consultant who does not have a veterinary medicine background. A technician with behavioral expertise is an excellent option for many clinics: their salary is less than a veterinarian's, and they can operate not only as a behavior expert but as a technician, enabling them to perform multiple jobs at the clinic. A veterinarian with an interest in and knowledge of behavior (possibly a member of the American Veterinary Society of Animal Behavior) or even a veterinary behaviorist (a DACVB or veterinarian with a CAAB) would be qualified to manage a behavior/animal welfare program at a clinic and would have additional skills enabling them to manage complex behavior cases. A behavior consultant or non-veterinarian behavior professional (certified by CCPDT, PPG, IAABC or ABS) would not necessarily have a veterinary medicine background, unless they were also a veterinarian or veterinary technician. Again, this may make them more able to see clinic operations with fresh eyes. However, they may also find understanding the complexities of clinic operation to be more challenging than someone who has worked in that environment previously.

While preferred, if hiring or training a staff behavior professional is not desirable or feasible for some reason, a veterinary clinic can work closely with/refer to a capable, experienced and qualified force-free behavior consultant in the community. Clinic leadership will need to interview and research these professionals carefully to ensure skills, experience and qualifications.

Such a consultant could help design and implement a new behavior program. This option may be best for clinics without the resources to devote a full- or part-time staff member to their behavioral program. However, without the insights from a team member who knows the clinic's existing protocols well and is also steeped in the world of animal behavior, important components of the behavioral program may be overlooked.

Degreed behavior certifications

Formal certification for behavior work is available to veterinarians, veterinary technicians, individuals with academic degrees (M.S. or Ph.D. in appropriate fields), and individuals without an advanced degree. When clinic leadership is seeking a program for a current employee who is interested in focusing on behavior or evaluating the credentials of a new hire with behavioral expertise, a referral or consultant, they may put considerable trust in these programs, which provide a high level of education and support for behavioral skills.

American College of Veterinary Behaviorists. Veterinary behaviorists are commonly diplomates of this college. They have completed a residency program and passed a board exam, and, importantly, have access to the college's resources, namely its other diplomates. Note that some veterinarians may have completed a behavior residency but not passed the board exam. ACVB diplomates (DACVBs) are highly trained in veterinary behavior medicine though they may not have extensive experience in hands-on animal training. dacvb.org

The Academy of Veterinary Behavior Technicians. This organization certifies a VTS (Behavior) specialty. Credentialed veterinary technicians wishing to specialize in animal behavior must work with behavior cases for several years and sit for an exam. A technician with a VTS (Behavior) could be an excellent candidate for managing a clinic's adoption of new behavior protocols. However, technicians working at a clinic without a veterinarian who currently sees behavior cases may find it difficult to log the necessary case hours to qualify to take the VTS (Behavior) exam, so this option may not be the best one for a technician working at a veterinary clinic who wishes to increase their behavior skills. avbt.net

The Animal Behavior Society. The ABS certifies non-veterinary animal behaviorists, as well as some veterinarians who want a behavior certification but are unwilling or unable to acquire a DACVB. Those with a Ph.D. in an appropriate field, or with a D.V.M. or V.M.D., are eligible to become a Certified Applied Animal Behaviorist (CAAB), and those with an M.S. degree are eligible to become an Associate Certified Applied Animal Behaviorist (ACAAB). ACAABs are, again, highly trained professionals. Those who are not veterinarians, are not able to prescribe behavior medications, but they are very capable of handling complex behavior cases. animalbehaviorsociety.org

Non-degreed behavior certifications

The Certification Council for Professional Dog Trainers. CCPDT is an independent (non-membership) organization that provides certification for dog trainers (CPDT-KA-knowledge assessed and CPDT-KSA-skills and knowledge assessed) and dog behavior consultants (CBCC-KA-knowledge assessed). Professionals certified through CCPDT are expected to follow the Humane Hierarchy, using positive reinforcement as their first training and behavior modification approach. They do not require any veterinary or other degree prior to application for certification. www.ccpdt.org

The Pet Professional Guild. *www.petprofessionalguild.com* PPG offers certification through the Pet Professional Accreditation Board (PPAB) for behavior consultants, again without requiring any advanced degrees. PPG certificants are expected to support humane and scientific practices. www.petprofessionalguild.com.

The International Association of Animal Behavior Consultants. IAABC provides certifications for behavior consultants. They do not require any veterinary or other degree prior to application for certification; however, veterinarians, veterinary technicians, and individuals with M.S. and Ph.D. degrees have obtained certifications from them. They provide a variety of certifications for consultants interested in working with various species. IAABC certificants are expected to follow the LIMA (Least Intrusive, Minimally Aversive) model in their training and behavior work. www.iaabc.org.

Independent training and behavior courses

There are several legitimate and well-regarded independent and scientifically sound certification courses for training and behavior professionals. While most focus on dogs, there are also some courses available for other species. Some are remote courses, some are hands-on. These include:

- **Academy for Dog Trainers** (Jean Donaldson) - https://www.academyfor-dogtrainers.com/
- **Karen Pryor Academy** (Karen Pryor/Ken Ramirez, Director of Training) - https://karenpryoracademy.com/
- **Victoria Stillwell Academy for Dog Training and Behavior** (Victoria Stillwell) - https://www.vsdogtrainingacademy.com/
- **Peaceable Paws Intern Academies** (Pat Miller) - https://peaceablepaws.com/peaceable-paws-intern-academies/

Identifying an appropriate behavior expert

A behavior expert with certification from any of the above programs is very likely to have a science-based understanding of modern behavior approaches. If clinic leadership is selecting an appropriate program for staff training, or debating a possible hire with a different certification, they will need to navigate the confusing array of animal training certifications. In the United States, there is no legislative oversight of animal trainers. Many certification programs are excellent and produce graduates with solid behavior skills based on scientific approaches. Others produce graduates who have had a smattering of online education mostly based on outdated techniques. Many fall in-between these two extremes, and many animal trainers have no certification at all, only their own experience.

Several organizations do not provide certifications but do provide support for individuals with an interest in veterinary animal behavior who seek to connect with others in the field, as well as providing educational opportunities. The American Veterinary Society of Animal Behavior (avsab.org) provides support to veterinarians with an interest in veterinary behavior, both with and without behavior residency backgrounds, and is an excellent resource for identifying a veterinarian with an interest in animal behavior. The Society of Veterinary Behavior Technicians (svbt.org) provides similar support to veterinary technicians and staff with an interest in animal behavior.

In some areas, certified behavior consultants may not be available, and excellent trainers and behavior experts exist who do not have certifications. To find these, search for consultants who:

- Identify as "positive," "reward," "force-free" or "reinforcement" based, incorporate the scientific principles of behavior and learning, and use food in training.

- Do not identify as "balanced," use dominance theory (the theory that much canine aggression stems from an attempt to dominate the owner), or use prong or electronic collars.

- Do not do anything to animals in their classes that would make you uncomfortable if done to your own animals – or your child.

- Actively continue to learn about animal behavior and can list recent educational experiences.

- Provide follow-up with their clients.

- Work as part of a team with clients' other animal-care professionals.

- Belong to professional association(s).

- Will provide a list of clients as references; the clients should assert that the trainer or behavior consultant successfully resolved the behavior problem, and that it remained resolved.

- Have at least several years' dedicated experience in the field.

- Have excellent people skills and understand that much of animal behavior modification is really owner behavior modification.

Additional resources for increasing behavior expertise

Just as with veterinary medicine, the behavior field is always growing and changing. Keeping up means engaging in high quality continuing education. Luckily, there are many opportunities for veterinarians and veterinary staff to learn more about behavior, both online and in person.

- Fear Free Pets is an initiative providing educational resources and certification for veterinary clinics that handle animals in a minimally invasive manner. It includes RACE-approved continuing education courses, a community with which to discuss the challenges of changing clinic protocols, and a directory for potential clients to search for Fear Free certified practices. fearfreepets.com

- IAABC offers an annual conference chock full of information about behavior modification, as well as online courses. iaabc.org

- ClickerExpo, from Karen Pryor Academy, is a massive semi-annual conference about animal training. While not completely focused on behavior problems or behavior modification techniques, it includes many opportunities to learn about these topics. clickerexpo.clickertraining.com

- APDT and PPG also offer annual conferences which include information about behavior. https://apdt.com/ and https://www.petprofessionalguild.com/

- Fenzi Dog Sports Academy (FDSA), an online dog sports school, often offers online courses on modification of dog behavior problems. Fenzidog-sportsacademy.com

- AVSAB and SVT, as previously noted, are excellent resources for veterinary-specific educational opportunities in behavior.

- Many animal trainers offer in-person seminars. To find some in your area, ask at local training clubs. Once you have found trainers whose content is useful to you, follow them on social media to learn who else offers similar content and discover when those trainers will be in your area. When attending in-person seminars, make new friends and ask them who else they enjoy learning from and what mailing lists you should be on to learn about upcoming opportunities locally.

The journey to building clinic protocols that make animals truly comfortable in a veterinary setting is a vitally important one, with many learning challenges. Taking that journey requires the support of someone on staff with a deep passion for animal behavior and a commitment to learning more about it, who can champion the team along the trip. This book contains a great deal of guidance but is only the first step on the road. Working with qualified animal behavior professionals can make that hill far less steep and that road much less rocky.

Chapter 4
The Hospital Environment
By Dr. Leslie Sinn, CPDT-KA, DVM, DACVB

The power of environmental management

One of the simplest, easiest and most powerful ways to impact behavior is through environmental management. Knowledgeable teachers and trainers continually assert that you must "set your learner up for success," while in applied behavior analysis there is a name for this process known as antecedent arrangement. The gist of this simple concept is that to a significant extent, you can control behavioral outcomes by setting the stage. In this case, the stage is the veterinary practice and by managing both the day-to-day flow that comes through the hospital as well as the physical plant itself, you have in your power the opportunity to provide a calm, quiet and supportive environment that minimizes stress for your patients, clients, staff and co-workers.

Seeing, hearing and smelling - the animal's point of view - the concept of Umwelt

Umwelt is a German word meaning surroundings or environment. It was first proposed as a concept by the biologists Jakob von Uexküll and Thomas A. Sebeok. Their idea was a simple one, which is that even though we share the same environment, our perception of that environment will vary based on how our senses interpret it. For example, since human vision is different from canine vision, which is different from feline vision, the perception of the same scenario by each species will vary. Add into the mix the learning history of each individual, and it becomes clear that there will be a great deal of variation between how each of us experiences our shared environment. Making the assumption that every species perceives things the same way humans do is, unfortunately, a common fallacy. If our goal is to provide a positive experience, then we need to attempt to see the world from the animal's point of view.

The physical plant

Take a tour of your facility and try to view it through a dog's or cat's eyes. This isn't a new theory. For years, hospital managers have been exhorting us to view our facilities through the eyes of our clients. The same principle applies, but in this situation, viewing your workspace through the eyes of your *animal* clients. An excellent way to approach this is by having a hospital team member walk through the hospital with a recording device held at dog/cat level and then reviewing and discussing the tape during a staff meeting. Undoubtedly there will be numerous improvements that can be made, most of them at low or no cost.

Space

The more space the better, but the reality is that in many facilities the amount of space is at a premium. This can create a management challenge. At a minimum, set your exam rooms and waiting areas up so that there is at least six feet (the length of a standard dog leash) between animals. In addition, take steps to create space. Ban flexi-leashes and provide simple slip leads for clients who forget to bring a standard leash. Prevent animals from going nose-to-nose by creating visual barriers with either furniture or plants. An often-overlooked way to create additional space is to provide stable shelves or tables in the waiting room where carriers can be securely placed (Carlstead, Brown, and Stawn, 1993). This takes advantage of vertical space that is often underutilized and allows for a greater feeling of safety for cats and other small animals (Kry and Casey, 2007).

Waiting area – note dividers between spaces to help reduce stress.

Prevent or limit patients from facing each other in the waiting room, cages, or kennels. This includes restricting roaming by your clinic cat! If feasible, provide separate dog and cat waiting areas. Another alternative is to offer a cat-only day, so that the two species can be kept apart.

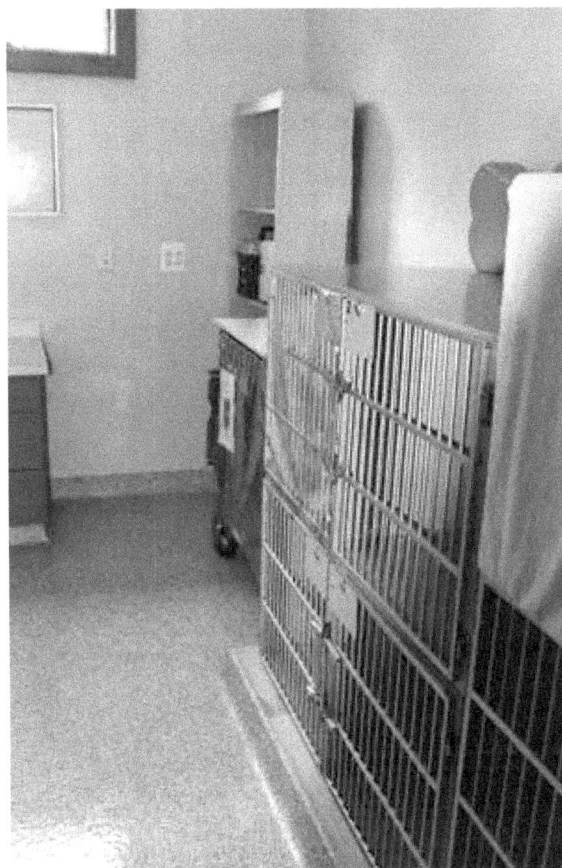

Cat kennel isolation – sound insulated and away from traffic, to minimize stress.

Surfaces

One of our primary concerns as veterinary professionals is disease control. This translates into flooring that is impervious for sanitation purposes. However, the same characteristics that make flooring impervious often makes it slick. It isn't uncommon to see a terrified dog standing splay-legged in a lobby or hallway too scared to move. Invest in some lightweight mats (this is often a great way to recycle yoga mats) that can be used as stepping stones to allow a dog to comfortably ambulate across the floor. In addition, providing towels, throw rugs or bathmats for resting and/or hiding once in the exam room will help mitigate stress. Install non-slip mats on walk-on scales, exam room floors (for larger dogs) and on tables (for cats and smaller dogs). Several easily cleaned non-slip mats are now commercially available.

Walk-on scale with non-slip surface to minimize stress.

Traffic flow

Develop a circular pattern for traffic flow such that clients don't have to cross over or double back when moving through the clinic, thereby minimizing unwanted contact with other patients. Have staff escort waiting clients into open exam rooms to cut down on congestion in the lobby. Another option is to have clients call or text when they arrive, wait in their cars and then have staff escort them directly to a consultation room. Creating a separate quiet room as shown in the photos on the next two pages where anxious animals can wait in peace is ideal Another effective way to reduce delays at the front desk is to have online booking, and wireless checkout that takes place in the exam room. Use technology to decrease stress-causing congestion and back-ups wherever possible.

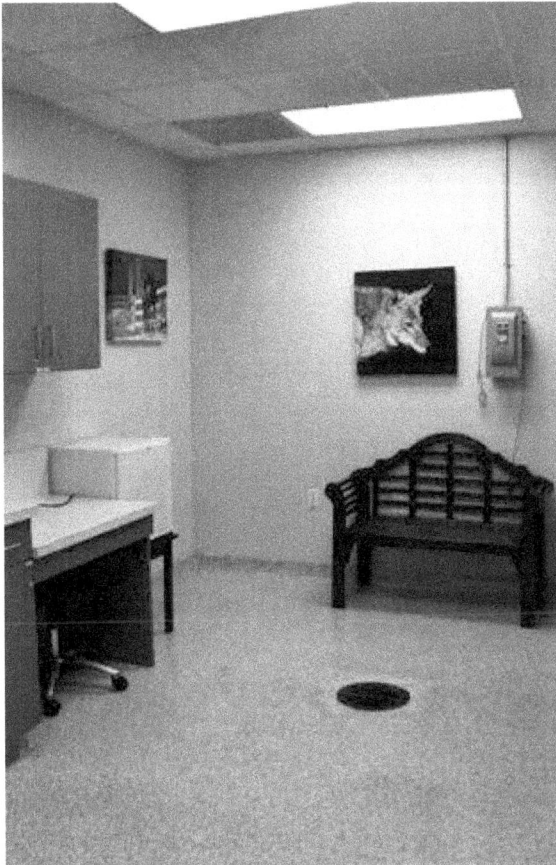

Three photos of exam rooms. The first two show an exam room with space for seating for human clients, and the third photo shows an outside exam as a creative alternative.

Through their eyes

Colors

Dogs and cats both have the ability to perceive color. The dog's vision is similar to that of people with red-green color blindness, while cats can perceive the same colors as humans as long as the stimulus is large enough. Cats have trouble perceiving the color of small objects, perhaps as an evolutionary adaptation that allows them to see past the protective coloration of their typical small prey (Loop and Bruce, 1978).

Calm, visually soothing cat exam room with cat toys.

The recommendation has been made to choose environmental colors based on what is perceived as 'soothing' by people (Fear Free Level 3), however, research to date on the emotional response of animals is limited. In addition, the verdict is still out on human perception of color. While it is true that some people have strong associations with specific colors, those associations are often at the individual level and are heavily influenced by cultural and personal associations (Gryzbowski and Kupidura-Majewski, 2019).

One color that often has a clearly negative association is white, specifically associated with white lab coats. A well-documented phenomenon in people, a number of research studies have also documented a 'white coat effect' in both cats and dogs (Belew, Barlett, and Brown, 1999; Marino et al., 2011). Remove your white lab coat before working with anxious or fearful patients or choose some other color for staff and veterinarian professionals to wear.

Patterns
Dogs are more likely to respond with submissive behavior towards people wearing shirts with narrow stripes than people wearing wider stripes or a broken, uneven or spotted pattern (Chamove, 1997). Although we do not have similar studies to refer to

in cats, it makes sense to avoid striped patterns for professional wear or decorating purposes. While 'submissive' is sometimes perceived as a positive response, it is, in fact, not – as it indicates the animal is uncomfortable and often fearful of the human with whom they are interacting.

Lights

Both dogs and cats are more sensitive to light than humans due to the tapetum lucidum, an anatomical adaptation in the eye which gathers and reflects available light back into the retina. Harsh, continuous lighting has been found to be stress-inducing in a variety of species, therefore soft/dim lighting is preferred (Morgan and Tromborg, 2007).

Dogs and cats have higher flicker fusion rates (the speed at which the retina updates a visual image) than people (Miller, 2001; Coile et al., 1989). This means that they perceive the flicker of fluorescent lights which are below our threshold. Malfunctioning fluorescent lights, those that we can perceive, will be especially bothersome to cats and dogs and should be replaced as soon as feasible. Where practical, non-fluorescent lighting should be used.

For both predators and prey, fast movements attract attention, and fast movements directed toward the recipient are likely to be perceived as a threat (Howard and Holcombe, 2010; Reid, 2009). Move slowly and deliberately. Avoid fast, jerky, unexpected movements that may trigger a fight or flight response.

One way to help control visual input includes the simple step of covering the carrier, cage or even the pet's head to help decrease or eliminate fearful or overwhelming visual input. For worried or reactive dogs, a Calming Cap/Thunder Cap® may be helpful. It is a stretch jersey hood that functions similar to the hood on a falcon, decreasing alarming visual input and helping the pet be more at ease. The difference between a Calming Cap and falcon hood is that the Calming Cap is a sheer nylon – so dogs can still see through it, but detail is blurred, so intensity of the stimulus is decreased, eliciting less of a reaction. A falcon hood is opaque – the dog could not see through it at all.

Through their nose

Pleasant scents

Scents associated with positive behavioral responses in dogs and cats include lavender, chamomile and the scent of the owner (Berns, Brooks, and Spivak, 2015; Graham, Wells, and Hepper, 2005; Wells, 2005). Catnip also has a positive response in those cats that are responders (Ellis, 2010). It may be helpful to use lavender oil on bandanas, towels and bedding. In one study, lavender helped to reduce excitement in dogs during car rides (Wells, 2006).

Noxious scents

Noxious smells may include the smell of harsh chemicals, alcohol, blood, bodily excretions and the scent of predators (Takahashi, Nakashima, and Hong, 2005). In the case of most cats, this would include the smell of dogs. Distinctive smells such as alcohol may become a classically conditioned stimulus indicating that bad things are about to happen. If the only time a pet smells alcohol is immediately before being pricked by a needle, a strong negative association is likely to be formed. This type of single trial learning is a frequent response to a fear-inducing situation and a common outcome in the veterinary setting.

Avoid harsh chemicals. Use enzymatic cleaners where practical. Wipe down contaminated surfaces, wash hands, switch clothes and remove the trash in order to eliminate noxious smells that are likely to trigger a fearful response.

Pheromones

Pheromones are chemical messengers that trigger a behavioral response. They are detected by the respiratory epithelium and the vomeronasal organ (Jacobson's organ) and are species-specific serving a variety of functions associated with social interactions (Pantages, 2000). Feline facial pheromone fraction (Feliway®; Ceva) is a synthetic copy of the secretion used by cats to rub against objects in their environment signaling familiarity and territory. Dog-appeasing pheromone (Adaptil®; Ceva) is a man-made copy of pheromones produced by the sebaceous glands in the intermammary sulcus of bitches shortly after birth. Both promote an overall calming effect in the respective species.

Research shows that the use of Feliway spray on the examination table improves the welfare of cats by reducing their stress during veterinary consultations (Pereira et al., 2016). A second study suggests that exposure to Feliway may be helpful in increasing grooming behavior and food intake in hospitalized cats (Griffith, Steigerwald, and Buffington, 2000).

Research conducted with dogs suggests that the use of Adaptil in the clinic was associated with greater relaxation of the dogs, but there was no effect on aggressive behavior during the clinical examination (Mills et al., 2006). Use of Adaptil in a clinical setting may also improve the recovery and welfare of dogs undergoing surgery (Siracusa et al., 2010).

Pheromones can be aerosolized via diffusers in the waiting, exam and recovery rooms. Using pheromone spray on bedding, bandanas, Thundershirts® and carriers is an additional option.

Through their ears

Species specific communication

There is some indication that in order for music to be an effective form of communication, it must be in the frequency range and with similar tempos to those used in natural communication by each species. Research in cats would suggest that species specific music is more effective in reducing stress than human directed music (Snowden, Teie, and Savage, 2015). Species specific soundtracks have been created for use in the clinic or home (Through a Cats' Ear ™ and Through a Dog's Ear™).

Music

Avoid hard rock, as this type of music has been associated with signs of stress in animals (shaking and increased barking) while classical music has been associated with signs of relaxation (less barking and more time spent resting) (Kogan, Schoenfeld-Tacher, and Simon, 2012; Wells, Graham, and Hepper, 2002). Playing audiobooks was also found to increase resting behavior in kenneled dogs (Brayley, 2016). It is important to note that playing classical music is associated with increased owner satisfaction regardless of the dog's behavioral score (Engler and Bain, 2017).

Noise

Stress associated with noise has been well documented in a variety of species including humans (Ackerman and Lloyd, 1959). Damage to hearing is associated with sound levels above 85 db. Unfortunately, a barking dog will often exceed 100 db while barking (Coppola, Enns, and Grandin, 2006). Continuous sounds are less disturbing than intermittent sounds. White noise can be stress reducing if below 85 db, otherwise the white noise itself can become an additional source of stress.

Talking

Harsh voices and reprimands can be perceived as punishing, increasing stress and leading to increased aggression (Herron, Shofer, and Reisner, 2009). Speak quietly, calmly and sparingly. Keep in mind that for feral or shy animals, speaking to them may actually be aversive and increase their anxiety level in any given situation.

Barking and other sounds of distress

In a study, physical examinations were performed on dogs with and without background noise playing that consisted of barking, talking and metal doors clanging. The presence of background noise affected a number of parameters including respiratory rate (Stellato et al., 2019). Behavioral signs of stress increased with noise including lip licking, avoidance and posture reductions. Based on the above findings, minimizing noise in the veterinary clinic is a must. This is done by having an awareness of and avoiding, as much as possible, the background-noise-creating conditions described above. Sound absorbing panels can also be helpful, as can cotton balls in the ears of animals who are particularly sound-sensitive.

Through their touch

Surface treatments

The disadvantages of slick surfaces have already been discussed. The use of easy to clean mats such as the Ezee-Visit Pet Vet Mat® (Limington, Maine) for conducting your physical exams either on floor or on the table will help pets be more at ease. Providing ample soft bedding for hiding and resting also allows for greater comfort and security.

The power of contact

In one study, having owners pet their dogs prior to separation helped to decrease the subsequent stress response (Mariti et al., 2018). In a second study, having the owner present during the examination attenuated the dog's stress response (Csoltova et al., 2017). The above studies indicate that, whenever possible, examination and treatment should occur in the owner's presence.

With cats, sociability varies considerably from one individual to the next. Depending on the cat, contact with a familiar person may be stress reducing (Vitale, Behnke, and Udell, 2019).

Providing a place to hide, such as allowing the pet to remain in its carrier while conducting and examination or procedure, can help to mitigate stress. Prior conditioning to a carrier significantly reduces stress during transport and handling (Gruen et al., 2013; Pratsch et al., 2018).

Through their taste

The use of food to help form positive associations with the veterinary facility and staff will be discussed in detail in Chapters 5 and 6. Keep ample supplies of high value treats in the waiting room, by scales, in the exam room as well as the front desk. Mounting shelves to hold a variety of treat containers may be useful in helping to provide easy access.

Looking at other species; Small companion animal behavior

Avian and pocket pets have special needs above and beyond what are typically required by cats and dogs. Of primary concern is that most of these small animals are prey species and feel exceptionally vulnerable when housed in close proximity to predators (dogs and cats). Providing separate species-appropriate housing is a must. As discussed with dogs and cats in the previous sections, all aspects of their environmental needs must be addressed: sight, smell, sound, touch and taste. For example, housing an avian patient in a cat room because it would be considered quieter is unacceptable. Keeping a rabbit in an exposed cage on a veterinarian's desk is an equally inappropriate choice. Think carefully before accepting these patients into your care. Make sure that you can truly provide for their needs: medically, environmentally and behaviorally (Warwick et al., 2018).

Conclusions

Our environment shapes our perceptions, and that same environment impacts our moods and our behaviors. The same applies to the animals under our care. Make the effort to see the world through their eyes. Adapt your facility to be more attuned to animal needs, and reap the many benefits of a calm, quiet and supportive environment that minimizes stress for your patients while maximizing their welfare. These topics will be covered with more specificity and details in the chapters that follow.

Chapter 5
The Patient-Friendly Reception Area
By Dr. Andrea Y. Tu, DVM

Introduction

While the previous chapters have provided us with a good understanding of feline and canine body language and how the veterinary staff can utilize that information to determine the emotional state of a patient at the hospital, we will now shift gears and attempt to understand the environment from the patient's point of view. In order to best prepare your waiting room for as low-stress of an experience as possible for our feline and canine patients, we must first gain an understanding of how cats and dogs perceive their environment. Undoubtedly, one of the easiest mistakes is to presume that the veterinary patient's perception of a room is similar to our human perception, resulting in an environment that is optimal for staff and clients, but does not meet the needs of our feline and canine patients.

We will first review the senses for the feline and canine patient in the order of least impactful to most impactful for the patient, both in terms of how well they serve as methods of obtaining information from conspecifics and the environment, and how this information can subsequently impact the recipient's emotional health once the message is received. Then, we will discuss ways in which to pre-emptively prevent overstimulation of our patients' senses both immediately prior to and during the entrance and waiting period in a veterinary clinic. Finally, we will also cover the check-out process, as well as reintroduction to any housemates once the client returns to their home. This will ensure that our patients have as pleasant an experience as possible prior to and after their exam and treatment and set both our patients and the veterinary team up for success.

Tactile sensation

Of all the senses, tactile sensation is much less impactful for the veterinary patient when compared to other senses such as sight, hearing, and smell. Despite this, it is still an important way for cats and dogs to obtain information from their environment, and tactile sensation plays a key role in the veterinary patient's comfort and stress level. Cats are highly tactile beings and appear to enjoy physical contact with familiar individuals with whom they have a social bond. Physical contact by the queen has been shown to have a calming effect on kittens, as they will bury their head in the queen's fur upon reunion after a period of separation. A similar calming effect can be obtained in an older cat if the owner covers the cat's face with their hands. Cats prefer gentle stroking or petting, respond better to minimal restraint instead of being held firmly, but can resent being handled near the base of the tail (Beaver, 2003).

With regard to temperature, in general, veterinary patients, especially cats, prefer warmer temperatures and are less tolerant to cold compared to humans, due to their higher body temperatures. Feline faces are about one third as sensitive to radiant heat as human faces, but a cat's nose is able to detect up to a 32.36° F (0.2° C) increase or a 32.9° F (0.5° C) decrease in temperatures. Cold temperatures result in increased somatic rage reaction and increased circling behaviors, suggesting an increase in spontaneous and evoked somatic motor activity, possibly resulting in a display of aggressive behaviors. However, excessive heat is also uncomfortable, as cats will be: lethargic with prolonged exposure to temperatures between 75° to 85° F (25° to 30° C); start to display signs of discomfort such as panting, hyperexcitability, circling at temperatures higher than 85° F (30° C); and will sense heat-related pain between 124° to 129° F (51° to 54° C), in comparison to humans who can detect pain at 111° F (44° C) (Beaver, 2003; Giammanco, Paderni, and Carollo, 1976; Kenshalo, 1964; Kenshalo, Duncan, and Weymark, 1967).

Cats and dogs also possess specialized tactile vibrissae, which are longer hairs attached to striated muscle that allows for voluntary control and are contained in larger follicles that have blood-filled sinuses and nerve receptors. These vibrissae are located primarily on the face (whiskers) and the ventral aspect of the carpus and can respond to as little as seven ounces (2mg) weight or directional movement against the natural direction of the hair (Beaver 2003). Facial vibrissae are used to scan the environment craniolaterally during ambulation and are folded along the side of the head during rest, greeting, defense or sniffing. Losing these hairs results in a cat becoming more dependent on vision. The carpal vibrissae, on the other hand, are speculated to be used during predatory behaviors and are not related to walking.

As a form of communication, tactile sensory input is valuable in that it is immediate, it is highly recipient specific and can be quickly altered as needed. However, it is a weak form of communication in that it requires close proximity to the recipient, and it lacks pertinence (Ley, 2016). To that effect, in the context of the veterinary clinic, one would expect that the communication resulting from tactile contact between conspecifics is minimal at best, and tactile comfort for the veterinary patient would focus more on appropriate room temperatures, adjusting the pressure of restraint to be most soothing for species-specific and individual preferences, and utilizing the calming effects of petting or physical contact with the owner when appropriate.

Visual sensation

It can be argued that vision is also a less impactful sense for our feline and canine patients. Most studies on feline and canine visual perception have been done in comparison to that of humans, and compared to humans, felines and canines are not as dependent on their visual senses as a means of communication as compared to, for instance, their olfactory senses. This is an important distinction to keep in mind; as highly visual beings ourselves, we may prioritize minimizing visual stimuli and forget the strong impact of the other senses discussed below.

Feline and canine vision also appear to perceive the world very differently compared to human vision. Cats have well developed visual abilities (Bradshaw, Casey, and Brown, 2012) and feline visual perception appears to be particularity adapt at detecting motion and in low light environments having an ability to detect the presence of objects at one-fifth the illumination that humans need to see an object (Ewer, 1973). This is in part due to the tapetum lucidum, present in both feline and canine eyes, which allows light to be reflected back through the retina, resulting in better detection of the presence of an object, but with decreased detail perception (Miller and Murphy, 1995).

When provided with television monitors, cats in shelters are noted to spend about 6% of their time watching them with the amount of time decreasing over subsequent exposures (Ellis, Sarah, and Wells 2008), indicating cats are both able to see and show interest in two-dimensional moving visual images, despite the higher critical flicker fusion of feline and canine visual abilities that results in the images appearing less fluid than to a human (Coile, Pollitz, and Smith, 1989).

Despite this, it should be noted that cats in shelters do not benefit from visual stimuli as much as primates do (Ellis, Sarah, and Wells, 2008). What is interesting is that environmental conditions in turn appear to impact the development of visual abilities, as caged cats are myopic (near-sighted, with far objects appearing out of focus) whereas free-range cats are hypermetropic (far-sighted, with close objects appearing blurry) (Belkin et al., 1977).

Like feline vision, canine vision is also more sensitive to rapid movements when compared to human vision (Coile, Pollitz, and Smith, 1989) and both have a lower threshold of light for vision (Miller and Murphy, 1995). Dogs also have the benefit of a wider field of vision when compared to humans (Miller and Murphy, 1995) and are better at differentiating shades of grey, but dogs appear to be less able to see sharp images from a distance and have a more restrictive binocular visual field when compared to their human counterparts (Miklosi, 2007). Depending on the breed, depth perception is also likely blocked by the nose, as the length of the nose can interfere with binocular vision in most breeds when they look below the horizontal (Miller and Murphy, 1995). When it comes to color detection, cats and dogs appear to view the world like that of a color-blind person, with cats possessing cones that detect green and blue colors, and dogs being able to see shades of violet, blue and yellow (Houpt, 2018).

Overall, feline and canine vision are well adapted for low light vision detection over wide fields, and are highly sensitive to movement, but at the expense of decreased detection of details and color. As a form of communication, vision is not as reliable as some of the other senses as it only travels a short distance and can easily be intercepted by a barrier, such as a panel or even one's dolichocephalic nose! Furthermore, diseases such as cataracts or corneal lesions, or even eye medications, can dramatically decrease or prevent the recipient from detecting a visual cue.

Visual stimuli do have the benefit of being quick acting as the information can be received immediately, but it does not have permanence and will not persist in the environment when compared to other stimuli such as olfactory scents (Ley, 2016). We can, however, use our understanding of feline and canine vision to help manage stimuli that can result in increased fear and anxiety. Reminding staff to move in a deliberate manner around the clinic and avoid fast, dramatic movements will help prevent visual overstimulation. The use of visual barriers such as strategically placed furniture or even room divider panels can further minimize undesired visual triggers. Keep in mind that our veterinary patient's visual field is much closer to the ground than ours, and either focus on preventing visual stimuli that are located at ground level or elevate the patient's carrier off the ground in order to place them in a less stress-inducing visual environment.

An understanding of feline and canine visual limitations will also be handy in our interactions with our patients. For instance, far-sighted cats may be more stressed by a nearby object as this may appear out of focus. A favorite treat offered immediately in front of a cat that has nasal discharge may be refused not because there is an increase in that cat's stress, but because the cat has trouble detecting the presence of the treat due to their hypermetropic vision and an olfactory sense that is compromised by illness. This example also highlights the need to consider the visual stimuli in the context in which it is presented. One cannot look at just the impact of the visual stimuli alone as this is not how the cat or dog is perceiving the environment. Rather, our patients will be obtaining information from various senses, and we also need to consider the information being communicated via the other senses in our effort to minimize stress and fear in the veterinary clinic.

Auditory sensation

Feline and canine auditory senses are more sensitive than that of a human and are believed to be more important than vision (Jane, Masterton, and Diamond, 1965). Cats can detect sounds from as low 48 kHz up to 85 kHz, which means they are able to detect sounds within the ultrasonic range. The cat's unique ability to hear well in both low and high frequencies also means they possess one of the broadest hearing ranges among mammals, barely exceeded only by cattle and porpoises (Heffner and Heffner, 1985; Neff and Hind, 1955). Dogs have a hearing range of 44 kHz to 67 kHz. In comparison, humans have a hearing range of 17 to 28 kHz in ideal laboratory conditions, but usually only up to 19 kHz in most conditions (Heffner, 1983).

Cats and dogs both have mobile pinnae, which allows them to localize the source of sound and significantly lowers the auditory threshold. In cats, this allows them to discriminate the source of the sound by an angle of 5 degrees (Beaver, 2003; Houpt, 2018). Dogs can localize sound to within 8 degrees (Miklosi, 2007). Cats also possess large tympanic bullae, and they have 10,000 times more cochlear nerve fibers between ganglion cells and the brain as compared to humans, both of which contribute to a superior auditory sense (Beaver, 2003).

Felines and canines are also able to discriminate one-fifth to one-tenth of a tone difference, especially at higher pitches (Beaver, 2003; Ewer, 1973). However, the heightened auditory ability to detect sounds does not equate to a superior ability to process complex sounds, which is required in understanding human language and key in our interspecies communication with felines and canines. Studies have shown that dogs trained to a cue appear to recognize only the first few phonemes of a spoken cue, as the chances of the trained behavior to occur was higher when the phonemes of the cue were unaltered at the beginning of the cue versus at the end of the cue (Miklosi, 2007). Furthermore, dogs have a harder time responding to cues when the cue is played back on a recording device, suggesting that they are utilizing other sources of information, such as visual senses, to determine context (Miklosi, 2007).

Despite this seemingly limited ability to understand human language, more recent studies have shown that dogs without explicit language training still possess a sensitivity to general vocal qualities of human speech and are more cautious around tones produced by a scolding human, an ability that appears to have developed or been learned by four months of age (Gibson et al., 2014).

In terms of being an effective communication method, auditory communication does have certain benefits. It is immediate and can travel large distances as it is not as easily hindered by barriers as visual stimuli are. Of course, the ability to detect the auditory cue also depends on the recipient's hearing abilities, and certain disease states or even aural medications may result in temporary to permanent loss of hearing and inability to receive auditory communications. On the other hand, auditory stimuli lack permanence and have poor recipient specificity as they will be received and have the potential to impact all individuals within earshot (Ley, 2016).

Given our understanding of how sensitive feline and canine auditory senses are, and the broad-acting effects of auditory communication, it is important in our veterinary setting to minimize distressing sounds as much as possible while maximizing soothing sounds. In the following sections, we will discuss more detailed ways in which to structure your waiting area to minimize the sound of conspecific vocalizations from permeating your waiting room. Interspecies auditory stimuli should also be managed properly.

Keep in mind that the ability to recognize general vocal qualities of human speech is present in un-trained dogs, as this further emphasizes the importance for all staff members to utilizing calm, soothing and quiet voices in the veterinary setting. Finally, many studies have shown the calming effects of certain types of sound stimuli, in particular music, on both veterinary patients and clients (Engler and Bain, 2014; Kogan et al., 2012; Wells, Graham, and Hepper, 2002), and one can utilize such auditory recordings to our advantage to best promote a comfortable auditory environment for our feline and canine patients.

Olfactory sensation

Feline and canine olfaction are superior to that of humans. Humans have an olfactory epithelium of 0.8-2 inches^2 (2 to 5 cm^2) in size, with 5 million receptors. Cats in comparison have 8 to 16 inches^2 (20 to 40 cm^2) in size, with 200 million receptors, which makes feline olfaction 20 times better than humans. However, that pales in comparison to the dog's olfactory epithelium, which is up to 60 to 67 inches^2 (150 to 170 cm^2) in size, with 220 million to 2 billion receptors, resulting in a sense of smell that is 50 to 1000 times better than that of the human (Ley, 2016; Miklosi, 2007).

In dogs, there appears to be a preference for the olfactory sense over vision, and a reliance on olfaction when other sensory stimuli is lacking. In studies, explosive detection dogs have been noted to rely on olfaction over vision as their main sense when engaging in bomb-detection work, both in low light and full light environments. The amount of ambient lighting present did not differentially affect the dog's detection ability, even in extreme (fully light and virtually dark) conditions (Gazit and Terkel, 2003).

Not only are scents important in exploring and habituating to new environments, but they also play a key role in social behaviors and in both intraspecies and interspecies communication (Beaver, 2003). Indeed, we commonly see cats and dogs greet each other first face to face, then face to anus in an attempt for scent detection. Unlike other carnivores, felids possess sebaceous glands in addition to apocrine glands, and as such, cats secrete unique oils in their anal glands that are used in olfactory marking and may be important in conspecific communication (Beaver, 2003). Studies have shown that cats will spend more time sniffing the fecal material of unfamiliar cats. (Nakabayashi, Yamaoka, and Nakashima, 2012).

Cats also have a unique plant-induced aspect of their olfactory sense, in that they will display a change in behavior when exposed to plants that contain 7-methylcyclo-pentapyranones, 7-methyl- 2-pyridines, and 4-methylbenzofuranones, the most well know of which is catnip (*Nepeta cataria*, catmint) (Tucker and Tucker, 1988). Cats are able to detect the active ingredient of catnip, *cis-trans*-nepetalactone, a monoterpene, at levels as low as one part in 109 to 1011. Exposure to catnip results in behaviors such as licking, chewing and eating the catnip, drooling, rubbing of the head in the catnip, to more intense behaviors such as rolling and leaping (Beaver, 2003). Response to catnip varies by individual, with 30 to 50% of cats not possessing the autosomal dominant gene for responding to catnip, and response in general can vary by age and experience. Furthermore, it is also worth noting that kittens younger than two months of age, fearful, and extremely stressed cats have a decreased response to catnip, and the vomeronasal organ is not involved in the cat's response to catnip (Beaver, 2003; Tucker and Tucker, 1988).

Canine olfactory sense also has unique qualities. Amazingly, canine olfactory sense has been shown to develop in dogs as early as *in utero*, as puppies have been found to prefer uniquely scented foods that were fed to their mothers during gestation. While this has been hypothesized to be used by the newborns to learn what 'safe foods' are, given the long canine postnatal period of being fed milk, then regurgitated food, then meat brought to them by the mother, it is more likely that the early learned olfactory scents play a part in intraspecies communication, identity, and social behaviors, especially during the first 10 weeks of life (Hepper and Wells, 2006; Miklosi, 2007).

Finally, it should be noted that the nose is lined with a mucous membrane that preferentially absorbs and binds hydrophilic molecules over hydrophobic odorants and is sensitive to different concentrations of molecules (Miklosi, 2007). Since odorants in the environment will degrade over time, the ability of our veterinary patients to differentiate between molecule concentrations means not only are they able to use their olfactory sense to gain information about an event that has occurred, but they are also able to obtain additional information regarding when this event occurred based on the concentration of the odorant.

Olfaction is a highly efficient and heavily relied on form of communication for our feline and canine patients. Cats and dogs often rely on olfactory signals in interspecies and intraspecies communication, in mate attraction and selection, and to locate prey and food. Olfactory cues are long lasting and can travel far distances as they are the least likely to be obstructed by a barrier.

Like other sensory stimuli, receipt of an olfactory cue may be hindered if the recipient has an ongoing illness that impacts their ability to detect olfaction, or if they are in a heightened state of stress, such as is the case with extremely fearful cats and catnip. However, olfactory stimuli tend to be transmitted slowly and, like auditory stimuli, olfactory stimuli can have poor recipient specificity (Ley, 2016).

We can utilize these properties of olfactory cues and communication both to encourage soothing effects by providing calming scents and decrease stressful effects by minimizing distressing scents in the veterinary clinic. For instance, studies have shown that scents, such as lavender, chamomile, ginger, coconut, vanilla, and valerian reduced behaviors that indicate stress in shelter dogs, suggesting that the use of these scents may have an overall calming effect (Blinks et al., 2018; Graham, Wells, and Hepper, 2005). Lavender scents have also been shown to have a calming effect on dogs during travel, resulting in a lower occurrence of barking and hyperactivity (Wells, 2006). Indeed, lavender and chamomile scents appear to be particularly calming for dogs, and the use of this in veterinary waiting rooms may help decrease stress in our canine patients.

Interestingly, exposure of shelter cats to lavender did not yield the same calming effects, however the difference in results may be due in part to the different modes of odor presentation (lavender air diffusers for the canines versus lavender-infused cloths for the felines), which likely resulted in different concentrations of the odorant (Ellis and Wells, 2010). Indeed, given the difference in olfactory concentrations, the gradient that can occur in the resulting olfactory stimuli and the cue that is communicated, it would be prudent to not only consider the type of scent to use in our veterinary clinic, but also the intensity of olfactory cue used, as a calming scent likely will be less impactful when diluted and one may need to increase the concentration of these odorants when used in a large room or in a room with increased air flow in order to achieve the desired soothing effects.

Semiochemicals - pheromones

In discussing feline and canine senses, one would be remiss to leave out semiochemicals: these are chemicals released by one organism into the environment to communicate and influence the behavior of another organism. Semiochemicals can be found in various species of insects and mammals and can be divided into allomones (impacting organisms of different species) or pheromones (impacting organisms of the same species).

Semiochemicals bind to receptors, and in the case of pheromone, these receptors are usually only present in the species producing that pheromone. They are organic chemicals secreted in small concentrations and can be found in various secretions such as urine, feces, sweat, and mucous secretions of genitalia, as well as specialized exocrine glands such as the intermammary sulcus, cheeks, foot pads, periaural regions and tail base. Pheromones are classified by the specific receptors they bind to and the behaviors they elicit, and not by their chemical compound.

Pheromones can be further subdivided into two types: releasers (which induce a specific behavior); and primers (which modify the emotional state of the recipient) (DePorter, 2016; Pageat and Gaultier, 2003). Pheromones can also be further classified as appeasing pheromones, identity pheromones, alarm pheromones, scratching-induced pheromones, and urogenital/sex pheromones. For our purposes, we will be focusing on mammalian primer pheromones, in particular the appeasing pheromones, the identity pheromones and the alarm pheromones as these will have the most relevance for a veterinary clinic setting.

Semiochemicals, such as pheromones, are very context specific and provide unconditioned signaling. In other words, a dog or cat does not need to have had a previous experience with or learn how to respond to a pheromone; their response is instinctive. Semiochemicals in the environment are inhaled by a cat or dog, and travel either via the nasal cavity, or via the mouth and through the incisive channel, to the vomeronasal organ.

The vomeronasal organ consists of two specialized tubular structures located in a small fossa on either side of the internasal septum, and dorsal to the hard palate, that is present in cats and dogs as well as other species such as horses and ruminants. Specialized receptor neurons in the vomeronasal organ respond to the semiochemical molecules, which are first inhaled during olfactory investigation. Certain species such as cats and horses will also display a Flehmen Response or a 'gape response' to further encourage gathering of semiochemicals into the nasal or oral cavity. This response in the cat consists of a partially open mouth, with a curling of the superior lip and occasionally a flicking of the tongue, often paired with a far-off gaze as the feline inhales deeply and gathers these molecules. See the next page for two examples of the Gape Response.

Two examples of the Gape Response.

Once in the nasal or oral cavity, semiochemicals stimulate the vomeronasal organ to open and are drawn into the lumen of the vomeronasal organ via a pumping action of the surrounding vascular tissue. It is worth noting that semiochemicals and odors are detected differently – perception of odors via the olfactory system is a passive procedure, whereas detection of semiochemicals is an active process as the vomeronasal organ must be stimulated to be opened first before the semiochemicals can bind to its receptors. Upon activation of the receptors in the vomeronasal organ, the signal is then transmitted via the vomeronasal nerve to the accessory olfactory bulb, as well as to the amygdala (via the limbic system) and the ventromedial hypothalamus. This pathway, as well as other specialized semiochemical chemosensory receptors, results in mediation of the limbic system and can impact the recipient's emotional, social and motivational processing and impulses in the environment in which the semiochemical was present (DePorter, 2016; Pageat and Gaultier, 2003).

As mentioned above, we will be focusing on feline and canine appeasing pheromones, identity pheromones and alarm pheromones. Appeasing pheromones are phero-mones secreted by the intermammary sulcus of mammalian mothers starting about 3 to 4 days after parturition. Both cats and dogs secrete an appeasing pheromone, with bitches secreting the canine appeasing pheromone up until puppies are about 4 months of age, and queens secreting the feline appeasing pheromone until kittens are about 6 to 12 weeks of age (DePorter, 2016; Pageat and Gaultier, 2003). Appeasing pheromones are believed to not only play a key role in maternal attachment but also have a comforting effect on the recipient, regardless of the recipient's age.

Identity pheromones are secreted from various glands, including the supracaudal gland at the base of the tail in both cats and dogs, the anal gland in both the cat and the dog, the ear gland in the dog, and facial pheromones of the dog, but the most commonly recognized versions are the facial pheromones secreted by the cheek glands of the cat. There are five known fractions of the feline facial pheromone – F1 to F5. F2 is used by tomcats in sexual marking; F3 plays a key role in special orientation and identifying geographical territories; F4 is used in allomarking and identity of known conspecifics. (The function of F1 and F5 is still undetermined.) These feline facial pheromones are often deposited by cats through facial rubbing or during allogrooming to help cats identify 'safe' territories and 'known' conspecifics.

Facial Rubbing

Facial Rubbing

Allogrooming

This ultimately results in decreased aggressive behaviors and decreased fear and stress resulting from novel environments (DePorter, 2016; Pageat and Gaultier, 2003).

Alarm pheromones are secreted by the supracaudal gland at the base of the tail in both cats and dogs, by the interdigital glands in the cat and by the anal gland in the dog (Pageat and Gaultier, 2003). These pheromones are emitted during fear reactions and can result in avoidance by other cats or dogs that subsequently encounter regions that have been marked with alarm pheromones.

Given their effects, appeasing pheromones, identity pheromones and alarm pheromones will have the most relevance for reducing stress and fear in a veterinary clinic setting. For instance, one can take advantage of the calming effects of the appeasing pheromones through use of commercially available synthetic versions of this pheromone (Adaptil for dogs; Feliway Multicat for cats), thereby reducing patient's stress and fear responses in the veterinary clinic (Gandia-Estelles, Mills, and Mills, 2006; Kim et al., 2010; Kronen et al., 2006; Mills et al., 2006; Pereira et al., 2016; Siracusa et al., 2010).

Similarly, the use of synthetic versions of the identity pheromone (Feliway Classic for cats) can counteract neophobia and help the veterinary clinic seem more familiar and less scary for the veterinary patient. Finally, ensuring alarm pheromones that may have been deposited by a previous patient are thoroughly cleaned and neutralized prior to the arrival of the next patient will prevent fear that results from the subsequent patient detecting the alarm pheromones. These will be discussed in more detail in the following section.

Waiting room set-up

Now that we have a better sense of how differently our feline and canine patients perceive the environment, we can structure our waiting room to prevent overstimulation of our patients prior to their examinations and treatments.

Using your front desk staff as your reception coordinators

One of the most crucial parts of the veterinary team is your front desk staff, as they are the stewards during your patients' (and clients!) first interaction with your practice. They are essential in setting the tone for how the rest of your relationship with that patient and client will progress, both for the day and for the years to come, especially when it comes to promoting and supporting your practice's dedication to a low-stress visit for both the client and the patient.

As with all behavioral interventions aimed at decreasing a patient's stress levels, they should be applied when the patient is not yet aroused or at a lower level of arousal. These interventions often are less effective when the patient is already agitated, and their stress coping methods have been initiated. As such, your reception staff's role in ensuring a low-stress visit starts early, prior to the day of the appointment.

For new clients who have not been to your practice before, the initial call to set up an appointment is your practice's chance to emphasize your dedication to your patients' emotional as well as physical well-being. In addition to obtaining the routine information required for setting up a new client, have your front desk staff take the time to discuss preparations for a low-stress visit. Ask the client what the patient's previous veterinary experiences have been like, and what has worked in the past and what has not. This will give your technicians and doctors the chance to make individual-specific accommodation for that particular patient prior to the day of the examination. Review if there are specific triggers for that individual pet, such as the presence of other animals in the waiting room, or interactions with specific types of staff members. Discuss preferences, such as whether the patient prefers to be examined on the exam table or on the floor. Your front desk staff can discuss with the client what their animal companion enjoys as a treat, or what their favorite toy is, and recommend they bring an assortment of favorite foods, toys, or long-lasting puzzle toys with them the day of the appointment. That way, you can ensure that food items or toys that are considered high value for that patient are available for your staff to use during that patient's exam.

For the clients who have never considered exploring what their pet prefers, it would be wise to have pre-prepared a list of commonly used treats and toys that your front desk staff can send the client. (Some clinics find it useful to further divide this list into items that would be appropriate for certain common medical conditions and by species, e.g., a section of treats that is appropriate for the feline patient with chronic renal disease, or for the canine patient with a history of pancreatitis). Your staff can encourage the client to explore which items their pet likes, then reports back the findings. (For all patients, their preferences for food items or toys should be ranked, then recorded in their medical records as part of their emotional health history so your technicians and doctors can easily reference this in the future.)

Finally, have your reception staff encourage new clients to bring their dog to your clinic's waiting room for 'happy visits' for a treat several times prior to their first visit – this will help their dog be less fearful of a new location the day of the visit. All pets can benefit from happy visits, but these are crucial for the neophobic pet who may have a harder time adjusting to new environments. For clients who are unable to come for a happy visit prior to the day of their appointment, consider e-mailing them a floor plan of your waiting room and parking lot (or a map with parking garages in your area). This will help them plan for the least stressful way to get their animal companion to your clinic, as well as the best entry point for the patient.

For established patients, your front desk staff plays an essential role in ensuring that all previously established pre-veterinary visit pharmaceutical (PVP) plans are implemented by the clients. When scheduling the appointment, reception staff will remind the client of the PVP plan. They, or your technicians, will review the doses of the medication(s) as listed by the doctor in their medical record. Remind the client what time the medication should be given, as most PVPs must be administered one to two hours prior to the veterinary visit. Have the client check that they have enough medication at home, and if not, arrange for them to pick up a refill beforehand so they have enough PVPs on hand for the day of their appointment.

Your front desk staff can also remind the owner of any special accommodations for the time of their pet's arrival, e.g., some will do better entering the practice through a quieter side door instead of the front door, while others may prefer to wait in the car with the owner until an exam room is available. When scheduling the appointment, your front desk staff should also keep in mind any other accommodations noted in the emotional health medical record, such as a preferred exam room or staff member, and schedule that patient accordingly so that the individual animal's preferences can be met.

Have your front desk staff ask the client to avoid feeding their animal companion several hours prior to their visit, as long as this is medically appropriate, since this will help encourage the patient to take treats at the clinic. In addition to favorite foods and toys, remind the client to also bring any other tools that can be helpful for the visit. For instance, a patient may have previously been desensitized to a specific basket muzzle or trained to a specific type of head harness. A specific mat or bed may help a patient remain relaxed during his or her vaccination. (These tools and toys should also be documented in their PVP plan as part of the patient's emotional health medical record.)

Finally, when determining the time of the appointment, your front desk staff can schedule more fearful patients for slower times of the day and adjust the length of the appointment to allow for extra time to provide support and accommodations. For feline and canine mixed practices, consider reserving certain days and times of the week for feline patients in order to create as much of a 'feline only' practice environment as possible. Ideally this would be a morning time, after your clinic has been thoroughly cleaned from the previous day so that your waiting room and exam rooms are not yet contaminated with the scent of previous canine patients.

Transport to the clinic

Your front desk staff will also review with the client how to best transport their animal companion, as a calm ride to your clinic sets the stage for a successful low-stress vet visit. Ideally, cars should have calm, quiet, familiar music or no music playing in the background. Compared to other types of music and the sound of human conversation, classical music has been shown to result in increased time spent resting and increased time engaging in behaviors that correlate to relaxation, suggesting that classical music may promote a relaxed state in dogs (Wells, Graham, and Hepper, 2002; Kogan, Schoenfeld-Tacher, and Simon, 2012). A good option would be the "Through a Dog's Ears" or "Through a Cat's Ears" audio series, comprised of classical music that has had the instrumentation and tempo psycho-acoustically designed to be most soothing for the feline and canine auditory systems (iCalmPet, n.d.; iCalmPet, n.d.). Also remind clients to avoid any loud, startling noises.

Proper restraint during travel is also essential. Your reception staff can remind the client that not only will proper, crash-tested restraint during transport ensure the pet and client's safety by minimizing driver distractions and injury in the event of a crash. It will also prevent the patient from becoming stressed due to slipping during transport movement, resulting in a patient who is already stressed and anxious before even arriving at the veterinary clinic.

The Center for Pet Safety is an excellent third-party source for carriers and harnesses that have been crash test certified (Center for Pet Safety, n.d.). For cats and some small dogs, this would involve use of a carrier or crate. The safest place for a carrier or crate is secured on the ground, on the floor of the back seat behind the front passenger seat. An ideal carrier is one that is large enough for the pet to turn around and lie down in, but not so big that the pet will feel insecure.

For cats in particular, recommend a carrier that has at least two entry options, with sides that can be broken down or a removable top. This may also help create a less stressful exam environment for the feline patient if parts or all of the exam can occur in the carrier. For larger dogs, an ideal carrier could either be a larger crate secured in the interior of the car, or a harness-type seat belt fitted to the size of the dog. Your front desk staff can remind the client that dog carriers should never be secured in any open, exterior space, such as on the roof luggage rack or an external cargo rack, and if a carrier is too big to fit in the interior of their car the client can look into obtaining a harness seat belt or borrowing or renting a larger car or van for the transport. If an external cargo area of a pick-up truck must be used, the crate must be properly secured and protected from environmental elements such as rain, wind and snow.

Review with the client the use of visual barriers, both for carriers that are secured within the vehicle and in the external cargo area of a pick-up truck, to minimize visual stimuli that may be stressful for the canine or feline patient. Ideally, three sides of the carrier should be covered, allowing the patient the option to look out or in, based on their preferred level of visual stimulation.

Once the client has chosen the best travel restraint to use for their pet and vehicle, it is worth taking the time to discuss with the client carrier and seat belt training prior to its use. Decreasing fear and anxiety surrounding the transport tool is not only a crucial first step towards a less stressed patient during your veterinary exam, but also an essential part of protecting your patient's overall emotional wellbeing.

Ideally, puppies and kittens should be trained from an early age to accept the seat belt or carrier. For harness seat belts, allow the animal time to get used to the tool first at home, then in a parked car, then finally in a moving car for short trips only. Each session needs to be paired with treats and positive rewards.

Clients should watch for calm, relaxed body language, and be advised to progress to the next stage only when their pet is consistently calm and relaxed in the prior stage. Warn them that for some animals, each stage may take several days or longer, and make sure they understand to never force the tool onto their animal companions or punish them for refusing to use the transport tool. (Refer to Chapter 6 for more information on how to condition a pet to a harness and car ride.)

Encourage the client to contact your staff for guidance if he or she has problems progressing with the training. Advise clients to leave the carriers out during the training, making it part of the home's furnishing and placing it in places that their animal companion already likes to rest. This will encourage the pet to spend time and sleep in the carrier. Some animals prefer the carrier to be placed on an elevated surface instead of the floor, and some prefer the carrier to be more open (in which case the client can consider removing the top of the carrier for the initial stages of carrier desensitization). Place food items and favorite toys in the carrier to encourage the animal to explore the space. (Refer to Chapter 6 for more information on how to condition a pet to a carrier.) Just like with harness seat belt training, remind your client to take their time and be patient, and to not force the animal into the carrier or punish them if they resist. If your client is having trouble with the desensitization protocol, encourage them to reach out to your staff for assistance. Finally, remind the client that even if their animal companion has already been trained previously, they may need to be re-acquainted with the harness or carrier a few days before the appointment.

Treats should also be used in the carrier for the day of the transport, assuming the patient is not too stressed to eat them. Uneaten treats in a crate with a stressed animal may sometimes result in a negative association with/aversion to those treats in the future for that animal. Encourage your client to use long-lasting treats, puzzle toys, or even automated food dispensing machines to provide the patient with something to do during the transport – again, assuming the animal isn't too stressed to make use of them. (For automated food dispensing machines, have the client devise a chute out of the cardboard tube of a used paper towel roll so that treats dispensed can fall into the carrier without the machine itself taking up space in the carrier.) Remind the client to offer additional high-value rewards for any calm behaviors observed during the transport.

Olfactory tools, such as pheromone sprays or lavender scents, can be used to further calm an animal during transport (Gandia-Estelles, Mills and Mills, 2006; Wells, 2006). This can be sprayed on the bedding used during transport, in the carrier or on the harness, on the client's clothing, or inside the car. Encourage clients to prepare this in advance of transport by spraying it with pheromone sprays or lavender scents 15 to 30 minutes prior to their time of departure. Carriers should be lined with a non-slip mat to allow for better tactile sensation and to prevent slipping or falling.

The individual transporting the carrier also needs to be aware of how they handle the carrier to ensure they provide their pet with a smooth, calm trip. They can be given the following instructions: Carriers should be carried like a delicate gift – with both hands, held close to the individual's chest for maximal stability, and never by the handle on top of the carrier. Do not swing, shake or jostle the carrier. Avoid using wheeled carriers that are designed to be dragged like luggage – this can make for a very jarring ride for the dog or cat! Walk slowly and carefully when carrying the carrier, and once the carrier is secured in the vehicle, follow the speed limit and drive calmly and carefully. Finally, for multi-pet households that use carriers, ideally each animal should have his or her own carrier. If a shared carrier must be used, this may be acceptable for the transport to the clinic, but it is not a good plan for the return trip as fights between the carrier-mates may occur post-veterinary visit due to the increased levels of stress in the patients.

All veterinary patients should wear collars with updated identification tags during the transport, and for animals with a history of escaping a carrier or harness, a double-leash method might be considered to prevent the dog from escaping when being placed into or taken out of the vehicle. (One person holds the leash outside the vehicle and passes the second leash to the person already in the vehicle, who restrains the dog while first person secures the dog in the carrier and/or closes the vehicle door.) For best safety and security, recommend to your client that prior to the day of the transport they replace any damaged or faulty collars, harnesses and leashes that may fail during transport. Your front desk staff can also offer to update any micro-chip information to reflect new addresses or phone numbers at this time, so that the animal has the best chance of being reunited with his or her human should he or she become lost during transport.

For the animal companion who simply cannot tolerate transport, consider offering a house call as an alternative option or referring to a house-call veterinarian if this is not a service you offer. Many pets, especially feline patients, will be much less stressed with an exam that occurs in their own home rather than in a veterinary clinic. Finally, have your reception staff remind clients to check their animal companion's level of stress and anxiety the day of the appointment. This can include monitoring for stressed body language (including panting, drooling, pacing), vocalization, and urinating or defecating in the carrier. If the client notes that the patient is having a particularly bad day, allow them to reschedule to a later appointment slot or another day to accommodate the emotional needs of the animal. If a visit cannot be rescheduled due to medical necessity, offer to have the client talk with the medical staff to arrange for more PVPs or a sedated exam, or arrange for a house call.

Arriving at the clinic

On the day of the appointment, your front desk staff will play a crucial role in ensuring that things run smoothly. Your front desk staff will first assist in client and patient arrivals. Before arriving at your clinic, encourage your clients to call ahead to notify your front desk staff of their time of arrival; this will help ensure that your team is prepared with any special accommodations for that animal, ranging from unlocking the side door for the dog or cat that prefers to avoid the main entrance to drawing up any injectable sedation drugs ahead of time. For patients who cannot tolerate the waiting room, encourage your clients to utilize your parking lot and their car as an alternative waiting room. The client can stay in close cell phone communication with your front desk staff and be updated on when the exam room is ready for them, thereby eliminating any need for the client and animal companion to spend time in the waiting area. Alternatively, have them wait in the exam room so that the pet can have the privacy she requires, and have more time to adjust to the environment. (Ideally the preference to go directly into the exam room would be noted prior to the appointment, and your front desk staff can schedule that client's appointment during a quieter time of day so that an exam room is available to be used as a waiting area.)

For the patient that can be in the waiting room, there are several things you and your front desk staff can do to help make the wait time as pleasant as possible for both the client and the patient. Arrange chairs and waiting areas so that there is a small buffer zone surrounding the main doorway. This will prevent an entering patient from startling an animal who is sitting too close to the doorway, and vice versa. If possible, the main doorway should be glass or have a window to allow your client to briefly glance in the waiting room before entering, thereby allowing them the opportunity to look for and avoid anything that may trigger fear in their animal companion. For example, if a small dog has a known fear of larger white fluffy dogs, and the waiting room is full of Great Pyrenees dogs that day, the client can observe this through the door, and choose to wait in the car instead of entering the waiting area. Remind dog owners to keep their companions close to them on a short leash while they are in the waiting area, and never allow their dog to explore the room off-leash or on a retractable lead.

Consider laying down non-slip flooring for your entire entrance and waiting area. If this is not possible, then at the very least provide a non-slip pathway from the entry to the front desk, and from the front desk to the general waiting area. Walkways made of non-slip substances such as heavy-duty galvanized rubber mats will provide better traction and tactile sensation for the canine patients, thus reducing their fear and stress. It will also prevent a client who is carrying a carrier from slipping and falling, resulting in jostling or even dropping the pet inside the carrier.

Have your reception staff be proactive in assisting clients with entering and exiting the clinic, including opening doors, helping hold a carrier, or assisting the client with multiple animals so that their companions, as well as the other animals in the waiting room, remain safe and stress-free. Finally, carefully consider paths of entry to ensure that there are multiple pathways to entering and exiting the clinic, to accessing the waiting area and the exam rooms, and so that no narrow areas or bottlenecks exist, as this could lead to increased fear and anxiety for the more nervous patients.

For the feline and canine mixed practice that cannot accommodate special "feline only" hours as detailed above, consider setting up separate check-in stations and waiting areas for the two species. If your front desk consists of one long desk with multiple staff members at adjacent stations, provide visual barriers that extend from ground level to waist or chest high between each check-in station so that canine patients on leashes do not have the opportunity to reach over and sniff the feline patient in the carrier checking in next to them. Also offer large, elevated surfaces on which your client can place the carrier so that it is not on ground level and easily accessible by other dogs on leash. For smaller clinics with limited space, consider foldable TV tray dinner tables and rolling room partitions that can allow for temporary configurations based on need. (Note: Select ones that are stable so that a stand does not fall down when a carrier is placed on top!) Advise the client to keep a hand on the carrier at all times for safety and to ensure that the carrier does not fall.

During the check-in process, have your front desk staff remind the client of your practice's dedication to their pet's emotional as well as physical well-being, and introduce the client to the tools your practice offers to help make their pet's wait time as stress-free as possible. Every pet should be welcomed into the clinic with a tasty treat (with owner's permission) while your reception staff points out the location of treat dispensers in your waiting area and clinic.

Offer canine patients a pheromone-infused bandana to wear while they are waiting. Feline and smaller canine patients that arrive via carrier can get pheromone-infused fabric carrier covers that fit over the carrier, thereby providing both the benefits of the calming pheromone as well as a visual barrier from the activity in the waiting room. These carrier covers can be as simple as a towel, or you can sew custom covers with elastic openings that fit snugly over standard-sized carriers. Even better, consider putting your clinic logo and contact information on the bandanas and covers as an easy way to help promote your practice should your client wish to take the bandana or carrier covers home with them!

To infuse these products with pheromones, spray them with either the Adaptil or Feliway Classic spray. These sprays are packaged in a medium that has a strong chemical smell when first applied, so one should never present a bandana or carrier cover to an animal within the first 15 minutes of application of the sprays. Once applied, these sprays will last a maximum of about four hours. It is recommended that your front desk staff spray the bandanas and carrier covers with the pheromone spray twice a day; once in the morning when they first arrive at the clinic for the day, and again when they break for lunch.

Finally, your reception staff should all be well-versed in feline and canine body language and trained to identify signs of fear and stress in the veterinary patient, both during the check-in process and throughout the animal's time in the waiting area. Oftentimes owners may misinterpret signs of fear and stress, and they may not be aware of the level of fear their companion may be experiencing at that moment. As your front desk staff gets to know each individual patient, your staff members may even be able to recognize unique signs of stress for a specific pet. This is important as your reception staff will play an essential role as your clinic's first line in detecting those stressed patients and relaying this information to the technicians and doctors working with that patient that day. This helps ensure that a gentler approach can be provided to accommodate an individual animal's emotional needs for that day, and that the medical team can provide additional coaching for the owner that needs more help on identifying and ameliorating stress in their companion.

Your front desk staff will make note of any specific experiences that resulted in increased fear and anxiety, and record this in the animal's emotional health medical records so that your staff can be better prepared for future visits. Furthermore, your front desk staff needs to be conscious of their own body language, and ensure they greet and approach patients in a non-threatening manner. It is important that they know never to lean over a patient, and to avoid approaching or facing head on with direct eye contact. Teach them to squat down from a distance, facing away from the patient (either sideways or obliquely), and use slow, smooth movements. Always allow the patient to approach on their own, even established patients that have met the staff previously, as their emotional state and behavioral responses may vary from day to day. Instruct your reception staff that if the patient does not approach on her own, they are to allow the patient the opportunity to move away, and to never corner a patient or lure them closer with treats. (Treats can be tossed from a distance, or the owner can offer the treat to the fearful patient so the patient is not required to get closer to a staff member who may be perceived as scary.)

Waiting area

Aside from the role your reception staff plays in ensuring an ideal start for your clients' and patients' visit to your clinic, there is another key element here – the waiting area itself! There is an art to setting up the waiting area to best maximize your space and optimize it to meet the sensory needs of the feline and canine patient. Many of the previously discussed considerations for your front desk check-in area should extend to the space that your clients and patients will adjourn to after they complete the check-in process.

Use chairs, plants, or room dividers to create multiple separated areas in your waiting room for dogs of different temperament or size. Consider providing separate areas for feline and canine patients; if this is not possible, utilize the same foldable TV tray dinner tables and rolling room partitions discussed above to provide room configurations that can allow for privacy areas for the non-canine-friendly feline. Alternatively, allow the client and cat to wait in the privacy of an exam room. Remind clients to never put a cat carrier on the ground as this can be very stressful for the feline patient, especially if they are stared at or visited by a curious (or worse!) adjacent canine patient, and to keep a hand on the carrier at all times for safety. Once a cat carrier is elevated off the ground, continue to use the pheromone-infused carrier covers or towels to provide an additional visual barrier and minimize visual overstimulation.

Room divider to minimize stress for waiting patients

Ensure there are plentiful treat dispensing stations placed at strategic and easily accessible locations in your waiting area, such as above the scale, by the main entrance to your clinic, near the check-in/check-out desk, and in each section of the waiting room. These can be comprised of a row of small bins with a sampling of various types of small, pre-cut pieces of treats in each bin. Place only one type of treat in each bin, and clearly label the contents, including all proteins in the treats, as these are the most common dietary allergens. Consider separating each type of treat with an empty bin to reduce cross-contamination between the different types of treats.

Treat bins

In addition to the stationary treat dispensing stations, make sure your staff members are equipped with treat pouches so they can be mobile treat stations! Treats should be offered upon walking into the clinic and frequently, as long as this is not contraindicated medically. Some animals will refuse treats when stressed or may take treats with a harder bite and in a more intense manner. Remind your staff and clients to keep in mind that if they observe this in the patient then there may have been an increase in that animal's stress level.

Avoid visual overstimulation when choosing decor for your waiting area. For example, avoid using realistic images of cats in the waiting area, as seeing other felines can cause increased fear and anxiety in some cats. Remember, one of the things that makes cats special is the fact that they are both solitary predators and prey animals, so the sight of either fellow feline predators or the sight of a predator who preys on cats can cause fear in your feline patient. For your canine patients, pictures of other dogs in the waiting room may trigger undesired behaviors from dogs with inter-dog aggression concern. Consider using abstract art in your waiting area instead of images of other animals.

Tactile sensations should also be taken into consideration when setting up the ideal waiting area. Non-slip floors will decrease fear and stress by providing dogs with better traction, and guard against slipping or falling. This is especially important for the scale, as the weigh-in process is often stress-inducing for the veterinary patient. Provide walk-on scales with non-slip surfaces, ideally ones that are recessed into the floor, so that a patient does not need to be picked up and placed on a scale. Do not place the scale in corners where the dog may feel trapped or enclosed, and as a result may refuse to enter. Use treats to encourage the animal to get on the scale, either by creating a treat trail, having your staff offer treats, or having the client offer the treat if their companion refuses to take treats from the staff. Never force or drag a pet onto the scale.

Do not take feline and smaller patients out of their carriers in the waiting area to be weighed; instead, wait to do this when the patient is in the exam room. If the weigh-in process is stressful for the patient, wait until the end of the visit to obtain the weight so that the stress level remains as low as possible prior to the examination. Ensure that the temperature of the waiting area is ideal for the patient and client and eliminate any drafts or areas of increased air flow that might be uncomfortable. Ensure that the tools the client is using to restrain their companion are not causing uncomfortable tactile experiences. Remove collars that can cause stress, pain or inappropriate interactions, such as shock or prong collars and retractable leashes, and replace these with flat collars and a fixed-length leash. Have these available at your front desk to loan to clients if they do not bring appropriate gear and consider spraying these with pheromones ahead of time to further decrease fear and stress. Finally, remind owners to keep the leash length short, but also loose, as much as possible, so that they are not applying leash tension that may result in increased stress for their dog.

Auditory stimulation should be kept at a minimum, and all team members will need to play a part in keeping overall noise level down by speaking in low tones with calm voices. Encourage your clients to do the same. Reduce noises that can be heard in the waiting room; strategically place any hospital equipment or HVAC systems far from the waiting room and exam room areas. Keep in mind the sensitive auditory systems of our feline and canine patients and remember to reduce any ultrasonic sounds that may not be detectable to the human ear.

Set front desk phones at a low ring level and ask clients to turn their phones to 'silent' and take calls outside if necessary. Reduce noises from barking dogs by distracting them with toys or a long-lasting food dispensing puzzle toy. Alternatively, ask these patients and clients to wait outside or in their cars for their comfort and the comfort of the other patients and clients in the waiting room. Consider installing sound absorbing acoustic wall and ceiling paneling to further reduce noise. You can further counter undesirable auditory stimuli by playing calming classical music or "Through a Dog's Ear" or "Through a Cat's Ear." Music has been shown to not only decrease stress, but it can also increase client satisfaction with veterinary visits (Engler and Bain, 2014; Kogan et al., 2012; Wells, Graham, and Hepper, 2002).

Finally, cater to your feline and canine patient's sensitive olfactory sense and ability to detect pheromones. Use pheromone diffusers such as the Adaptil, Feliway Multicat or Feliway Classic diffusers in your waiting area, as these emit synthetic versions of appeasing and identity pheromones that can help soothe and calm cats and dogs in a veterinary setting (Mills et al., 2006; Kim et al., 2010; Kronen et al., 2006; Siracusa et al., 2010). Pheromone sprays can also be applied to the furniture and on staff clothing to decrease stress (Pereira et al., 2016). A lavender diffuser may also help promote a calmer, more relaxed state in both the veterinary patient as well as the client (Wells, 2006). Just as important as infusing the waiting area with a calming scent or pheromone, it is also essential to remove any offensive smells or alert pheromones left by a previous patient that may trigger stress or fear in a subsequent patient. These can include true alarm pheromones (such as those from the interdigital glands of the cat), anal gland secretions that were released by an anxious dog, urine or fecal material in the waiting room, or even the scent of blood from a bleeding patient. Ensure all are cleaned promptly and thoroughly with an enzymatic cleaner, consider wiping down surfaces with a pheromone wipe after cleaning, and make sure all sharp containers and used venipuncture tools are enclosed and kept far away from the lobby to prevent the smell from entering the waiting area.

Use the time while the client is waiting wisely. This is a great opportunity to further educate your clients and provide resources on ways to promote their animal companion's mental health. This can include teaching dogs and cats to lie down on cue, and conditioning/desensitizing them to various handling procedures and tools such as muzzles. Consider providing your first-time clients with a brief behavior survey and treat and handling preferences questionnaire that can then be attached to that patient's emotional health medical record. Have handouts available in your waiting room for the client to read and take home on first steps towards desensitization and counter conditioning for common behavioral concerns. Prepare a list of recommended training and behavior professionals in your area who do not use aversive techniques, who can further help your clients with their behavioral concerns in their homes. If there is a veterinary behavior service in your area, also provide their business card and a brochure explaining their services, so that your client can become familiar with all their options when it comes to behavior professionals.

Checking out

Your front desk staff will also play a crucial role at the end of your patient's visit, as they are the last point of contact for your client and patient prior to leaving your practice. It is important to make sure that the check-out process and departure is just as efficient and stress- free as the arrival. This will impact how the patient (and client!)

perceives future visits. You want the visit to end on a high note so that they look forward to their next visit.

The same care should be taken to provide assistance upon departure, including creating separate private transaction areas at the check-out desk, using room dividers, elevated surfaces, chairs and planters as previously discussed. Alternatively, consider checking the patient out in the exam room – this may be beneficial for the patient who is experiencing increased fear and anxiety after their examination, and for the client who is trying to manage their companion's emotional state during the check-out process.

Consider having your staff escort certain pets out of the exam room and out of the clinic to prevent any interactions that could result in conflict between the exiting patient and an incoming patient. If needed, have your front desk staff coordinate the flow of client entry and exit around your clinic entrance. They might, for example, ask an incoming client and patient to briefly step out to let the departing client and patient pass first. When the coast is clear they can then invite the incoming client to return.

Finally, your front desk staff should take time to discuss the patient's reunion with other household companions and ensure that a plan is in place before returning home. Advise that during the re-integration period household inter-dog aggression can sometimes occur. It is best to separate other dogs while a patient returns home, especially for patients who will need time to recover from sedation.

For canine patients, provide time for about 30 minutes of quiet relaxation and re-acclimation in a safe space with minimal stimulation upon returning to the home before attempting reintroduction. For a patient who received sedation, advise the client what to watch for at home, including signs of dysphoria, and let them know how long the sedative effects are expected to last. Advise that the private acclimation period will need to be extended until the patient is fully awake.

Suggest that upon arriving at home, they consider keeping other dogs outside in a yard, enclosed in a separate area of the home, or outside on a walk with another family member. Once the patient is ready to be reintroduced to his housemates, it may be beneficial to meet housemates outside on a neutral territory first, or have housemates go on a 10-to-20-minute walk together before entering the home. Encourage play and use treats and verbal praise during the reunion (as long as neither pet has a history of food-related aggression) but remove any high value food items or toys that the housemates could fight over prior to reintroduction. Watch the dogs closely to ensure that they are getting along, and intervene before a problem occurs, but remind the client to never punish an undesired behavior. Advise your client that if the housemates are not getting along after 24 hours, keep them separated and call the clinic to discuss next steps with your medical team.

For feline patients who recognize conspecifics via smells and identity pheromones, the reintroduction of a housemate who smells differently may be similar to introducing a stranger cat to the household. Furthermore, the patient may not be feeling well, or may be recovering from sedation, further adding to the stress and anxiety of all members of the household and resulting in household inter-cat aggression.

Clients should closely monitor cat housemates and ensure that all members are coping well with the reunion. Advise your client to provide the returning feline patient with a safe, quite place to recover privately (e.g., a small bathroom with a closed door) for at least 30 minutes after returning home, and not to attempt to reintroduce a cat who had received sedation in the clinic until the effects of the sedation have worn off and the patient is fully awake.

Prior to reintroduction, have the client rub down all cats with the same towel or with a piece of the owner's clothing to create a common scent, or use a synthetic identity pheromone and/or appeasing pheromone such as Feliway to help decrease reunion-related stress. They can distract the cats with food or parallel play in the same room during the reintroduction. If needed, the client can also set up short, supervised reunion periods, and separate the cats in different areas of the home at other times to prevent unsupervised interactions until they can ensure that the housemates are getting along. As with the canine patients, the client will need to monitor the cats closely to ensure that they are getting along, and intervene before a problem occurs, but never punish any undesired behaviors. Advise your client that if the housemates are not getting along after 24 hours, keep them separated and call the clinic to discuss next steps with your medical team.

Conclusions

Ensuring as low stress a visit as possible for both patients and clients starts early, even before the patient arrives at your clinic. Feline and canine emotional health needs must be addressed at the first point of contact when the client schedules the appointment, through preparation for the visit, transport to the clinic, checking in at your clinic, and the time the client and patient spend in your waiting room. Furthermore, the check-out process at the end of a veterinary visit and the reintroduction to any housemates will also set the tone for the next visit. This pre-handling and waiting room experience is an essential precursor to reducing fear and anxiety during the veterinary visit and exam. By properly minimizing stress and anxiety for both the client and patient during this crucial period, you can support the emotional well-being of your patients, promote satisfaction, enhance your relationships with your clients, and ultimately ensure a successful veterinary experience for the patient, the client, and your veterinary team.

Chapter 6
Patient-Friendly Handling in the Exam Room
By Dr. Ashley L. Elzerman, DVM, DACVB and Katelin Thomas, CDBC, CPDT-KA

A little planning goes a long way

We often find ourselves in the middle of a busy day at the clinic and a multitude of things are pulling our attention in just as many directions. When trying to create the best visit possible for our patients, a little planning and preparation go a long way.

The amount of planning and preparation for each patient will vary depending on the needs of the patient, the guardian and the clinic team. Some owners will be on board with starting their preparation at home whereas other owners may not have the time or interest to do any preparation prior to appointments. Regardless, the end goal is to create a positive experience for the patient and to provide excellent medical care today as well as to set the patient up for success for at-home care and future visits.

Pre-appointment preparation

Reviewing the patient's history prior to the appointment helps the team form a plan based on the patient's previous reactions to restraint and procedures. Some options to maintain this information are to include it in the patient's medical record or have the owner fill out a pre-visit questionnaire on the patient's previous experiences. This can be added to the patient's record and additional insights can be added with each visit. It is also helpful to keep track of patient allergies or dietary restrictions and if there is a peanut allergy or other severe allergy in the family.

As the owner prepares for the visit, a pre-visit checklist can help ensure that all aspects of the visit are considered. Often these checklists include items the owner will bring with them, procedures to reduce stress during transportation to the clinic, instructions on what to do when arriving and entering the clinic as well as any specific preparation such as fasting prior to the appointment.

An example of an owner's vet visit preparation package. Note that this pack contains a variety of treats, some chews and toys, a basket muzzle and a harness. A mat or towel familiar to the patient would also be a good addition.

Providing clients with a menu of add-on items and services that could potentially reduce stress during their visit is a great way to give the client choices and allow them to choose the level of care they are comfortable with for their pet. Laying out these options prior to or during the appointment is also a great way to inform them of any additional charges that would be incurred with each add-on service. Some examples of add-on services that could be offered include sedation, a longer visit, low-stress packs with special treats, enrichment items, and other stress-reducing options, 'happy or victory' visit packages, and planning and preparation for the next visit. Creating package options can help cover the costs of buying, preparing, and sterilizing any items used during the visit, such as Kongs or other food treats in addition to the extra time required to prepare for and execute the visit.

The visit

Exam room options

As was discussed in Chapters 4 and 5, we want to create an environment that is conducive to a relaxed, calm patient, guardian, veterinarian and team. In the exam room, we want to particularly focus on decreasing auditory, olfactory and visual stimuli as well as pay attention to the surfaces, places, and overall environment that we create for patients. Bright lights, noxious odors, and loud noises are to be avoided. If a scale is being used in the exam room, a non-slip mat should be placed on the scale so that the patient does not slip when they step onto the scale. Classical music played at a low volume in the exam room was found in one study to increase client satisfaction with their visit (Engler and Bain, 2017).

For anxious patients, allowing the guardian to set up the room prior to bringing in the patient may decrease the patient and the caretaker's fear upon entering the room. If safe to do so, the guardian could leave the patient in the car for a couple of minutes while they set up the room with some comfort items including a blanket familiar to the patient and pre-filled treat toys or small piles of treats. The piles of treats can be strategically located in areas of the room where the patient will be for procedures. This will encourage the patient to explore these areas and will start creating positive associations right from the start.

Ideally, a patient who may be fearful or reactive in the waiting room can be brought straight into an exam room instead of remaining in the waiting area where they may be exposed to unnecessary stressors. Upon entering the room, advise the guardian to give the patient some treats to create a positive emotional experience. If treats were pre-placed in the room, the guardian can allow the dog or adventurous cat to do a 'treat hunt.' Some animals will not eat treats in high-stress environments. Not eating a treat that the patient would normally eat at home is usually a sign of stress or fear. Higher value treats may be tried in these situations but continued inappetence indicates a need for additional stress decreasing techniques or consideration of a nutraceutical or medication to reduce anxiety.

Patients who have a strong history of responding to trained cues and enjoy performing the learned behaviors may exhibit a decrease in their anxiety by performing a cue familiar to them and being rewarded by their guardian. If the guardian gives a cue and the patient does not immediately offer the behavior, have the owner pause and try again in a few minutes, or try a behavior the patient loves and may offer more easily, such as a paw shake or nose touch. Some animals are unable to respond to cues when they are fearful or anxious, so failure to execute behaviors that the patient is usually quick to perform should also be taken as an indication that the patient may be stressed or fearful. In cases where the animal has a history of being trained using aversive techniques or has experienced fear or pain while learning, you may see an increase in stress or anxiety when the guardian gives a cue. In these cases, opt for interactive treat toys or simply continue to reward the dog without giving any additional cues to build positive associations during the visit. The use of treats to help a stressed dog perform learned behaviors are illustrated in the set of photos beginning on the next page.

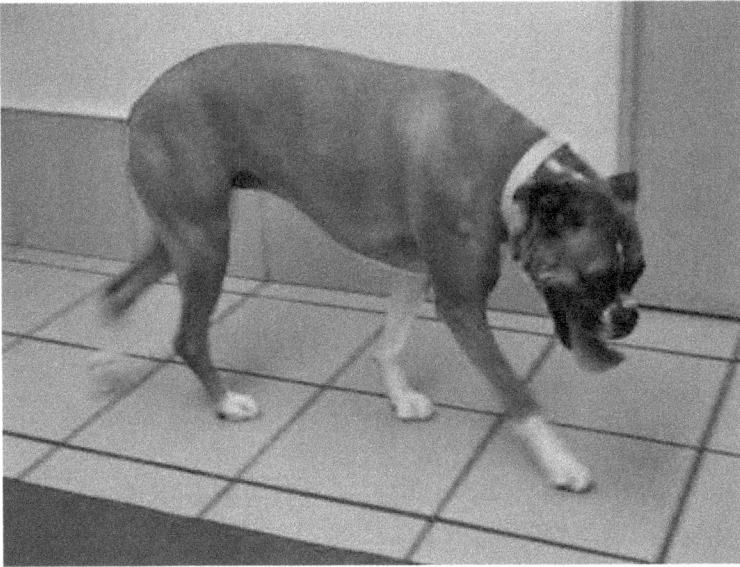

The patient was showing signs of stress (pacing and panting) in the exam room.

Treats were first offered on the non-slip mat where the physical exam would later be performed.

Can you identify the signs of stressed body language from Chapter 2?

After the patient ate the treats, a previously learned behavior was cued.

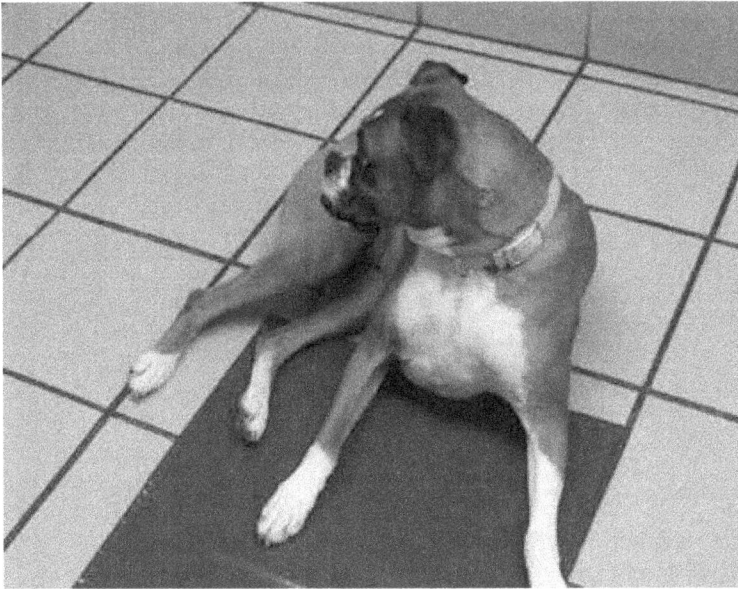

After a couple of repetitions of the cued behavior, the patient settled on the mat still alert to noises outside the room but with a more relaxed posture.

Due to the degree of anxiety at the beginning of the appointment, this patient may be a good candidate for pre-visit pharmaceuticals prior to future visits.

Some hospitals allow patients who are particularly fearful of entering the clinic to be examined outside of the hospital in a secure garden or dog-walk area. In some locations this is not feasible due to weather or other constraints but may seasonally be an option.

Depending on the flow of the hospital and if the patient is a dog or a cat, the clinical staff can either be in the room as the patient and caretaker enter or can plan on entering the room after the patient has settled. If the caretaker is creating a positive experience for the patient while waiting for the clinical staff, they may find that this time allows the patient to acclimate to the environment. If the clinical staff enters the room after the patient and client, the staff member should quietly enter the room with non-assertive body language and treats ready.

Once the clinical staff has entered the room, allow the patient a chance to acclimate to the presence of the new person before approaching the patient. This is a convenient time to obtain history or ask the guardian any questions needed prior to the examination. Observe the patient's location in the room relative to you and any anxiety signs during this time.

The exam

Before initiating the physical exam or other physical contact, communicate your plan with the guardian and anyone assisting you. Acknowledge or confirm the patient's previous responses to handling. If the patient has a history of aggression during veterinary handling, communicate with the owner about using a muzzle for safety.

Ideally, the patient should be conditioned to wear a muzzle prior to the visit (see Chapter 8 for more detailed information on muzzle training). If the patient was not muzzled prior to entering the building and the client is going to apply a muzzle, give them time to follow their normal protocol and apply the muzzle. It is helpful to have some tasty treats available in case the owner does not have a sufficient supply.

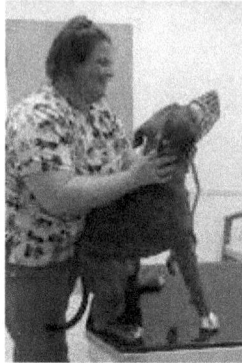

A muzzle can in some cases be a necessary tool to assure everyone's safety. This dog appears a bit stressed by the application of the muzzle. Be sure to talk to your clients about conditioning the dog to love a muzzle prior to its use.

Location of the exam

The location of the physical exam will vary based on the patient, the client, the procedures planned, and your exam room features. Ideally, we want to perform the exam in the location where the animal is most comfortable, and we can feasibly complete the planned procedures. Always approach the patient in a calm, quiet, non-threatening manner.

This practitioner created a comfortable location for the patient to receive a laser treatment.

Monitoring body language

Throughout the physical exam and procedures, it is important to monitor the patient's body language to assess if the emotional state of the animal is changing, how quickly it is changing, and if some handling techniques escalate the animal's fear (see Chapter 2). In general, the physical exam should proceed from least invasive to most invasive with areas suspected to be painful at the end of the exam. Another option is to complete the most urgent procedures first so that you can stop if the patient becomes overly stressed, reactive, or fearful. The examiner should adjust the exam as needed based on the animal's response. With practice, we can learn to anticipate an animal's threshold based on their response to handling, but each individual may vary, and their behavior may be affected by other events of the day, health status and pain level. Animals who are in pain are more likely to escalate to aggression with handling than healthy, non-painful animals.

When the veterinary team is working with an anxious or potentially aggressive patient, we need to have our full focus on the animal, their body language, and the potential for a rapidly changing situation. During these interactions, it is best to minimize distractions. If talking can be kept to a minimum, or at least if calm, quiet tones are used, then the team can hear any vocalizations from the animal as well as more easily communicate with each other about the patient's anxiety level.

If a patient's anxiety signs are escalating, give the patient a break, change handling techniques, or if the escalation continues, consider sedation or anxiolytic medications.

To complete a physical exam and procedures, we may need to use a combination of restraint and distraction techniques to keep the animal from moving excessively and have the patient experience the least distress possible. High value treats or toys can be useful for distraction.

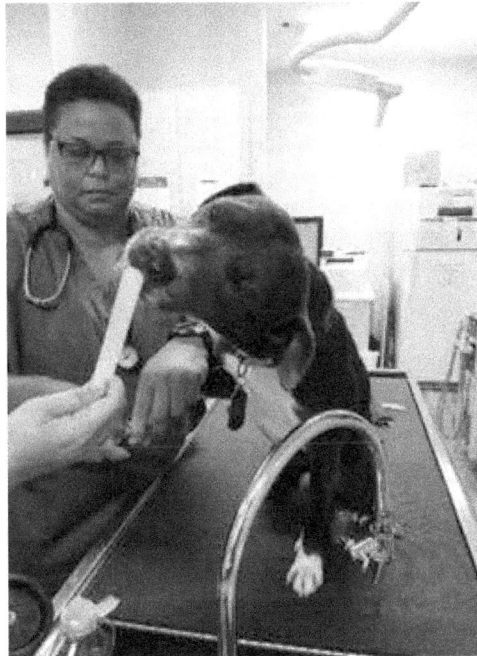

Using a 'lollipup' in this and the following photos - cheese or peanut butter smeared on a stick - to keep the dog occupied and happy during various procedures.

105

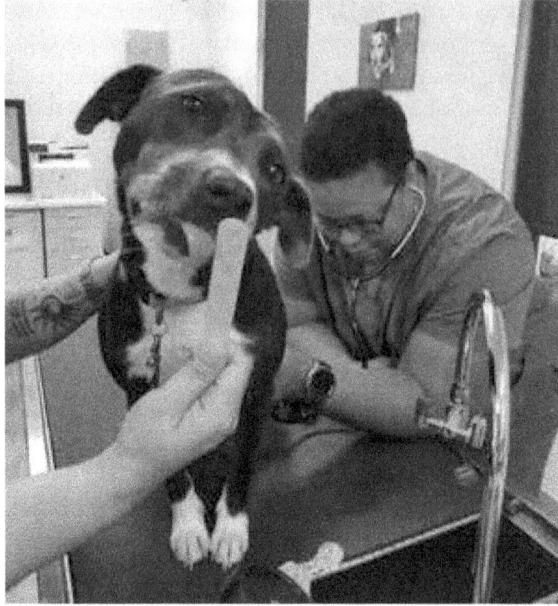

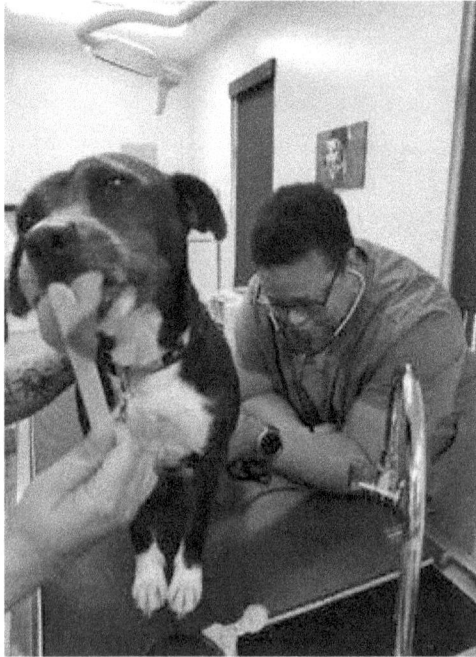

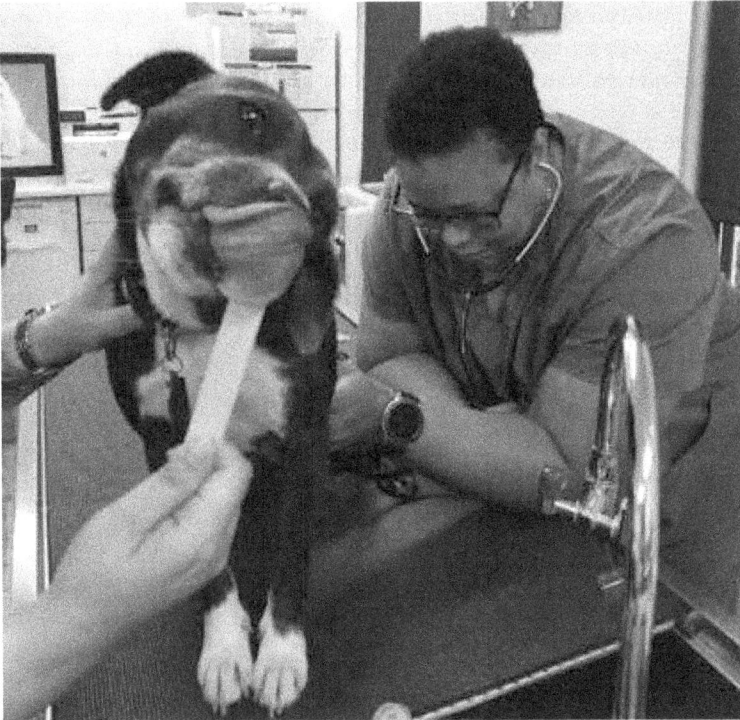

Make a mental list

At the beginning of the exam, the veterinarian will ideally have a mental list of next steps needed to diagnose the animal's clinical signs or complete planned preventive care. As information from the physical exam is obtained, the animal's anxiety level and tolerance for handling assessed, and the ability and willingness of the client to complete recommended care ascertained, the list of needs and wants should evolve into a plan for care. Clients, patients, and medical situations may require a different balance of the three elements that contribute to the final plan for care.

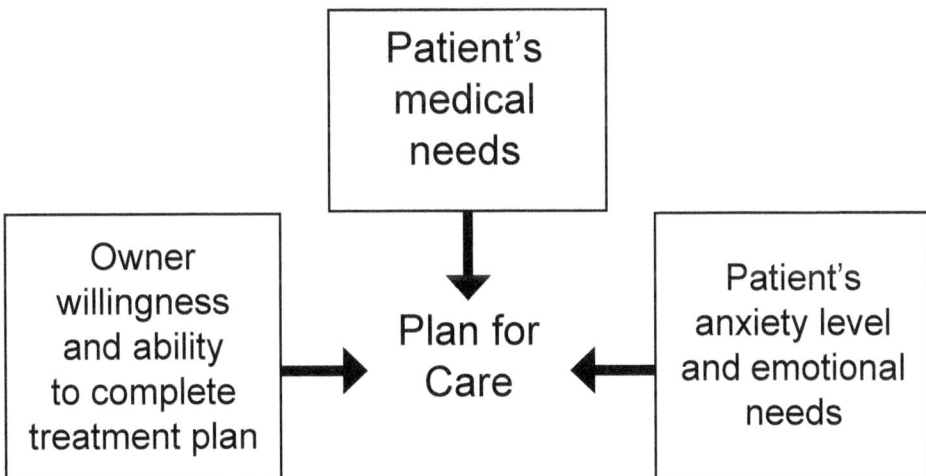

Three considerations contribute to the final plan for care:

For example, during a preventive care visit, the emotional needs of the patient may outweigh the urgency of the patient's medical needs, but if the patient is experiencing a life-threatening emergency, the patient's medical needs may outweigh the patient's emotional needs (although addressing the patient's anxiety, if possible, will aid in the treatment of the medical emergency). See Chapter 9 for more information about addressing anxiety in an emergency setting.

Veterinarians should always abide by local practice acts and regulations, but when warranted, based on their assessment of the animal, there may be times when a part of the physical exam is unable to be performed without extreme stress to the animal. In this case, it may be appropriate to note that area or system as "not examined" instead of subjecting the animal to undue stress.

Two common procedures that tend to cause stress to our patients include rectal temperature and fecal collection. Cats were found to be most stressed during veterinary visits at arrival to the clinic and when the rectal temperature was taken (Belew, Bartlett, and Brown, 2008). Since activity and anxiety can both cause elevations in body temperature in an otherwise apparently healthy patient, it may be difficult to differentiate between a true fever and stress-induced hyperthermia. Dogs have been found to have increased heart rates, rectal temperatures, and blood pressures at the veterinary versus at home (Bragg et al., 2015). Collecting a fecal sample using a fecal loop is also a common cause of stress for patients that can be avoided by asking the owner to bring a fecal sample to the appointment or asking them to bring one by the clinic at a later time.

For patients with a history of fear of handling in the veterinary setting, it can be helpful for the client to bring videos of any gait abnormalities or photos of areas of concern if these can be safely obtained at home. For example, it may be difficult to have an anxious or very active patient hold still long enough in the veterinary setting for the veterinarian to focus on a lesion or to assess the gait of a dog who is lunging and barking at the sounds of dogs or people. In a video or photograph, they may be able to take a good look and then confirm their assessment with a shorter look at the area of concern.

Handling techniques

There are many techniques used for handling veterinary patients in the hospital and different patients may react favorably to different techniques. In the following sections about dogs and cats, we will discuss some of the techniques in detail. We want to strive to use techniques that allow the patient to be comfortable, minimize the patient's fear, and allow the veterinary staff to work safely with the patient. When working with patients, we want to keep in mind our relative location in relation to the patient's head, mouth, and legs or claws. We should avoid placing our face near our patient's faces since some animals find this threatening and it puts us at risk for a bite. As discussed in Chapter 2, most animals do not consider 'kisses' as a sign of affection, so the veterinary team should avoid perpetuating this myth.

Cooperative care

Cooperative care, also known as consent training, is the process of training and empowering animals to be active, willing participants in all aspects of their care, including during invasive handling or otherwise stressful procedures. What the animal may find most aversive in the veterinary setting and during husbandry activities is the lack of choice and inability to predict or control what happens to them. Providing the animal an opportunity to be an active participant in training allows the animal to be given the maximum amount of control and autonomy while increasing safety and comfort for the animal as well as the clinic staff. This communication can also help the veterinary team to more easily read the emotional state of the animal and react accordingly.

During this process, the animal is taught how to signal when they are ready to start, stop, or pause at any point during their exam or procedure. The animal uses a behavior they already know to act as their "go" signal, often being a chin rest or holding their nose to their handler's hand. This tells the veterinary staff the animal is giving permission to begin or continue the interaction. To give the "pause" or "stop" signal, the animal simply removes or lifts his head or chin, indicating they need a break, are not comfortable, or would like the procedure to end. The animal is rewarded regularly for engaging and completing each part of the exam or procedure. Because choice is a natural reinforcer for animals, allowing the animal to drive each interaction makes the experience not only low stress but fun for the animal.

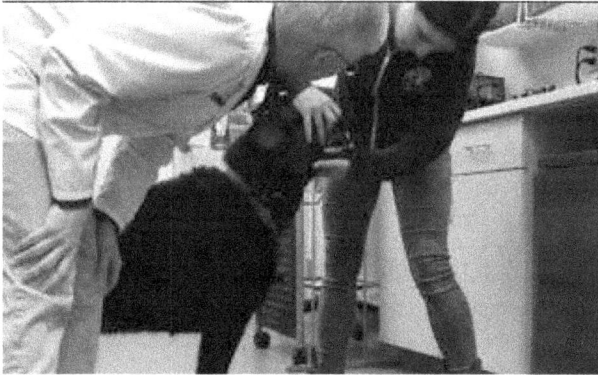

Owner using chin rest to assure dog's consent and cooperation while holding up lip for dental exam.

Many guardians are anxious about their companion's behavior at the veterinary clinic. Chapter 8 will detail the client's role in the clinic. Veterinarians and clinical staff need to recognize our role in helping the caretaker feel comfortable. Reassure the client that it is appropriate to comfort their dog and that the dog's behavior gives us information about his or her anxiety level. We want the guardians to feel that they are part of a team trying to provide the best care possible. This often requires empathetic, nonjudgmental communication from the veterinary team about the animal's behavior. For example, "jumping up like this is normal behavior for dogs and often they will do it more when they are anxious." Clients are also often concerned that when their dog does not respond to training cues in the clinic it reflects poorly on their training skills. A gentle reassurance that many dogs don't respond to their training cues during times of stress will often reassure the guardian and open a dialog about the dog's other signs of anxiety in the clinic.

Canine-specific recommendations and techniques

Each hospital is unique in its design, but when possible, using the exam room closest to the entrance door for an anxious patient will minimize the patient's exposure to a busy reception or waiting room area. The exception to this would be if the room closest to the door has more noise and the dog reacts to noises. In that case, a quieter room a little further from the door would be preferred.

It is important to create a calm environment free from noxious odors and sounds to set our patients and their humans at ease. Multiple yoga mats or other non-slip surfaces available in the exam room will allow for flexibility in the physical exam location if needed. If the patient has been trained at home with a specific mat for cooperative care, use the patient's mat as a surface for procedures, if the dog appears most comfortable on this mat. The goal of the non-slip surface is to provide the patient security and assurance that they are not going to slip, as well as to provide padding and a comfortable surface.

Depending on the flow of the hospital, allow the dog time to acclimate to the room and explore briefly as well as eat some treats before the veterinary staff enters the room.

For most reactive dogs, knocking on the door before entering will increase their arousal level, so in most cases knocking should be avoided. To alert the client to your entrance, slowly open the door an inch or two, gain the owner's attention with a hello, pause to assess the situation, and then enter the room. For patients with a history of aggression or aggressive displays in the hospital setting, make sure to allow the caretaker a moment to confirm their hold on the leash and begin giving the dog treats as a distraction before you open the door fully and enter the room. Unless the client already has the dog's attention with a treat distraction, be prepared to toss treats to the dog as you enter the room. You want to toss the treats instead of handing them to the dog to avoid immediately approaching the patient before you have assessed their anxiety level.

If a patient has retreated under the table or bench, give them time to emerge from the hiding location instead of cornering them in a tight location. Some dogs may be willing to come out if their guardian starts to walk away and offers a treat to the patient or calls them over.

The location of the exam should balance the dog's comfort and the veterinary team's ability to perform the necessary procedures. Most larger patients can easily and comfortably be examined on the floor while small patients may be comfortably examined on the table. When placing the dog on the table, ensure that the body is well-supported and the client or a team member is paying attention to the dog to ensure that she does not attempt to jump off the table. Escape attempts off the table or moving away from the veterinary team on the floor are signs of fear and should cause the team to re-evaluate the patient's stress level and address any needed modifications to the situation.

A study examining anxiety during physical exams found that dogs exhibited fewer anxiety signs when their humans were encouraged to pet and reassure the patient during the exam versus guardians who were present but were asked not to pet or reassure the patient, so having the client touch or reassure the dog may be useful to calm the patient (Csoltova et al., 2017). The physical exam should progress from least invasive to most invasive, with attention being paid to the dog's reaction to each step. When comparing heart rate and behavioral responses to handling, one study found that petting dogs on the chest caused less heart rate elevation than other areas of the body so this may be a good place to start a physical exam (Kuhne, Hobler, and Struwe, 2014). A gentle, smooth, consistent touch should be used. The initial touch can often cause a patient to startle, so repeatedly removing the hands and replacing them should be avoided as much as possible.

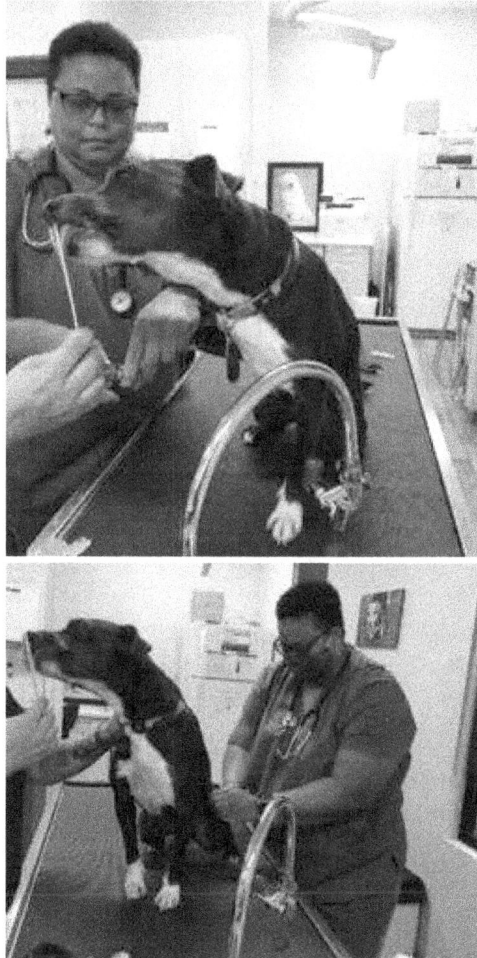

Another example of using food to keep the dog calm during a medical procedure.

The goal of restraint during the physical exam and procedures should be to maintain comfort and safety for the patient, client, and veterinary team. The least amount of restraint needed should be used to achieve these goals.

Restraint for blood collection depends on the position most comfortable to the patient as well as the volume of blood needed. A lateral saphenous blood collection from the back leg is often tolerated by patients who become anxious with crowding of the face or handling of the feet.

For clients who are willing to work with their dogs at home, training a consent cue or other cooperative care techniques can be beneficial to achieving veterinary care with the least stress possible. (See the "Bucket Game," Chapter 1.) Patients who react to specific aspects of the visit such as restraint can benefit from a desensitization and counter-conditioning program to improve the emotional response to these situations (see Chapter 1 and, for more on this, see Chapter 7.)

Feline specific recommendations and techniques

Feline appointments should ideally be seen in the quietest exam room of the hospital. If possible, the examination area should be far from barking dogs and the noises of the waiting area. Cats should be put directly into an exam room and waiting in the lobby should be avoided whenever possible.

In preparation for the appointment, training cats at home to be familiar with their carrier can reduce the stress of the veterinary visit (Pratsch et al., 2018). When coming to the veterinary clinic, it can be very helpful to have the guardian include a small blanket or towel that has the cat's scent on it in the carrier (see Chapter 7).

An ideal exam room for cats will have minimal odors, soft surfaces, vertical spaces, and dim lighting. Cats have an excellent sense of smell, so strong scents or the odors of other animals should be avoided in feline exam rooms. Cleaning products used to clean the room between procedures should have as little scent as possible. Cats prefer soft surfaces for resting (Crouse et al., 1995), so a soft surface should be provided on the examination table for the cat to rest upon. Many hospitals find it convenient to use a towel as a soft surface on the exam table so see that a towel is readily available if needed to facilitate restraint, or, ideally, have the client bring a towel from home. Application of a pheromone product such as Feliway may also help reduce the cat's stress during the veterinary visit (Pereira et al., 2016). The Feliway should be applied to the towel or surface and the alcohol base allowed to evaporate prior to exposing the patient to the towel or the surface.

Vertical spaces allow the cat to climb up and feel more comfortable in the room. Cat shelves or cat trees that are made of non-porous surfaces that can be cleaned between patients are preferred to carpeted or porous surfaces. A towel or non-slip surface can be placed on the shelf or cat tree to provide comfort for the cat while maintaining an easy to clean set up.

Once the client and the cat are in the exam room, instruct the caretaker to open the door of the carrier and allow the cat to exit the carrier on their own. Give the patient some time to acclimate to and explore the room before handling begins. If the cat has not exited the carrier on its own, removing the top of the carrier is preferable to reaching in and pulling the cat out or turning the carrier up on its end to dump the patient onto the table.

The cat can be lured onto a baby scale in the room to obtain a weight. If the cat will not willingly get onto the scale, she can be lifted and placed on the scale. For patients who are stressed by handing in the exam room, an alternative is to weigh the cat and the carrier as they are brought into the room, and then weigh the carrier (and any blankets) without the cat after she has exited the carrier. Then subtract the weight of the empty carrier from the carrier-and-cat weight to obtain the weight of the cat.

Because many cats prefer to remain in one location during their exam, examining the cat in the bottom half of its carrier or on the client's lap may be most comfortable for the feline patient. The client can be guided to provide reassurance to the cat or allow them to 'hide' against their guardian or under a towel if appropriate. If it is necessary to move the patient, make sure that the body is well-supported.

The physical exam for felines should progress from least invasive to most invasive with attention being paid to the patient's reaction to each step. Use a gentle, smooth, consistent touch throughout the exam. A study looking at responses of cats to the handling of different body regions found that they respond most negatively to the caudal region being handled (Ellis et al., 2015). Since familiar cats often greet each other by extending nose to nose and then bunting on or licking the head, extending a finger to a social cat may entice the patient to come forward to interact. From here, start the physical exam at the cat's head and work toward the caudal region. If there is an area of priority, you may need to examine this area earlier in the process, in case the patient does not tolerate a full, in-depth exam. If a more in-depth exam is needed and the cat is exhibiting signs of stress, you may need to consider sedation or anxiolytic medications.

Respiratory rates for cats can be significantly higher in the veterinary office than at home. If there are concerns about the cat's respiratory system, it may be helpful to have the guardian count respirations at home or for them to bring a video of the cat sleeping and the cat resting so that an accurate respiratory rate can be obtained (Dijkstra, Teske, and Szatmari, 2018). The goal of restraint during the physical exam and procedures should be to maintain patient comfort and safety for the patient, client, and veterinary team. Use the least amount of restraint needed to achieve these goals. A study comparing full-body restraint to passive restraint found that the odds of a cat struggling were greater in cats being placed into full-body restraint than passive restraint. During the physical exam, cats undergoing full-body restraint had higher respiratory rate and signs of stress and the full-body restrained cats were less likely to stay on the examination table when released from restraint (Moody et al., 2018).

Towels can be useful for restraint with feline patients, either using a formal towel wrap technique as described by Dr. Sophia Yin (Yin, 2009) or as an aid to provide the cat with a place to hide. If given the opportunity to hide, some fearful cats will remain hiding on the table or in their carrier instead of trying to escape and jump off the exam table. If you need to move the patient to the scale or elsewhere in the exam room, a towel can provide a feeling of security to the cat. Towel wrap techniques can be useful for handling cats but should only be used on patients who are otherwise tolerating their visit without signs of escalating stress. A cat who is struggling against a towel wrap or exhibiting other signs of distress during handling (growling, hissing, yowling) may need sedation or anxiolytic medication before continuing. To use a towel wrap, lay the towel open on the exam table and place the cat several inches from the front edge of the towel, about a foot in from one end. Wrap the short end of the towel snugly around your cat's neck, like a scarf. Lift the short end of the towel over the cat, so that her entire body is covered except for her face. Pull the front edge of this end of the towel forward and wrap it under the cat's neck. Once the end is wrapped all the way around her neck, grasp the other end of the towel, pull it over the cat, and wrap it snugly in place. This technique will be most effective if your client has taken the time to condition the cat at home with gently treat-related towel-wrap activities.

Current vaccine guidelines for cats suggest that veterinarians may want to consider administering injections in the distal limbs instead of between the shoulder blades. The guidelines advise that caution should be taken when vaccinating cats resting in a crouched position to ensure that the injection is given lower on the leg, and not in the skin fold of the flank (Scherk et al., 2013). To access the distal portion of the leg in a crouched cat, it may be necessary for the person administering the vaccine to gently extend the leg while an assistant is supporting the rest of the patient. Restraint for blood collection depends on the position most comfortable to the patient, as well as the volume of blood needed. Many cats will tolerate a jugular blood draw with gentle restraint.

For clients who are willing to work with their cats at home, training common procedures can be helpful to decrease the stress of husbandry procedures and veterinary procedures. All kittens should be introduced to force-free nail-trimming, brushing, and non-stressful medication strategies at a young age, so comfort with the procedure and a positive emotional response can be established early before the kitten undergoes negative experiences. A study examining the effects of operant conditioning for blood draws found that cats who were trained in a recumbent blood draw technique had lower heart rates when released from restraint than cats who were not trained, indicating that cats may benefit from cooperative care training prior to any veterinary procedures (Lockhart, Wilson, and Lanman, 2013).

Conclusions and creating a flow of care

Each hospital has a unique flow of care through the hospital and different priorities or philosophies about patient care. A useful exercise is to think through the flow of your hospital and design a go/no-go decision tree for your team and hospital. A decision tree can be helpful so that as the hospital team identifies patients who are experiencing stress or fear in the hospital setting, everyone is on the same page about next steps and options. The patient's stress level is fluid throughout the visit, but most decision trees include pauses along the way to assess body language and the stress level of the patient. A couple of these assessment points where the patient's stress level may change would be any change in environment (entering the clinic, entering the exam room, when the veterinary staff enters the exam room) when contact is initiated with the patient, and throughout the physical exam and any procedures.

Depending on the clinic, these assessment points may be recorded on the patient's emotional health record for the visit, or assessments may be more informal. With practice, the assessment of patient stress in the hospital becomes second nature and requires very little time. An example of an algorithm for creating happier visits and healthier pets by Colleen Koch, DVM, DACVB appeared in *Veterinary Medicine* (Koch, 2015). This algorithm may be a useful starting point to create a decision tree specific to your hospital.

In conclusion, improving our patient's exam room experience improves our client's experience in the clinic, client compliance, and our ability to provide the best care for our patients.

Chapter 7
The Client's Role in Patient Transportation
By Dr. Ariel Fagen, DVM, DACVB

Introduction

Veterinary clinics across the country are working hard to make the patient experience a less stressful one. Veterinarians and animal welfare professionals agree that we need to improve the patient's welfare in the clinic environment. If you have gotten this far in the book, then you understand already the importance of safeguarding the emotional well-being of our patients. Changing how we design our buildings, enacting new protocols and standards, training employees and upgrading how we practice medicine with behavioral health in mind are all a huge part of this effort. No matter how well we do this, at some point or another we may need to touch the patient in ways that they do not understand or are painful and thus find scary.

We know that client perception of perceived patient stress can decrease the frequency of veterinary visits. Yet only 24% of veterinarians surveyed in 2014 were providing instruction to clients (always or often) on how to make their animal companion's visit to the veterinarian less stressful and only 18% of clients reported receiving this information. Clients are the ones with the powerful opportunity to effectively prepare their family member for a potentially scary experience. What are we not saying and what are our clients not hearing?

Getting clients involved in the preparation process can empower them to be active members of the healthcare team. They can play a key role both in advance of the appointment, and during the appointment, in helping their animal companion voluntarily participate in their own care. Their presence during moments the patient may experience as difficult could ease both the client and patient's minds (Herron and Shreyer, 2014). The patient may experience comfort in having their social support present, and the client may feel comforted knowing that they were given every opportunity to help their loved one. Furthermore, having this transparency builds trust with the clinic and holds practices accountable for excellent patient care.

Veterinarians and animal welfare researchers concur that there is significant room for improvement in our ability to use positive reinforcement-based training techniques, species-specific handling, and 'pre-training' our patients for the veterinary experience. This chapter provides a deep dive into this pre-training and how you can educate and partner with your clients to help prepare your patients, as best as possible, for the veterinary experience. Conditioning pets in advance to what they might experience over their lifetime is the best way we can 'explain' to our patients what is happening. This chapter can give you and your healthcare team a roadmap to start a client education program on how they can help prepare their loved one for the vet.

No time like the present – The Patient Prep Plan

There is no better time to start a program like this than right now. From the very first appointment with your practice, you can help put into action a Patient Prep Plan for each patient. Whether a new puppy exam, a new rescue adoption or just a new patient to your practice, that first appointment is your first opportunity to incorporate the client as an active member of the healthcare team. And for your current clients, what better way to communicate with them that you are serious about transforming your practice into a low stress experience than by getting them involved in the preparation process? The earlier in an animal's life that you start teaching these skills, the better (Doring et al., 2009).

The exercises and skills described here are not just for animals who are already exhibiting fear, anxiety or stress at your office. In fact, the process of teaching some of these skills and getting the patient acclimated to veterinary procedures will be significantly easier for those who do not already have negative associations with the veterinarian. You will find in this chapter a variety of different techniques that will enable you to tailor a plan for every patient that walks through your door.

Implementing a Patient Pre Plan

To effectively implement a client education program, all doctors and support staff need to be aware of the benefits a program can provide, when to recommend it and how to work within the parameters of a Patient Prep Plan to get their jobs done. Only select support staff need to be skilled enough to implement the client coaching part of the service. This does not need to be a doctor. Instead, this is the perfect role for a veterinary technician or assistant who has received further education in reading body language, learning theory, training and behavior modification.

The bulk of this preparation requires at-home management changes or skills practice *before* a client brings their animal companion into the veterinary clinic. Research shows that clients are more likely to do this at home practice than repeated in clinic visits anyway (Stellato et al., 2019). Clients need expert guidance on how to do this effectively. Here lies a unique opportunity for veterinary clinics to provide a preventative behavioral medicine service that is good for their patients, good for employee safety and improves quality of patient care. With appropriate staff knowledge, coaching can be provided one-on-one to clients through technician appointments or via group classes to guide them through the process.

Fear of lack of compliance should not stop you from creating a program. In one study with dogs showing mild-moderate fear at the vet, clients were asked to practice handling only twice weekly for 3 to 4 out of 4 weeks. Even with only partially tailored plans, the probability of clients reporting decrease in fear was 86.7%! (Stellato et al., 2019). This client perception was supported by a decrease in fearful body posture as assessed by professionals (Stellato et al., 2019), despite some barriers avoidable in real-life. Imagine what outcomes your patients could get with more tailored plans and expert guidance! This hands-on coaching is a valuable service and should be charged appropriately, so it can be a new revenue stream for the practice.

For patients showing aggression or anxiety, or if your clinic simply does not have the capacity to provide the needed client coaching, it may be in the pet's best interest to get a board-certified veterinary behaviorist involved. If a patient is showing significant aggression or anxiety at the vet's office, then he also may be experiencing anxiety that the client does not recognize as such in other areas of his life. A veterinary behaviorist can do a comprehensive assessment and then help design the veterinary plan, as well as evaluate if the animal's quality of life at home is compromised by anxiety or fears. Alternatively, or additionally, a qualified force-free behavior professional can be invaluable in helping a client implement training and behavior modification protocols at home. (See Chapter 3 – Working with a Behavior Professional.)

Preparing for cats as well as dogs

Don't forget the cats! Dog training is a common and well-accepted practice in today's culture but is less known as an option for cats. Because of this, it may be tempting to implement a Patient Prep Plan for dogs and ignore the dire need for felines to have Patient Prep Plans as well. This would be a mistake. Clients have identified that feline resistance and stress over being put in carriers, transported to the veterinary hospital and undergoing veterinary care are primary barriers to veterinary visits. Cat guardians felt more negatively than dog guardians about every aspect of taking their cat to the vet, even depicting images of frightened and tortured cats in focus groups. Clients often have noted behavior changes in their cats for several days after a veterinary visit, indicating lasting behavioral effects in the home from a scary veterinary experience. Multiple statistics support that felines on the whole receive less veterinary care than dogs do:

- 40% of cats had not been to their vet in the past year in one study, compared to 15% percent of dogs; 52% of cats had not been to their vet in the past year in a second study.

- Only 83% of cat caretakers reported having a primary care veterinarian vs. 91% of dog caretakers.

- Dogs had visited the veterinarian a mean of 2.3 times/year, compared to 1.7 times/year for cats.

The veterinary industry recognizes that cats are not coming in as frequently as they should. Therefore, addressing feline stress associated with transportation and veterinary visits may be a critical way to ensure that your feline patients are receiving medical care. Sure, it may feel foreign to cat guardians to work on conditioning exercises. You may have concerns about cat guardian compliance. However, this does not alter the fact that it may be even more needed amongst our feline population than canine. The veterinary industry recognizes that cats are not coming in as frequently as they should. According to a 2014 study, only 65% of veterinarians report that cats are easy to work with (compared to 90% for the same question about dogs). Additionally, only 18% of cat caretakers reported receiving any direction from their veterinary healthcare team as how to make the veterinary experience better for their cat. Here may be the most impactful place for clear and thorough guidance from you and your veterinary team. You may be surprised at how relieved a client might be to have a plan in place.

Foundation information for your plan

Before embarking on coaching any clients through the techniques below, there is some foundational knowledge that is essential for any veterinary care provider to understand. First is fluency in reading dog and cat body language (see Chapter 2). You must be able to identify even subtle signs of anxiety, so you understand when you are pushing a patient beyond their comfort level. Failure to notice these subtle signs could mean many of the plans in this chapter will backfire on you and you could accidentally sensitize a patient to handling (Stellato et al., 2019). This is one of the reasons why clients need coaching to help them through these protocols. Left to their own devices, they very frequently push too fast through protocols out of impatience, and then suddenly the plan fails. Whoever coaches the client through these protocols must be able to identify the anxiety, help the client identify it and slow the protocols down so that they can be effective.

Secondly, you must have a clear understanding of learning theory to be able to apply these protocols correctly. Outlined here are guidelines, not a cookbook, for evoking the behavioral change you wish to see. You must understand where to flex them, why and how to accommodate the individual patient. The only way to have that skill is to become a learning theory nerd. For a thorough review of the learning principles involved in teaching these skills, see Chapter 1. In this chapter and the next, we will default to treats as the reinforcer being used because they have been shown to be effective for just this type of practice (Stellato et al., 2019), because for many animals they are highly reinforcing and generally easy for clients to administer. However, all these skills can be taught using other reinforcers when needed, such as play or grooming, depending on the preferences and medical conditions of the patient.

In many of the protocols listed here, a clicker is recommended as a marker, a bridge or a secondary positive reinforcer. The clicker is used to mark the moment something happens, or the pet does something that we hope to reward with our primary positive reinforcer (treats) (Mazur, 2016). Thus, the clicker 'tells' the animal that what they just did or what just happened was what we are looking for and has earned them a treat. It provides a clear method of communication and thus can be particularly helpful for modifying behavior. However, it can add a layer of mechanical difficulty, as clients must negotiate using the clicker along with whatever else they are doing when they only have two hands. In addition, some sound-sensitive dogs and cats can find the 'Click!' of the clicker to be aversive. For those who prefer not to use a clicker, the 'click' can be replaced with a distinctive verbal marker, such as "Yes!" or a tongue cluck. If a replacement is needed, swap this out in your head for all the protocols written here where you see the word click.

Prior to initiating a Patient Prep Plan, clients should develop a Hierarchy of Reinforcers, so they know what is for their pet generally a low value, moderate value, and high value reinforcer. This, of course, may change over time as the novelty wears off or with satiation, so it may need to be constantly updated. The highest value reinforcer can be reserved as an 'emergency' reinforcer. Using it only in emergency situations can maintain its novelty and thus its power.

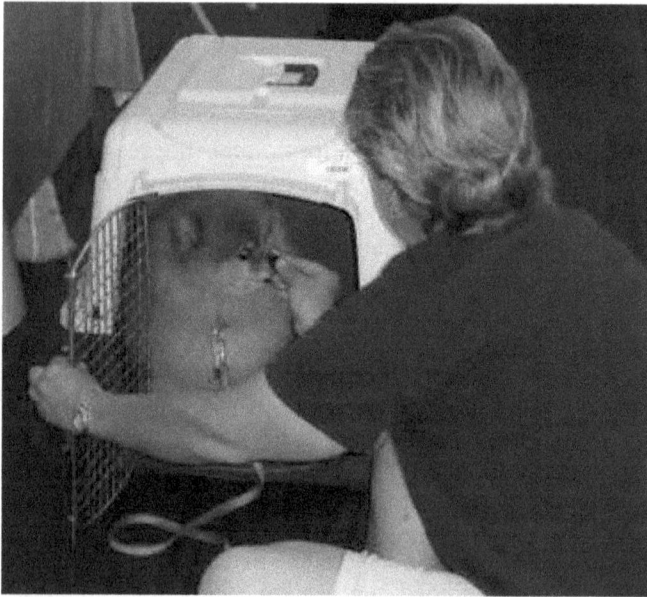

Using counterconditioning to help this Pomeranian become comfortable in his crate.

Generally speaking, low-to-moderate value reinforcers can be used at home when teaching new skills if the animal does not have a prior negative experience with the skill or tool at hand. If the dog or cat has had a negative prior experience or has demonstrated fear in the past, then moderate-to-high value reinforcers may be needed. With counterconditioning, the reinforcer needs to be of significant inherent value (aka palatability with treats) for the most efficient and best learning (Mazur, 2016). Once you are utilizing these skills in the veterinary environment for actual handling and procedures, moderate to high-value reinforcers should be used. The emergency reinforcer should always be brought with the client, just in case, but reserved for when things do not go as planned. You can also keep a variety of high-value reinforcers on hand, again, just in case.

For patients with special dietary needs due to medical conditions, treats should remain within the bounds of what they can eat. For animals on limited ingredient diets, acceptable foods can be their fresh-cooked protein source cut into small chunks, baked into treats or made into purees. (Pureed foods can be delivered as treats via a camping food tube, or a turkey baster with the tip cut off to widen it.) If the dog or cat typically receives the kibble version of a diet, then the canned version can be used as is, or baked into treats or made into a puree. For dogs on prescription hypoallergenic diets, the cat version of the diet may prove more palatable and acceptable to use as treats in limited quantity. Single ingredient human foods without animal proteins may be an option as well, e.g., sweet potatoes or watermelon, or simple grain-based foods such as plain breakfast cereals or pasta.

For patients undergoing anesthesia, while advanced practice at home can utilize the patient's Hierarchy of Reinforcers, on the actual day of the procedure there are a few options. Toys or the opportunity to smell interesting or novel smells can be used as strong reinforcers in some patients. Frozen chicken stock or frozen chicken, turkey or sweet potato baby food can be offered in a cup or jar for the patient to lick. Each lick acts as a reinforcer and minimal amounts of food might actually be consumed. Recent research (Savvas et al., 2016) questions the previous standard that providing food prior to anesthesia is higher risk of causing aspiration problems. Thus, using small amounts of the patient's regular treats may be judged as a relatively safe and necessary option in some cases.

This chapter and the next will focus on a few key areas where we can prepare our patients that can result in a much lower-stress veterinary experience. The first is to ensure the patients arrive at the veterinary clinic calmly. The second is strategic use and training to get them accustomed to various tools that can be helpful to increase safety and decrease stress for everyone involved. The third area incorporates the various skills that can be implemented for teaching patients to become partners in the handling itself.

Getting to the vet safely and calmly

If a patient's sympathetic nervous system is already activated before she even arrives at veterinary office, we cannot possibly expect that patient to have a low-stress veterinary experience. Carriers and the transportation experiences have been shown to be stressful for many companion animals. One survey revealed that cat owners believe 77.8% of cats know they are going to the veterinarian before arrival (Mariti et al., 2016). This same survey revealed that over half of these guardians observed stress signs before even leaving the home. If arousal levels are already increased when they are sitting in their living room an hour before the appointment because that carrier came out, then we need to start there.

Carriers

Conditioning animals to carriers has well-established benefits that can have real effects on your experience, the patient's experience, and the client's experience. Cats hiding from carriers, or physically and aggressively resisting being put into carriers have been established as barriers to veterinary care. The practice of conditioning cats to carriers has been shown to decrease examination time (Pratsch et al., 2018). Hiding and escape attempts during veterinary examination were lower in cats taught to accept their carriers (Pratsch et al., 2018). Comfort-indicating behaviors (milk treading, purring and scent marking via body rubbing) were present during car rides in carrier-trained cats, and certain stress behaviors such as panting and hiding were eliminated in the car rides (Pratsch et al., 2018). To get more of these comfort-indicating behaviors, let's first set ourselves up for success.

Carrier selection

Choosing the correct carrier is an important step in maximizing its potential to help make the veterinary experience as least stressful as possible. The carrier needs to provide both safety and comfort for the patient and provide safety and utility for the client. The carrier should be large enough that the patient can stand up normally, turn around and then lie down comfortably. It should have adequate ventilation such that it is safe even on hot days and can allow for dissipation of odors, in case the carrier gets soiled. Carriers should be set up to maximize pet comfort and safety. A soft, absorbent lining should be placed on the bottom, such as a blanket or towel that the animal is regularly wiped down with (Anseeuw et al., 2006) or routinely lies on. A water bowl should be provided for any extended use. Toys and chews can be provided for any period the patient is enclosed when it is medically acceptable.

The plastic airline-approved clamshell carrier is an excellent choice. The bottom shell should easily unscrew or unclip from the top shell to allow for separation of the two halves (Mariti et al., 2016; Moffatt, 2008). This provides easy access to a patient who is inside (Pratsch et al., 2018) and unwilling to exit on his own without staff needing to risk sticking hands into a carrier and cornering the animal. Many patients remain in or retreat to the bottom half of the carrier when made available for an exam (Pratsch et al., 2018). Once the top is removed, a blanket or towel can immediately be placed over the animal, (Lloyd, 2017; Anseeuw et al., 2006) for those who feel safer hidden. The towel can be moved aside as needed to access specific body parts, allowing the patient to remain partially covered throughout the exam. Options that include both top and front-loading provide the additional benefit of multiple ways of loading and retrieving the pet if they are unable to walk in and out comfortably on their own (Anseeuw et al., 2006). Following are photos of a number of crate options.

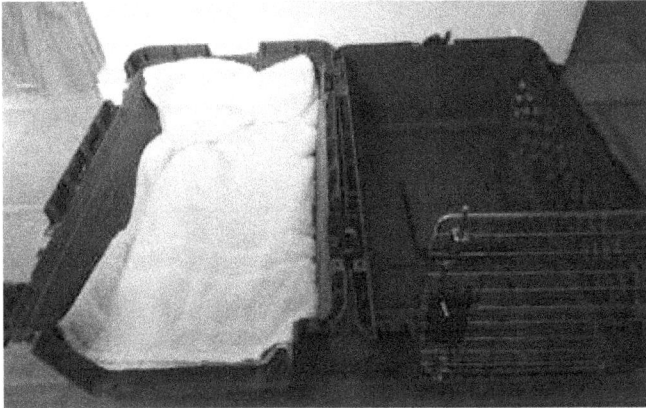

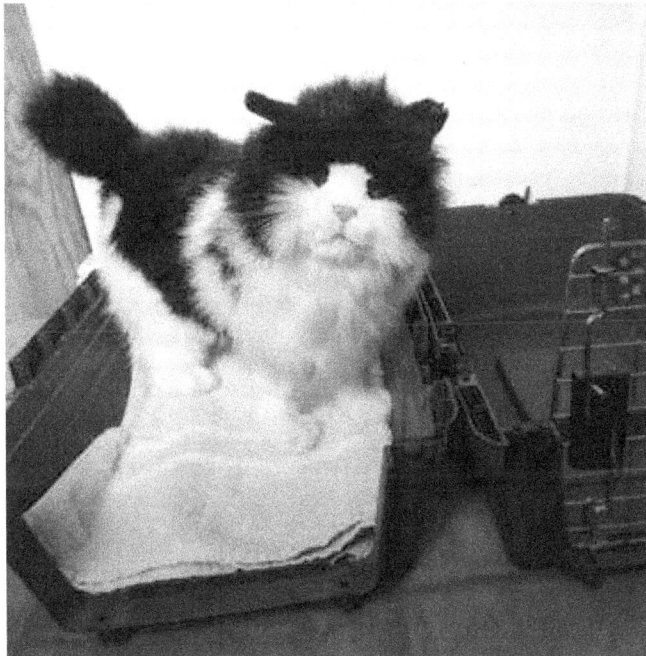

Removing the carrier top can help the cat become more comfortable in the carrier

Certain circumstances may warrant alternative carriers. Soft-sided carriers can be useful for patients who need intramuscular sedation for exams. For example, the cat can stay inside the familiar carrier, and the side of the carrier can be flattened against the cat and the injection given through the carrier mesh. There are carriers that have a 'squeeze cage' mechanism built in. This essentially means that the patient can be pushed against the side of the wire frame carrier by a moveable door. This can allow for intramuscular injections while keeping the handlers safe. If it is known that this is a useful tool for a particular animal, then that patient could be conditioned to tolerate this type of carrier and the moving mechanism so that the squeeze action is relatively low stress. However, for many animals, if such an effort is needed to condition this tool, similar time could potentially be invested to teaching the patient to tolerate handling in other ways, making the necessity of such a carrier questionable.

Several different methods can be used to teach an animal to feel safe in the carrier, including habituation, conditioning, counterconditioning and a combination desensitization and counterconditioning.

Carrier habituation

The simplest and easiest way to get a companion animal acquainted with his resting area is for it to become just another piece of furniture in the house. This means the carrier is out all the time with its comfortable bedding (Anseeuw et al., 2006). This may be all that's needed, especially for kittens or puppies or naive, confident dogs. The patients for whom habituation may be enough will most likely be those who have had no prior negative experience with the carrier, and who naturally gravitate towards enclosed spaces. To start, either take the door off completely or fix it in the open position. The door accidentally banging open or shut could easily frighten an animal and cause this plan to fail. (See below for tips on how to get the animal accustomed to the door closing.)

Some companions may do better with only the bottom half of the carrier presented as furniture. The enclosed carrier may be too intimidating for animals who are not drawn to enclosed spaces. Both halves of the carrier can be presented concave side up with comfortable blankets inside. Slowly, over time, these two halves can be moved closer and closer into the assembled position (really making this part a desensitization plan). While the animal may still need to be taught to be comfortable with the carrier assembled for transport using one of the methods below, this approach will at least familiarize him with the individual parts, despite the altered arrangement. An added benefit may be the familiar scent that could accumulate with sufficient use.

Conditioning and desensitizing the patient to the carrier

To step it up one notch, you can pursue a basic life-integrated classical conditioning (Lloyd, 2017) or a counterconditioning approach. In reality, these look very similar to each other; the difference is the animal's prior association with the carrier. If he already has experienced the carrier as aversive, then this is functionally a counterconditioning plan – changing the already existing association. If he has no prior or neutral experience with the carrier then it is technically a conditioning plan – creating the initial association. Either way, the life-integrated conditioning plan should simply be a change in how a client interacts with their companion around the carrier and not take up a significant part of a client's day.

At the core of it, the client picks out a few of the patient's favorite activities, such as meals, brushing, massage, play, delivery of chews and delivery of treats. These wonderful life occurrences now happen in the carrier. Excellent things, such as new toys or treats should just 'magically' appear in this special spot. (Anseeuw et al., 2006). In this way, the animal companion is conditioned to have positive associations with the carrier.

If the patient already has a strong conditioned negative response to the carrier, or the life-integrated plan seems insufficient to change how he feels, then a desensitization and counterconditioning plan will be needed. In this way we slowly work towards the patient spending time in the carrier in a graduated fashion, using preferred activities, ideally mealtime or receiving treats if the animal is food motivated.

The first step is to determine the threshold – the first point in the getting into the carrier process that the patient finds slightly anxiety-provoking or scary. For example, as you take the carrier out of the closet, you see your Chihuahua lip-lick and look away the moment the carrier comes within 10 feet of him. This is your dog's threshold. You start your protocol one 'step' before the threshold. Play the whole scene in your head like a movie. Press pause when you see the first conflict sign and then rewind the movie a moment. This is your starting point for the protocol. In this scenario the threshold is 10 feet so the starting point would be when the carrier is 11 to 12 feet away from the dog's body. You want your starting point to be the last point where the handling is not scary. Better to err on the side of caution or too early in the process (rewinding the movie a little too much), than too late in the process.

Below are a few protocols that can be used as a rough outline, but modifications can and will likely be needed for individual patients. If the animal can tolerate looking at the carrier but any movement of the carrier toward him is triggering, then start at the beginning of the protocol below. If the threshold is farther along in the process, you can skip some initial stages. If the patient cannot even tolerate looking at the carrier, you may need to back it up even further to work on reaching toward where the carrier is stored. You might need to start with just presenting the bottom of a clam shell carrier and then add the top in later (Pratsch et al., 2018).

Stage 1 is getting the pet to be willing to be in the crate – a few techniques are described. For this stage, always start with the crate door fixed open so that it does not suddenly bang closed and accidentally frighten the pet. Stage 2 is working on closing the door of the crate. Stage 3 is building duration of the pet staying in the crate calmly. Stage 4 is acclimating the pet to the carrier moving while they are in it.

Note that I am now referring to the carrier now as a crate. Most clients use the term "crate" and may find this more applicable to this training even though most professionals prefer the term "carrier."

Implementing crate protocols

Stage 1- Entering the crate
Option #1: Lure method with meals. In this simple plan, the crate is stored out of sight between sessions, so the presentation of the crate becomes the cue for entering. To start, place the crate in view across the room and then within one to two seconds put the meal down for consumption. Each day, the meal is placed one foot closer to the open door of the crate. Once at the entrance to the crate, place the meal half inside and half outside the crate. Then, just on the inside of the door. Then, on subsequent days move the meal one to two inches deeper inside the crate until the patient is readily walking into the crate for a meal placed all the way in the back of the crate. If at any point in this process the animal shows any hesitancy about the proximity to the crate, back up a step and feed a few days at this easier level before progressing.

You can continue with this and move onto the next stage, but recognize that each time the patient needs to get into the crate the meal would need to be placed in the crate first to lure him in. This may be sufficient for some, but if you want to teach the animal to enter without the food (e.g., for situations like undergoing anesthesia where you may not be able to feed), then you will have to transition off the lure. To do this, when the patient will readily enter for a meal, present only half the meal. The moment the animal steps all the way into the crate, deliver the second half of the meal. The next day, only provide ¼ of the meal as the lure, then provide the remainder of the meal after the patient is in the crate. Next, provide an empty bowl and the moment the patient steps in provide the full meal. Repeat for a few sessions. After five to seven successes with the empty bowl, try presenting the crate without the empty bowl inside and follow up with the full meal reward.

This plan can work well for people who do not want to do specific training sessions but can modify how they do their regular feeding. The animal companion needs to be interested enough in their regular meals for this to work and consume their meals in actual meals - so it is not a great option for grazers or picky eaters. This is a slower process because each meal is essentially just one repetition, so weeks or months may be needed to get in enough repetitions.

Option #2: Lure method with treats. This plan is essentially the same as above except using special high value treats instead of the patient's meal. The advantage is that we can use this even with grazers or picky eaters but it does take specific training sessions. Another advantage is that multiple repetitions can be performed in one session, so progress can be much faster. Treats can be placed directly on the ground; they do not need to be in a bowl. A clicker can optionally be added in to mark the moment the animal steps into the crate.

Option #3: Capture and shape being in the crate:

1. Present the crate.

2. Click at the moment of presentation.

3. Deliver treats or a few bites of the meal.

4. Put the crate away.

5. Repeat until the patient exhibits no body language signs that indicate concern at least three times in a row – not even subtle ones! Ideally, the patient looks expectantly at the crate on presentation, understanding that a treat is imminent.

6. Put the crate down on the ground far enough away that your animal companion is not concerned (this may be across the room for some patients, this may be a few feet for others). The moment your companion takes one step towards the crate, click and reward. You can pick up the crate and re-present it in a slightly different location at that same distance again. When the pet re-approaches the same distance away, click and reward. Repeat until the patient approaches from that distance away at least three times in a row with no body language signs of concern.

7. On your next repetition, click and treat for the animal companion approaching a few inches closer.

8. Repeat in this fashion until he can approach right up to the crate entrance at least three times in a row with no conflict behaviors.

9. Then, click and treat for one paw inside the crate, then two paws, then three paws, then all four. You can wait to let your animal companion exit the crate on his own and then mark and reward for each entrance into the crate. To speed up the process, some people drop one treat in the crate (or wherever their animal is) then either call the patient out or toss a second treat out of the crate to reset for the next rep. You can also click and treat multiple times for staying in the crate, so he doesn't think the game is just about going in and coming back out, but that he also gets reinforced for staying in.

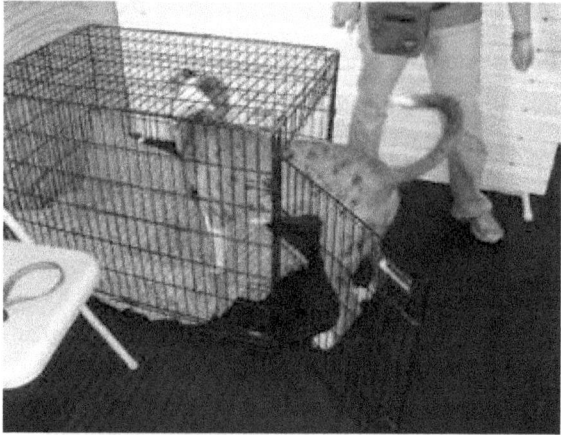

Using shaping to teach a dog to go into a crate.

For all these options a verbal or hand signal can be added to cue the patient to enter the crate. Once he is reliably entering with the crate presentation, then the moment before presentation (or opening the door for the animal), the client would cue the patient to enter.

Stage 2 – Closing the door

Once the patient can enter the crate, we must teach him to tolerate having the door closed. Do not block his ability to exit the crate. If he attempts to leave the crate, allow him to do so. The ability to choose to leave the crate is an important part of giving him control of the situation. If he does choose to leave, this is valuable information about his comfort level or motivation in the moment. At each step in this process watch for body language signs of concern, and if noted, back up to an earlier step. Do not move on to the next step until you obtain at least three repetitions in a row with no conflict behaviors:

1. When the patient enters the crate with all four paws and will stay for at least several seconds, touch the door without moving it. Click the moment of the touch and toss a treat into the crate. Repeat several times.

2. On your next repetition, move the door one to two inches towards closed, click, toss a treat and then immediately open it again. Repeat several times.

3. Close the door halfway, click, toss a treat in and immediately open again. Repeat several times. Close the door ¾ of the way, click, treat, open. Repeat several times.

4. Close the door completely without latching, click, treat (toss through the door), open. Repeat several times.

5. Close the door, latch, click, treat, and immediately open the door. Repeat.

The patient can remain in the crate for this entire process if he chooses or he can leave at will and the protocol can be continued at the next opportunity. Option: to add a verbal cue to exit the crate (which might be very helpful once you get to the veterinarian), the client would add a word like "exit" the moment the animal stands up or starts to move towards the open door when given the opportunity. (Timing is important: the word should come just before the patient exits, but ideally only when the client sees that he is exiting.)

Stage 3 – Build duration

1. Have the patient enter the crate, close the door, count to one second in your head, click, treat, count another one second, click, treat and count another one second, click, treat and open the door. Allow him to exit if he desires. Repeat several times.

2. Cue him to get back in the crate if he chose to leave. Close the door, count two seconds in your head, click, treat, count another two seconds, click and treat, then count another two seconds, click and treat and open the door. Allow him to exit if he desires. Repeat several times.

3. Continue working up the time interval in this fashion. Once you reach five second intervals, generally you can increase the interval by three second increments. Once you reach 15 second intervals you can try increasing the interval in five to 30 second intervals until you reach a goal of the patient getting a treat once every few minutes.

The total duration you build up to will depend on the amount of time needed for the client to get their animal companion into the veterinary clinic. Typically, once a patient can tolerate about 10-15 minutes of duration in the crate, extending that time is not a hard task. The patient learns to settle in, and if needed, long-lasting chews, toys or other fun distracters can be provided.

Stage 4 - Acclimating to movement

When the patient can remain calmly in the crate for your target duration, start teaching him to tolerate the movement of the crate. Start by picking the crate up a few inches off the ground, putting it back down and then delivering a treat. Slowly progress to picking it up completely. Then progress to walking to the car or other mode of transportation. Monitor the patient's body language this entire duration for signs of stress. For clients who are unable to make approximations for all these steps due to the limits of accessible transportation, then they do the best they can and if any 'leaps' are needed to be made for real life transport, a safe stuffed food puzzle or long-lasting chew can be provided to distract the patient.

Transportation

Much as we need to get our canine and feline friends accustomed to riding in a crate, similarly we need to get them accustomed to whatever mode of transportation they will be taking to get to the veterinarian. This will allow us to start our exams with our patients in the best possible emotional state. We will go through the details of conditioning animals to be comfortable riding in cars, but all of the following information can be modified to ensure that those patients commuting by bus, train or walking also arrive at the vet's office calm, cool and collected.

Cats who otherwise never leave the home may be particularly sensitive to the distressing effects of a car ride when their only experience riding in cars is to go to the veterinarian. Twenty-one percent of cat guardians assessed their cat as stressed in the car ride to the veterinary clinic (Mariti et al., 2016). Cats who were reported to be anticipating the car ride were less calm in the waiting room, on the exam room table and once returned home (Mariti et al., 2016). By the time of arrival on the veterinary exam room table, fewer than one quarter of cats were calm enough and motivated enough to eat (Mariti et al., 2016). This illustrates the level of stress they must experience in the process of transporting to the clinic and through the waiting room. Cats crying during transportation was noted as a distressing experience for clients and one barrier to cats receiving medical care. Let's remove this barrier to care and coach clients on the importance of helping our feline friends through each step of the preparatory process.

Our feline companions may not be the only ones who find getting into the vehicle worrisome. Animals who are not routinely lifted in and out of vehicles must be able to enter and exit securely. Those with mobility concerns or who may not be able to jump directly into vehicles smoothly should be provided a stable, non-slip set of stairs or ramp – and be taught how to use them. For those patients fearful of these mobility aides, additional conditioning protocols may be needed for these to be of use. If a patient is to be lifted into and out of a vehicle, then ideally a consent cue would be instituted so the patient can indicate he or she is ready to be loaded and unloaded. This increases the patient's control over the process, and thus can decrease anxiety (Lindsay, 2000). This can be accomplished by teaching an "in" cue and "out" cue via positive reinforcement training techniques. Multiple methods can be used to teach the in and out – simple lure methods, shaping methods and targeting are all common options.

Remind your clients that once safely in the vehicle, the patient needs a comfortable, safe space to ride. For animals in carriers, they can secure the carrier on the floor behind the driver or passenger seat (https://www.centerforpetsafety.org/pet-parents/pet-travel-tips/). Patients should have enough room in their appropriate-sized carrier/crates or harness to lie down, stand up and turn around during transport.

Temperature regulation is also critical for patient safety (https://www.weather.gov/safety/heat-children-pets), so ensure that vehicles are climate controlled. Check that surfaces such as seats and crates are comfortable to the touch if the vehicle has not been in a climate-controlled garage. Provide blankets if needed. For any animals who need to be in the vehicle for extended periods of time, water and litterboxes should be available and breaks provided as needed for pets to relieve themselves. (Note that the author does not recommend leaving animals in vehicles for extended periods of time due to potential for stress, and ill effects from cold or overheating. Leaving the engine running with heater or air conditioning on is not a safe solution – these can break down and shut off.)

Patients who are expected to enter the crate after it is placed in the vehicle (as opposed to loading up in the home and then being carried to the car), will need to be conditioned to be comfortable with this loading procedure and confinement. The lure and capture methods described above can be used to teach animal companions to tolerate crating in the car. Conditioning can be very situational, so while a patient may be comfortable in his crate at home, he may need to be taught to be comfortable in a crate in a car (or vice versa).

Some patients have minimal anxiety about riding in the car. For these, it may be as simple as providing a stuffed food puzzle, container smeared with cream cheese or anchovy paste, or providing a long-lasting chew for each car ride. Similarly, if most car rides result in an exciting adventure (e.g., hiking, dog parks, visiting loved ones, beach time, etc.), over time patients can be classically conditioned that car rides mean great things. For these, a formal conditioning protocol may not be needed.

For patients who are fearful of riding in the car or associate car rides with scary experiences (such as groomer or veterinary visits), the following protocol can be modified to the individual's needs. Rewards can be delivered via tossing or hand delivering treats directly to the animal. Generally, a passenger is needed to be the treat deliverer so the driver does not get distracted, though automated remote treat dispensing devices may be useful.

As with any desensitization and counterconditioning protocol, the client will need to pick a starting point one step prior to where the individual animal starts to demonstrate body language signs consistent with fear or stress. Caution them to not move onto the next step until the patient is enthusiastically participating in that step, multiple repetitions in a row, with no conflict behaviors. As a general rule of thumb, if a patient demonstrates mild conflict behaviors twice in a row at any step in the protocol, they need to back up to an easier step (or to an intermediate step between the last one and the one they had been working on). If he demonstrates marked signs of stress, the client should stop practicing and return at a later time to an easier step. Some patients may be able to skip some of the following steps, depending on what is challenging for them. Others may need an even more incremental approach.

Protocol for conditioning car rides (with multiple repetitions at each step)

1. Dog looks at the car, client marks and rewards.

2. Dog approaches car, client marks and rewards.

3. Dog gets in the car, client marks and rewards, unloads.

4. Dog gets in the car, client closes the door, marks and rewards, unloads.

5. Dog gets in the car, client closes the door, sits in the driver's seat, marks and rewards, unloads.

6. Dog gets in the car, client sits in the driver's seat, starts the car, marks and rewards, turns off car and unloads.

7. Dog gets in the car, client starts the car, drives down the driveway, marks, rewards, returns home, unloads.

8. Dog gets in the car, client drives around for two to three minutes giving a reward every one to two seconds along the way, returns home, unloads. Practice on a few different routes.

9. Dog gets in the car, client drives around for two to three minutes giving a reward every five seconds along the way, returns home, unloads. Practice on a few different routes.

10. Dog gets in the car, client drives around for two to three minutes giving a reward every ten seconds along the way, returns home, unloads. Practice on a few different routes.

11. Dog gets in the car, client drives around for two to three minutes giving a reward every 20 seconds along the way, returns home, unloads. Practice on a few different routes.

12. Dog gets in the car, client drives around for two to three minutes giving a reward every 30 seconds along the way, returns home, unloads. Practice on a few different routes.

13. Dog gets in the car, client drives around for two to three minutes giving a reward every 45 seconds along the way, returns home, unloads. Practice on a few different routes.

14. Dog gets in the car, client drives around for two to three minutes giving a reward every 60 seconds along the way, returns home, unloads. Practice on a few different routes.

15. Client gradually takes longer rides and spaces out treat delivery more and more.

Here is a protocol to share with clients for those patients who generally find the car a pleasurable experience but 'just know' when they are headed to the veterinarian on the car ride over:

1. Take a drive to the vet and watch your companion's body language carefully, looking for the first sign of distress. Note where in the ride this is – this is her starting threshold for this exercise.

2. Drive one block before her starting threshold. Toss her a handful of treats, then head on a different route towards some place fun – an adventure, to a friend's house or even back home for a game of ball. Repeat until she exhibits body language signs consistent with excitement that you have reached this location.

3. Repeat Step 2 driving to what was her original starting threshold.

4. Then, drive one block closer to your veterinarian, repeating Step 2.

5. Proceed in this fashion until you can drive all the way to your veterinarian's office without your animal companion exhibiting any signs of stress.

Chapter 8
The Client's Role in At-Home Preparation
By Dr. Ariel Fagen, DVM, DACVB

As discussed in the previous chapter, there is much your client can do at home to make life easier for the patient, as well as for you and your staff. The more comfortable the patient is with commonly used tools and handling procedures prior to arriving at your clinic, the less stressful it is for all concerned. The less stressed the patient is upon arrival and during handling, the more smoothly things will go during the visit – and that is our goal, to have smooth, low-stress encounters with our clients and patients.

Tools and restraints

Muzzles
It is incredibly valuable for any patient to be conditioned to happily wear a muzzle. Muzzles provide the handlers with the security of knowing that they are not going to be bitten, and sometimes are critical to ensure a patient can get the medical treatment he needs. Having this safety tool in place can expedite treatment and reduce staff stress, thereby making it a less stressful experience for the patient. As Herron and Schreyer so deftly write, "The key to successfully integrating handling tools [like muzzles] into the veterinary practice is using them correctly, using them often, and using them early" (Herron and Schreyer, 2014, p. 465).

If our goal is to make our patients as comfortable as possible during the veterinary experience, then placing a muzzle without pre-conditioning is the exact opposite of our goal. Just slapping a muzzle on a patient, and thereby removing opportunity for behavioral expression, can lead to frustration (Lindsay, 2000) and potentially fear, and can compound the fear already associated with the rest of the handling that is being performed, not to mention the distress the patient is feeling due to pain or discomfort from a medical problem. With proper conditioning, the muzzle can be perceived as a comfortable or even fun piece of clothing or a delicious food basket. Without proper conditioning, the muzzle simply becomes associated with and amplifies the stress of the veterinary experience.

As a standard recommendation, every dog should be conditioned from puppyhood to be comfortable in a muzzle. This way if a veterinary team needs to place one on, the dog can cooperate in its placement. Many veterinarians have been in situations where they were not able to provide gold standard medical care because they were unable to successfully muzzle a patient. Standardizing muzzle conditioning as part of the package of essential puppy skills would virtually eliminate this as a barrier to treatment. Any dog, even the most friendly and cooperative patient, could be in a situation in his or her life where a muzzle is advantageous. Pain-related aggression is a defensively aggressive response to a painful stimulus (Landsberg, G., Hunthausen, W., and Ackerman, L., 2011) and can commonly occur in veterinary environments in a wide variety of cases, from treating broken toenails, painful cases of otitis externa and bad teeth, to accident-related injuries and structural pain – and everything in-between.

The same could be said for cats as well – it would only benefit the cat and the veterinary teams to have every cat conditioned as a kitten to be comfortable wearing cat muzzles. The caveat is that cat muzzles can provide a layer of protection to veterinary teams from cat bites, however they do nothing to protect veterinary teams from the four other defensive weapons cats have – their claw-studded paws! That being said, many cat muzzles on the market provide visual obstruction which may not only add a small element of increased safety for handlers but may also help some cats feel more secure by providing a visual blockade (Herron and Schreyer, 2014; Moffatt, 2008). If properly conditioned, cats, just like dogs, can develop a strong positive conditioned emotional response to muzzles.

Muzzles for dogs

There are a few features that are essential to consider when choosing a muzzle. First, we want the dog to be able to thermoregulate appropriately (meaning they need to be able to pant effectively) with any muzzle that might be worn longer than a few minutes. In order for us to practically use many of the other skills and techniques described in this chapter, we need the patient to be able to eat through the muzzle. For this reason, a basket muzzle is recommended (Moffatt, 2008).

With the standard basket muzzle, there is a formed cross-hatch or grid frame around the dog's whole snout. Basket muzzles do not hold the dog's mouth closed, so they are able to pant, lick and chew inside the muzzle. Treats can be delivered through the holes, and the dog can submerge the end of the muzzle into a bowl of water to drink. This is not possible with standard sleeve muzzles (usually made of cloth or leather) that loop around the dog's mouth to keep the mouth closed. Sleeve muzzles may allow for limited licking at the open end but not for panting or effective drinking.

There are many types of basket muzzles made from a variety of materials, including rubber, leather, metal and plastic. Features to consider that make different basket muzzle brands more or less user friendly include: 1) the stiffness of the muzzle; 2) the general shape of the muzzle (e.g., intended for more dolicocephalic or brachycephalic snouts); 3) the type of clasp on the strap; 4) the size of the holes in the muzzle; and 5) the washability of the material (e.g., rubber vs. leather). There are many brands out on the market, and choice will depend on the individual case.

Ultimately, patient comfort and fit are of paramount importance. Ensure that the straps are sufficient for keeping the muzzle on correctly and that no rubbing or injury occurs secondary to wear. The muzzle should not be so big that it bumps against the patient's eyes or flops around on the patient's face. Nor should it be so small that it prevents the dog from opening her mouth effectively or squishes her nose against the end. For difficult to fit patients, custom-made muzzles are also available in a variety of materials.

One limitation of basket muzzles is that very brachycephalic patients (English Bull-dogs, Pugs, French Bulldogs, etc.) may not have sufficient snout for standard basket muzzles or even custom-made ones to fit effectively. There are mesh-based muzzles that are intended for brachycephalic patients, but these do not provide all the advantages that basket muzzles can. Open-ended globe muzzles that fit over the patient's entire head are an option (Moffatt, 2008) depending on the medical interventions needed. Elizabethan collars can work well for some patients (Moffatt, 2008) and may be the best option for some of these dogs.

Muzzles for cats

Many inventions have been introduced on the market in recent years to address feline muzzling needs, from opaque cones with openings at the end, full face masks (without a hole in front of the mouth), to the open-ended globes that fit around the cat's entire head. Similar considerations are important when selecting a cat muzzle as when choosing a dog muzzle. The ability of a muzzled cat to be able to eat and breathe effectively essentially eliminates full-face masks as a viable option. Finding a muzzle that allows the cat to drink is even more of a challenge, so it's important to have time limitations in place. Your best options are the cone-shaped muzzles with openings at the end through which food could be provided, or the open-ended globes. Some cats may appreciate the visual blockade provided by opaque cones (Herron and Schreyer, 2014; Moffatt, 2008) and others may feel more secure if they are able to see the handling. Stiffer plastic or leather muzzles are safer than mesh or cloth ones that the cat may be able to bite through (Herron and Schreyer, 2014). Comfort is important for muzzle use to be as low stress as possible, so it is important to make sure there are no areas of irritation or rubbing.

Conditioning the muzzle

There are two general approaches to getting a patient to be comfortable with a basket muzzle. The first is a simple, straight forward conditioning protocol, and the second a participatory desensitization and counterconditioning protocol. Straight conditioning would be a reasonable option only for selected patients who have not had any prior negative experiences with muzzles and are generally non-fearful, easily habituated, well-adjusted patients who generally do not mind wearing 'clothing.' A trained professional should be involved in identifying these patients, as it requires adequate knowledge of body language to identify subtle signs of stress. The average client might think the above statement describes their companion, when in reality a desensitization and counterconditioning protocol might be more appropriate for their animal. Any patient who does not meet the above criteria should be guided through a desensitization and counterconditioning protocol.

Simple classical conditioning for the muzzle. Classical conditioning is fairly straightforward. The muzzle is placed on the patient and then good things immediately happen – rapid fire delivery of treats, a few minutes of licking peanut butter off a spoon, a fun game of chase, etc. After a few minutes, the muzzle is removed and the fun stops. This is repeated until the patient looks enthusiastically and expectantly for the fun thing when the muzzle is brought out. When this happens consistently, the patient has obtained the positive conditioned emotional response to the muzzle.

Once the muzzle placement has been conditioned, the duration the muzzle is left on the patient can gradually be extended, and over time the rate of reinforcement can decrease and become randomized. Any signs of stress or discomfort during this process, including pawing at the muzzle, moving away, ears moving backwards, lip licks or other signs are indicators to stop this protocol and switch to the participatory desensitization and counterconditioning protocol.

Desensitization and counterconditioning for the muzzle. Any patient for whom a straight classical conditioning approach is not sufficient needs be guided through a graduated incremental protocol to become comfortable with the muzzle. Any patient who dislikes 'clothing' on their body, is face or head shy, has underlying anxiety, or a history of a negative experience with muzzles will benefit from the more graduated approach. Here are two different protocols that can be implemented to condition an animal to be comfortable wearing a muzzle.

The first protocol is based primarily on shaping and is an excellent procedure for patients and clients who have prior history implementing secondary positive reinforcement and enjoy the process, especially if they have learned targeting in other contexts. These patients can speed through the initial stages of this process. Stage 3 may need to be skipped for animals who find sudden or quick movements frightening instead of fun, or for clients who have mobility restrictions.

Muzzle protocol 1

Stage 1: Conditioning the sight of the muzzle

1. Hold the muzzle behind your back.
2. Remove the muzzle from behind your back.
3. The moment the patient sees it, deliver a reward within one to two seconds.
4. Hide the muzzle again behind your back.
5. Repeat until the patient looks enthusiastically for a reward when s/he sees the muzzle.

Stage 2: Targeting the open end of the muzzle

1. Sit on a chair or stool with the muzzle behind your back. Bring the muzzle out from behind your back and hold the open end of the muzzle toward the animal with the straps secured back and your elbows resting on your knees. DO NOT move the muzzle towards the patient. When the patient orients his nose or moves his nose toward the open end of the muzzle, mark and reward.
2. Place the muzzle behind your back.
3. Repeat Steps 1 and 2 until the patient repeats this successfully at least three times in a row.
4. On the next rep, repeat Steps 1 through 3, but wait until the patient moves his nose one inch closer to the opening of the muzzle before you mark and reward. This is the new criteria.

5. Repeat until the patient repeats this successfully at least three times in a row.

6. Continuing in this fashion, gradually reinforcing for closer and closer nose position until the patient's nose is fully inserted into the muzzle. As you proceed, part of the criteria becomes rewarding only for gradually orienting and inserting his nose into the open end of the muzzle.

Stage 3: "Catch me if you can!" – helpful for pets that find chase games fun

1. On your next repetition, when you offer the muzzle, slowly move it away from the patient so he has to follow to 'catch' it. Repeat until the patient successfully follows the muzzle a few inches to place his nose into it.

2. Repeat several times while you are standing instead of sitting.

3. Repeat while you walk slowly backwards away from the patient with the muzzle presented.

4. Repeat several times while you walk quickly backwards away from the patient with the muzzle presented.

5. Repeat several times while you jog backwards away from the pet with the muzzle presented. (Don't trip!)

6. Build up the speed and excitement so this turns into a fun game of 'catch the muzzle.' Play in different rooms in the house, in the yard, in the hall, etc. When the patient is enthusiastically chasing you to stick his nose in the muzzle, move on to the next stage.

Stage 4: Build duration

1. For this stage you will vary how the muzzle is presented – sometimes run away for chase, sometimes stand still, sometimes present the muzzle in your seated lap. When a patient's nose is in the muzzle, count to one in your head, then mark and reward. Remove the muzzle.

2. Repeat until the patient keeps his nose in the muzzle for a one-second duration at least three times in a row.

3. Repeat for a two-second duration.

4. Repeat for a three-second duration.

5. Continue to increase duration to at least ten seconds.

Stage 5: Clasping the neck straps

1. Offer the muzzle in your lap between your knees with the open end facing the patient and the straps dangling. (Alternatively, smear peanut butter or other lickable treat on your refrigerator, vinyl floor or Licky Mat®-type product and let your dog lick at it.) This will leave you with two hands free to work on clasping the neck straps. When the patient's nose is in the muzzle, raise the right strap up halfway to the patient's ear, mark while strap is raised, release the strap, deliver the reward through the muzzle and remove the muzzle. Repeat until you have at least three successful repetitions in a row.

2. Repeat Step 1, raising the right strap all the way up behind the patient's ear.

3. Repeat Step 1 with the left strap.

4. Repeat Step 2 with the left strap.

5. Offer the muzzle in your lap (or use the peanut butter). When your patient's nose is in the muzzle, raise both straps up behind the ears, mark while the straps are raised, release the straps, deliver the reward through the muzzle, and remove the muzzle. Repeat until you get at least three successful repetitions in a row.

6. Offer the muzzle. When the patient's nose is in the muzzle, clasp the straps behind the ears, mark the moment the straps are buckled, deliver the reward, release the straps, and remove the muzzle. Repeat until you get at least three successful repetitions in a row. If you need to keep the patient busy while you clasp the straps, spread peanut butter or squeeze cheese on a cleanable surface and let her lick while you close the straps.

Patient comfort and staff safety is of paramount importance when choosing a muzzle, so ensuring the correct fit for the dog is crucial. A well-fitted basket muzzle allows your dog to take treats, drink, and pant comfortably - it should not cover their eyes and the dog should not be able to pull it off or slip out of it

Muzzle protocol 2

This second protocol is based on a lure method of 'spiking' the end of the muzzle with a smearable treat. For patients and/or clients who have less experience with secondary positive reinforcement-based conditioning, this may be an easier protocol to follow. Some patients and clients may do just fine never fading off the lure in Stage 3 if a shortcut is needed. Clients need to understand that a lure treat may always be needed for the animal to put his nose in the muzzle. Most times that a patient needs to go to the veterinarian a small amount of lickable food needed for this process would not be problematic. On the rare occasion where a patient needs to be completely fasted this may be limiting. As in the prior shaping protocol, Stage 4 can be skipped for patients who would not enjoy the 'chase me' game.

Stage 1: Condition the sight of the muzzle

1. Hold the muzzle behind your back.

2. Remove the muzzle from behind your back.

3. The moment the patient sees the muzzle, deliver a reward within one to two seconds.

4. Hide the muzzle again behind your back.

5. Repeat until the patient consistently looks enthusiastically for a reward when s/he sees the muzzle.

Stage 2: "It's a treat basket!"

1. Spread some peanut butter, cream cheese or other lickable treat at the nose end of the muzzle.

2. Sitting in a chair or on the floor, hold the muzzle with the straps open and your elbows against your own knees. DO NOT move the muzzle towards your companion. Let the patient approach the muzzle.

3. When your patient's nose is all the way in the muzzle, mark and reward through the muzzle.

4. Gently remove the muzzle and place it behind your back. Your patient does not need to finish the lickable treat at the end of the muzzle on each repetition; you can leave some for the next rep. Restock as needed.

5. Modification: If your patient is suspicious of the muzzle, he may not be willing to put his nose all the way in at first. You may need to smear the lickable treat on the open end of the muzzle. Mark and reward when your patient has his nose in line with the first 'rung' of the muzzle. Remove the muzzle and repeat until you have success at least three times in a row. Then, proceed to the next rung, or one inch deeper into the muzzle. Continue in this fashion until your patient is putting his nose all the way into the muzzle.

6. Repeat until your patient enthusiastically sticks his nose all the way in the muzzle at least three times in a row.

Stage 3: Fade the lure

1. For this repetition, smear about half the amount of the lickable treat you normally apply inside the end of the muzzle. When your patient sticks his nose into the muzzle, mark and reward. Remove the muzzle and place it behind your back.

2. On your very next repetition, ensure there is less lickable treat on the end of the muzzle. Repeat until you are not smearing any lickable treat inside the end of the muzzle.

3. When your patient enthusiastically sticks his nose into the end of the muzzle at least three times in a row for the mark and reward without any lickable lure treat present, move on to the next stage.

Stage 4: Catch Me If You Can! – Helpful for pets who enjoy chase games

1. On your next repetition, as soon you offer the muzzle, slowly move it away from the patient, so he has to follow you to 'catch' it. Repeat until the patient successfully follows the muzzle a few inches to place his nose in it.

2. Repeat multiple times while you are standing.

3. Repeat multiple times while you walk slowly backwards with the muzzle presented.

4. Repeat multiple times while you walk quickly backwards with the muzzle presented.

5. Repeat multiple times while you jog backwards with the muzzle presented. (Don't trip!)

6. Increase speed and excitement so this turns into a fun game of "catch the muzzle." Play in different rooms in the house, in the yard, in the hall, etc. When the patient is consistently and enthusiastically chasing you to stick his nose in the muzzle, move onto the next stage.

Stage 5: Build duration

1. For this stage, vary how the muzzle is presented – sometimes run away for chase, sometimes stand still, sometimes present the muzzle in your seated lap. When the patient's nose is in the muzzle, count to one in your head, then mark and reward. Remove the muzzle.

2. Repeat multiple times until the patient keeps his nose in the muzzle for a one-second duration at least three times in a row.

3. Repeat multiple times with a two-second duration.

4. Repeat multiple times with a three-second duration.

Stage 6: Clasping the neck straps

1. Offer the muzzle in your lap between your knees with the open end facing the patient and the straps dangling. Alternatively, smear peanut butter or other lickable treat on your refrigerator, vinyl floor or LickiMat®-type product to keep your patient's nose oriented in one direction and stable. This leaves you with two hands free to work with clasping the neck straps.

2. When the patient's nose is in the muzzle, raise the right strap up halfway to the patient's ear, mark while strap is raised, release the strap, deliver the reward through the muzzle, and remove the muzzle. Repeat until you have at least three successful repetitions in a row.

3. Repeat Step 1 with multiple repetitions, raising the right strap all the way up to behind the patient's ear.

4. Repeat Step 1 multiple times with the left strap.

5. Repeat Step 2 multiple times with the left strap.

6. Offer the muzzle in your lap (alternatively, smear peanut butter or other sticky treat on your refrigerator, vinyl floor or Licky Mat®-type product). When

your patient's nose is in the muzzle, raise both straps up behind his ears, mark while the strap is raised, release the straps, deliver the reward through the muzzle, and remove the muzzle. Repeat until you have at least three successful repetitions in a row.

7. Offer the muzzle. When his nose is in the muzzle, clasp the straps behind his ear, mark the moment the straps are buckled, deliver the reward, release the straps, and remove the muzzle. Repeat until you get at least three successful repetitions in a row.

Stage 7: Increasing duration

1. Offer the muzzle, wait one second, mark, reward, and remove the muzzle. Repeat multiple times until you have at least three successful repetitions in a row.

2. Offer the muzzle, wait two seconds, mark, reward, and remove the muzzle. Repeat until you get at least three successful repetitions in a row.

3. Increase the time lag by one-second increments with multiple repetitions until you reach ten seconds and have at least three successful repetitions in a row.

4. Increase the time lag by five-second increments with multiple repetitions, until you reach 30 seconds and have at least three successful repetitions in a row.

5. Increase the time lag by ten-second increments with multiple repetitions until you reach 60 seconds and have at least three successful repetitions in a row.

6. Reward once every 60 seconds for three minutes *without* taking the muzzle off in between with multiple repetitions until you reach 60 seconds and have at least three successful repetitions in a row.

7. Continue to increase the time the patient can wear the muzzle, reinforcing approximately once a minute until you reach ten minutes with multiple repetitions and have at least three successful repetitions in a row.

8. Decrease your frequency of reinforcement until the patient can wear the muzzle around the house for 10 to 15 minutes with only a few random rewards.

The relaxation mat

The purpose of the relaxation mat is to help the patient emotionally self-regulate and calm down in stressful circumstances. The mat is transportable, so can be taken to any appointment at any doctor or groomer, or any other away-from-home venues. It can also be a helpful station that gives animals information about where to be and what to do when there are circumstances that could inadvertently escalate anxiety or arousal levels. For example, the mat can first be used in the car, to help a dog lie down and snooze during the 20-minute car trip over, instead of panting and whining while looking out the window. In the waiting room, the mat can help encourage a patient to calmly lie down instead of barking at the nearby dog or pulling on leash to sniff a nearby cat carrier. In the exam room before the doctor walks in, the mat can help the patient relax instead of pacing around the room. Too many patients go into a physical exam already stressed and highly aroused because of all the stressors that have been encountered on the way in. The mat can help mitigate some of the over-arousal before, during and after veterinary handling, so the whole experience is as smooth and non-traumatizing as possible. The relaxation mat can keep a patient calm prior to veterinary handling as well as help a patient recover after veterinary handling.

Patient selection

Most patients can benefit from a relaxation mat protocol. The versatility of this tool can go well beyond the veterinary environment. Other applications can include visitors in the home or family picnics at the park. The protocol is not a short one, and to do it well clients do have to make a commitment to investing some time, consistency, and perhaps some finances to get the appropriate professional coaching to be successful. This tool might be particularly helpful for those patients who find the car ride, waiting room and waiting process to be challenging, as well as for patients who have a difficult time recovering from stress episodes. Owners may choose to skip this exercise for those patients who generally are calm and relaxed at the veterinary office and simply find the moment of handling slightly stressful, but easily recover afterwards. These owners may want to spend their modifications and training efforts on the veterinary handling protocols presented later in this chapter.

Mat selection

There are three criteria to meet when selecting a mat: 1) functionality; 2) patient comfort; and 3) portability. You want the mat to have a non-slip bottom surface so it can be laid out and look and feel the same each time it is presented. It needs to be large enough and comfortable enough so the patient can lie in lateral recumbency with legs fully extended with most of their body on the mat. How much cushion to provide may vary depending on the individual patient's preferences, body condition score, and orthopedic or dermatologic conditions. The mat needs to be lightweight enough that it is easy for the client to bring with them to the clinic and store at home between sessions. For larger dogs, this may mean a mat that can be rolled up. Yoga mats or bathmats are great options for many dogs. For cats, a cat bed, bathmat, or cushioned placemat can serve well.

Conditioning relaxation

The protocol for obtaining a positive conditioned emotional response of relaxation to a mat is a multi-stage process. The following protocol is one the author uses at The Veterinary Behavior Center (www.vetbehaviorcenter.com) modified from a protocol used at the Florida Veterinary Behavior Service (www.flvetbehavior.com). Share this with your clients so they can teach the protocol to their animal companion.

Use low-to-moderate value treats no bigger than the size of a pea. If the patient is motivated for their regular kibble this is a great option. Between sessions, store the mat out of sight. This protocol requires the animal to already respond reliably to a down cue. If he does not, the protocol can be modified accordingly – contact a qualified force-free training/behavior professional for help. Each stage must be done completely and thoroughly in order for the protocol to succeed. Skipping or rushing through stages can result in the client investing significant time and not accomplishing the emotional self-regulation that is so valuable. Advise the client that if they get stuck on a step, they can contact a qualified force-free training/ behavior professional for guidance.

Relax on a mat protocol

Stage 1: Building association and intensity, also known as 'This mat causes treats to fall from the sky.'

1. Put the mat down.

2. When the patient steps on the mat – one foot at first, eventually building up to all four feet, drop one treat on the mat every second for ten seconds.

3. Call animal off the mat verbally - do not use treats for this.

4. Pick up the mat, place it down in a different location.

5. Repeat until the animal companion steps onto the mat immediately at least three times in a row when you place it down in a different location.

Troubleshooting tip: If a treat accidentally rolls away from the mat and your patient leaves the mat to retrieve it, then just take this as an opportunity to reset the mat.

Stage 2: Make sure it's really about the mat

1. Put the mat down, then slightly turn your body angled 45 degrees away from the mat. Don't look at the mat.

2. When the patient steps on the mat, drop one treat on the mat every second for ten seconds.

3. Call the animal off the mat verbally - do not use treats for this.

4. Pick up the mat, place it down in a different location, angling your body slightly differently each time. Repeat the treat-dropping procedure in each new location.

5. Repeat steps one through four until the patient steps on the mat immediately at least three times in a row when you place it down and angle your body away.

6. Repeat Steps 1 through 4 with your body angled 90 degrees away from the mat until the patient is successful at least three times in a row.

7. When your companion steps on the mat, drop one treat on the mat every second for ten seconds.

8. Call patient off the mat verbally - do not use treats for this.

9. Repeat Steps 4 through 6 above, taking one step away from the mat each time.

10. Repeat, taking three steps away, then five steps away. Walk in a different direction each time with your body angled differently each time.

Troubleshooting tip: If your animal companion lines up in front of you instead of on the mat, wait for 30 seconds to see if she will think it through and offer to step on the mat. Reward immediately if she does and continue with the protocol. If she does not step on the mat after 30 seconds, pick up the mat and place it down again. Angle your body only 15 degrees away from the mat this time. Gradually build up to a 90-degree turn. Put the mat down, take one step away from the mat and angle your body slightly away from the mat. If the patient attempts to follow you, pick up the mat, reset and stay a little closer to the mat for the next few repetitions. Gradually increase distance.

Stage 3: Default down on the mat

1. Place the mat down.

2. The moment the patient steps on the mat cue the 'down.'

3. The moment she lies down, drop a treat on the mat between her front paws every one second for ten seconds, as long as she stays in the down position. From now on, being in the down position is the only way to elicit treats when on the mat.

4. Call the patient off the mat, pick up the mat, place it down in another location.

5. Repeat until the patient lies down immediately when cued at least five times in a row.

6. Place the mat down. When the patient steps on the mat, start counting to 30 in your head. you are waiting for her to guess that she has to lie down to make the treats happen.

7. The moment she lies down, reward with a small handful of treats and then continue with one treat every second for ten seconds. Then call her off the mat and pick up the mat.

8. Place the mat down. Wait until she steps on the mat and automatically lies down without you giving any cues. Reward with one treat every second for ten seconds. Call her off the mat, pick it up and repeat until she automatically lies down at least three times in a row when the mat is placed down. If she does not automatically lie down the first time when you are trying to wait her out, after 15 seconds pick up the mat and replace it one more time without cueing the down. If she is unsuccessful again, return to cueing the down until you get another five successful repetitions in a row. Then try again without cueing the down, this time giving her 30 seconds to figure it out.

Troubleshooting tip: If she stands up at any point before the ten seconds are over, stop delivering treats, call her off the mat, pick it up and repeat. If this occurs again, drop treats faster on the mat - your dog needs a higher rate of reinforcement at this time.

Stage 4: Building duration

1. Take a seat in a comfortable chair.

2. Place the mat down next to you. The patient should automatically step onto the mat and lie down on her own at this point.

3. Count one second in your head, *then* drop the first treat on the mat. Count another second, then drop a second treat, then count another second and drop a third treat.

4. Increase to two seconds between treats. Repeat at least two times.

5. If the patient is still lying on the mat, increase to three seconds between treats.

6. Continue on in this fashion, increasing to five seconds, then eight seconds, then 12 seconds, then 16 seconds, then 20 seconds, etc. until she can stay on the mat in a down position for a treat once every minute for three minutes in a row for at least three repetitions in a row.

7. At each new session, start at a slightly shorter interval than you ended at the last session. If you successfully worked up to 30 seconds, on your next practice session start at 25 seconds and gradually work up to 30 again.

Troubleshooting tip: If the patient gets up or walks off mid-session, pick the mat up and reset it. When your companion lies down again, start your next repetition at a shorter interval. If she gets off the mat after 12 seconds, reset the mat, count to nine in your head and deliver the first treat. If successful, repeat at least two more times, then slowly work your way back up to 12 seconds.

If you find your patient 'popping' off the mat frequently, double check that you are counting your interval before delivering the first treat when your patient drops into a down. If you are dropping a treat the moment she lies down, your pet may learn that she actually earns treats faster by getting up and lying back down rather than just staying down.

Stage 5: Building a conditioned emotional relaxation response

1. Take a seat in a comfortable chair. Do not look directly at the patient; use your peripheral vision.

2. Place the mat down next to you. At this point, your companion should automatically step onto the mat and lie down on her own and be able to stay there for a full three minutes, getting only one treat every minute. If she cannot do this, revisit earlier stages before moving on.

3. Using your peripheral vision, watch for any body language signs of relaxation. These can include: a hip shift, head lowering, head resting, half-closed eyes, lying on her side, muscle tension relaxation, taking a deep breath, etc.

4. Any time the patient exhibits any body language sign of disengagement or relaxation, drop a treat right in front of her nose. Purposefully try to reward a variety of different body language signs, not just one. The goal is to reward a compilation of outward behaviors that are associated with an inner feeling of relaxation. If you reinforce only one behavior, then your companion will only learn to offer that one behavior and is not as likely to actually relax.

You know you have successfully reached the end of this protocol when you put the mat down and your pet immediately lies down and settles into a fully relaxed position.

Towel restraint

Towels can be a useful and gentle restraint method that can increase the safety of the veterinary staff and minimize patient arousal levels (Moffatt, 2008). Some animals will appreciate the use of towels, especially cats, as the restraint method can capitalize on their natural instinct to hide when they are fearful. Felines in the clinic environment have been shown to exhibit more hiding behaviors than when veterinary handling is performed in the home environment (Herron and Shreyer, 2014). Thus, towels used appropriately in some animals, even without prior conditioning, can decrease anxiety and fear by making them feel safer.

Towels become even more powerful as a tool when owners put in the time up front to teach their animal companions that this type of restraint is safe and makes good things happen. Towels can be used with dogs in multiple ways as well, including providing a visual blockade to handling, and a gentle restraint method. For cats, there are a variety of towel wrap techniques that can comfort cats and increase the safety of the handlers. Many of these towel wraps were initially described by Sophia Yin (Yin, 2009) and her materials can be referenced for further detail.

Towels as a visual blockade

For some patients, not seeing what is happening 'back there' can make it easier for them to cope with handling. This is most effective and humane when combined with chin rest consent (or see Chirag Patel's Bucket Game in Chapter 1) along with desensitization and counterconditioning to handling – both described below. Those two protocols can be quite effective on their own for many patients for standard handling, but it is difficult to prepare for all types of unusual handling. This is where the towel as the visual blockade is useful – for quicker, unusual handling, such as an intramuscular injection. The visual blockade allows the intervention to occur with as little anxiety as possible commonly associated with the anticipation, restraint and approach to the procedure. Visual blockades may virtually eliminate or minimize the need for restraint, especially when used in combination with tools like a handling mat. Robustly pre-conditioning the visual blockade can help the patient expect the unexpected.

Patient selection

Patient selection for towel as a visual blockade includes an assessment of a dog's previously displayed behavior. Dogs who have responded well in the past to a form of visual barrier are perfect candidates. For example, they may have done well with a gentle "veterinary hug" restraint, where a technician or assistant faces the lateral aspect of the dog with arms around the dog's neck and chest, hugging the patient to her chest. With this restraint technique the body of the technician provides a visual barrier to handling of the dog's hindquarters when the doctor is located on the same side of the dog as the technician. Alternatively, a dog may have been noted to bury his head in between the client's knees, or in an armpit, while handling is happening. Perhaps a visual blockade tool such as a Calming/Thunder Cap has been successful in the past. Dogs who offer to bury their heads are communicating already that they do not want to see what is happening – much like a human who closes her eyes for a blood draw from her arm. For these patients, either the Towel Wall or an Eye Pillow approach (see below) can be conditioned as part of the veterinary plan.

For some patients a visual blockade may not be a useful tool. For patients who have a medical condition necessitating repeated, frequent handling, e.g., subcutaneous fluids in a chronic kidney disease patient or insulin injections in a diabetic, conditioning the patient to that specific handling should be the priority. Repeated painful or uncomfortable manipulations with a visual blockade may result in a negative association with and intolerance to the visual blockade. Other patients for whom you may want to avoid utilizing this technique are those who have demonstrated that visual access decreases their stress levels. Look for hints of this in past handling experiences and during other stressful events.

Conditioning the visual blockade

Two common types of visual blockades are the Towel Wall and the Eye Pillow. In the Towel Wall, a towel or other opaque blanket is held up above the patient's neck, hanging down to drape at the level of the shoulders or caudal neck. This requires two hands of the client or a technician to hold the towel up, so a second person needs to be in charge of reward delivery. For the Eye Pillow a small towel is folded up and placed over the patient's eyes. This may require one person to hold the pillow, and a second person to feed treats.

If the patient does not have a pre-existing fear of toweling procedures, then conditioning these are relatively straightforward:

1. Place the towel in the appropriate position.
2. Feed treats rapidly for three to five seconds.
3. Remove the towel and stop feeding.
4. Repeat until you see consistent body language signs indicative of a positive conditioned emotional response (e.g., loose body, tail wag with caudal movement, looking at the treat source, ears cocked forward with interest, etc.) as soon as the towel is put into place.

If the patient has had negative prior experiences with towels, then start by using an alternate appropriate fabric that the patient will perceive as significantly different. Options might include small blankets, felt fabric squares, dish towels, scarves, old t-shirts, etc. If a full desensitization and counterconditioning plan needs to be implemented, you can help your client decide if this is a good procedure to use, or not.

Towels for physical restraint – the Doughnut Restraint

Towels can also be used for physically restraining patients to prevent them from injuring caregivers. Patients can be conditioned to feel very comfortable with these restraints. This is important so the restraint itself does not become an added stressor. The Doughnut Restraint is one such method that also provides the benefit of at least a partial visual blockade. The Doughnut Restraint technique can be a highly effective, gentle, and safe restraint option, to provide head control in patients large and small. This technique is of particular utility in brachycephalic patients for whom muzzling is not an option or for patients who may still be working on muzzle conditioning.

A towel is rolled to create a soft tube, then the middle is draped under the patient's chin while the ends are held behind the dog's head. The towel creates a thick, soft, doughnut around the dog's neck so the patient is unable to whip his head around. The towel should be held tight enough that lateral head movement is limited but loose enough that there is no obstruction to the airway. Doughnut Restraint can be combined with a handling mat, chin rest consent, desensitization and counterconditioning to handling and other techniques described in this chapter, for a comprehensive approach. To condition Doughnut Restraint, follow the protocol described above for the visual blockade methods.

Towel wraps in cats

The simplest towel wrap for cats is called **The Drape**, which is much like it sounds. A towel is simply draped over the cat. The weight of the towel and the visual blockade can calm many cats and reduce flight behavior. The veterinary staff can then access different parts of the cat's body by lifting corners or reaching their hands under the towel. The Drape can be used in combination with light head restraint over the towel, if needed. The Drape can also be used with the cat inside the bottom half of a hard-sided carrier or in a comfortable cat bed or box. This tool allows for a minimal restraint/minimal stress form of handling and is an excellent first choice.

The next option is **The Scoop**. This too, is much like it sounds. With this technique, the cat is already located on the table or examination surface – there is no need to pre-place towels. In this technique, you start with The Drape, then the handler stands with forearms held in parallel, the width of the cat, and brings arms straight down on either side of the cat, holding the cat snugly between them. The handler's hands can be used to scoop the front of the towel underneath the cat's head and forelimbs. From here, the cat can gently be rolled into lateral recumbency.

The Burrito is a more significant towel restraint. This is ideal for situations when the veterinary staff feels more comfortable having protection from the forelimbs and mouth, and for cats who feel safer hiding inside or underneath something. This technique is more complicated and, as with all techniques, works best in cats who are still calm. When a cat is already in 'fight' mode, successfully completing a Burrito wrap will be stressful for all parties, and very likely unsuccessful. This makes it an ideal candidate for pre-conditioning.

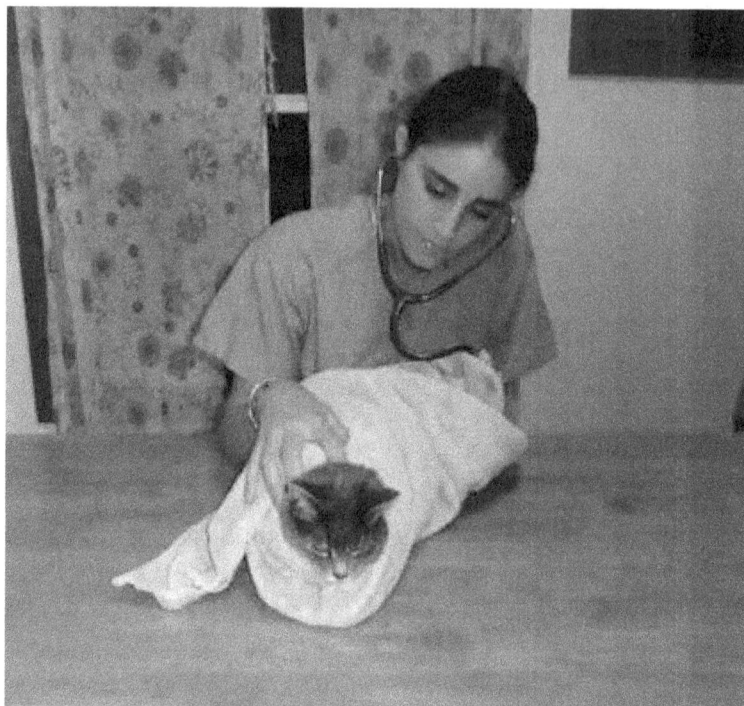

Burrito Wrap

For this technique a towel is preplaced on the table, spread out with the length of the towel extending side-to-side and the width of the towel extended in front of the restrainer. The edge of the towel is lined up along the edge of the table closest to the handler. The cat is placed in ventral recumbency in the center of the towel with her hind end close to the edge of the table directly against the handler's stomach. There should be approximately one-third to one-half of the width of the towel to use in front of the cat's face. Take the edge of the towel directly in front of the cat and fold it up and over the cat's head, somewhat loosely to ensure an air pocket remains in front of the cat's nose. Then, each of the wings to the right and left are folded snugly up and over the cat in turn. The handler's body acts as a wall so the cat cannot back his way out of the towel. Double-check to make sure there is an effective air pocket. The cat should look like it is wrapped inside a burrito. Once wrapped, the cat can be gently rolled onto her side if needed. The end of the towel near the cat's hind end can be lifted or rolled forward for the veterinary staff to work with the cat.

The Half-Burrito is a variation of the Burrito that leaves the cat's head exposed but folds all the legs into the wrap. The set-up is the same, but when the first fold is made, instead of drawing the towel up and over the head, the towel is brought over the cat's forepaws and under the cat's chin. Then, each side is wrapped as before.

The Scarf Wrap is another alternative to the Half-Burrito. The cat is placed on the towel much like with the Burrito wraps. The front left corner of the towel is then grasped and crossed over the back of the cat's neck, then wrapped over and around the right side of the neck and swooped under the cat's chin. This will look like you are wrapping a scarf around the cat's neck. The left forelimb is covered in this process. The same thing is repeated with the right front corner of the towel in the opposite direction.

The Half-Scarf Wrap is the same procedure but can be used to leave one of the forelimbs out. This can be very helpful for a cephalic blood draw, catheter placement or working with the paw or nails. Start with a regular scarf wrap on the opposite side of the limb you want to work with. Then, on the side you want to work with, take the corner of the towel and bring it behind the forelimb, then proceed with the remainder of your scarf wrap, looping the towel over the back and neck and then around the neck and chest as before.

Conditioning the towel wraps

For all of these towel techniques a simple conditioning plan can be undertaken with those patients that do not have a fear of a towel being used in this manner. Have your client place the towel in position and then provide high value treats for a few seconds while in the restraint, then release the animal. For the Burrito wrap, treats need to be pre-placed before the front fold is made. As with the other towel wrap techniques, if the cat already has a negative conditioned emotional response to towels from previous handling, the client can experiment with alternative materials. If this is not successful, a full desensitization and counterconditioning plan can be designed.

When a consistent, positive conditioned emotional response is occurring, a simple protocol can be implemented to increase the duration of time the patient tolerates the restraint. The client will put the towel and cat in place, and after one second release the restraint and provide a treat. After repeated success at a one-second interval, the client will slowly increase the time interval with multiple repetitions at each increment, until the tool is functional for extended duration and real-life use. A one-minute duration is a good starting goal.

The Handling Mat

If you are going to make the effort to teach a patient that handling is comfortable, and enjoyable, establishing a Handling Mat is an easy and useful start. The goal of the Handling Mat is to teach the patient that all handling that happens on the mat is safe. The mat becomes a safety signal. Additionally, it ensures your patient is stationed where you want them to be. You want this mat to be a non-slip surface that is transportable to whichever doctor's office or grooming facility the patient might need to visit during his lifetime. Any patient could need the services of a specialist doctor one day, so having a tool that travels with the animal is advantageous. This mat becomes associated with handling that feels safe to the patient and becomes part of the environmental stimuli that can signal the patient that the same rules that applied during practice sessions can apply at the vet's office too.

This tool all by itself does little to provide comfort to an animal during handling. It must be used in conjunction with the methods for conditioning handling to be particularly effective. Note that if the patient has a relaxation mat discussed earlier, these mats serve two different purposes and should be distinctly different for the patient.

Patient selection and utility

Any patient who is undergoing conditioning for handling would benefit from having a Handling Mat. This is an easy tool to implement with minimal time investment. We should, however, be more selective about when to use the mat. The utility of the handling mat is for more routine, more 'expected' and generally minimally painful manipulations which the patient has been taught to largely accept already. It can be especially useful for helping a patient tolerate a minor variation in the type of handling they have been taught. For example, if a patient has been taught to tolerate standing restraint and injections to the forelimbs, then the mat could potentially be used in the same patient for standing injections in the hind limbs (assuming the patient does not have any sensitivities that would make hindlimb injections particularly painful or scary).

The Handling Mat, however, should not be used if this animal is going to be rolled into dorsal recumbency for radiographs or a cystocentesis. Dorsal recumbency is far outside the scope of what this animal has learned 'happens' on the mat. The pain or discomfort associated with this may end up damaging the message of 'safety' the animal has learned is associated with the mat.

Occasionally, something might happen on the mat accidentally that is not something the patient is accustomed to, such as a new type of handling or an injection. Depending on the severity of the animal's anxiety, prior experience, the severity of this 'breach of the expected' and the history of the mat being used in safe situations, the mat could potentially be spoiled as a useful tool. To avoid this, any handling that is expected to be too much for the patient to tolerate – based on painfulness or discomfort associated with the procedure or history of known patient sensitivity – should be performed off the mat under an appropriate anxiolytic and sedation protocol. Alternatively, one could pre-condition the mat to be associated with novel handling where unusual and unexpected handling routinely occurs and is generally safe and comfortable.

Conditioning the Handling Mat

This is the easy part. To start, your client first simply obtains a positive conditioned emotional response to the mat just like was done in Stage 1 of the Relaxation Mat, where the patient learns that the mat 'magically' makes treats fall from the sky. (See the Relaxation Mat protocol earlier in this chapter.) Once this is complete, have them start putting the mat out and practice all the handling exercises on the handling mat. After each session, they will roll the mat up and put it away.

Other tools

There are other tools available that can potentially decrease patient stress with the veterinary experience. One such tool is the CalmingCap/ThunderCap which is basically an elastic cloth hood that covers a dog's eyes. The goal is to limit stress associated with visual stimuli, such as other dogs in the lobby (Moffatt, 2008). Another option is the compression products available on the market, such as the Thundershirt (ThunderWorks, Durham, NC) or the Anxiety Wrap (The Company of Animals LLC, Broomfield, CO). These products are designed to decrease anxiety by applying even pressure to the body, much as swaddling a baby reduces stress for the child. Another tool that is common in veterinary practice but could be conditioned more proactively before use is the Elizabethan collar (Herron and Shyer, 2014). These collars can protect veterinary staff from bites and may be better tolerated than muzzles by some patients. They are an excellent option for brachycephalic breeds and cats. Many patients will need conditioning to be comfortable with these tools. Although the rare patient may happily accept them the first time they are put on, it's better to be safe than sorry – have your client do a pre-conditioning protocol before you need to use them in real life. Conditioning protocol choices need to be made based on the patient's fear level and following all the principles of desensitization and counterconditioning previously described.

Veterinary handling

Handling affects the veterinary experience for both the patient and the client. Evidence indicates that there is room for improvement during this part of the visit. In one study, only 15% of cats were assessed to be calm during veterinary handling by clients and fewer than 15% of cats tolerated all of the intended veterinary handling and interventions (Mariti et al., 2016). More than two-thirds of cats refused to allow the veterinarian to examine at least one part of their body (Mariti et al., 2016) and approximately one-third of cats refused injections and/or having their temperature taken. 79 percent of dogs were observed to be fearful (body language signs consistent with fear) during a veterinary experience, whereas only 17.8% were judged as relaxed (Doring et al., 2009). Younger dogs were significantly less fearful than older dogs, suggesting that experience worsens the level of fear over time (Doring et al., 2009).

While involving clients in restraint and making a respectful approach might be helpful, these efforts are insufficient to avoid stress levels significant enough to cause aggressive responses and have reverberations back in the home environment. Forty-four percent of cats who exhibited aggression during veterinary handling did so despite being held by their guardians, and in 24% of cases the cats bit or scratched the guardian in the process (Mariti et al., 2016). Cats who were more stressed on the exam room table were also more stressed when they returned home (Mariti et al., 2016). Simply attempting to 'make friends' with the cat prior to handling is judged to be insufficient by clients in changing the behavior of their cats. If they were already stressed, the stress-related behaviors of the cats on the exam table and back home were not affected, even when veterinarians took time to talk to, stroke or offer the cat food prior to initiating their veterinary exam (Mariti et al., 2016). Low-stress handling techniques can make a difference. One study demonstrated that cats have lower cortisol levels on subsequent veterinary visits after low- stress handling when minimally stressful restraint was used on the first visit with the same veterinary team.

Beyond low-stress handling, clients can contribute significantly by teaching their animal companions to participate in and tolerate veterinary handling. For some animals, the restraint is significantly harder for them to tolerate than the procedures themselves (Herron and Shreyer, 2014,) This conditioning starts at home. Before we can expect a patient to tolerate a stranger touching them, we first need to help them to be comfortable with their family handling them in ways that may initially feel weird, unusual or uncomfortable to them – procedures that replicate veterinary handling. If the client can teach their companion that this type of handling is safe and good by developing a positive conditioned emotional response to the handling itself, then we set everyone up for success. We cannot possibly expect an animal to be comfortable with a total stranger 'hugging' them, if they don't even like when their own human hugs them! Step number one when thinking about all the conditioning that goes into veterinary handling is to condition the patient to accept, participate in and even enjoy the handling with their own human first. Then we can start generalizing this positive association to other individuals, including the veterinary health care team.

Consent communication

Consent communication is one of the most powerful tools you can give a patient who is worried about veterinary handling. The reason is because this is one skill that gives the animal control over his or her body. Veterinarians with additional training in animal welfare and animal welfare researchers appreciate the impact on their welfare of an animal having more control in the veterinary environment (Nibblet et al., 2015). Anxious animals feel less stressed when they have control. The goal of consent communication is primarily to give the patient a way to control the pace of the exam and handling and let us know (calmly, without aggression) if we are entering intolerable waters. If the animal is engaging in consent behavior, then that means the veterinary health care team has the green light to proceed forward. The moment the patient stops engaging in the taught behavior (lifts his head out of the chin rest), then that means 'stop.' We work consent communication in combination with all the other techniques discussed here, especially conditioning to the handling, to increase the likelihood that the patient gives us the green light for as many types of handling as possible.

Many different types of behaviors can be used for consent communication. The author's preferred method is a duration muzzle or chin target, where the animal is taught to place his chin in a cupped hand or on a washcloth or other soft surface. As long as the patient's chin is resting on the surface, he is consenting; the moment he lifts his head up off the surface, he is not consenting. Variations that can be equally effective can include chin resting on other surfaces, a muzzle placed inside an inverted cupped hand or 'hand tunnel' and more. The details of this can be varied based on the patient's prior experiences, known cues, the guardian's mobility and dexterity, and the patient's medical conditions.

The criteria in choosing how to set up a consent communication behavior includes: 1) the patient is able to comfortably rest in the location for a few minutes at a time; 2) the patient can easily and quickly decline consent with a small movement and; 3) the consent behavior could be performed with the patient standing, sitting, lying down in sternal, lateral and dorsal recumbency.

Though not a requirement, it can be advantageous in some circumstances for the guardian to have two hands free while the patient engages in the consent behavior. For this reason, a chin rest on a washcloth that, when needed, can be draped over the guardian's lap can be an ideal choice. This washcloth provides also a relatively easy way to transfer the chin rest consent between handlers with a little practice. Chin rest consent can be paired with visual blockades (previously discussed) and can be performed with a muzzle on, if needed. Chin rest, or any other consent communication, can also be paired with the handling mat.

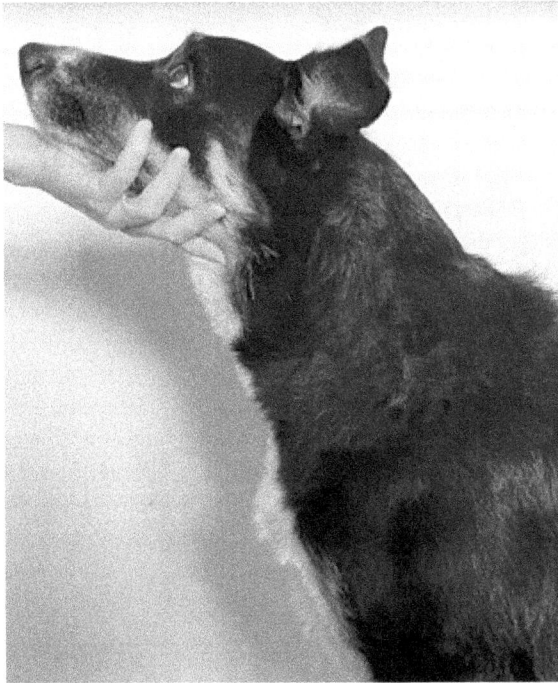

Chin rest

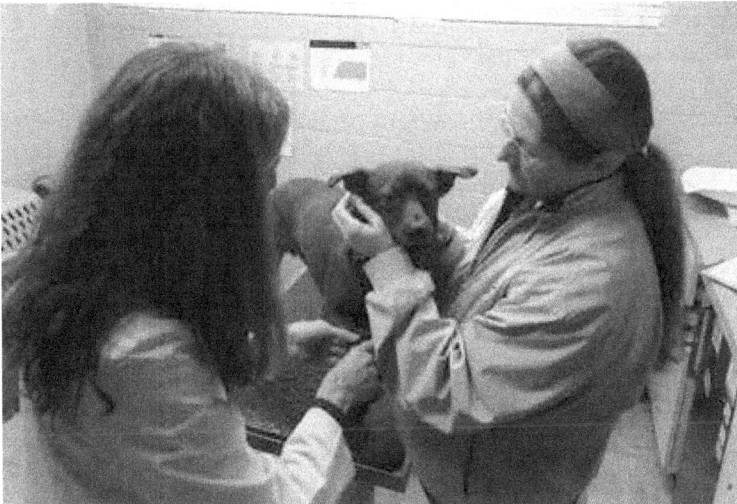

Chin rest with visual blockade

Patient selection

Any patient can benefit from consent communication, and teaching this as a foundational skill to all puppies and kittens could cause a tidal wave of change in our low-stress handling efforts. The protocol is more advanced in that it is a multi-step process, so it requires a good skill level of the person coaching the client, and some investment of time on the client's part to successfully complete the program. This may not be a priority skill for some clients who may have difficulty committing to the full plan. There are some 'shortcuts' the client may be able to take with certain companions that, while not 'proper,' may be functional enough for this to still be useful. If shortcuts are taken and the skill is proving insufficiently useful, then you may need to go back and re-teach the full protocol.

Utility

For chin rest consent to remain powerful, we must respect the rules of consent. If we breach those rules, then we remove the control from the animal and potentially spoil all the hard work the client has done to teach this tool in the first place. We only use chin rest consent when it is possible to take the time, to move at the animal's pace and stop if the patient says 'no.' Good examples might be physical exams, ear swabs, tape preps, subcutaneous injections or non-urgent blood draws. This means if we are engaging in handling that we know the patient will not consent to, we should not ask for the consent in the first place. If we are engaging in something painful that might cause the animal to startle out of position, or something that we cannot stop if the patient declines after we start, we should not ask for chin rest consent for this procedure in the first place. For example, avoid using the consent communication in longer and necessary blood draws, catheter placement, or any handling procedure that historically has been challenging for this patient, and for which the clients have not done conditioning work.

Cooperative care behaviors

Cooperative care behaviors are specific operant behaviors that we teach patients so they can assist with their own veterinary care and general veterinary handling. Some of these behaviors are ones that many patients already know or are included in basic manners education, while others are not. Many can be used in multiple circumstances and combined with conditioning for specific procedures, basic restraint and all the other techniques described in this chapter. Whenever possible we want the patient to be able to choose to actively participate in a learned cue.

While the classical conditioning to handling described below is essential as well, the functional goal is for the patient to passively tolerate (or hopefully enjoy) the handling. Participation in practicing classical conditioning exercises is always voluntary too, as described here, but wherever we can we want the patient to be an active participant instead of a consenting body. Operant conditioning inherently involves elements of classical conditioning too (Lindsay, 2000), so if we can harness the power of both, we should.

Simple, helpful operant behaviors and cues

Five operant body position behaviors that can be very helpful are: stand, sit, sternal recumbency, lateral recumbency and dorsal recumbency. If you need to narrow this list to prioritize, then drop out the stand and dorsal recumbency.

Stand is relatively easily lured in most patients without physical manipulation so if we don't have it on cue the position can generally still be obtained without force. Dorsal recumbency is rarely truly needed for veterinary handling in circumstances where duration is not needed. For example, one of the most common times dogs are rolled into dorsal recumbency is for urinary cystocentesis but this procedure can be performed standing or in lateral position. Other times are for abdominal ultrasounds and radiographs, both of which generally require duration and thus pharmaceutical help may be most appropriate. That is not to say you cannot teach a duration dorsal recumbency - of course it can be taught - but the time investment may not be practical given the frequency with which this occurs over the average patient's life and the time it would take to teach it. That said, if a patient has specific medical needs that might warrant many instances of a duration dorsal recumbency, then it very well may be a good idea to teach it.

Targeting is a skill where the animal learns to touch a specific target with a specific body part. The target can be an outstretched hand, a target stick, a post-it note, a container lid or really anything else you want to use.

Commonly, animals are taught to target with their nose. The value of this is that you can use targeting to help orient a patient in space without using physical manipulation. You can move them from room to room, have them get up on a scale or table, align their body so a certain side is facing the doctor and more. Nose targets are generally extremely easy to teach and can be used in countless ways. Targeting can also be applied to other body parts too. For example, you can teach an animal to target a back leg or a hip so you can get even more fine-tuned with how you position the body.

Operant conditioning can be used to teach presentation of specific body parts. One such skill is a duration "give paw" cue where the patient places their paw in a person's hand and allows it to be held for some duration. This can be useful as a precursor for nail trims, paw or leg exams, cephalic blood draws, catheter placement, etc. Patients can be taught to file their own nails by scratching at a large, stationary emery board. These can easily be made with a block of wood, sandpaper and glue. A duration "open mouth" cue can be used to have the patient open their mouth for visual or manual exam.

These body part cooperative care behaviors are very commonly used in zoo animals (Davis and Audubon Zoo, 2006; Coleman et al., 2008; Desmond and Laule, 1994; Bloomsmith et al., 2003; Fagen et al., 2014). It makes sense then, that they should be able to be easily taught to companion animals! Examples include targeting a hip against cage bars for intramuscular injections or inserting a tail into an opening for blood draws. These behaviors can be taught using capture, lure, shape and targeting techniques. The precise details of how to teach these behaviors would take up too much space here and can be easily found in other resources but a veterinary behavior technician or a qualified force-free behavior professional could be contacted if additional help is needed.

Teaching consent communication

To teach consent communication, have your client follow this general outline using all the techniques and skills discussed thus far in this book.

1. Shape and/or lure the patient into the chin rest position.

2. Ideally one would fade the lure if one was used. Functionally, if the client has difficulty fading the lure, the lure's presence may not be problematic, at least for some patients. (Note, if you ever want to be able to use this in a situation where the patient is not able to eat, then you would need to fade off the lure.)

3. Build duration on the chin rest by spacing out the rate of reinforcement. Aim for a total two-minute duration hold to start (where the reward comes at the end of the held position). Shorter intervals between rewards while the patient maintains the consent position may be functional enough for many animals in many situations.

4. Add in handling work with a second person. If the patient needs a formal desensitization and counterconditioning plan, work that plan in this position following the consent rules. If the patient is generally comfortable with handling and the consent work is being instituted prophylactically, then practice a variety of veterinary handling following the consent rules.

5. Absolutely important final consent rule. Any time the patient lifts his head from the consent position, all touch or handling ceases immediately until the patient offers consent again. If he continues to revoke consent, either stop the procedure and try again later in a less challenging environment or initiate a non-consent set-up if the procedure must be done now.

For troubleshooting help on teaching consent communication, contact a veterinary behaviorist, a veterinary behavior technician, or a qualified force-free behavior professional.

Conditioning basic restraint positions, handling and specific procedures

When the patient has learned the operant cues we want them to know, we can layer in some classical conditioning techniques to address the other behaviors we need. The starting place would be the multitude of basic restraint positions we use every day in our veterinary handling. Then, specific procedures can be conditioned based on patient need, and may be extremely valuable in effecting medical outcomes.

For dog restraint, the three main body positions to focus on are a restrained lateral recumbency, seated position with chin up for jugular blood draw and what affectionately can be known as the standing Veterinary Hug. For these, ideally the dog would be taught with operant cues to either stand, sit or lie down in lateral recumbency and then consent communication would be used to continue to make sure the patient was comfortable throughout the procedure. If the animal does not have these skills, we are left with conditioning them to tolerate being rolled into lateral recumbency and having their floor-side legs restrained, just in case.

The Veterinary Hug position is the classic standing restraint position whereby a technician or assistant faces the dog who is oriented laterally to them, places one arm across the chest and around and up over the neck, with the other arm over the back scooping under the chest to hug the dog towards their body. This may end up being modified to hand-only restraint in a similar configuration for little dogs. For cats, a seated or sternal recumbent gentle restraint around the collar is one position and again, lateral recumbency with the underside legs held. For both species, much more minimal restraint of a reminder hand being placed on the chest or back of the shoulders can be conditioned as well.

Handling of all body parts can also be conditioned. A list of common maneuvers to work on would be:

- Lifting ear flaps and touching entrance to the ear canal
- Holding open the eyes
- Lifting lips, opening mouth
- Touching skin all over body
- Abdominal palpation (one-handed or two depending on size of animal)
- Lifting and touching feet
- Lifting and touching tail

For all these handling and basic restraint tasks either classical conditioning and/or a desensitization and counterconditioning plan can be instituted depending on patient need. The same patient may be able to handle a classical conditioning plan for certain types of restraint and handling while needing the more graduated plan in other scenarios. Classical conditioning, when appropriately selected, is a faster process so should be the first choice if you are able to utilize this method.

Classical conditioning

It is relatively straightforward to utilize classical conditioning with a novice, non-frightened, compliant patient. You simply assume the position, feed treats for a few seconds while in position, and then release. One person may need to be the restrainer while a second person provides the treats. If practicing alone, a lickable treat such as peanut butter, anchovy paste or pureed meat may be placed in front of the patient's mouth on a long wooden spoon, smeared plate or container, or purpose-designed licking mat to aide in the process. Give the patient a verbal cue ('Hug!') just before initiating the restraint and they can learn after enough repetitions that the restraint (and treats!) is about to happen. This way the patient can brace himself for the contact (and happily anticipate the treats), much like you would if your doctor said "this may be cold" before placing a stethoscope to your back.

Desensitization and counterconditioning

For most patients, especially those who have had frightening experiences with handling in the past, you need a desensitization and counterconditioning plan. If the patient shows any conflict or stress signs at any point in the restraint, then stop and reassess your protocol. You risk sensitizing the patient to the handling if you push too far too fast without taking the appropriate desensitization steps.

Begin by identifying your patient's starting point as described previously in this chapter. Once you have determined your starting point, follow the protocol below. How graduated the protocol needs to be depends entirely on the patient's fear level and how quickly they are able to get comfortable as they proceed through the protocol. Some patients will need a very incremental approach, and some will be able to make bigger jumps. As a general rule, if conflict signs are seen twice in a row at any step in the protocol, you should either drop back to an easier step or split the difference between the last step and this step and drop back to there.

We certainly do not want patients practicing being scared at any step. This is where the value of experience in leading these protocols becomes apparent. A skilled and experienced person can coach clients through these protocols deftly and efficiently, not pushing the patient too far too fast while also not wasting time by going slower than the patient can handle.

Desensitization and counterconditioning to handling protocol

1. Move your body into your starting point position.

2. Deliver a treat within one to two seconds.

3. Back off from the starting point position.

4. Repeat until no signs of stress or avoidance are observed at least three times in a row.

5. On your next repetition, move your body/hand one increment closer to your goal body position, e.g., move your hand an inch closer. Repeat Steps 1-3.

6. Continue in this fashion until you reach your goal position.

7. When you reach your goal position, incrementally increase the pressure of your touch until normal handling pressure is applied. Repeat each pressure level until no signs of stress or avoidance are observed at least three times in a row before increasing the pressure. Continue in this fashion until you reach your goal pressure (e.g., a gentle squeeze).

8. When you reach your goal position with normal pressure, increase duration of your touch by holding the position for longer periods until you reach the duration needed for real life handling. Proceed in one-second increments until you reach ten seconds. Then use five-second increments from ten to 30 seconds. Beyond 30 seconds, increase in ten-second increments. Repeat each duration until no conflict signs are observed at least three times in a row before increasing the duration.

Once the basic restraint positions are in place, specific procedures may be added depending on patient need. Common procedures that many patients will likely be exposed to in their lifetime include:

- Being placed on an exam room table

- Loading up onto a scale for weighing

- Auscultation with a stethoscope

- Otoscopic exam with aural specula
- Ocular exam with light source
- Injections
- Cephalic, jugular and/or saphenous blood draws
- Placement of an Elizabethan Collar
- Taking oral medications
- Eye drops
- Ear drops

All these procedures could potentially get harder, not easier, for a patient over their lifetime with repeated exposures, especially if pain is involved. Injections seemed to be the most stressful part of the typical veterinary visit (Mariti et al., 2016). Forty-four percent of cats were reported to be intolerant of injections from the very first injection (Mariti et al., 2016). Approximately one quarter of cats worsened in their response to injections over time, while only 6.6% of cat guardians reported that their cats became more tolerant of injections over time (Mariti et al., 2016). Given this reasonable likelihood that handling only gets more difficult with time, begin designing a desensitization and counterconditioning protocol at the first sign of a problem.

When conditioning for these specific procedures, the handling itself needs to be conditioned as well as the implements or instruments involved, and the sensations they evoke. For painful procedures like needle sticks you can progressively work towards simulating the feeling of the stick by using capped needles, pens and other non-injurious pointy objects. You can do a limited number of repetitions by actually sticking the patient with a needle. If practicing the actual needle stick is uncomfortable or contraindicated or just too limited, one option is to teach the animal to expect the unexpected: one repetition they feel a cold sensation, the next a pinching sensation, the next a hard push, the next a hot sensation, the next a gentle pressure, etc. (Ramirez, 2013). In this way the patient builds resiliency to novel sensations in this context.

When creating a desensitization and counterconditioning protocol, there are clearly many specifics that can alter the plan. Each protocol should be tailored for the individual situation and then modified as needed as you proceed through treatment. Expect that different patients might zip through some parts of the protocol and find other sections harder than you anticipated. Stay flexible and rely on your knowledge of the science and troubleshooting skills to modify as you go.

Designing a plan

Clearly, there are many skills for a client-patient team to work on to help prepare the patient for veterinary visits. The options can be overwhelming so creating a Patient Prep Plan can be a valuable service your team provides in addition to coaching clients through the process. To help provide some guidance, here are some lists of fundamental and more advanced skills for dogs and cats. These can be further tailored based on an individual's medical conditions, lifestyle, personality, anxieties and fears and even breed. For example, it might be on every Cocker Spaniel puppy's plan to do conditioning to ear cleaning, every indoor-only cat to do nail trims, every dog who is a picky eater to accept oral medications and every diabetic's plan to start conditioning for injections.

Fundamental Skills	Advanced Skills
Target (nose to designated object)	Consent communication
Muzzle	Relaxation mat
Sit	Specific procedures
Ventral Recumbency (on cue)	Stand
Lateral Recumbency (on cue)	Dorsal Recumbency (on cue)
Condition to car	Towel wrap restraint
Condition to carrier (small dog/cat)	
Condition to basic restraint	
Condition to nail trims	

Implementing the plan

When a client-patient pair has some of these skills ready to put into action, have the client do some practice runs in the veterinary environment. If the patient has a negative conditioned emotional response to the veterinary clinic itself, then the client-patient team may be working on a separate plan to counter condition the veterinary environment and staff (covered in the next chapter). If this is the case, then practice sessions on all the ideas presented here should first occur in the patient's home where they are most comfortable (including introduction of veterinary clinic odors), and then in other novel environments with which the patient does not have any negative associations (e.g., friend's house, quiet park, etc.). The client will take any tools they need with them, including their high value reinforcers, and do a run-through of their skills in these novel environments. This will help generalize the skills for the patient in non-stressful locations, so she learns that these skills work in environments outside the home.

When the team is ready for the veterinary environment, have them practice in the clinic in advance of any upcoming annual exams. The more practice sessions in the environment before anything scary or painful needs to happen, the better. With a plethora of positive experiences in the real world as well as the veterinary clinic, you have a higher likelihood that the skills will be successful in a real-life moment.

Life is not perfect, and inevitably, sooner or later, you will accidentally push a patient too far. Even the most experienced handlers can make errors in judgement when evaluating whether the patient is ready for a procedure. Sometimes we know a pet is not ready for a particular handling experience, but the medical situation is critical enough that we need to proceed. Perhaps you are already mid-procedure, and discontinuing is not possible or is determined not to be in the patient's best interest. Maybe the procedure really cannot be delayed, or there are unacceptable financial consequences to stopping a procedure and trying again on another day.

There are a few ways to address this situation. Do only what is needed from a medical perspective so the experience can be completed as quickly as possible – and make it clear to the patient that this is not a 'consent' procedure. (Save consent work for when the patient's 'no' can and will be honored.) Abort the rest and return to it another day. Every effort should also be made to implement appropriate anti-anxiety, anti-pain and sedative medication protocols as quickly as possible, so the patient is not traumatized. Fast acting injectables may be most appropriate in these situations. See Chapter 9 for more information on pharmaceutical plans. You do not want to undo hours of practice the client-patient team has done at home! Doctors need to stop and think about whether or not there really is time to let medications take effect.

Regardless of medication choices, as long as the patient is conscious and it's safe for him to eat, 'emergency' counterconditioning should be implemented immediately. This means the client or another familiar handler will rapid-fire deliver the highest value treat (the 'emergency' treat) on the patient's Hierarchy of Reinforcers until the handling can quickly be completed. Think of this emergency treat as loading the 'positive experience' side of the scale while the handling is loading the 'negative experience' side of the scale. The more the patient values those emergency treats and the more of them that happen, the more you tip the scales in our favor. If the patient is so stressed he cannot eat, then continue to offer the treat as the odor may have some impact but it is important to recognize that the patient is in severe distress at that point (Lindsay, 2005).

If a situation like this occurs, the client may notice some relapse in the patient's skills. This can be quite disheartening for all involved. How quickly a patient is able to rebound from a situation like this depends on the patient's level of underlying anxiety, how traumatizing the event was, how difficult the skill was for them in the first place, how thoroughly the patient was prepared prior to the event and the quality of recovery efforts after the event. If sufficient conditioning work was done before the accidental event, then recapturing a positive conditioned emotional response and compliance with handling may not be too difficult. Most patients without significant anxiety disorders should bounce back with remedial conditioning. As the client practices again at home, they will likely need to back up to an easier step in the process and work back up to the full expression of the skill. Assessing what a patient needs in this situation requires deftness in troubleshooting these protocols, perceptive body language reading and an openness to meet the patient where she is. Professional guidance in this can be the difference between a successful and non-successful recovery of skill. Here is a chance for your team to really shine!

Conclusions

All the techniques listed here can be used both independently and in combination to create incrementally more powerful impacts on the veterinary experience for both the patient and the client. Client emotions have an important impact on the patient's clinic experience so empowering clients to take an active role can significantly affect the patient experience as well. Clients should be perceived as partners in the veterinary experience. If clients come in having practiced some of this material, veterinarians should follow their lead in how to approach and utilize these techniques. When these skills are in place, veterinarians must do their part and commit to following the protocols established.

Certainly, emergencies happen, and our patients may not always be prepared for everything. In this case, with anxious patients, use appropriate pharmaceutical plans to minimize the emotional trauma. Be a champion of stress-mitigation. Applaud your clients for their amazing efforts. Praise your co-workers for their respectful and conscientious handling. Listen to what the animals are communicating to you, and always be prepared to adjust your plan accordingly.

Chapter 9
The Client's Role in the Clinic

by Dr. E'Lise Christensen, DVM, DACVB and Jolanta Benal, PCMT2, CPDT-KA and CBCC-KA

Your clients may be accustomed to taking a passive role at the veterinary clinic – standing aside (and, perhaps, worrying) while you and your staff 'do things' to their animal companion. We hope to encourage you to enlist them as active participants instead – think of it as cooperative care for your human clients as well as for your animal patients. Like other forms of cooperation, it calls for some investment of time; like other forms of cooperation, it can help you provide the best care for your patients.

Lay the groundwork for a low stress visit

Nobody knows their animal's personality and needs better than your client does. That knowledge, shared with you and your staff, can lay the groundwork for making visits as low-stress as possible.

Since, as we've mentioned, many clients will have a history of being expected to stand by passively while veterinary staff make all the decisions about how their companion animal is handled, you will likely have to start the discussion of their role as participants and as experts –not experts in veterinary medicine, but experts in their own animals' personalities and histories. By explaining the benefits of lower-stress approaches to veterinary care, you can encourage them to offer helpful information, and guide decisions about handling and medical care. Additionally, you can advise them on teaching cooperative care behaviors (see Chapter 7).

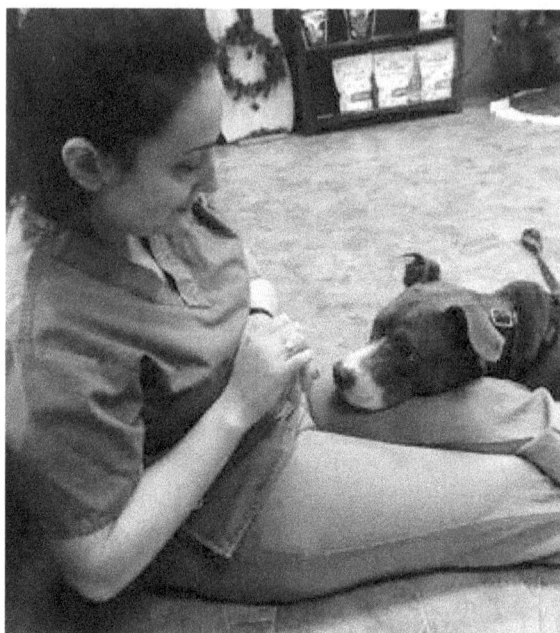

Josie performing a chin rest (trained by her owner, Jenny Chun, at home) with technician, Nicole, at Healing Paws Veterinary Care, Elmwood Park, NJ.

For our part, it's important to be open to our clients' requests and suggestions, and to bear in mind that they may not be able to communicate even the most reasonable requests or the soundest ideas clearly or 'correctly.' This goes double if they're anxious or frightened; if they're unfamiliar with scientific or medical terms; or if English is not their first language.

Before the first visit

You can start building a fruitful relationship even before the client brings their animal in. When someone calls to make an initial (non-emergency) appointment, it should be a routine practice to ask a few basic questions:

- Is your animal companion generally fearful or relaxed during vet visits? (The client can describe the pet's behavior in words, or on a numerical scale, as they prefer.)

- Does your companion eagerly approach unfamiliar people? Is this the same if you're at the veterinary hospital?

- Does your companion stay for petting by unfamiliar people? Does your pet stay for petting by unfamiliar people if you're at the veterinary hospital?

- Is there any body part that your companion avoids letting unfamiliar people handle? Is this response the same if you're at the veterinary hospital?

- Does your companion eat treats at the vet's office?

- Is there anything that makes your companion stop taking treats?

- What parts of the exam are hardest for your animal companion?

- Some patients pull away when their mouth is opened so their teeth can be examined. Or an animal may snarl or scratch when their temperature is taken. Does anything make your companion growl, snarl, snap, bite, hiss, or scratch?

- Has your animal ever been prescribed any medications specifically for use before a vet visit? Do you give your companion any over the counter or herbal treatments before a vet visit? (Of course, any intake questionnaire will inquire about the animal's medications; we stress pre-visit medications because of their significance in the context of low-stress veterinary care.)

If the initial appointment is made by e-mail, the online form can include a short questionnaire. Hopefully, people making online appointments will be comfortable enough with the written word to provide useful information; but if not, a brief phone call may elicit more, as well as establishing your office's genuine concern for the patient's comfort and well-being.

As you see, we strongly suggest asking in advance about the animal's demeanor and behavior. But as any veterinary behaviorist or behavior-modification trainer knows, few laypeople are accustomed to describing their companion animals' behavior in specific and explicit language. Also, many laypeople aren't well versed in reading animal body language, even if they have lived with cats/dogs/rabbits/psittacids or any other species for many years.

Consequently, your client may tell you, in all sincerity, that their dog is 'fine' during vet visits, and you may find yourself with a patient who pants throughout the exam and leaves sweaty pawprints and shed hair all over the exam room floor. To help minimize these miscommunications, take every opportunity to draw clients out in describing their animal's behavior and, as needed, to educate them. Post videos, photos, and diagrams on your website and include links and illustrations in online registration forms and questionnaires. Include illustrations on your hard-copy intake forms. Be sure that your office staff knows to ask about behavior in specific terms and to make clear notes of the answers they get.

This dog's wide eyes, tense facial muscles, and panting suggest he is fearful, but people who are not trained in behavior may not recognize these signs of fear.

More is more

The more you can learn about your client's companion animal, the better, of course. If time permits, and you can elicit more detail before the first visit, we suggest giving the following subjects priority:

- How does the animal respond to the presence of unfamiliar animals? (Our earlier comments about clients' potential difficulty describing behavior and body language obviously apply here as well.)

- Does any vet visit stand out as the best one ever? What made that visit so good?

- Does any vet visit stand out as the worst one ever? What made it so bad?

- If the animal is uneasy during vet visits, or in anticipation of vet visits, can the client think of anything that has helped put the animal at ease?

- Can the client think of things that have made the animal more uneasy?

- Does the client know whether the animal is more or less at ease in the client's presence during vet visits?

When an animal is more stressed in a family member's presence

This is a particularly sensitive issue which has been the subject of some recent research (Girault, C. et al., 2022). Some dogs appear more at ease when family members are not present (or when a particular family member is not present). That's to say not only that any aggressive behavior is less intense, but also that muscles are more relaxed; occasionally you'll even find prosocial behavior with strangers that you don't see in the family's presence.

The difficulty is, of course, in telling the difference between an animal who's less outwardly defensive and one who genuinely feels better away from the family member/owner. It has to be acknowledged that some owners increase their companion animals' stress. Owners who punish the animal certainly do. Repetitive petting and repetitive, high-pitched talk are possible (not invariable) stressors. And it can be difficult to get stressed owners to stop these coping strategies even if you are skilled in soliciting and encouraging incompatible behaviors in humans.

Most of us have heard the advice that conversations about sex are best not initiated during sex, when emotions may be running high, and people are likely to be feeling vulnerable and sensitive to perceived criticism. Similarly, the vet visit itself is probably not a good time to tell your client that repetitive rapid patting paired with anxious-voiced injunctions to "behave" is less likely to calm most companion animals than to agitate them. Offer your clients helpful information at times when they're more likely to be able to hear it without feeling personally undermined or criticized and remember to phrase your suggestions as "to do" information, rather than "don't do." For example, "What often works well is to manage your animal like this," rather than "Don't manage your animal like *this*."

Preparing for the visit

During visits, clients who are not professional or skilled amateur trainers are likely to need your and/or your staff's help with the cooperative care behaviors they are (hopefully!) teaching and practicing at home. Set your client up for success: Elicit information about what their animal companion finds reinforcing – foods, games, toys, physical contact – and establish a reinforcement gradient, so that you and your client both know when you may need to bring out the big guns to help her through a more challenging situation.

For the same reason, ask what cues the patient has already learned and can perform in different environments. In this context, it's important to remember that punishment-based or 'balanced' dog training still holds sway in many places, with unfortunate effects on both dog and human (See "Training methods and their implications for low-stress vet visits" below.) You may be able to exploit the fact that some old-school trainers who see 'tricks' as trivial use positive reinforcement to teach them even though they otherwise cling to punitive methods. For obvious reasons, this advantages tricks or obedience behaviors as stress relievers.

Training methods and their implications for low-stress vet visits

Command-based (or punishment-based, old-fashioned or 'balanced') training – mostly of dogs, but also of other animals, in particular psittacines – is an approach to teaching animals that require them to perform specific behaviors in order to avoid an unpleasant consequence. This can be a yank on the neck, a shrill sound, a spray of water, an electric shock, or anything else the animal would prefer to avoid. This kind of training can increase stress and aggression, with obvious potential consequences for veterinary visits.

This dog's lowered head, stiff body, and hiding are strong signs of fear that many lay people downplay during training sessions. Training new behaviors should be fun for handlers and animals.

Additionally, an animal taught via punishment to perform a specific behavior may experience stress from the fear caused by the original punishment (and by the punisher), even if neither the punishment nor the punisher is obviously present. So, for example, a dog trained with punishment may experience stress simply from being asked to sit.

On the other hand, animals taught with reward-based methods most often appear to enjoy their training sessions and are usually eager to perform the behaviors they've learned. Clients who have clicker-trained their animals, for instance, can often help keep them calm and distracted by asking them to perform manners behaviors (such as sit or down) and (during breaks) do tricks, even if they haven't taught any specific cooperative care behaviors.

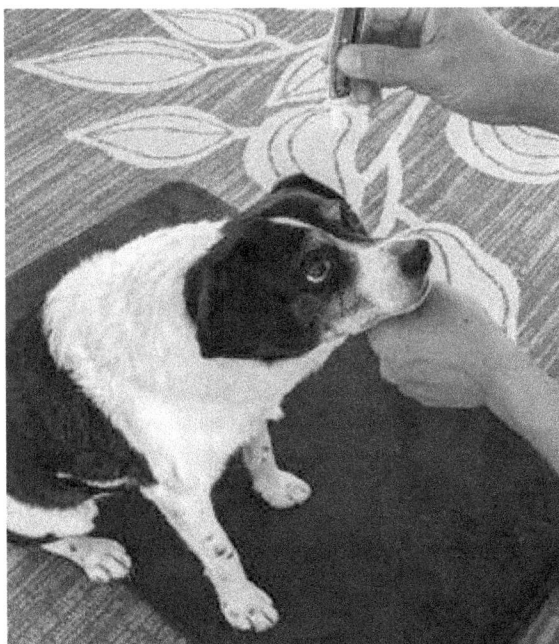

Scout and Ferdie are practicing a "chin rest" at home so Scout can receive eye drops comfortably. Ferdie cues the chin rest by putting out his hand in a fist. When Scout rests her chin on his fist, he picks up the eye drops (this is a human formulation for training purposes). Scout gets a treat. Having staff and owners learn to train and practice cooperative care cues at home can help them feel more confident when using the cues in the veterinary hospital.

Planning visits

Consider asking your client to help you plan the visit and to address bureaucratic paperwork matters in advance. This can be especially useful if anything other than a routine exam is expected, if the patient can be expected to aggress, or if either the client and/or the patient is particularly anxious. The more advanced knowledge the client has, the better they can prepare themselves and their companion animal.

You can discuss what procedures may be desirable or needed, how long they are likely to take, their risks and benefits, and their probable costs. (Much or all this information should be supplied in writing, both to prevent misunderstandings and to save time, but respectful conversation helps build a relationship of trust.) Dealing with finances ahead of time leaves the client free to concentrate on medical matters, and of course getting the patient out of the office as fast as possible is high on the list of ways to decrease stress.

Help the client prepare a checklist of items (blanket or mat, treats, and so on) to bring with them to the clinic – especially if they're not accustomed to active participation in cooperative care – and go over with them any list of items you expect to be sending home with the patient.

Some clients will appreciate (and their animals will benefit from) the extra preparation afforded by a walk-through practice visit with you, but without the animal present.

Minimizing stress during the visit

The two keys to successful low-stress veterinary visits are (1) planning, and (2) being ready and able to change plans fluidly.

Make sure the hospital and the client prepare supplies before the appointment. (Consider individualized checklists that can be automatically e-mailed or texted to the client along with appointment confirmations.) Useful supplies might include a relaxation mat or bed the owner has been training with at home (or even that the animal favors, in the absence of training); special treats the animal enjoys and that don't cause gastrointestinal or skin reactions; and favorite toys.

There are special considerations for bringing items into the hospital. Hospital staff may have allergies to ingredients in treats (peanut butter, for instance); depending on the degree of sensitivity, it may not be possible to allow such ingredients in the exam room, or in the clinic at all. Toys that elicit any aggressive behaviors in an animal will not only increase everyone's stress but also may endanger your staff, your client, and other animals at the clinic, so these should not be brought to the hospital no matter how much the patient enjoys them.

Decide ahead of time whether the animal should come in fasted for the sake of any possible diagnostic tests or procedures. Although, to make food more motivating, some vets encourage complete fasting before a visit, hungry animals may also be more irritable. If the patient doesn't need to be completely fasted for medical reasons, consider feeding half the usual breakfast ration. This can help increase interest in food while, perhaps, avoiding hunger-related irritability. Bear in mind, too, that some animals find food so motivating that there's no need to fast them at all except for medical reasons, whereas others may be too anxious to find food motivating no matter how hungry they are. In the latter case a pre-visit anxiolytic will be more to the point.

If a patient needs special accommodation, such as a private entrance to limit or prevent exposure to other animals or people, coordinate that in advance. Give the client a plan for their arrival – if they arrive early, where should they wait? By which door will they be entering the clinic? Make sure other staff are aware of the time of the appointment and of the patient's needs, so they can avoid the area if advisable, or help reassure the client that these arrangements are in place. Signs along the route can be helpful for communicating between team members and clients, not only guiding clients on where to go but also reminding everyone to keep the space quiet and clear of people and animals.

Supplies for appointments, provided by owner:

- Carriers for small animals (coach both staff and owners on appropriate handling)
- Leash
- Body harness, head harness, or collar
- Basket muzzle (for previously trained dogs)
- Special, allergy-safe and stomach-friendly treats in ¼-in or smaller pieces, or in a container that will allow easy licking

- Bed or mat
- Preferred toys

Supplies provided by hospital:

- Carriers for small animals (coach both staff and owners on appropriate handling)
- Leashes
- Body harnesses, head harnesses, collars
- Basket muzzles (for previously trained dogs)
- Very motivating food in ¼-inch or smaller pieces, or in a container that would allow easy licking
- Beds or mats
- Easy-to-clean toys: balls, Frisbees, puzzle toys, and snuffle mats
- Special, allergy-safe and stomach-friendly treats (both chewy and lick-able)

Arrival at the clinic

For most patients, especially those who have stress issues, it's best to wait outside the hospital, especially if an exam room is not immediately available. Cats are generally much better off waiting in their carriers, in a car kept at a comfortable temperature, with quiet music playing, than they are stressing out in a busy waiting room. Dogs arriving by car may benefit from an opportunity to take a walk before they enter an exam room. This can be especially helpful if the walk includes play or training that the dog and handler truly enjoy together.

Most clients have cell phones these days and can call or text from outside to let your reception staff know they've arrived. The reception staff can then use computerized census programs or analogue alerts to let other staff know of the patient's arrival, location, and preferred exam room. When the room is ready, they can contact the client, who can then bring the animal directly inside to the exam room. As mentioned before, clear, prominent signs can guide the client and help your staff communicate from a distance to maintain a clear, quiet pathway to the correct exam room. Place a sign on that door with the client's and patient's names to guide them into the room.

If staying in the waiting room is the only option, then staff and clients can choose a waiting-room seat in a way mindful of the animal's comfort and security, and reserve it using a sign. Forward-thinking reception staff can assign locations ahead of time.

If the client or staff have identified stressors for the animal, minimize or avoid them if possible. In this vein, waiting room management is a critical and often overlooked skill for reception staff. For example, if a dog is sniffing a cat carrier, the dog and handler should be moved away, or the cat should be removed.

Staff can coach clients on appropriate ways to interact with other clients and patients. This is especially important for clients who may not understand what their companion or other animals need (more space, quiet, etc.). Appropriate, upbeat signage can help with passive client education, which can then be reinforced with guidance from reception staff. Staff should bear in mind, too, that many people find it difficult to assert themselves strongly enough to protect their animals from unwanted and potentially threatening overtures, whether from people or from other patients. (One of us [JB] used to advise her more timid clients, "Be rude so your dog doesn't have to be.") Tactful support and coaching can not only help keep everyone safe and reduce stress but also encourage clients to exercise their right to look out for their animal's well-being.

Use signs, videos, and direct coaching by reception staff to encourage clients to practice known cues or games (using positive reinforcement) and other good management skills during any wait time.

During the exam and/or procedure

Ideally, the DVM or staff have had the opportunity to describe the steps of any procedures before a patient's appointment. This will allow the clinician and the client to troubleshoot the best ways to get the needed handling accomplished for each individual animal. Often appointments can't be prepared for as thoroughly as we might like; but even if thorough preparation is feasible, it's a good idea to check in again on the day of the exam/procedure.

Remind the client that many patients aggress during vet visits and that this is normal for many animals, especially during veterinary handling, which can be frightening and uncomfortable or even painful. Clients and staff appreciate honesty and are better able to keep themselves and the animal safe when everyone has all the details. Your reassurances will help the client feel comfortable being more forthcoming about her companion's potential for aggression.

Use the information your client gives you to decide what is and isn't necessary. For example, if the patient accepts all handling easily except for having temperature taken, can that part of the exam be skipped or done last? Or the rectal temperature might be eschewed in favor of an aural or axillary temperature.

Save it for me!

It's common for staff and clients to come up with useful plans for patients and then forget to implement them from visit to visit. A clear record of how the patient responded to different approaches will improve everyone's experience – but only if the information is consistently used. You can help the client implement successful plans by setting pre-appointment reminders (e-mail, phone, and/or text) that include relevant information – for example, pre-visit medications or supplements and when the client should give them; what treats and toys to bring; a recap of the plan for entering the clinic; and whatever else is pertinent to the individual client and patient.

Both your staff and the client should make notes about what helps – or doesn't! Be sure to keep notes on successful strategies in your alerts or in an easy-to-find area of your medical record so any staff member can replicate those strategies whether or not you're present.

After the visit

If the visit goes badly or is likely to have been traumatic (emergency visit, e.g.), offer aftercare suggestions to the client.

First, consider a benzodiazepine before, during, and after appointments to stop panic and fear before they kindle, generalize, and become more difficult to relieve, and to help promote retrograde amnesia of the event. It's best all-around that the animal forgets a scary experience at the hospital. As always, it's preferred to test anti-anxiety medications before triggers to assess possible side effects. Some animals may be sedated, activated, ataxic, or aggressive in new ways when an anti-anxiety medication is administered. However, lack of experience with a patient and a specific medication shouldn't stop rational use. Results should be recorded so the medication can be used proactively in the future if helpful, or not re-tested if there were objectionable side effects.

Fun is the enemy of fear. As soon as possible, after a potentially traumatic veterinary experience, have your client engage the animal in medically appropriate play, training, or petting they truly enjoy in order to help them recover more quickly.

Patients commonly lose training progress immediately after a stressful event, especially if that event is directly related to the training. Be sure to make your client aware of this possibility. If the owners have been working on cooperative care and/or medical handling at home, they should backtrack in their training plans, returning to steps the patient can easily handle. Success will help the patient and the handler relax and reconnect, and generally enables them to return relatively quickly to the previous level of training.

An 'after action review' is critical to the success of the next visit. The important questions are:

- What can be improved for next time?
- What went surprisingly well and should stay in the plan?

Record the answers both for the client and for the medical record.

Other considerations

Clients restraining animals for exams and procedures

Few clients are familiar with proper restraint techniques, and improper techniques can result in human injury or injury to the patient. This, of course, also presents a liability risk for the veterinarian. However, with the advent of low-stress handling, many practices are cautiously including clients in handling for exams and procedures, at least to the extent of having them give treats or supply other distractions, and sometimes by doing examinations on clients' laps or on the floor. Of course, if you know that the client does have extensive experience with appropriate restraint techniques, consider allowing them to play a larger role in the procedure.

Expect to coach clients on strategy and hand placement, especially if they're doing more than giving treats or providing a distraction. If pain is likely or inevitable – for instance, if you're removing a foreign body from a dog's nose or trimming the nails of a cat with arthritis – there may also be an increased risk of biting or scratching; the client's participation in restraint should then be considered with great caution.

Client education

Clients are best able to participate when they have multiple opportunities to learn about the many ways they can help their animal companion at the veterinary hospital. Some useful topics include not only low-stress handling but also waiting room etiquette (give other animals space), appropriate ways to transport carriers (not like suitcases and not with cross body straps, but instead holding steadily horizontal in two hands), types of treats to bring to a consult (tiny, soft, high-value smelly ones!), etc. Posters and videos can be used in the clinic, both for on-the-spot demonstrations and to give clients something helpful and informative to look at during any wait time – if they don't happen to have their phones! Of course, you will also be posting pictures and videos on Instagram and Twitter.

Make sure all hospital staff and educational materials model cooperative care, empathetic rhetoric, and gentle handling. Actions and words need to be consistent. Staff interactions with patients will often trump all other attempts at client education. Strive to identify the staff members who are the best fit for each patient. For example, many clinics have a few employees who adore cats and many who are not comfortable with them. When possible, schedule cats with cat fanciers so that everyone can have the best experience.

There are many ways that clients can help their animal companion at the veterinary hospital, including bringing high-value treats and providing a non-slip surface, such as a towel, for patients to stand or lie on during exams."

Be explicit in pointing out what works for each patient. For example, "Your cat is easy to handle for the initial exam if she can sit in her carrier with the top off" is much more helpful than "She really doesn't like it when she's taken out of the carrier." The latter offers no information about what does work.

A trip to the veterinarian can be stressful for clients, and people often take comments about their companions very personally. There's good reason for this: many humans are accustomed to being held responsible for absolutely everything their animals do, and dog owners in particular are often blamed and stigmatized, even by supposed experts, for any 'problem' behavior. Practice delivering information so you don't elicit defensiveness and pushback. For example, instead of asking whether a dog is ever 'aggressive' at the veterinary clinic, ask about signs of distress, such as moving away, ignoring favorite treats, shaking, panting when not hot, growling, snarling, snapping, or biting. Instead of calling a dog mean, report on the behavior you see, and open a conversation about alleviating stress. For instance, "I notice your pup is shaking, growling, and not interested in these amazing treats you brought. I bet he's feeling stressed. That makes sense. Seeing the veterinarian can be scary. Let's see if we can change things up so he can feel more comfortable."

The back, a.k.a., the treatment area

When possible, it's generally best to keep patients with their family members, and to keep them in the same room rather than moving them around. Many animals are calmer and less stressed if their humans are present. Many human caretakers are quite skilled at managing their animals and can participate in low-stress handling procedures, even doing something as simple as feeding treats, freeing your team members to assist with other aspects of the treatment. Additionally, it builds trust with your clients when they are able to observe how their animals are handled and how the animal responds. (Exam rooms should be fully stocked with the basics so that staff need not shuttle back and forth to complete procedures.)

However, there are times when separating animals from their families is wise:

- Patients may respond to a very anxious client's emotional state by becoming more anxious themselves. This is especially a problem if the client is touching the animal repeatedly and in places on the body, or with an intensity, that makes the animal move away or appear more agitated.

- In a crowded room, staff may simply need the space to maneuver.

- If clients become woozy at the sight of needles or blood, it may not be safe for them to be present.

- Stage fright can make it harder for staff to perform high-skill work (such as venipuncture or IV catheter placement), with the result that these procedures end up being repeated unnecessarily. Many clients understand this, especially if a trusting relationship with clinic staff has already been established and they will be willing to step out of the room briefly. You might also consider having a more confident staff member perform the procedure if the client is adamant about staying with the patient.

- In emergency situations, talking clients through life-saving procedures as they happen can divert medical attention from the issue at hand and make it difficult for veterinary staff to act quickly and efficiently.

- Separation is appropriate, even preferred, when a patient needs a procedure such as rapid start of an IV and may struggle to get to a guardian who's present in the room.

- In some cases, it is illegal to have clients in the room for some procedures, such those involving chemotherapeutics or radiation. In this case it can be helpful to have a window through which the client can watch the procedure.

Help clients prepare for emergency visits

Emergencies are not good times to learn new skills or to troubleshoot new approaches. When possible, clinicians should call ahead and send records ASAP to any urgent or emergency care facilities for patients who need special handling. Additionally, coach clients on how to deliver information about their animals' special handling needs. Clients may wish to keep a laminated "what works well" information sheet with their carrier or veterinary trip supplies. We recommend that you (or the primary care veterinarian) print this information on a letterhead and sign it, in hopes of increasing the chance that it will be taken seriously by a colleague unfamiliar with your client and their animal.

Conclusions

At first glance, careful preparation and guidance such as we have described don't come cheap: Clients may need to schedule extra exams, and some exams may take longer and consequently cost more. That said, our suggestions outline a path to better medical care, and perhaps to saving the client money (and your clinic time and resources) over the long haul. While not everyone can afford every level of care, a client who is aware of their animal's behavioral needs, who has learned to read their body language, and who has used reward-based methods to teach them a few (or several!) cooperative care behaviors is in a good position to stretch their budget as far as possible. An animal treated respectfully will be better able to allow a complete exam, and complete exams allow for better preventative care and early screening.

One more bonus for you: The client who knows how to advocate for their companion animal and how to decrease the stress of vet visits to the greatest extent possible is also helping to educate your colleagues and their staff. We hope you'll appreciate their work as much as they appreciate yours.

Chapter 10
The Role of Medications in the Clinic
By Dr. Amy L. Pike, DVM, DACVB

Introduction

Psychotropic medications and products can be a useful adjunct to a patient's behavior modification program as well as helping them cope with the veterinary medical exam. Before intervention with medications or products is considered, however, a veterinarian should rule out any medical disorders which could either be contributing to the problematic behavior, or those disorders which could affect the metabolism or excretion of the chosen psychotropics (Overall, 2003).

A full physical examination, including orthopedic and neurologic examination, should be performed along with a complete blood count, chemistry profile and urinalysis. Other tests may be warranted based on symptoms or results of screening tests, including diagnostic imaging and endocrine testing.

Once the patient has been medically cleared, or any underlying medical disorders have been appropriately diagnosed and treated, intervention with psychotropics can be instituted. It is important to note that all psychotropic medications and products should be combined with an appropriate behavior modification program and environmental management as they otherwise will likely not affect the desired long-term changes.

Delivering medication to a dog.

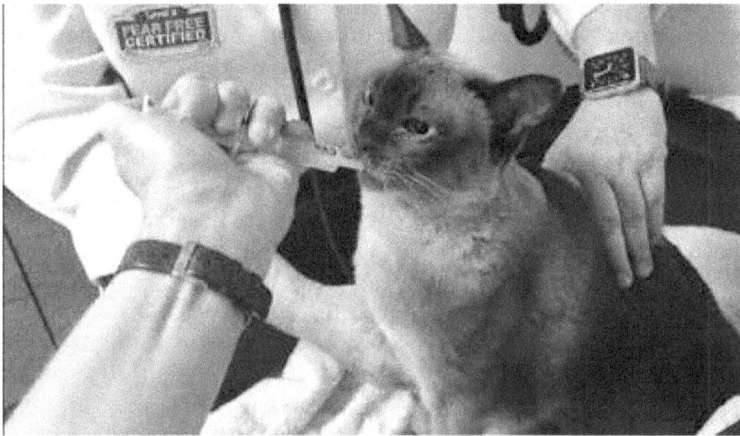

Delivering medication to a cat in an oral syringe

Uses of psychotropic medications and products

Psychotropic medication and products play a vital role, as does the behavior modification plan, in decreasing the emotional underpinning that is driving the patient's behavior. This is even true for aggression, since most aggression stems from underlying fear and the patient's desire to control the outcome of a situation that it finds stressful. In addition, there are genetically driven behaviors, such as compulsive disorders (Dodman et al., 2010) and ontogenetic factors such as poor neonatal nutrition (Wauben and Wainwright, 1999), that may only be overcome with the use of psychotropic medication to alter key neurotransmitter levels that may be deficient or in excess due to factors beyond the patient's or owner's control.

It is important to remember that psychoactive products are not a panacea or a magic wand that cause the behavior to disappear completely and should never be used without a comprehensive behavioral modification protocol. The goal of these products is to target key neurotransmitters and receptors that allow the patient to better cope in their environment and with the triggers that induce fear, anxiety or stress. Psychotropic products can decrease the emotional arousal that causes the patient to choose behavioral strategies such as fight, flight, freeze and fidget. Decreasing this arousal thus allows the patient to learn better coping strategies, to employ alternate behaviors, and can facilitate changing the negative emotion experienced when faced with a trigger to either a neutral or positive one through the process of counterconditioning. Since arousal and anxiety inhibit learning from taking place, intervention with products can make training and behavior modification proceed more efficiently. In addition, the intervention can increase the time and distance from the patient's baseline to their threshold making management and modification significantly easier to accomplish.

Successful intervention with psychotropic medications can be broadly measured by looking at three factors of the targeted behavior: the intensity of the behavior, the frequency of the behavior and the time it takes the patient to recover after a stressful event has concluded or the trigger is gone. These factors should decrease through the course of treatment, however, with some patients only one or two of the three will successfully be reduced. It is important that owners keep a log of incidences of the patient's behavior and monitor intensity, frequency and recovery in order to objectively evaluate the success or failure of an intervention throughout treatment.

Classes of non-medication psychotropic products

Pheromones

Pheromones are innate signals, or chemical messages, that are 'sent' to members of the same species in order to change that individual's behavior. The various pheromones can transmit a whole host of different information including sexual status, food sources, delineate a territory, and even create a better bond between mother and offspring. Synthetic versions of the pheromones that we have available for clinical use include the inter-mammary pheromones of dogs and cats, facial pheromones of cats, and the interdigital pheromones of cats.

Inter-mammary pheromones are appeasing pheromones that mothers produce when they are nursing their young. These pheromones help promote bonding between the mother and young and can create a sense of calm and security in any age animal in the species they target. Inter-mammary pheromones have been shown to have a wide application for clinical use, including for veterinary visits or hospital stays (Kim et al., 2010; Mills et al., 2006), noise phobias (Sheppard and Mills, 2003; Mills et al., 2003; Levine, Ramos, and Mills, 2007; Levine and Mills, 2008), for inter-cat conflict in the home (DePorter et al., 2019), for calming dogs in shelter settings (Tod et al., 2005; Osella, Bergamasco, and Costa, 2005; Grigg and Piehler, 2015; Barlow and Goodwin, 2009), to promote learning (Graham, Mills, and Bailey, 2007; Schroll, Dehasses, and Palme, 2005), to decrease social isolation stress (Taylor and Mills, 2007; Gaultier et al., 2008; Densenberg, Landsberg, 2008), for separation related distress (Gaultier, et al., 2005), and for car ride anxiety (Estella, Gandia, and Mills, 2006).

The F3 fraction of the facial pheromone is what cats deposit when they rub their face and whiskers on objects within their environment when they are feeling comfortable and secure. The synthetic copy of this pheromone has been shown to reassure and comfort cats in numerous situations, including when cats are urine marking as a result of stress (Mills and Mills, 2001; Ogata and Takeuchi, 2001; Pageat, 1996; White and Mills, 1997; Frank, Erb, and Houpt, 1999; Mills and White, 2000), for travel or in novel environments (Pageat, 1997; Gaultier and Pageat, 1998), at the veterinary hospital (Griffith, Steigerwald, and Buffington, 2000; Kronen et al., 2006), and in cases of interstitial cystitis (Gunn-Moore and Cameron, 2004).

The inter-digital pheromone is deposited when cats scratch their claws onto surfaces and serves as a means of delineating territory. The synthetic version of this pheromone is available in a product that also contains a visual attractant (blue dye) and a scent attractant (catnip) to encourage cats to scratch on appropriate, as determined by the owner, surfaces. More than 80% of cats are drawn to scratch on the treated surface within the first week of using the product. In addition, 90% of cats adopted into a home where the product was in use did not engage in destructive scratching on inappropriate items (Beck et al., 2018).

Nutraceuticals

The word nutraceutical is defined as something with medicinal properties or health-giving benefits that is derived from food. The two nutraceutical products that are used clinically in behavioral medicine are L-theanine, an amino acid found in green tea, and alpha-casozepine, a tryptic bovine alpha-s1 casein hydrolysate found in cow's milk.

L-theanine, in the form of Anxitane and Veggie-Zen (Virbac), have been shown to alleviate dogs' fear of humans in laboratory beagles, symptoms associated with thunderstorm and noise phobias in dogs, stress associated with veterinary visits, and a variety of emotional disorders in cats. L-theanine acts to increase concentrations of GABA, serotonin and dopamine, and inhibits binding to glutamate receptors (Araujo et al., 2010; Pike, Horwitz, and Lobprise, 2015; Michelazzi et al., 2010; Dramard et al., 2007; Pike et al., 2019).

Alpha-casozepine, in the form of Zylkene (Vetoquinol), has been shown to be just as effective, but with fewer side effects, as the medication selegiline hydrochloride to alleviate symptoms of anxiety in dogs. In cats, it has been shown to help alleviate fear of conspecifics, fear of humans, generalized fears and fear-based aggression. It has additionally shown benefits for comfort and compliance in horses experiencing mildly aversive routine health care procedures (Palestrini et al., 2010; Landsberg et al., 2017; McDonnell et al., 2014; Kato et al., 2012; Beata et al., 2007). The alpha-casozepine molecule is structurally similar to GABA and shows affinity for the benzodiazepine receptor, GABA-A.

Diets

There are several diets available with neuroactive compounds to help with behavioral disorders.

The first group of diets contain alpha-casozepine (see above information regarding this molecule) and added levels of tryptophan, a pre-cursor of serotonin. By feeding the pets these diets, it allows for easy administration of the key ingredients and research has shown the diet to help dogs under stressful conditions and fear in cats placed in an unfamiliar situation/location (Landsberg et al., 2017). Royal Canin Calm (available in both feline and canines less than 30lbs formula) and Hill's Prescription Multi-Care Urinary Stress (feline only) are currently the only brands with these key ingredients.

The second group of diets have been shown to help with cognitive dysfunction (Cotman et al., 2002; Milgram et al., 2002; Pan et al., 2010; Landsberg et al., 2017). Hill's Prescription b/d contains antioxidants that have been shown to alleviate signs of cognitive dysfunction as a result of beta-amyloid deposition and oxidative damage. Purina Pro Plan Veterinary Diets NeuroCare contains medium-chain triglycerides, an alternate energy source for the brain, and Brain Protection Blend to target several risk factors for cognitive dysfunction including reduced cerebral glucose metabolism, docosahexaenoic acid deficiency, chronic oxidative stress and chronic inflammation.

The advantage of dietary therapies is the ease of administration for the owner, but one of the disadvantages is that many patients may already be on a medically necessary prescription formula that cannot be changed.

Cannabinoids

Many cannabidiol (CBD)-rich hemp plant extracts are emerging on the veterinary market and recently with massive force likely as a result of many states being able to legally sell medicinal marijuana for human patients. The problems associated with using or prescribing these products are numerous. First, the Drug Enforcement Administration (DEA) has limited the research of these products by classifying them as Schedule 1, such that there are only three published studies in veterinary patients currently in existence at the time of this manuscript (Deabold et al., 2019; Wakshlag et al., 2018; Samara, Bialer, and Mechoulam, 1988). The federal government has further limited the study and use of these products by making it illegal to use CBD in animals. Veterinarians must understand the current legal ramifications prior to recommending, carrying, selling or prescribing such products. As far as CBD use for its psychoactive properties, there are CB1 receptors in the gut which cause release of GABA, an inhibitory neurotransmitter. Thus, CBD could have benefit to decrease anxiety responses.

Probiotics

The gut-brain connection is an area of emerging research in both human and veterinary medicine. There are multiple studies showing how an abnormal or sterile gut microbiome is implicated in such disorders as autism, Parkinson's disease, depression and suicide, Alzheimer's disease, weight gain, pain perception, and epileptic seizure control in humans. Two recent studies in dogs have shown that an abnormal or peculiar gut-microbiome may play a role in aggression disorders (Kirchoff, Udell and Sharpton, 2019; Mondo et al., 2019). A product targeted at helping anxiety and fear through introduction of good bacteria is Purina Pro Plan Veterinary Supplements Calming Care. Calming Care contains Bifidobacterium longum (BL99), a probiotic, a strain of beneficial bacteria, that was shown to decrease stress parameters in a group of dogs (Trudelle-Schwarz, 2018).

Classes of psychotropic medications

Daily

Daily medications are those that must be given on a daily basis and may take some time to reach peak effect based on pharmacokinetics and pharmacodynamics in the patient.

Selective serotonin reuptake inhibitors - SSRIs. This class of medication acts to increase the amount of serotonin in the neural synapse by blocking its reuptake back into the presynaptic neuron. Although side effects and some clinical effects may be seen as early as the first several weeks, true clinical effect may not be seen until six to eight weeks after starting the medication or after any dose change. This is a serotonergic drug and should be used cautiously with other serotonergic medications such as TCAs, SSRIs, MAOIs, Amitraz-containing parasiticides and Tramadol. The most common drugs in this class are fluoxetine (Reconcile by PRN Pharmacal), sertraline (human brand - Zoloft), and paroxetine (human brand - Paxil). In dogs, fluoxetine has been shown to alleviate aggression, compulsive disorders, anxiety disorders and separation anxiety (Dodman et al., 1996; Irimajiri et al., 2009; Ibáñez and Anzola, 2009; Pineda et al., 2014; Landsberg et al., 2008). In cats, fluoxetine has been shown to help reduce urine spraying (Hart et al., 2005; Pryor et al., 2001).

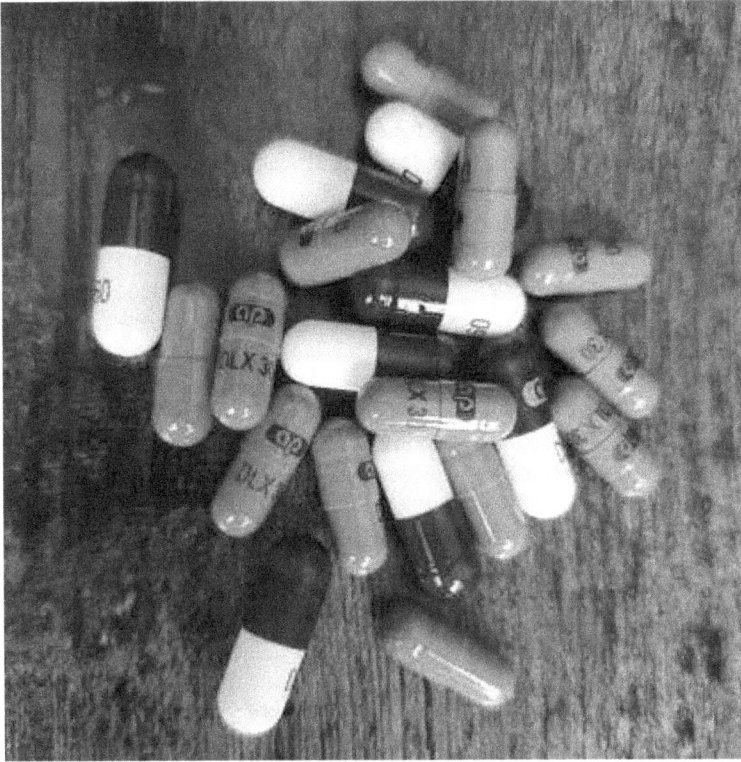

Tricyclic antidepressants - TCAs

Tricyclic antidepressants. This class of drugs alters neurochemistry in the brain by increasing serotonin. It helps to reduce anxiety and decrease repetitive behaviors. It may take four weeks to see its maximum effect after starting or after any dose change. This is a serotonergic drug and should be used cautiously with other serotonergic medications such as TCAs, SSRIs, MAOIs, Amitraz-containing parasiticides and Tramadol. The most common drugs in this class are clomipramine (Clomicalm by Novartis) and amitriptyline (human brand - Elavil). Clomipramine has been shown in dogs to help thunderstorm phobia, separation anxiety, compulsive disorders and aggression (Crowell-Davis et al., 2003; King et al., 2000; Hewson et al., 1998; Seksel and Lindeman, 2001; Moon-Fanelli and Dodman, 1998; White et al., 1999). In cats, clomipramine has been shown to help anxiety and compulsive disorders, and urine spraying (Hart et al., 2005; Sekel and Lindeman, 1998; King et al., 2004; Mertens, Torres, and Jessen, 2006). Amitriptyline has been shown to help idiopathic cystitis in cats (Chew et al., 1998; Kruger et al., 2003) and aggression in dogs (Virga, Houpt, and Scarrett, 2001; KuKanich, 2013) but has fallen out of favor due to its higher side-effect potential and lower clinical efficacy relative to clomipramine.

Serotonin and norepinephrine reuptake inhibitors – SNRIs. SNRIs are a class of medication used to treat behavioral disorders such as depression, anxiety, compulsive disorders, neuropathic pain, and fibromyalgia in humans. Their efficacy with chronic pain has led many veterinary clinicians to reach for these medications when there are comorbidities such as pain and anxiety, or pain and compulsive disorders (KuKanich,

2013). Venlafaxine (human brand - Effexor) is one of the top toxicosis seen in cats, as cats appear to readily consume this medication (Pugh et al., 2013).

Azapirones. Buspirone is an azapirone antianxiety medication that acts as a partial serotonin agonist. It may take two to four weeks to see a behavioral effect and is best administered two to three times daily for best efficacy. Side effects include irritability, gastrointestinal effects, increased affection and sociability, and occasional paradoxical increase in anxiety and/or excitement. It is considered anxioselective and therefore should not be sedating. Buspirone has been used in urine spraying and feline inappropriate elimination (Hart et al., 1993) and in cases of intercat aggression where it is most commonly given to the victim because it appears to not only reduce fear but increase assertive behaviors.

Monoamine oxidase inhibitors – MAOIs. MAOIs are irreversible inhibitors of monoamine oxidase and are most commonly used to treat cognitive dysfunction in dogs (Anipryl by Zoetis) and also used off-label in cats with cognitive dysfunction (Landsberg, 2005). Due to the high level of medication interactions seen with MAOIs, caution must be exercised when switching from another class of medication and appropriate washout periods must be strictly adhered to.

Situational/Event medications
Event medications are those that can be given on an as-needed basis prior to a stressful event. While considered situational in use, patients may benefit from their usage every single day at the appropriate dose interval as they often target different neurotransmitters than the daily medications.

Serotonin antagonist and reuptake inhibitors – SARIs. Trazodone is the most prescribed SARI, a class of drugs that in humans is used as an antidepressant, hypnotic and anxiolytic. It acts by blocking select serotonin receptors and inhibiting the reuptake of dopamine, serotonin and/or norepinephrine. It has a mildly sedating effect which can be very advantageous in pets who panic and/or are destructive. Research has shown efficacy for post-surgical confinement purposes where behavioral calming is needed, as an adjunct for chronic anxiety disorders, and hospitalization (Gruen et al., 2014; Gilbert-Gregory et al., 2016; Gruen and Sherman, 2008). In cats, it has been shown to be helpful with sedation for veterinary procedures (Orlando et al., 2016). Although traditionally used as a situational medication, there are some patients who need to have this administered twice daily. This is a serotonergic drug and should be used cautiously with other serotonergic medications such as TCAs, SSRIs, MAOIs, Amitraz-containing parasiticides and tramadol.

Alpha-2 agonists. Clonidine is the most common oral alpha-2 agonist used in veterinary patients. It has traditionally been used in human medicine for its antihypertensive effects but has been used off-label by psychiatrists for its action on hyperarousal, hypervigilance, PTSD, ADHD and impulsivity. It blocks norepinephrine release by activating the alpha-2 receptors in the locus ceruleus. It has been shown to be effective as a situational medication prior to stressful events (Ogata and Dodman, 2011) including veterinary visits, but caution must be exercised when using it in conjunction with general anesthetics or in cardiovascularly compromised patients due to its potential hypotensive effects. A recent addition to the pharmaceutical market, dexmedetomidine gel (Sileo by Zoetis), is an oral transmucosal (OTM) preparation of dexmedetomidine that is FDA approved for use in noise phobias (storms, fireworks) (Korpivaara et al., 2016; Amat et al., n.d.). It has a rapid onset of action after OTM absorption but only a 25% bioavailability which results in its anxiolytic effects without the profound sedation seen in hospital usage of IM or IV Domitor.

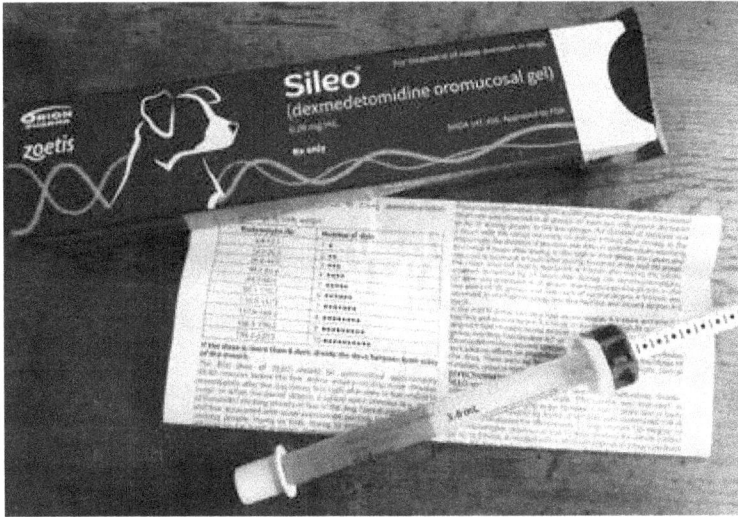

Sileo (approved for noise phobias in dogs)

Benzodiazepines. This class of medication (alprazolam, for example) facilitates behavioral calm by its action on GABA, at the GABA-A receptor, an inhibitory neurotransmitter. It is used situationally for acute panic disorders (Ibanez and Anzola, 2009; Pineda et al., 2014) since its onset of action is 60-90 minutes and depending on the particular medication, may only last for four hours. There may be paradoxical excitation associated with any situational medication and thus it must be tried at home prior to the patient experiencing the stressor/trigger. Although bite disinhibition can occur with any psychotropic medications, as a class, benzodiazepines appear to cause this more frequently and caution should be exercised when using benzodiazepines in dogs with aggression. Care should be taken with how many pills are dispensed at one time and how often the drug is refilled due to the highly addictive nature and potential for abuse by owners.

Alpha-2 delta ligands. This class of medication binds to the alpha-2-delta subunit of presynaptic voltage sensitive calcium channels and blocks the release of glutamate when there is excessive neurotransmission. Gabapentin is the most common drug in this class used in veterinary behavioral medicine. Since the mechanism of action of gabapentin is vastly different than the SSRIs, TCAs, SARIs, or benzodiazepines, this medication may be of benefit for those patients that have been intolerant of the other classes, or as an adjunct for incomplete resolution of clinical signs when using other agents. Gabapentin has been shown to decrease anxiety, aggression, avoidance behavior and inappetence associated with pain. There are two current studies on its use for cats prior to stressful events (Van Haaften et al., 2017; Pankratz et al, 2018), and it is anecdotally used by many behaviorists, anesthesiologists, and feline practitioners at 50 or 100 mg/cat or 20 mg/kg 60-90 minutes prior to examination. It appears to be palatable when a capsule is broken open and mixed with a small amount of canned food, and it appears to be well-tolerated clinically. No studies are currently available at the time of writing to support dosages or usage in specific behavioral situations in dogs.

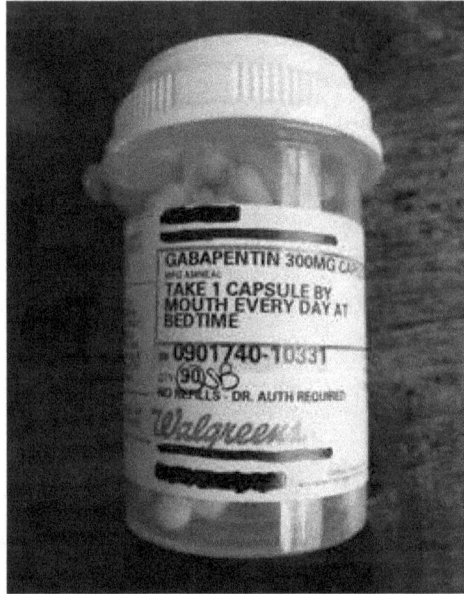

Gabapentin

Precautions with psychotropic medications

Off-label usage

Currently, there are only five FDA approved psychotropic medications for companion animals. These include Reconcile (approved for separation anxiety in dogs), Clomicalm (approved for separation anxiety in dogs), Sileo (approved for noise phobias in dogs), Anipryl (approved for cognitive dysfunction in dogs) and the newest, Pexion (approved for noise phobias in dogs). This means that if you prescribe these medications for another disorder, for another species other than indicated or for any other disorder than listed above, you are doing so off-label. While off-label usage is common in veterinary medicine, it is important that owners are made aware that the medication you are prescribing is being used in a manner that has not been tested nor approved for the species or disorder that you are prescribing it for. Informed written consent is highly recommended.

Common side effects

Thankfully there are very few side effects when it comes to psychotropic medication.

The most common side effects target the gastro-intestinal system and include vomiting, diarrhea, constipation, and lack of appetite. One main reason for this cohort of side effects is the sheer number of serotonin receptors in the gut compared with the rest of the body, including in the brain. Most of the common side effects are mild and self-limiting and will resolve without treatment if administration is continued. However, there are some patients that may benefit from a lower dosage or frequency of administration depending on the severity of clinical symptoms.

Serotonin syndrome (Crowell-Davis and Poggiagliolmi, 2008) is essentially an "overdose" of serotonin.

The syndrome encompasses a wide variety of symptoms and can be fatal if left undetected and untreated. Owners should be advised of the possibility of serotonin syndrome whenever serotonergic agents are prescribed. This is especially important when prescribing multiple serotonergic agents together (such as a daily medication and an event medication) but has been seen clinically by the author in patients only currently taking one serotonergic agent and at doses below the recommended dose ranges. It is possible that certain individuals may be more sensitive to the effects of serotonin and therefore more likely than others to develop the syndrome, but more research is needed in this area.

Treatment for serotonin syndrome includes supportive care and careful monitoring. Cyproheptadine can be given as a serotonin antagonist, and benzodiazepines and acepromazine can be used to calm agitation and tremors. If acute ingestion of a serotonergic agent is suspected, force emesis and treatment with activated charcoal should be implemented.

Symptoms of serotonin syndrome

- Diarrhea
- Dilated pupils
- Rapid heart rate
- Rapid breathing
- High blood pressure
- Excessive panting
- Sweating
- Fever
- Exaggerated reflexes
- Tremors
- Rigidity
- Confusion
- Agitation
- Excitement
- Seizures
- Hypersalivation
- Hyperaesthesia
- Depression

Bite disinhibition. Many clinicians have anecdotally heard that prescribing psycho-tropic medications can lead to increased aggression in some cases. As such, this has led them to be cautious in using medication to treat aggression disorders. The definition of bite disinhibition is that if anxiety is inhibiting the patient from becoming more aggressive, the medications may lower that inhibition causing an increased risk of impulsivity and aggression. The most common class implicated in bite disinhibition are the benzodiazepines because of their action on the GABA receptor. While the phenomenon of bite disinhibition is thankfully rare, clinicians should warn owners that it can occur. Strict management should be implemented prior to starting medica-tion and products, especially in households with at risk individuals such as children, the elderly, and the mentally impaired.

Long term side effects
There are few to no concerns about the long-term safety profile of the majority of psychotropic medications. Clinicians are advised to perform routine laboratory moni-toring including a complete blood count, biochemical profile and urinalysis annually (and every six months for seniors). Benzodiazepines are the class of medication most commonly implicated with long term side effects including dependency. Caution is advised when using these medications for more than an as-needed basis.

Switching medications
Should the need arise to switch medications, the clinician must be aware of the phar-macokinetic and pharmacodynamic properties of both medications, focusing espe-cially on the half-lives. Fluoxetine has the longest half-life of any of the clinically relevant SSRIs and a full five-week washout period after weaning is needed prior to switching to an MAOI or serotonin syndrome may result. It is important to note that many of the medications used by boarded veterinary behaviorists are being used extra-label and the exact half-life in our patients may be unknown, thus extreme cau-tion is advised when switching.

Weaning off medication
When clinical resolution or stability of the targeted behavior has been achieved, owners and clinicians may wish to wean the patient off the psychotropic medication. Severe withdrawal side effects can occur when psychotropic medications are abruptly stopped. It is advised to continue therapy beyond clinical resolution for approximately 6 to 8 months or until behavioral maturity is reached (approximately three years for our companion small animals) or whichever is longer. Then, a slow wean of about 25% every 6 to 8 weeks can be implemented. Should clinical signs return at any point in the weaning process, increase the medication back up to the most recent effective level. Recurrence of behaviors are more likely to occur if resolution was due to heavy reliance on the medication versus combined with effective behavior modification. Due to the long-term safety profile of most psychotropic medications, patients may remain on medication life-long if desired and appropriately monitored. Due to with-drawal symptoms, it is advised to not stop any psychotropic medications even prior to general anesthesia (see below).

Cytochrome P450 is an enzyme system critical in hormone synthesis, biotransformation, and metabolism of many different types of medication. Psychotropic medications are competitive inhibitors of many P450 enzymes, and when a patient is on another drug that is also metabolized by P450 enzymes, altered plasma levels and potential toxic side effects are possible.

Transdermal administration

At the present time only one study of transdermal administration of psychotropic medication has shown that this method is efficacious (Chavez et al., 2016). Ciribassi and colleagues showed that although fluoxetine was absorbed through the skin in cats, the relative bioavailability was only 10% of that for the oral route of administration, but higher doses of the medication resulted in severe dermatologic reactions (Ciribassi et al., 2003). Mealey and colleagues looked at the systemic absorption of amitriptyline and buspirone after oral and transdermal administration to healthy cats and found that systemic absorption of both drugs was poor when compared to the oral route of administration (Mealey et al., 2004)). Based on these studies and the lack of others (Eichstadt et al., 2017), an appropriate dosage for transdermal administration of psychotropic medications has not yet been established and this route of administration is currently not recommended.

Reformulated preparation

No formal studies are available to assess the potency and absorption of psychotropic medications once they have been reformulated into a liquid or some other distribution vehicle. For medication to be effective when given orally it must be soluble and stable in the stomach and intestines so it can absorb appropriately into the blood stream. When a medication is altered by reformulation it is unclear if the absorption has been altered as well and, if so, to what extent. Medication failures may be due to lack of availability of the medication rather than unsuitability as a treatment for unwanted behavior. Anecdotally, many veterinary behaviorists find a significant difference between efficacy of the brand versus generic medications currently available on the market.

Use of psychotropic medication and general anesthesia

Most psychotropic medications can be used safely with general anesthesia and should not be discontinued prior to any anesthetic events, especially due to the possibility of withdrawal symptoms. Appropriate monitoring including non-invasive blood pressure is recommended to ensure safety. Use of reversible medications for pre-medication and induction are recommended, including opioids and other alpha-2 agonists, so that should problems arise, partial or full reversal of the agents is possible. Drug interactions should be checked prior to usage of any anesthetic agent.

Conclusions

Psychotropic medications play an important role in the treatment of behavioral disorders among our veterinary patients. They should always be used in conjunction with environmental management, behavior modification and rewards-based training to affect the most change possible and for the best possible outcomes.

Dose chart

Drug Name	Medication Class	Canine dose	Feline dose
Alprazolam	Benzodiazepine	0.01-0.2 mg/kg PO q 6-8 hrs	0.05-0.25 mg/kg PO q 6-8 hrs
Amitriptyline	TCA	1-2 mg/kg PO q 12 hrs	0.5-1 mg/kg PO q 12-24 hrs
Buspirone	Azapirone	1-2 mg/kg PO q 8-12 hrs	0.5-1.0 mg/kg PO q 8-12 hrs
Clomipramine	TCA	2-4 mg/kg PO divided q 12 hrs	0.5-1.5 mg/kg PO q 24 hrs
Clonidine	Alpha-2 agonist	0.01-0.05 mg/kg PO q 8-12 hrs	
Clorazepate	Benzodiazepine	0.55-2.2 mg/kg PO q 8-24 hrs	0.2-0.5 mg/kg PO q 12-24 hrs
Diazepam	Benzodiazepine	0.5-2.2 mg/kg PO q 4-6 hrs	
Fluoxetine	SSRI	1.0-3.0 mg/kg PO q 24 hrs	0.5-1.5 mg/kg PO q 24 hrs
Gabapentin	Alpha-2-delta ligand	20-40 mg/kg PO q 8-24 hrs PRN	10-20 mg/kg PO q 12 hrs
Lorazepam	Benzodiazepine	0.02-0.1 mg/kg PO q 8-12 hrs	0.125-0.25 mg/kg PO q 12 hrs
Paroxetine	SSRI	0.5-2 mg/kg PO q 12-24 hrs	0.5-1.5 mg/kg PO q 24 hrs
Pregabalin	Alpha-2-delta ligand	3.0-4.0 mg/kg PO q 8-12 hrs	1.0-2.0 mg/kg PO q 12 hrs
Selegiline	MAOi	0.5-1.0 mg/kg PO q 24 hrs in AM	0.25-1.0 mg/kg PO q 24 hrs
Sertraline	SSRI	1.0-4.0 mg/kg PO q 12 hrs	0.5-1.5 mg/kg PO q 24 hrs
Trazodone	SARI	2.5-10.0 mg/kg PO q 12 hrs	25-50 per cat
Venlafaxine	SNRI	1.0-2.0 mg/kg PO q 12-24 hrs	0.5 mg/kg PO q 24hrs

Chapter 11
Emergency Treatment and Critical Care Patients
By Dr. Karen van Haaften, DVM, DACVB

In emergency and critical care contexts, it can be easy to discount the importance of caring for the emotional well-being of patients. This area of veterinary practice deals with the most urgent and debilitated patients, and often life-saving procedures necessarily take priority over all other consideration in what is often a highly stressful environment.

However, the emotional state of our patients can have a strong influence over their ability to recover from illness. With knowledge, planning, and training, providing good emotional experiences for patients does not have to take up valuable time. The benefits to the patient experience, client satisfaction, and staff morale are well worth the effort required.

The stress response and effects on compromised patients

Physiologic effects of stress

Stress is a biological response that is elicited when an individual perceives a threat to homeostasis (Moberg, 2000). The purpose of the stress response is to allow the animal to survive an acute threat. The trigger for the onset or prolongation of the stress response is the perception of a threat. Whether or not a true physical threat exists is irrelevant: if the animal perceives there is a threat, the stress response will be triggered (Moberg, 2000; McEwan, 1993).

The stress response includes behavioral and physiologic changes. Behavioral responses are described in greater detail below but are typically used for animals to remove themselves from stressful situations, such as moving away from a threat. When behavioral responses are limited, as with confinement in hospitalized patients, the stress response will endure, and the animal may be unable to return to homeostasis (Moberg, 2000).

The stress response is mediated through the autonomic nervous system (norepinephrine) and the hypothalamic-pituitary-adrenal axis (cortisol) (Russell, 1979). The acute effects of the stress response include immediately available energy, increased blood flow to skeletal muscle, bronchodilation, and decreased pain perception. Other bodily functions, including digestion, reproduction, and immune function are inhibited by a stress response (Moberg, 2000).

The behavioral and physiologic stress response may impair the clinician's ability to diagnose medical conditions (Tynes, 2014; AVSAB, 2019). Behavioral responses to stress such as escape behavior or aggression may interfere with a clinician's ability to perform a complete physical examination. Physiologic effects on respiratory rate, heart rate, blood pressure, or sensitivity to pain may interfere with diagnostic testing (Quimby, Smith, and Lunn, 2011; Bragg et al., 2015; Robertson et al., 2018).

Continuous stress can adversely affect emergency and critical care patients in a variety of ways. The immunosuppressive effects of stress can impair animals' ability to fight infections, diseases, increase wound healing time, and increase the risk of acquiring nosocomial infections. Shelter cats showing signs of chronic stress are at higher risk of developing upper respiratory infections (Tanaka et al., 2012). Idiopathic cystitis is an inflammation disorder of the bladder that has been associated with chronic stress in cats (Stella, Lord, and Buffington, 2011; Westropp, Kass, and Buffington, 2006).

Stress has also been associated with decreased gastro-intestinal function, including decreased gastric emptying, increased intestinal contractility, increased gut permeability, reduced water absorption in the gut, and more (Bhatia and Tandon, 2005). This response could slow patient recovery from gastrointestinal upset. Stressed animals are often less likely to eat, which may delay healing (Hewson, 2008).

Fearful and stressed animals who need to be sedated or anesthetized often require higher doses of sedatives to achieve adequate results compared with calm animals. Side effect profiles of anesthetic drugs are often dose dependent. This combined with other physiologic effects of stress (tachycardia, increased BP) tend to make the anesthetic risks for stressed patients higher. (Bednarski et al., 2011),

Recognizing fear

Behavioral responses
Behavioral responses to stress and fear can be highly variable, and are influenced by the animal's genetic predispositions, environmental factors, and learning history (Steimer, 2002). Veterinary team members need to be familiar with body language and behavioral signs of fear. For more on body language, see Chapter 2: Body Language.

In cats, common behavioral signs of stress include decreased appetite, social isolation, decreased self-maintenance behaviors such as grooming, and increased frequency and intensity of hiding behavior (Stella, Lord, and Buffington, 2011; Carlstead, Brown, and Strawn, 1993; Rochlitz, Podberscek, and Broom, 1998; Stella, Croney, and Buffington, 2013).

In dogs, behavioral responses to fear include avoidance behaviors, freezing, and trembling (Stephen and Ledger, 2005; Beerda et al., 2000; Rooney, Clark, and Casey, 2016; Blackwell, Bradshaw, and Casey, 2013). Some dogs may also use aggressive behavior as a coping mechanism when experiencing fear or feeling threatened (Von Borell et al., 2007).

Physiologic measures of stress
Much research attention has been given to measuring physiologic measures of stress, but unfortunately the clinical utility of physiologic stress markers is limited.

Cortisol levels in the blood, urine, saliva, and hair follicles have been used to gage HPA axis activity. High variability is common with intra and inter-animal cortisol levels, and levels are also easily influenced by stress during collection and diseased states (Polgár, Blackwell, and Rooney, 2019; Mormède et al., 2007). Another important consideration when interpreting cortisol levels is that cortisol levels rise with general arousal levels, regardless of valence. Excitement and positive experiences (eustress) can result in cortisol increases which are impossible to differentiate from distress caused by negative or aversive experiences. Therefore, cortisol levels should be interpreted in conjunction with behavioral responses (Mills and Marchant-Forde, 2010).

Heart rate (HR) measures the number of heart beats per minute and increases in response to sympathetic nervous system activation. Heart Rate Variability (HRV) measures the time between heart beats and is used to measure the activity of the autonomic nervous system. Higher sympathetic nervous system activation is associated with a decrease in HRV (Von Borell et al., 2007). Both HR and HRV can be significantly affected by body position and other physiologic stressors (Maros, Dóka, and Miklosi, 2008). HRV requires specialized equipment and software to monitor and analyze results and is a better metric of psychological distress than HR alone.

Other physiologic measures that have been studied include rectal temperature (Ogata et al., 2006), infrared thermal imaging (Travain et al., 2015; Rigterink, Moore, and Ogata, 2018), immune function (Gourkow and Phillips, 2016; Gourkow and Phillips, 2015; Gourkow, Hammon, and Phillips, 2014; Protopopova, 2016) and oxytocin (Mitsui et al., 2011; Pekkin et al., 2016). Other physiologic parameters (Part et al., 2014) have been investigated but not fully validated as measures of stress response in dogs or cats.

Despite a lack of accurate laboratory monitoring data, the importance of stress on animal health and well-being is too important to ignore.

Differentiating fear, pain, and illness

A common source of confusion in emergency practice is differentiating between fear behavior and pain-related behavior. While the motivation is different, both pain and fear can cause an animal to become uncomfortable with handling, socially withdraw, or use aggressive behavior (Epstein et al., 2015).

It may be helpful to take a short behavioral history from the owner, including questions about the animal's behavior at the vet hospital, and comfort levels with handling. If the sensitivity to handling is new and associated with recent illness or trauma, then chances are good that pain is the cause. Also, if the animal is comfortable with handling in general except for a localized area, the uncomfortable area should be investigated for pain (Epstein et al., 2015).

Pain assessment and scales

Pain has been described as the fourth vital sign, after temperature, pulse, and respiration rate (Epstein et al., 2015). Patients should be assessed for pain on initial physical examination and on a regular basis for hospitalized patients.

Pain scales can be useful for monitoring ongoing pain levels in hospitalized patients. In dogs, the Glasgow Composite Measure Pain Scale has been developed and validated for clinical use. This scale uses dog's posture, demeanor, and response to touch to assign a pain level (Reid et al., 2007). In cats, the Glasgow Acute Pain Scale has been validated and uses the cat's behavior, response to touch, and facial expressions, including ear and muzzle positions, to estimate pain levels (Reid et al., 2017). Pain assessment tools are an active area of research, and several other scales exist or are in development using the pet's behavior (Brondani, Luna, and Padovani, 2011; Brondani et al., 2013; Calvo et al., 2014; Guillot et al., 2011) and/or facial expressions (Holden et al., 2014; Keating et al., 2012; Langford et al., 2010; Sotocina et al., 2011; Dalla Costa et al., 2014). In the papers cited, the scales were validated against a surgeon's opinion of whether the dog or cat required analgesia, which may be a less-reliable standard than validation against a biological assessment.

Communication

Client communication

In the sometimes-chaotic emergency medicine environment, taking steps to minimize stress of clients can have a beneficial effect on patient's stress levels. When wait times are long, reception staff can explain to waiting clients why they are not being seen right away.

Non-critical patients with stressed or disruptive animals should be given the option to wait in the car or an empty exam room without losing their place in triage. Allowing the owner to stay with the patient until sedation has taken effect, or for as long as possible, can have a positive impact on client and patient stress levels.

Communication between members of the veterinary team

Medical records should be designed to track a patient's emotional state, preferred restraint and distraction methods, preferred treats and toys, areas they enjoy or object to being petted, and any other information that would be useful for helping members of the patient's care team to optimize emotional well-being. Information that does not fit on the medical record should be communicated during hospital rounds.

Procedures

Physical restraint

In general, the minimum amount of restraint needed to keep the patient and staff safe should be used. Humane restraint techniques described for other types of veterinary practice are also effective for emergency practice. However, some disease processes might require special consideration for restraint methods. For example, dyspneic animals should not be restrained with a burrito or scarf wrap as that may interfere with their ability to ventilate.

Chemical restraint

Patients exhibiting significant signs of fear or anxiety should receive appropriate sedation prior to stressful procedures such as radiographs or catheter placement, typically with fast-acting injectable medications. For more information on useful injectable medications, see Anxiety-Reducing Medications on page 206.

Use of treats. Where medically appropriate, use food treats to distract or counter-condition a pet for potentially stressful procedures as they are used in other areas of veterinary practice. Due to the nature of the conditions a patient presents to emergency practices, treats are often not medically appropriate, so sedation may be needed more often.

Injections. Limiting the number and level of invasiveness of injections improves patient comfort. Obtaining patent intravenous (IV) access for any patient requiring repeated injectable medications should be a priority in emergency and critical care patients. Once placed, IV medications given through the catheter are generally painless. Appropriate aseptic technique and daily monitoring of the catheter site can reduce the risk of catheter complications and reduce the number of times a catheter needs to be placed (Tan, Dart, and Dowling, 2003).

For patients who are uncomfortable being handled, the use of IV tubing or an extension set with a distant IV port can allow nursing staff to inject medications from a distance, limiting the number of times they have to enter the animal's personal space. The fluid volume of the tubing (listed on the product packaging) should be considered when flushing the line.

For outpatients, try to limit the number of injections given. If a rapid time of onset is not necessary, and the patient takes oral medications well, injections may be avoidable. For cats, pilling is often a stressful experience, so depending on the cat's historical response to pilling, there may be a stress net-benefit of injecting long-acting medications, such as maropitant or sustained-release buprenorphine. Using these preparations, owner compliance is not an issue and the patient will be spared stressful pilling sessions at home.

If subcutaneous fluids are administered, other subcutaneous injections can be given along with the fluids, reducing the number of injections that need to be given. This is particularly useful for medications that are known to cause painful reactions when injected.

Cerenia® is a very effective anti-emetic medication and commonly used in emergency medicine. Cerenia can be given via oral or subcutaneous routes (package insert), with the subcutaneous route being more common in emergency patients with gastro-intestinal upset. It is commonly reported to cause a painful reaction on injection (package insert) but this side-effect is less common when the medication is refrigerated rather than administered at room temperature (Narishetty et al., 2009), or when preserved with benzyl alcohol (Deckers et al., 2018).

Hospitalization concerns for critical care patients

Emergency and critical care patients are more likely to be debilitated and experiencing physiological stress caused by uncontrolled pain, polyuria or diarrhea, nausea, and hunger. It is essential to ensure that the patient's physiologic stress is relieved, or controlled as much as possible, in order to provide a positive emotional experience.

Pain control

Adequate pain control is determined in large part by the nature of the condition the animal is suffering from. Even if the presenting complaint isn't inherently painful, patients with underlying conditions such as arthritis may experience more pain than usual if they are spending a lot of time lying down in a debilitated state.

Constant Rate Infusions (CRIs) are an excellent tool for delivering multi-modal pain control medications. Some medications that can be used in CRIs may have anxiolytic or sedative effects in addition to analgesia. See Anxiety-Reducing Medications on page 207 for information on specific CRI medications.

Local anesthetics administered through epidurals, wound diffusion catheters, or sometimes injected into body cavities or surgical sites during a procedure, are effective and under-utilized options for pain control. Topical local anesthetics such as lidocaine-prilocaine or liposomal lidocaine cream can be used to reduce skin sensitivity for injections or diagnostic procedures.

Elimination behavior

In general, hospitalized dogs should be taken outside for elimination breaks every four to six hours. Patients receiving fluids, diuretic medications, or with underlying disease conditions causing polyuria, will likely need to relieve themselves more often. If possible, supporting animals outside for elimination behavior is preferred over urinary catheter insertion, due to high risk for the development of nosocomial infections with urinary catheters. However, in some patients, a urinary catheter may be the only option for relieving urinary discomfort and preventing urine scalds. Indwelling catheters pose the lowest risk for the development of nosocomial infections, and for patient comfort are preferable over repeat catheterization options. Length of catheterization should be minimized (Bubenik et al., 2007).

Defecation behavior can be highly specific in some dogs, requiring time to sniff and prepare to defecate. Also, body positions for defecation can be difficult to achieve for dogs in slings or with physical limitations such as ataxia. Medications such as opioids can pre-dispose animals to constipation due to inhibition of intestinal motility. Time and special care must be given to dogs with defecation problems recovering from major illness.

Cats need access to a litter box. Ideally, litter boxes should be larger than the length of the cat (bigger if possible). Clay, clumping litter is generally preferred, about 1.5 inches deep. Cats with mobility issues, bandages, or IV fluids need a low-sided litter box they can step in and out of easily.

Hunger, nausea and feeding behavior

A common concern with hospitalized patients is the competing demands of nausea and hunger. Stressed patients may be less likely to eat, even if nausea is not a concern. Links have been found between the gut microbiome health and psychological well-being (Foster and Neufeld, 2013). Anti-emetics should be used as first-line treatment in all inappetant patients (unless contraindications exist, e.g., suspected intestinal foreign body).

When an anorexic patient needs calories, enteral feeding options are considered superior to parenteral (intravenous) methods. Enteral feeding not only provides calories, but it also prevents atrophy of the intestinal villae, encourages GI motility, and supports the microbiome. In rare circumstances, such as comatose patients or those at extreme risk of aspiration, parenteral nutrition may be the only option.

Tube-feeding options such as esophagostomy, naso-esophageal or naso-gastric feeding tubes can allow enteral feeding for patients that are either too ill or too stressed to consume calories orally. Placed under anesthesia or sedation, tube feeding options are generally well-tolerated by patients, and allow the delivery of calories without potentially stressful feeding interactions with the animal's care team. Once the patient starts eating on their own, the tubes can be removed.

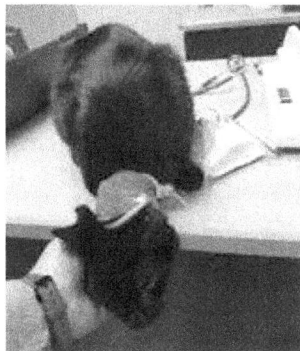

For inappetant animals who need calories, feeding tubes are usually indicated over force-feeding and/ or appetite stimulants. This patient is enjoying chin scratches during a visit with his owner during a hospital visit. He is tolerating both his esophageal tube and loose protective neck bandage well.

As appetite begins to return in the recovering patient, new food aversions may become apparent. Animals can develop food aversions at any time in their lives, particularly after significant GI upset. Offering a smorgasbord of food options, including wet and kibble varieties of food can be helpful. Warming the food to body temperature can increase its appeal, particularly for cats. Hand-feeding small amounts of food as kibble or meatballs can encourage some pets to eat.

Appetite stimulants and force-feeding are two very controversial practices in emergency medicine. Appetite stimulants rarely induce patients to consume enough calories (Pachtinger, 2016), and their use risks worsening welfare by increasing hunger in patients who are inappetant for good reason. Appetite stimulants are more appropriate for the treatment of chronic disease conditions such as chronic renal failure (Quimby and Lunn, 2013), than for acute emergency and intensive care patients.

Force-feeding has many drawbacks. Risk of aspiration is higher with force feeding. The process is usually very stressful for the patient and the caregiver, leading to conditioned fear, food aversions, and potentially defensive aggression (Pachtinger, 2016; Zoran, 2006).

In general, force-feeding should be avoided in favor of more humane options such as feeding tubes. However, there is a spectrum of assisted feeding methods and some more gentle practices can be beneficial. For example, some patients will not eat food out of a bowl, but if food is provided in a syringe held near the mouth the patient may voluntarily lick and swallow small amounts. Another trick that sometimes works is placing a small amount of food on the patient's lips or nose. They will normally lick it off, and sometimes, if the taste is agreeable, they will accept more. Some hospitals practice the One Hand Rule: Feeding patients from a syringe can only be done with one hand. This rule guarantees that the patient is not restrained and is a willing participant in syringe feeding sessions.

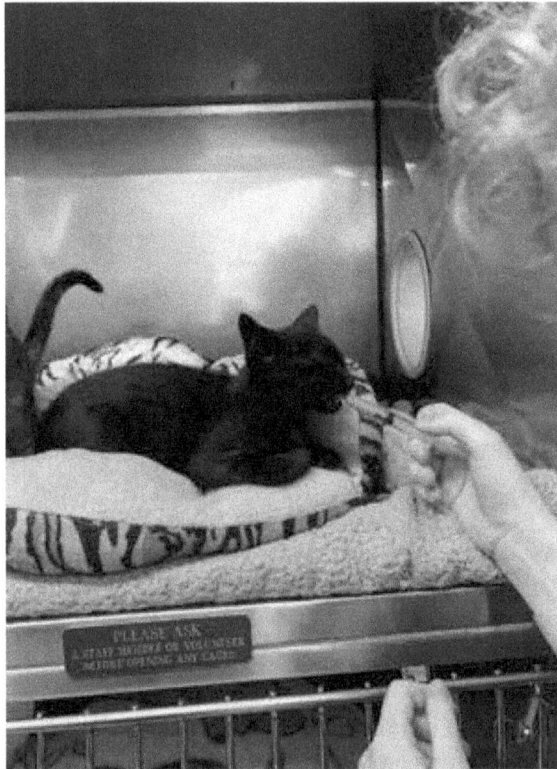

One-handed syringe feeding allows the patient to be a willing participant in assisted feeding. The kitten has the choice to back away from the syringe and avoid the feeding if it prefers.

Environmental sources of stress in hospitals

Sensory stressors

Olfactory. Cats and dogs are more sensitive to scent than humans, so environments that are comfortable for humans may contain odors that are unpleasant and stressful for patients. Some odors of particular concern are: scents of predator species (cats who can smell dogs, rodents who can smell cats or dogs); unfamiliar conspecifics, alcohol, cleaning chemicals, laundry detergent, and citrus scents. (Stella and Croney, 2016). As much as possible, efforts should be taken to house animals in species-separated wards, use low-scent cleaning products, dispose of soiled bedding and odorous hospital waste quickly. Garbage containers with lids may help to reduce odors in animal housing areas.

For cleaning within the patient's cage or kennel, spot cleaning is preferred, unless the cage space is soiled to an extent where spot cleaning is unreasonable (ASPCA, 2019; Fear Free, 2019). This method is preferred because it allows the animal's familiar bedding pheromone markings to remain in the environment (Ellis et al., 2013).

To prevent nose blindness, effective low-odor cleaning products are preferred. Activated Hydrogen Peroxide cleaners formulated for veterinary use have a low odor and are effective against pathogens including unenveloped viruses when used as instructed (Fear Free, 2019; Sattar, Springthorpe, and Rochon,1998). Prompt cleaning of soiled areas will remove odor sources such as waste and biofilms.

Visual access to other animals can be stressful, particularly for prey species (cats, small mammals, exotics). Where possible, house animals in species-specific wards. If this is not possible, use visual barriers such as towels or curtains over cage doors to provide privacy and an opportunity to hide.

Auditory. Emergency treatment and ICU areas can be busy, loud environments, with near-constant human and machine noises. Cats and dogs have an auditory frequency range that exceeds that of humans, meaning noises that humans cannot perceive may pose a welfare risk to patients. Sound intensity of 60 dB or below (quiet conversation level) have been proposed to maintain patient comfort. Phones and paging speakers often have volume settings which can be turned down. Alert noises on medical equipment can often be turned down or switched to alert lighting. Staff and visiting clients should be asked to keep their voices down in patient waiting, housing and treatment areas.

It may be beneficial to mask noises that cannot be reduced or eliminated using background noise, such as classical music, that can be used to reduce stress from noises audible in other parts of the hospital. Masking noise should be played at a low volume (quiet conversation level) (Fear Free, 2019).

Lack of circadian rhythm and consistent schedule

Circadian Stress (interference with an animal's normal sleep-wake cycle) has been associated with morbidity and mortality in human literature (Grandner et al., 2010; Grandner, et al., 2013; Puttonen, Härmä, and Hublin, 2010). An unpredictable schedule and macroenvironment has been associated with decreased affiliative behaviors, increased sickness behaviors, and decreased maintenance behaviors in caged cats (Stella, 2014).

For hospitalized patients in 24-hour care facilities, care should be taken to provide patients with a consistent 24-hour schedule, including scheduled sleeping time when noise, light, and activity are minimized. Treatments should be scheduled to provide patients with hours of uninterrupted rest at consistent daily times.

Lack of familiarity

The sights, smells, sounds, staff, and other animals the patient is being exposed to in the emergency care facility are all unfamiliar, which can be a significant source of stress. Some novelty stress is unavoidable, but there are steps that can be taken to provide some familiarity for the patient.

Allowing the owner to leave familiar items with the patient, such as items of the owner's clothing, toys, or bedding, may provide some comfort. Because it is easy for items to get lost or soiled in a veterinary hospital, your staff should counsel owners to leave only items they do not mind losing.

Allowing owners to visit their pets during a hospital stay can provide comfort to the patient. In addition to the comfort the presence of a familiar person can provide the patient, owners often experience significant stress when their companion is hospitalized. Allowing the client to visit a hospitalized patient also allows them to experience the high level of care their animal is receiving and allows for greater transparency regarding their companion's condition and care.

There are two major barriers to allowing owner visits: concerns for the privacy and confidentiality of other patients in the hospital; and interference with treatments and/or workflow in the hospital area. Privacy concerns can be avoided by covering charts and training staff not to disclose private information about other patients or clients to visitors. To ensure that workflow is not interrupted, rules for visitors should be decided on by hospital staff and discussed with owners who wish to visit their companions in the hospital area. Examples of visiting rules may include visiting hours that avoid shift changes, not allowing visitors to restrain patients for procedures, and an understanding that if there is an emergency, visitors may be asked to leave on short notice.

Rarely, owners visiting and leaving can be a significant source of distress for patients, most often dogs. In these situations, having an honest conversation with the owner, and providing video evidence of the distress their departure caused can be helpful. Perhaps these patients should not receive visits from their owners during hospitalization. If the emotional benefit outweighs the anxiety cost for owner and patient, anxiety-reducing medication can be given so that the time of peak onset matches the owner's departure time.

If the client cannot visit the patient physically but still wants to check on their condition, video streaming with webcams or smartphones can be a good alternative.

Staff can also try to provide comfort by interacting with the patient in a manner that is familiar to them, including actions such as using the patient's name and engaging familiar games and training routines. If the patient's family speaks a different language, try to use words the animal will recognize. Ask the owners if the patient knows any tricks or other trained behaviors, and if the animal is feeling well enough and able to take treats, engage in some rewards-based training using familiar cues.

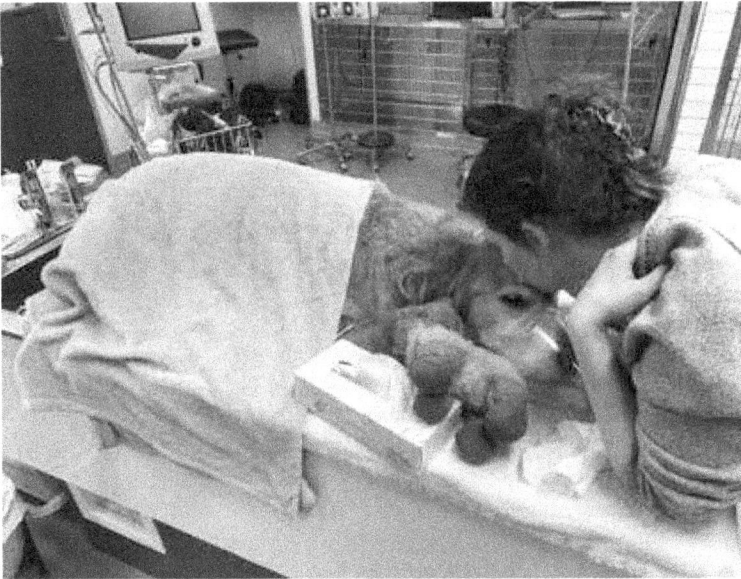

Allowing clients to visit pets and bring familiar items can provide comfort both to patients and owners.

Lack of social interaction

Some patients are accustomed to and have a need for a high level of social attention from humans. For these patients it can be stressful to be restrained away from people, or to have people around them who are not interacting with them. Separation from the owner and lack of adequate social interaction may be more stressful for animals who are accustomed to a high level of attention in the home environment (Stella and Croney, 2016; Wagner, Hurley, and Stavisky, 2018). Cats often prefer social interaction with people over playing with toys (Vitale, Mehrkam, and Udell, 2017).

When patients are stressed by lack of social attention, spending some time out of the cage or kennel with people may be helpful. Some opportunities include attending rounds in a staff member's lap or spending time with staff during meal breaks.

Conversely, for stray, feral, and non-domesticated animals, forced proximity to humans can be a highly stressful experience (Morgan and Tromborg, 2007). Housing options that limit exposure to people should be used for these animals.

Lack of control and predictability

A commonality among all the stressors discussed above is the patient's lack of control over their exposure to these stressors: their frequency, intensity, and duration. Lack of control has been proposed as one of the most significant sources of stress for captive animals (Morgan and Tromborg, 2007; Mineka and Kelly, 1989; Rochlitz, 2005).

In most cases, hospitalization necessitates confinement, and confinement creates lack of control. Veterinary treatments and diagnostic tests are often aversive to patients, but they are given no choice but to comply. Confined animals have restricted movement, meaning they are not able to move away from experiences or sensations they find aversive.

203

For confined animals, stress is minimized when schedules are highly predictable (Stella 2014; Hemsworth, Barnett, and Hansen, 1987; Bassett and Buchanan-Smith, 2007). Studies show that animals are better able to cope with aversive events if they are able to predict when they will happen (Gliner, 1972; Seligman, Maier, and Geer, 1979).

Finding opportunities to introduce choice and control into the lives of hospitalized patients can make a big difference in their overall welfare. Where their medical state allows, hospitalized animals can be offered choice in food options, bedding substrate, elimination substrate, level of physical interaction with owners and staff, level of privacy, and more.

Some aversive treatments (such as administering a necessary oral medication with a bitter taste), are unfortunately unavoidable. In these cases, making that event predictable and distinct from other handling sessions is recommended (e.g., wear a bandana during these treatments). This will give the animal an environmental cue that the aversive event is about to occur (increases predictability) and will also provide a safety cue letting the patient know that all other handling will not include this aversive treatment.

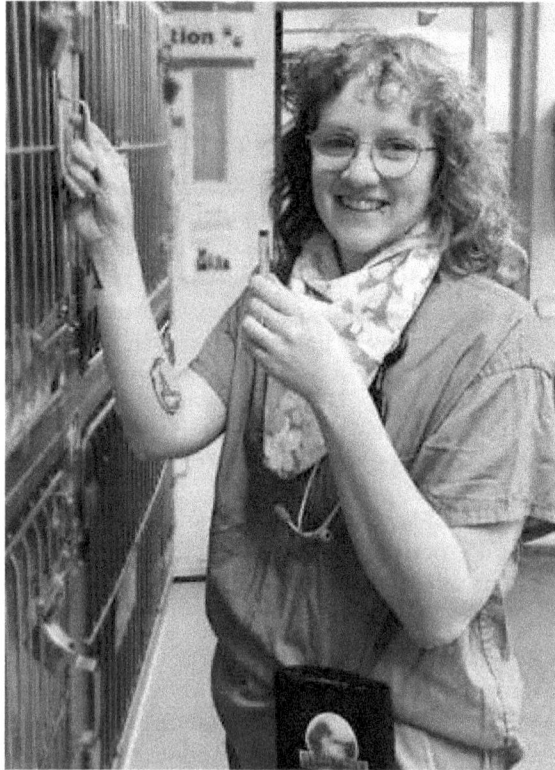

Unavoidable treatments that are expected to be stressful for the patient should be made as predictable as possible. Here the technician is wearing a bandana while administering oral medications. If the bandana is only worn during stressful treatments, the patient will learn to differentiate between visits that involve stressful interactions and social interactions that do not involve treatments.

Keep in mind the definition of what is 'aversive' to the patient is not always predictable and can be highly variable between individuals. In general, any treatment that is consistently met with fearful body language, distance-increasing behavior, or attempts to escape, can be considered aversive to the patient. Where possible, obtaining this information from the owner when admitting the patient can be helpful. Questions like "How does Rover handle eye drops and bandage changes?" can provide a lot of useful information for treatment staff.

Animal housing considerations

Cats, dogs, and small companion animals should be housed in separate wards if possible (Wagner, Hurley, and Stavisky, 2018). For cats, exposure to dogs (even if only auditory) is a proven stressor (Stella and Croney, 2016; McCobb et al., 2005). In an ICU environment, complete isolation from dogs is often not possible, but interventions such as visual blockers can help reduce stress. Treatment and ICU areas can be designed such that cats and dogs can be housed in the same room, but not have visual contact.

Cages and runs should be large enough for the animal to stand up and move around comfortably. Dogs should have enough room to stand up and turn around without touching the sides of the kennel. There should also be enough room for an animal to move away from soiled bedding.

Cats require a cage large enough to allow separation of food, water, and resting area(s) from litter box (Wagner, Hurley, and Stavisky, 2018). Multiple resting areas with different bedding options is preferred.

Resting areas should be made of soft, easily drainable material, such as synthetic fleece. Cats often prefer an elevated vantage point, such as a platform (Rochlitz, 2005; Rochlitz, 1999) and/or a bed with sides. This can also help with thermal regulation – elevated sides of the bed help retain heat when cats are resting.

Caging should be designed to reduce noise and vibration. Stainless steel cages can be insulated by placing foam board or insulation batting between cages. Low noise locking mechanisms should be chosen, or care should be taken by staff to open and close cage doors carefully to avoid unnecessary vibration and noise.

Tethering is not recommended as a restraint mechanism unless patients can be directly monitored at all times. If tethering is used, a loosely fitted harness is preferable to a collar to attach the tether to the patient.

Housing is an opportunity to give hospitalized animals some level of choice and control by offering a variety of in-cage enrichments such as hiding boxes, toys, familiar items, flooring/bedding choices, etc.

Privacy and hiding spaces

Many studies have confirmed that feline patients have better welfare, lower stress, better immune system function, and more affiliative behaviors when provided with an option for hiding in their home cage (Gourkow and Fraser, 2006; Kry and Casey, 2007; Vinke, Godijin, and Van Der Leij, 2014). A hiding area can be provided using the cat's carrier, a cardboard box, a milk crate, or a small plastic stool. Commercial hide and perch cage accessories are also available.

Hiding boxes may not be suitable for cats with IV or urinary catheters, but these patients can still be given privacy options such as a shallow-entry box, or curtain or towel covering a portion of the cage door (ASPCA, 2019). Animals on seizure watch can be provided with privacy by attaching bells to their collar. If they seize, ICU staff will be alerted by the sound of the bells.

Temperature

Hypothermia is physically uncomfortable for the patient and may pre-dispose patients to reduced metabolism and drug/toxin clearance (Robertson et al., 2018), and delayed wound healing time (Reynolds, Beckmann, and Kurz, 2008; Clark-Price, 2015).

Body temperature is influenced by the external ambient temperature, and internal thermogenesis (Klein, 2012). The thermoneutral zone is the ambient temperature range in which the body can maintain body temperatures without expending energy to increase heat production or loss. The thermoneutral zone for cats is 86 to 100 degrees Fahrenheit (30 to 38 degrees Celsius) (National Research Council, 2013). For dogs the thermoneutral zone varies by breed and coat type, but ranges from 68 to 86 degrees Fahrenheit (20 to 30 degrees Celsius) (National Research Council, 2006). Young, geriatric, and sick animals may have impaired thermoregulation. Febrile animals may have elevated temperatures, but still feel cold and seek heat sources. Animals under or recovering from anesthesia have impaired thermoregulation and require exogenous heat sources until anesthetic medications have been metabolized.

Most animal housing areas are maintained at 70 degrees Fahrenheit (22 degrees Celsius) (National Research Council, 2013) so it is safe to assume that all cats and most short-coated dogs would benefit from an exogenous heat source in their housing area. If the animal is mobile, providing a heat source in one resting area, and a separate resting area without a heat source is recommended. This way, the animals can self-regulate to reach homeostasis. Providing bedding with elevated sides (such as a box) for cats also helps with thermoregulation (Stella and Croney, 2016).

Hyperthermia may be associated with excessive exogenous heat and the administration of certain medications (opioids, ketamine) (Niedfeldt and Robertson, 2006). Treat according to source, by removing exogenous heat sources or treating with acepromazine (vasodilation) (Niedfeldt and Robertson, 2006). Hyperthermia due to drug reaction normally resolves within 1 hour without treatment (Niedfeldt and Robertson, 2006).

Anxiety-reducing medications

The emergency and critical care setting introduces unique challenges to the use of medication for the relief of stress and anxiety. Patients under emergency or ICU care often require a combination of analgesia, anxiolysis, and sedation.

Oral pre-visit medications are of limited utility for emergency examinations because most visits to the emergency room are unplanned. Stable hospitalized patients that are able to take oral medications may benefit from anxiety-reducing medications such as Trazodone for dogs (Gilbert-Gregory et al., 2016) or Gabapentin for cats (Pankratz et al., 2018; van Haaften et al., 2017). See Chapter 9 for further details on oral medications.

Some patients are too ill to take oral medications, or need to be fasted for medical reasons, but still have significant anxiety that cannot be relieved through environmental modifications and behavioral interventions. Injectable anxiety-reducing medications are needed for these patients. Some medication considerations are particularly important to consider for emergency and critical care patients. The ability to reverse anxiety-reducing medications if needed is particularly important for critical or unstable patients. Side-effect and drug interaction profiles of medications must also be carefully considered, as emergency and critical care patients are often receiving multiple medications.

Constant-rate infusions (CRIs) have several advantages over intermittent bolus injections: they reduce stress to the patient associated with repeated treatments, they avoid peak and trough drug concentrations caused by metabolism of the drug, they improve the ease of dose titration so the patient receives the minimum effective dose, and they can be used with polypharmacy.

Injectable medications with anxiety-reducing effects

Benzodiazepines. Benzodiazepines (e.g., diazepam, midazolam) work by potentiating the effects of GABA, an inhibitory neurotransmitter in the Central Nervous System (CNS). Benzodiazepines have anxiolytic, mildly sedating, appetite-stimulating and anti-convulsant effects. At high doses they can produce ataxia. Paradoxical effects are frequently reported with oral formulations of this class of medication. While generally considered safe, chronic use of oral diazepam has been associated with fulminant hepatic necrosis in cats.

Benzodiazepines are a good first-line anxiolytic for significant fear or panic-related emotional states (Herron, Shofer, and Reisner, 2008; Crowell-Davis et al., 2003). They have no significant analgesic effects, so use in combination with pain-control medications when needed. Benzodiazepines are reversible (flumazenil).

Opioids work by acting on opioid receptors and are used most often in veterinary medicine for their analgesic and sedative properties. Opioids also have mood-altering effects, generally producing peaceful or euphoric emotional states, but in some patients, paradoxical effects (dysphoria) can occur. Opioids, especially mu and kappa agonists such as morphine and hydromorphone, can be associated with respiratory depression, gastro-intestinal hypomotility, and nausea/vomiting. Mu agonist effects can be reversed with naloxone.

Butorphanol is a kappa agonist/mu partial antagonist, which can be used as a partial reversal agent for mu agonists. Due to the short length of action, its utility as an analgesic is limited. The most common use for butorphanol in emergency medicine is to treat distress in patients with respiratory distress, and it is often used to facilitate diagnostic tests such as thoracic radiographs.

Buprenorphine is a partial mu agonist with a long duration of action. Because it is not a full mu agonist, side effects such as respiratory suppression are markedly reduced. It can be administered transmucosally in dogs and cats. There is also a sustained-release formulation that lasts 72 hours in cats (Catbagan et al., 2011).

Alpha-2 adrenergic receptor agonists

This class of medication blocks norepinephrine release from presynaptic neurons in the CNS, reducing sympathetic tone. Alpha-2 agonists have anxiolytic, analgesic, and sedative effects (Valtolina et al., 2009). Dexmedetomidine produces hypertension with compensatory bradycardia, which may be followed by hypotension. Peripheral vasoconstriction alters mucous membrane color and may interfere with catheter placement or blood collection.

Dexmedetomidine is an excellent first-line choice for producing anxiolysis and analgesia for stable patients. At high doses, it can produce near-anesthetic levels of sedation, facilitating minor surgical procedures, or handling for fractious or highly fearful patients. Alpha-2 agonists are reversible (atipamezole).

Phenothiazines, including acepromazine and chlorpromazine are neuroleptic antipsychotic medications that block dopamine receptors in the CNS. Their main effects are sedation, reduced motor function, reduced awareness of external stimuli, and antiemetic. Their side effect profile includes vasodilation, impaired thermoregulation, decreased seizure threshold, bradycardia, ataxia, and extrapyramidal motor signs (Landsberg, Hunthausen, and Ackerman, 2013; Pypendop, 2012), which limits their use for unstable patients, and those with neurologic or cardiovascular compromise.

While this class of medication is an effective sedative, particularity when combined with other medications such as opioids or benzodiazepines (Hart, 1985), their effects on anxiety and aggressive behavior are variable. Some animals may become more sensitive to noise or exhibit aggressive responses without warning. For these reasons, acepromazine is not recommended as a first-line or solitary intervention for treatment of anxiety in hospitalized patients.

Chapter 12
Other Small Companion Animals and Exotics

By Dr. Marion Desmarchelier, DMV, IPSAV, DES, MSc, Diplomate ACZM, DACVB

Small companion animals have become incredibly popular over the last decade. This group of patients that used to consist mainly of rabbits, guinea pigs and ferrets has dramatically grown to include a long list of other species often called "exotics." Companion birds include budgerigars, cockatiels, cockatoos and larger parrots, as well as toucans, mynah birds and lorikeets. The ectotherm patients are also a very diverse group, from the smaller geckos to the popular red-eared sliders and bearded dragons to the rarer uromastyx and poison-dart frogs. Progress has been made in understanding the behavior and basic needs of these numerous species. However, due to their irregular sizes and the large variety of species, providing them with a low-stress environment in the hospital remains challenging.

All the behavior science principles apply to all species, and we should aim at elevating the level of care we offer to exotics as much as to more traditional species. Reducing fear in these fragile individuals can make a huge difference in the hospitalization outcome. Stress-induced anorexia causes gastrointestinal stasis in small mammals, with potentially serious to fatal consequences. In addition to improving their overall hospital experience, adjusting to the specificities of exotic patients is likely to significantly reduce morbidity and mortality.

This chapter will first provide tools to be able to assess exotic pet body language and behavior in the hospital. Appropriate ways to transport exotics to the clinic will be described, followed by how to adapt various areas of the hospital for them. Gentle handling for veterinary procedures will be reviewed. Finally, specifics of human-animal bond in the case of exotic pets will be presented.

Assessing body language and behavior in the hospital

Every species has its own complex communication system. Our goal here is to provide relevant information on how to read exotic pet body language and interpret their behavior in the hospital. This is the first and key step to reducing their stress and improving the way we provide the best care to them.

Small companion mammals

Most small mammals are prey species, with the notable exception of the ferret which is both prey and predator. They are generally quiet communicators, mainly using subtle facial expressions and inactive behaviors, especially in presence of humans in a stressful environment. The ability to read their body language will be helpful for two main reasons – to assess their level of stress and determine how they are coping with their hospitalization, and to differentiate pain from stress or sedation.

Rabbits and rodents

Rabbits and several species of rodents tend to freeze when handled. This should not be interpreted as them being relaxed and tolerant of manipulations, as they will often take any opportunity to suddenly jump or run away if given a chance. Freezing with tense muscles is usually a sign of intense fear. Many predators start chasing based upon prey movements, and more injuries will occur when the prey tries to escape once caught. If not killed when caught, there is always a chance to be accidentally released. Most rabbits will appear immobile when observed in their cage.

Paying attention to more subtle signs will help differentiate between stress-induced immobility, pain-induced immobility, or sedation. Ears will be flattened with the eyes bulging, and body posture crouched with feet beneath the abdomen in a fearful rabbit.

Rabbit with eyes bulging, tight ears and general muscular tension compatible with fear.

Pain can be associated with orbital tightening, cheek flattening, whiskers pulled back, and ears can appear more curled or tube-shaped than normal.

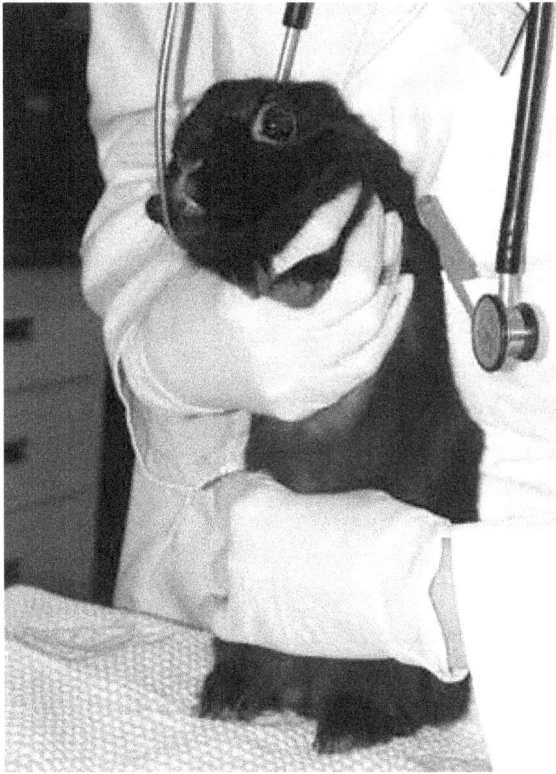

Rabbit showing eye bulging, flattened ears, cheek flattening, whiskers pulled back, tension in the nose and lips, compatible with pain.

Rabbits in discomfort may also push their abdomen towards the ground, grind their teeth, twitch, wince, stagger, or flinch (Leach et al., 2009).

Inactive pain behaviors were found to be the best indicators of post-operative pain in rabbits after an ovariohysterectom (Leach et al., 2009). Grooming should not be considered as a sign of comfort as it can also be performed in painful and stressed rabbits (Leach et al., 2009; Keating et al., 2012). Sedation with appropriate pain control is characterized by muscle relaxation, eyes closed or half-closed without flattened cheeks and ears, or pulled whiskers.

Sedated rabbit showing half-closed eyes, relaxed ears, normal round cheeks, relaxed nose and lip muscles and normal position of the whiskers.

Lying down with hindlegs extended, in sternal or lateral recumbency, is generally associated with physical comfort and mental relaxation.

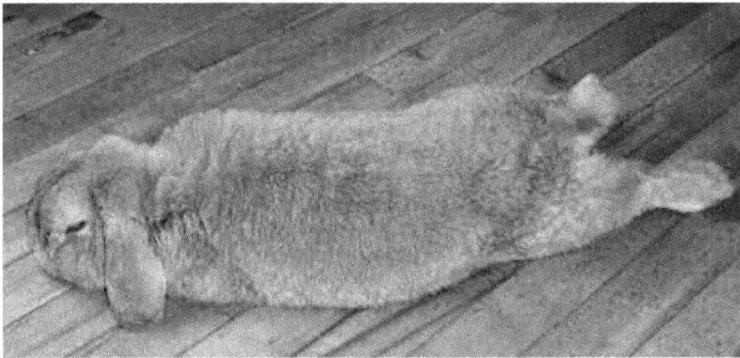

Non-sedated calm rabbit lying down with extended back legs, showing half-closed eyes, relaxed eyes and absence of general muscular tension.

Thumping is not very frequently heard in hospitalized rabbits but should be considered as a sign of fear. Stressed rabbits are rarely aggressive but lunging and bite attempts could happen if they were to be caught in a small enclosure with no possibility to escape. Vocalizations are rare in rabbits and are usually associated with intense pain.

Guinea pigs, on the other hand, are highly vocal. Normal guinea pigs will scream when handled, even if no painful procedure is performed. Absence of vocalizations can be a sign of comfort, or the opposite – a sign of abnormal mental state or shock. Chinchillas, degus, rats and mice will try to escape any uncomfortable handling situation, and they rarely freeze like rabbits or guinea pigs do. Grimace pain scales have been described in rats and mice and can be applied in a similar way as previously described in rabbits (Langford et al., 2010; Sotocinal et al., 2011).

Normal behavior of rabbits and rodents in the clinic varies with the species. However, they should generally be actively foraging for their ad libitum hay and other food items for several hours a day. Chinchillas, degus and other small rodents are very playful when comfortable and might use the enrichment items offered during their hospitalization (sand baths, tunnels, cardboard to chew, etc.). If they are hiding all day, the environment probably needs to be adjusted. It can be normal that they do not interact with hospital staff if they are not accustomed to them, but they should interact with their environment after about an hour of adjustment. Hamsters are nocturnal and could spend more time sleeping during the day than the other species. All these species should normally rouse very quickly if disturbed during a restful time.

Ferrets

Ferrets appear generally more tolerant and less fearful than other small mammals during handling. They can try and escape when uncomfortable but will readily escalate to aggression if the fearful stimulus is not removed. Calm ferrets will spend a lot of time sleeping, showing muscle relaxation.

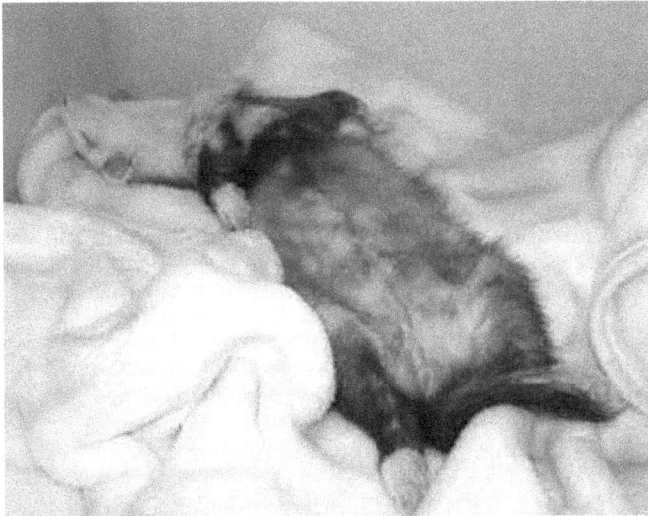

Non-sedated ferret sleeping in a position showing complete muscle relaxation.

Ferrets can sleep very deeply and be difficult to wake up, in contrast to rabbits and rodents. They are also more expressive in their behavior but will only be lethargic with severe conditions. Normal ferrets should explore their hospital environment immediately and thoroughly, which is why they are so excellent at escaping various types of cages. After this very active phase, ferrets will usually spend a lot of time sleeping if provided with a comfortable place to rest (hammock, towel, box, etc.).

Companion birds

The body language of companion birds varies between species and within individuals. Parrots have a very complex acoustic and gestural communication system based on vocalizations and body language (Moura et al., 2014). Though difficult to generalize such an evolved system, a few key features appear to be helpful while interacting with a companion bird in a hospital setting.

Body posture is generally straight with the head possibly turning from side to side when a parrot is alert and visually exploring a new environment.

Calm and alert green-winged macaw with a slight head tilt commonly displayed by parrot being attentive to their environment.

When the bird bends forward towards someone, with the beak and wings open, it is compatible with an aggressive display, though it could also be an attention-seeking behavior. Fanning of the tail can be seen before aggression. Pinning of the eye, characterized by the voluntary rapid and repeated contractions of the pupil, is indicative of high arousal, whether positive or negative, and can be seen with fear-induced aggression (van Zeeland, Friedman, and Bergman, 2015).

Erection of the head feathers and/or the crest is another sign of excitement.

Forward posture, erected feathers, open beak and voluntary contractions of the pupil is indicative of high arousal in this African grey parrot.

Birds will try to fly or move away from fear-inducing stimuli. Aggression can occur if the parrot is frightened and has no escape alternative. Vocalizations from loud calls to screaming can precede aggression. Parrots who talk in the hospital and readily take treats from hands are usually comfortable. They should spend time foraging for food, playing with enrichment items, exploring the environment and interacting with people.

Normally, parrots will perch on a high location in their enclosure to rest and observe the environment. Loud but interrupted calls can be contact calls, emitted by an isolated parrot who is trying to contact another one. This can be a sign of distress in a hospitalized parrot. A low body posture on a perch or a bird staying on the ground is very abnormal, and is often associated with pain or lethargy, but rarely fear.

Jandaya conure displaying a low body posture, half-closed eyes and ruffled feathers compatible with pain or lethargy.

Keeping the head tucked under a wing in the presence of an unfamiliar person is very abnormal and indicative of serious sickness. If the parrot was trained to perform simple behaviors at home, he should be able to perform them as well at the hospital if he is not experiencing undue stress.

Companion ectotherms

Reptile and amphibian behavior is extremely diverse, and no-one can be assumed to be knowledgeable about all species. It is very important to request information from the owner before the consultation, as is researching the normal biology of the species.

Absence of normal behaviors is usually an indicator of stress in reptiles. However, as some reptiles and amphibians spend a significant amount of time hiding or resting, it can be very challenging to assess in a hospital setting. Exploration of the environment, curiosity towards enrichment items, resting or basking, especially with limbs stretched for lizards and turtles, and using different areas of the enclosures, are considered normal behaviors.

Turtles benefit from a basking spot for their health and welfare like shown with these red-eared slider turtles.

Aggressive posture in fearful reptiles includes mouth/beak opening, inflating their body, throat or neck while standing erect, hissing and spitting. Fearful reptiles can also lie flat on the ground, feign death, or try to hide (inside their shell or in their enclosure). They can try to escape, squeak, whine, void feces or urine on the handler, as well as other secretions (musk, blood, stomach content). Some reptiles will also change color when undergoing stressful events.

Normal color veiled chameleon

Sick veiled chameleon with pale colors.

Stressed veiled chameleon with darker colors.

More subtle signs of fear include clutching, loop pushing (when a snake uses the arch of his body to avoid/deflect physical contact from the human), freezing, grating of the jaws in chelonians, projection of hemipenes and voluntary regurgitation of food.

When left alone in a hospital enclosure, most reptiles and amphibians will try to hide. Time needed to habituate is very long, usually longer than the hospitalization period. We should therefore aim at diminishing the stress as much as possible but should not necessarily expect to see them display normal comfort behaviors during their stays.

Transporting small companion animals to the hospital

Transport is the first stressful time in the chain of events occurring when taking an exotic animal to the veterinary hospital. Several adjustments can be made to reduce fear and anxiety while transporting small companion animals.

Small companion mammals

Small mammals are submitted to many different stressors during transportation such as confinement, novelty, changes in temperature and light condition. Multiple studies have shown long lasting effects of transportation on physiological parameters and cortisol/corticosterone concentrations in rodents, up to 16 days after a three-hour transportation in rats (Arts, 2012; Stemkens-Sevens et al., 2009). In one study, rabbits lost 6.4% ± 2.2% of their body weight during a 13 to 14-hour transport (Tasaki et al., 2019). Though stress is well documented, and guidelines exist on how to transport laboratory rabbits and rodents, very few studies have tested how to reduce these transportation-associated side effects (Swallow et al., 2005).

Transport time should be reduced as much as possible. If longer than about half an hour, it is ideal to provide a transporter in which the animal will be able to eat. Providing preferred items, such as fresh greens for rabbits and guinea pigs, might help decrease the transport-associated fast. Prolonged fasting can lead to gastrointestinal stasis or hypoglycemia in many species and should be avoided as much as possible.

The type of preferred cage has not been studied but cages that are well covered, with minimal visual exposure to the outside, appear to be recommended. Cages that open through the top are preferred, as it can be difficult to get rabbits through small frontal openings. Appropriate ventilation and protection against temperature variations is important.

We can hypothesize that getting small mammals habituated to their transport cage by feeding them in it on a regular basis would help decrease stress. Motivated clients could do a desensitization/counterconditioning program in which they train their small companion animal to get into the transporter and slowly increase the time spent in it, as well as the movement of the transporter. Gentle handling of the transporter and proper placement in the vehicle is required, to avoid any additional stress and decrease the risk of injury.

Companion birds

Transport-associated effects on physiological parameters have been studied in multiple production bird species, but only one study documented these effects in companion birds (McRee et al., 2018). Hematologic changes compatible with stress, as well as corticosterone increase, occurred in Hispaniolan parrots after a short transportation (McRee et al., 2018). However, no study has documented how to decrease stress while transporting companion birds. We can hypothesize that training companion birds to get in and out of a transport cage and using desensitization and counterconditioning to short transportation, could help decrease stress. A cage in which the bird can feel protected from potential predators may be preferred. Avoiding temperature change stressors is also ideal. Prolonged fasting can be a problem for very small species, so clients need to make sure their birds are comfortable enough to eat during transport. It may be beneficial for longer transports to stop regularly and provide them with preferred food items.

Companion ectotherms

Transport-associated stress is less documented in reptiles. However, there is no reason to think they would not be as sensitive to the effects of transportation as mammals and birds. Thermal stress might be one of the more important stressors in ectotherms. Avoiding rapid and important temperature changes is critical.

Reptiles and amphibians can be transported in boxes placed into insulated containers as long as the volume allows for appropriate ventilation. A heating pad or a cold pack can be placed in the cooler that contains the pet transporter but should be well protected to avoid any direct contact resulting in burn or frostbite. Gentle handling is required as in all other species. Training reptiles to voluntarily go into a transport box, through target training or other techniques, every time their enclosure is cleaned for example, could help decrease the stress they experience during transport.

Adjusting the hospital environment for small companion animals

Small animal veterinary hospitals are often designed with cats and dogs in mind and may be more or less exotic pet friendly. However, simple adjustments can significantly improve the experience of small companion animals and their owners at the clinic.

Small companion mammals

Reception and waiting area. As previously mentioned, small mammals are mainly prey species. Visual, auditory or even olfactory contact with predators like cats and dogs adds to the stress already caused by the transport to an unfamiliar environment. It would seem to be ideal to have a place designed for exotics. However, keeping a ferret next to a rabbit is not appropriate either, and most clinics do not have enough waiting room space to allow room for specific species groups.

On a case-to-case basis, small mammals can be either placed in a calm cat area of the waiting room if the room is relatively empty or brought to a quieter area while the owners wait at the reception desk or in the waiting room. There is always a quiet area, even in the smallest clinic. A cabinet, a bathroom or a freezer room can provide safe and quiet places with less predator threat for small mammals. Rabbits and chinchillas, and to a lesser extent other rodents, are heat sensitive. Should the reception area not be air conditioned on a hot day, these species should be placed in a cooler area immediately upon arrival. Drafts can predispose them to respiratory infections and should be avoided. A towel can be provided to cover the transporter and make the small mammal feel more secure.

Examination rooms. Disinfect floors and tables thoroughly (although table use is discouraged) to remove the odors of predators as much as possible. Examinations could be performed on the floor, since being at table height can be very stressful to ground or burrowing species. A large towel placed on the ground can provide traction on slippery floors that can make some individuals uncomfortable. Noise and light should be kept within an appropriate range to avoid additional disturbances of these very sensitive species. Materials and equipment should be organized to allow for rapid examination in one location.

Hospitalization. Small mammals can easily be kept in small animal wards with a few adjustments. First, the proximity of predators remains a significant issue. If possible, hospitalize the small mammal in a different room, even if this room was not originally designed for hospitalization. Place a towel in front of the cage door to provide an additional feeling of safety. If the animal requires frequent monitoring, a camera can be placed, or the towel pulled aside to leave a small opening through which the animal can be observed without being startled. Appropriate items should be placed in the enclosure. For example, hiding spots made of syringe boxes are appreciated by guinea pigs and other rodents and ferrets can enjoy a hammock or towel placed in a cardboard box.

Cardboard boxes make great hiding spots for small rodents like this guinea pig.

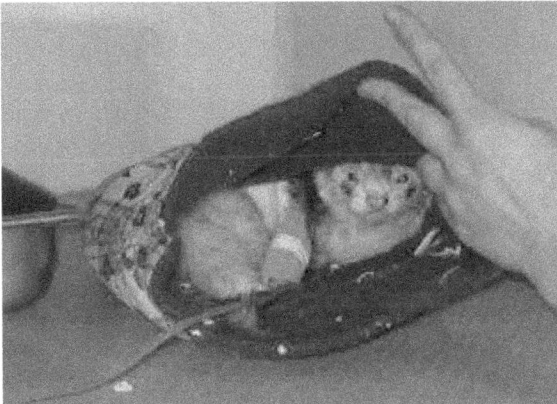

Ferrets often choose to hide if provided with appropriate places such as this fleece bag.

Many items found in the recycling box can safely be used to make small mammals more comfortable during their stay at the hospital. For example, paper towel rolls can be used to feed hay.

Chinchillas and degus will enjoy sand baths if they can be provided for about an hour a day. Temperature needs to be adjusted to the animal's condition. Though hypothermic patients may benefit from warmer wards, healthy rabbits and rodents should not be kept with exotic birds who require temperatures of 82 to 86 degrees Fahrenheit (28 to 30°C) as they could suffer from heat stress. Light should be minimal, especially at night. Maintaining the animals in bright light 24 hours a day can affect mood in rodents (Fonken et al., 2009). Noise disturbances should be assessed from the animal's perspective. Mouse hearing extends into the ultrasonic frequencies and ranges from one to about 100 kHz, whereas the human hearing range is between 20 Hz and 20 kHz (Reynolds et al., 2010). Hearing is most sensitive for humans at frequencies of approximately one to four kHz, and approximately 16 kHz for mice (Reynolds et al., 2010). Therefore, loud noises for us might not be that disturbing to them, while sounds inaudible to us can be stressful to them (Reynolds et al., 2010). Ultrasound-emitting tools should not be used in proximity to hospitalized small rodents (i.e., motion detector for lights, oscilloscopes, monitor, computers, etc.) (Sales et al., 1988).

Finally, allowing a companion to come in with his cage mate can help decrease stress in some circumstances.

Rabbits can develop very strong social links and could benefit from the presence of their cage mate during hospital visits and stays.

Companion birds

Reception and waiting area. Many healthy pet birds will feel more comfortable in the middle of a noisy group of people and other animals, even if unfamiliar with them, than isolated in a quiet area. For these birds, a hospital waiting room can be full of enrichment. However, sick and anxious parrots would benefit from being placed in a warm incubator, in a quiet area, with a cover on their cage, as soon as possible upon arrival. If bird owners brought their birds on a harness or let them out of their carriers in the reception area, they should be reminded of the numerous hazards present in a veterinary hospital (cats, dogs, fans, open doors, large windows, ventilation, etc.) and the birds should be immediately placed in a safe enclosed area. Owners can be woefully unaware of their parrot's body language and might not recognize how fearful their companion birds are when surrounded by predators in a small area.

Examination rooms. Being a prey species, companion birds are highly vigilant of their environment. Reducing the amount of space that they need to visually inspect to feel safe will help decrease their stress. Shut curtains and work in a small room to improve the bird's safety during the examination. It is critical to ensure that the environment is completely birdproof before handling the parrot or other bird. Turn off all fans, close all doors and lock them, or post "Do Not Enter" signs. Remove electrical devices from the room or stow them safely in a cupboard. You must never assume that the bird will not escape handling. It is even more critical with birds than it is for small mammals to have everything on hand to be able to perform a very quick and efficient examination. Catching them is often the most stressful part, so giving them a break during the exam is not always the best option.

Hospitalization. Sick birds strongly benefit from being hospitalized in an appropriate incubator. This allows them to rest in a safe enclosed area that can be supplemented with oxygen and humidity and kept at an appropriate temperature. Although regular bird cages are open on all sides and on the top, they can still be used if covered by a blanket in a warm room. Perches should be present and placed according to the bird's specific needs. If a bird is weak, the perch can be tipped over and placed on the ground. Most birds will prefer this set up over the bottom of the cage when they cannot reach a higher perch because of their condition. Healthy birds can have higher perches that will make them feel safer.

Cages and incubators should be of appropriate size with perches high enough to allow birds to turn around without breaking their tail feathers. (This can be challenging when keeping long-tailed large parrots such as macaws.) Position bowls at a level where the sick bird can easily feed.

Providing food and water at the bird's height may help return to normal food intake during hospitalization.

Offer a variety of preferred foods if the medical condition allows it. Many companion birds will eat better when outside of their cages and sharing food items with humans. Some birds require a lot of human attention and will benefit from contact time with staff and their owners, who should ideally be allowed to visit their bird. Hospitalized parrots often appreciate enrichment items such as pieces of paper or cardboard to chew on, and toys. Background noise is usually good for most birds and will decrease startle responses that are more obvious and disturbing in a quiet environment. Turn off lights for the night to allow birds to sleep. Sleep deprivation appears common in companion birds and can negatively affect immune functions and normal healing.

Companion ectotherms

Reception and waiting area. As previously mentioned, most reptiles should be transported in safe enclosed carriers that maintain a constant temperature. These carriers are often also well sound-insulated. Reptiles often can be safely kept in these carriers in the waiting room. However, if transport was long and the temperature in the carrier is not optimal, they should be placed in a warm incubator or heated room. Reptile owners might want to display their companion animal in the waiting room, as they often attract a lot of attention. However, they should be kindly instructed on how to observe subtle signs of stress in their animal's body language and reminded of the risks of escape and injury in this area shared with other species.

Examination rooms. If they escape from their handlers, reptiles can flee through very small ventilation holes, or hide behind furniture. As with birds, never assume that this will not happen. Make sure adequate safety measures are taken before taking the animal out of the transporter. Even if the reptile patient freezes during the examination and appears to tolerate handling well, stress is most likely present. Attention to subtle signs often reveals a much higher amount of stress than expected. Therefore, as with mammals and birds, perform the physical examination as quickly and efficiently as possible, with good advance planning. Temperature can drop rapidly if small reptiles are examined in a room at ambient temperature for too long. Decrease cold stress by placing them or their small enclosures on a warm pad.

Hospitalization. Because of the variety of size, husbandry requirements and potential medical conditions of this large group of species, creativity is called for when hospitalizing reptiles and amphibians. Terrestrial species like bearded dragons and green iguanas can be kept in regular cages, in a warm room, with a heat lamp safely secured next to the cage to provide a basking spot. If hospitalization is prolonged or if metabolic bone disease is suspected, a UVB light should be added to the individual's favorite spot.

Humidity should be adjusted to the species' needs. However, it is difficult to attain 80% humidity in a large open cage that houses an adult iguana. Regular spraying of the enclosure and bathing the animal several times a day can help with proper hydration in these cases. Keep substrate simple (paper or cardboard sheets) to avoid accidental ingestion of sand, rocks or other items. Arboreal species like some snake species should be offered branches to climb on. Aquatic species should be provided with an aquarium if their medical condition allows it.

Decreasing stress and fear during handling and veterinary procedures

The less amount of physical handling used, the less stressful the experience will be for the exotic animal. There are many ways to do parts of a physical examination with minimal to no restraint. When handling is necessary, proper technique and time efficiency are critical.

Small companion mammals

Gentle physical restraint

Several studies have focused on appropriate handling of companion rabbits. Many rabbits display fear behaviors when lifted from the ground. Estimates from owner surveys suggest that about 60% of companion rabbits struggle if lifted (Schepers, Koene, and Beard, 2009; Rooney et al., 2014). Lifting without hindquarter support can result in lumbosacral fracture and paralysis of the rabbit (Flecknell, 1983). The Rabbit Welfare Association and Fund states that a rabbit should be "lifted gently and securely, with one hand across the shoulder blades, fingers gently supporting the chest of the rabbit, whilst the other is under the rabbit's bottom, taking the bulk of the weight (Bradbury and Dickens, 2016). This technique is widely supported in the literature as the least stressful and safest handling technique for pet rabbits (Appleby, 2016; Fischer, 2010; Graham and Mader, 2012).

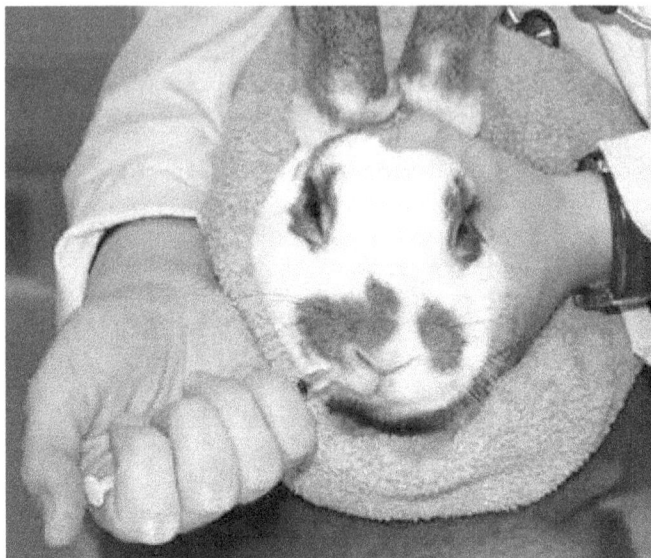

Proper positioning to reduce stress during drug administration in rabbits.

If a rabbit must be held, she should be held firmly and gently. Hesitant restraint promotes struggling, which can cause injury (Poole and English, 1999). Allowing the rabbit to have her paws in contact with a surface rather than hanging down decreases struggling and distress (Magnus, 2005). Most rabbits resent being touched on their abdomen, therefore, providing support under the back legs is preferred to supporting the ventral abdomen (Bradbury and Dickens, 2016). Tonic immobility in rabbits is a state of motor inhibition induced by inverting the rabbit onto her back (Bradbury and Dickens, 2016). It is believed to have evolved as an anti-predation mechanism, movement being the primary motivator for attack by canids, as previously mentioned (Fox, 1969). A pilot study showed significant elevations in respiration, heart rate and plasma corticosterone after induction of tonic immobility (McBride et al., 2006). The use of tonic immobility for veterinary procedures should be avoided, as many other less stressful techniques exist. Some authors argued that tonic immobility poses less risk than anesthesia and could be used for procedures such as radiographs (Varga, 2013). However, in our experience, sedation for radiographs is safe even in sick animals, and allows for much better quality of imaging compared to any physical restraint technique. Finally, rabbits never lift their heads up. Forcing them to do so can be stressful and painful, and result in avoidance response. When examining the oral cavity, the examiner should adjust their height to the rabbit to avoid having to raise the rabbit's head.

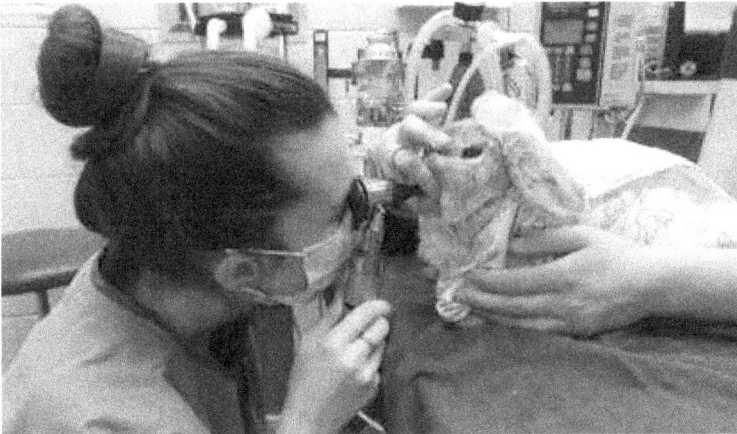

Proper positioning to examine the oral cavity of a rabbit by keeping the head in a horizontal position that is more comfortable for the patient.

Approach rabbit patients from the side when examining the head and oral cavity. The blind spot in front of the rabbit triggers the startle response observed when approached head-on.

Guinea pigs are often easy to handle, as they will freeze. This behavior should not be confused with relaxation of the animal, as was well demonstrated in a study on animal-assisted therapy guinea pigs (Gut et al, 2018). Heart rate and respiratory rates are often increased during even gentle restraint and screaming often results from firmer handling. Many guinea pigs are very sensitive to handling-related stress and should be examined as quickly as possible. Additional procedures such as oral examination, blood work, and radiographs are best performed under isoflurane flash anesthesia.

Many chinchillas are not accustomed to being handled and will struggle during physical restraint. In most cases, you can accomplish gentle handling with one hand under the thorax while keeping the two hind limbs on a non-slippery surface.

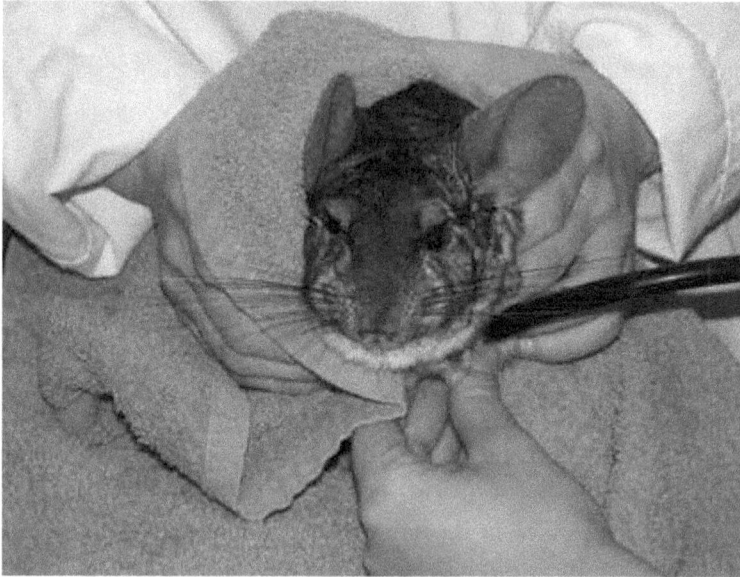

Gentle handling of a chinchilla using a towel.

Highly stressed chinchillas can be anesthetized with isoflurane in an induction chamber.

Anesthesia-associated risks are often inferior to the risk of trauma during rough handling. Even a short anesthesia will allow you to perform a more in-depth physical examination and obtain higher quality images and samples. Though reported as an appropriate technique in the literature, we do not recommend picking up chinchillas by the base of their tail (Quesenbery, Donnelly, and Mans, 2012a). Fur slip is a protective technique against predators in chinchillas (Quesenbery, Donnelly, and Mans, 2012a). They will release a large patch of fur, revealing the underlying skin. This rarely occurs in clinical situations and is most likely associated with intense fear or improper handling technique.

Small rodents range from being very tractable to difficult-to-handle without anesthesia, depending on the amount of handling they have experienced at home, and their current emotional and physical condition. In general, rats tolerate gentle handling very well, and most rat physical examinations can be performed with the use of a small towel if needed. Do not attempt scruffing with rats, as they do not have extra cervical skin and this technique could hurt them.

Some hamsters have undergone extensive manipulation and training and behave similarly to rats. However, hamsters can also be fearful and may bite. Hamsters have a very large surface of cervical skin that will allow scruffing if required. As for other species, scruffing can be stressful and should be reserved for very rapid procedures, and only if absolutely necessary.

Mice share some similarities with hamsters. They can be fearful and may bite if they feel threatened. Mice can be gently grabbed by the base of their tail while their forelimbs are on a non-slippery surface. Use of a tunnel, especially a familiar tunnel, is an alternative to tail grabbing, and has been shown to reduce anxiety in laboratory mice and increase willingness to interact with handlers (Gouveia and Hurst, 2013). Mice can also be scruffed for short examinations, but flash anesthesia is often preferred.

Gerbils struggle a lot when restrained. They can be cupped in one or two hands. Though they can technically be scruffed, they have less neck skin than other rodents and do not appear to show any muscle relaxation while being restrained with this technique. Their tails are very fragile and should never be used for handling. Flash anesthesia is generally preferred when a complete examination is required. The AHWLA website presents several tutorials on how to gently handle laboratory rodents. These techniques can often be utilized with companion rodents (AHWLA, 2019).

Ferrets have exceptional spinal flexibility and tend to struggle when restrained (Ivey and Morrisey, 1999). As with cats, the least amount of restraint is often preferable. Ferrets can often be distracted with food for examination and even for subcutaneous injections.

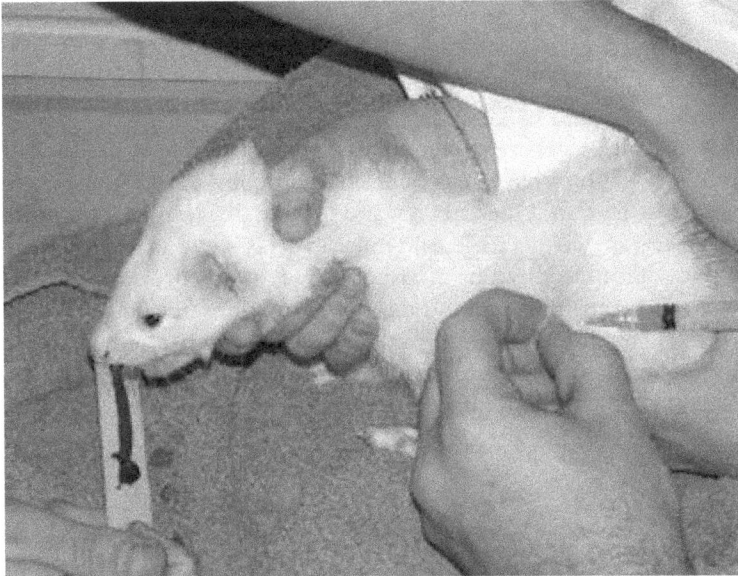

Using treats during subcutaneous injection decreases resistance and increases cooperation from this ferret.

However, auscultation, abdominal palpation, oral examination and many other procedures will require more stillness from the ferret. This can be accomplished with many ferrets by gentle handling on a table, with one hand supporting the thorax, and the ferret's feet standing on a non-slippery surface.

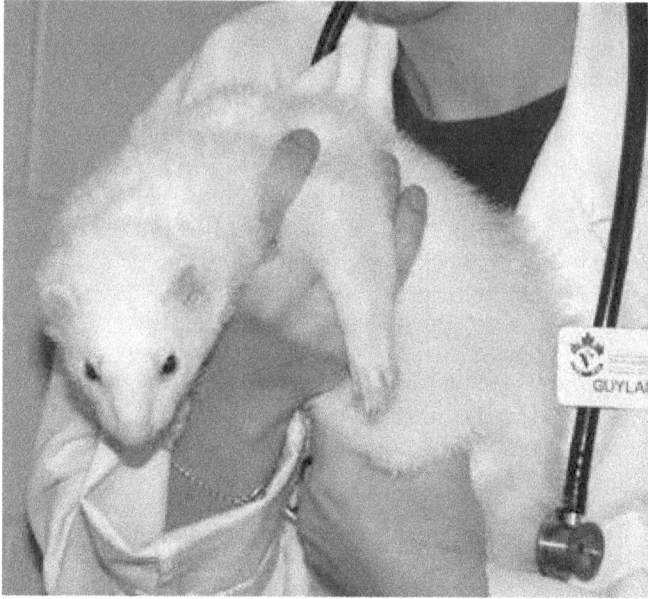

Gentle handling of a ferret for a physical examination.

If the ferret struggles excessively or attempts to bite, scruffing by the back of the neck with all four legs off the table often results in immobility, allowing, for example, thorough cardiac auscultation (Quesenberry and Orcutt, 2012b). Though in the author's experience, heart rate will decrease, and muscles relax while a ferret is scruffed, there are no studies indicating that this is associated with a comfortable position for the animal. Therefore, scruffing should be reserved for those difficult cases requiring a very short period of immobility that would not justify the use of sedative agents. For mask induction or rapid head examination, you can roll the ferret's body in a towel to make a ferret "burrito" as described for cats in Chapter 5.

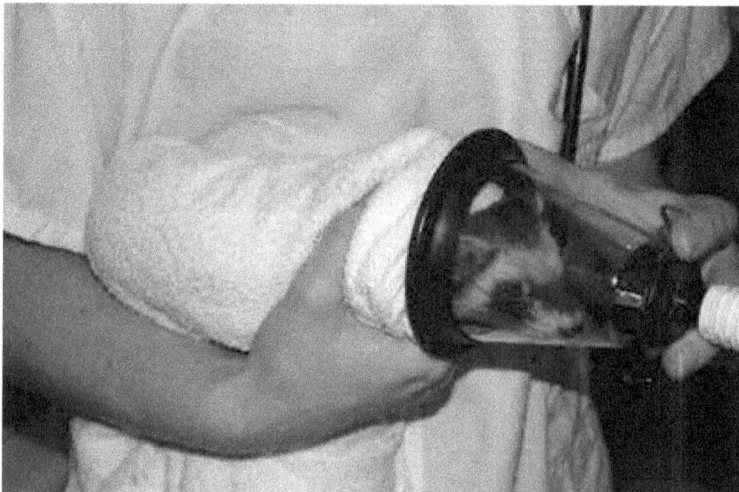

Wrapping a ferret in a towel for mask induction of anesthesia.

Sedation should be performed with the rare ferrets that prove difficult to handle, show excessive signs of fear (i.e., defecate or urinate while handled) or display aggression. Often the only warning a ferret will give before biting is struggling to escape, as they do not snarl, growl, or hiss. North American ferrets have been selected for docility and rarely bite. However, when they do, they can hold the bite and cause painful injuries. Proper reading of the ferret's behavior should help avoid aggression.

Adjustments to decrease stress during procedures

The first way to decrease stress while examining small mammals is to reduce the actual handling time. Parts of the examination can be performed with minimal to no restraint. Small or flighty individuals can be placed in transparent boxes that will allow for hands-free, very close evaluation, including of the ventral parts of the body and feet.

The use of a towel to gently and safely restrain small mammals as described for cats in Chapter 5 is helpful. Performing assessment and procedures on a blanket on the floor reduces the risks of falling off the table, which makes the handler generally more relaxed and allows for the animal to take breaks, safely walking around. Toys (mainly for ferrets) and treats can be used during the examination. It is preferable to move the examiner around the patient, rather than turning the animal in all directions during the examination. It is important to choose a calm, quiet room to handle small mammals, in addition to adjusting the lighting as needed. Remember to clean the examination space to reduce predator odors. Focus the examination on obtaining useful data and avoid unnecessary procedures (such as taking temperature in a healthy active individual).

Despite best handling techniques and environmental adjustments, veterinary procedures continue to be very stressful for many small animals. Sedation with a combination of opioids (butorphanol or buprenorphine) and midazolam provides a safe relaxation that should be considered in all cases requiring procedures beyond a physical examination. Flash anesthesia with isoflurane or sevoflurane, administered through an induction chamber, reduces the risk of trauma during handling and is considered very safe in non-critically ill patients.

Training cooperative care

Training small mammals to participate voluntarily in their medical care is extremely useful to reduce stress. This can be achieved in many different ways, starting with what the owners are most interested in, or what is most needed for the current situation. Always use operant conditioning with positive reinforcement. Utilize treats based on each animal's individual preferences.

Ferrets can enjoy commercial ferret treats, hairball paste, coconut oil, watermelon, cooked meat, baby food, etc. Rabbits can be easily trained with small pieces of dried fruits (pineapple, papaya) or with fresh fruits, fruit or vegetable juices (unsweetened), grains, nuts, etc. Chinchillas and degus love raisins, but these should be cut into very small pieces, as these species are sensitive to diabetes. Other rodents enjoy various treats ranging from cheese, fruits, and commercial rodent treats to nuts, mealworms, and more (Brown, 2012). Target training, perhaps with a Clikstik or equivalent, is easy and rapidly learned by most small mammals.

Crate training for transport can be accomplished via target training or shaping. Reinforcing calm behavior during handling in the hands or in a towel can also be helpful. To train the patient to drink water from a syringe in order to facilitate oral medication, first dip the syringe into any preferred food (apple sauce, yogurt, nut paste, etc.) and have them lick the syringe. Then you can gently push water out of the syringe while they are holding it in their mouth. When they swallow the water, you can mark the behavior if you use a clicker or any other bridge, then deliver a reward. By learning this drinking behavior, small mammals will be more likely to accept less tasty medication, as they expect the reward to come after the drinking behavior rather than being rewarded solely by the sweetness of the liquid.

Companion birds

Gentle physical restraint

Routine handling and transportation have been used as a stress model to document physiological changes in birds (McRee et al., 2018). However, techniques to reduce handling-associated stress have not been well-studied in birds. As previously mentioned for small mammals, reducing handling time is the first important step in reducing stress. You can make many good observations with the bird in a cage (feather quality, eyes, legs, posture, lameness, etc.), or perched on a hand if more comfortable for the individual bird. Birds can be trained for almost all parts of the physical examination (see Training Cooperative Care below), which significantly improves their experience in the hospital. However, when presented with an untrained bird, gentle and rapid restraint in a towel is usually well-tolerated, unless the bird had previous negative experience with the towel. If this is the case, handling the bird in your hands can sometimes be easier.

The handlers need to adjust their technique with the species. When handling small birds with one hand, extend the neck to prevent the bird from moving his head forward in an attempt to escape. This allows for a better and faster examination and is to be preferred. In all cases, position hands in order to prevent inappropriate movements from the bird, but never apply any pressure. Parrot skin is very thin, and marks can be observed when inappropriate pressure has been applied, especially on some macaw jaws. For multiple reasons, hands should never be positioned against the ventral part of the bird. First, the absence of hands in front of the animal allows good visualization of the breathing pattern. Second, humans will naturally apply pressure where their hands are when the bird starts struggling. Compressing the celomic cavity of a bird will not prevent him from escaping the restraint but can dangerously interfere with breathing.

Focus restraint primarily on the parrot head, then on the wings and finally, when needed for the examination, on the legs. Even when the bird is wrapped in a towel, the hand holding the towel in place should not be tight against the bird's ventral body. Good handling technique allows the bird to rapidly learn in which position he will be more comfortable. He will feel some pressure when trying to escape, with his movements restrained by the handler's hands, but he should feel the release provided by the appropriate positioning. If a bird keeps struggling to escape during an entire procedure, confirm that the handler is not applying pressure when the bird stops moving.

Adjustments to decrease stress during procedures

Many birds will have a very short tolerance to prolonged physical restraint for medical procedures. Hydrotherapy on wounds can be performed without sedation and with minimal gentle restrain in some avian patients. However, most wound care and other minor procedures are better performed under sedation or anesthesia.

Flash anesthesia is often safer than prolonged restraint of a very stressed bird and will improve the quality of the procedure. Intranasal or intramuscular injections of midazolam have been associated with reduced vocalizations, flight, and defense responses, and is reversible with flumazenil (Mans et al., 2012; Sadegh, 2013; Schaffer et al., 2017). Minimize rapid movements and noise around the parrot during medical procedures. Dimming lights may also help. Probably the most important factor is to proceed rapidly with gentle technique. It is critical that you read the bird's body language and interrupt the procedure if the animal shows signs of distress. Finally, always focus on what is relevant to the situation, and avoid unnecessary procedures that would lengthen handling time.

Training cooperative care

Most parrots are easily trainable, regardless of whether they were hand-raised or parent-raised. If the bird will accept treats, owners can be shown how to start the training process with very simple behaviors that can be taught during the consultation (Cook, 2012).

To train turning around on a perch, first lure the bird with a treat, then put the behavior on a finger cue. When the parrot understands that his behavior controls the treat delivery, a variety of useful behaviors can be trained. These include getting under a towel, offering feet for nail trim, opening the beak, targeting to stand still during auscultation, opening the wings, and voluntarily taking water from a syringe. The author recommends training birds to take water from a syringe and get a food reward after the drinking behavior is offered. (See the description in the previous section on training rodents to drink from a syringe; the procedure is the same.) If the bird is trained to drink fruit juice from a syringe and expects the syringe content to be the reward, the behavior can quickly extinguish when a less tasty liquid has to be administered. If trained to drink a neutral liquid such as water and expect a reward afterwards, birds are more likely to tolerate the poor taste of medication, as they expect to be rewarded after drinking. If the bird has a syringe phobia, it can help to place food such as peanut butter on the tip of the syringe.

Though counterconditioning and desensitization can work to help birds learn to tolerate being held in a towel, training them to voluntarily get into the towel often offers more long-term benefits. The bird can start by moving into a large tunnel made with the towel. Gradually reduce the diameter of the tunnel until the bird makes his own way under the towel to get to the treat.

Training can be more difficult in birds with previous negative experience with humans, towels, syringes, or veterinary procedures. Fearful and anxious birds might refuse to interact positively with humans and may refuse to take treats. In these situations, we recommend starting the training process in protected contact.

By placing the bird in a cage or another environment where he knows that he cannot be caught or hurt, you will increase his feeling of security, and therefore the likelihood that he will take treats offered through the bars. As an added benefit, the fact that the parrot has no physical opportunity to bite increases the human's confidence in the training. At any time, the bird is allowed to move away from the trainer with no negative consequences. He will quickly learn that this set up allows for safe delivery of treats. When the parrot consistently accepts treats in this context, basic behaviors can be taught through the bars, such as presenting feet, taking water from a syringe, or any easy behavior, even if not medically relevant. The parrot will come to understand the process of positive reinforcement training and will gain trust in the trainer. When the bird and trainer relationship is strong enough in protected contact, trained behaviors can be practiced outside of the cage.

Companion ectotherms

Gentle physical restraint

As with mammals and birds, the least amount of restraint is ideal in reptiles. Small reptiles can escape the handler and injury may result. Observe the animal in a transparent box to accomplish a very good initial evaluation of the body condition, skin, shell, limbs, external masses, celomic distension, swelling, spinal malformations, breathing pattern, lameness, etc. Snakes can be placed in a transparent tube to avoid coiling.

Remember to adjust your reptile handling techniques to the species. Safety measures are important to avoid human injury with some species. The snouts of medium-sized and large crocodilians are routinely taped to prevent biting. Take care to leave the tape on only when handling is required and not for prolonged periods of time. Should the crocodilian require a long, fearful and/or painful procedure, sedation should be considered.

Handling techniques for lizards share some similarities with avian techniques. Apply a firm but gentle hold, with pressure being released when the animal remains in the appropriate position. Lizards should never be held by the tail, as many species can perform autotomy.

Many techniques have been described on how to get a chelonian out of her shell for a physical examination. Most of them involve applying pressure or a fearful stimulus or using physical strength (i.e., pushing on a leg to get the head out, pulling on legs, presenting an object in front of the beak in order to get the turtle to get her head outside of the shell to bite the threatening object, etc.). These techniques are often successful but are likely associated with stress. Consider sedation if prolonged or forceful handling is required. Allowing snakes to wrap around an object or an arm, if appropriate, appears to decrease struggling and escape behaviors during the examination. Handle amphibians with care, using non-powdered gloves and dechlorinated water. Most of them are rarely handled by their owners and are likely to be very stressed during physical examination.

Adjustments to decrease stress during procedures

It can be challenging to keep reptiles in their optimal temperature range during a physical examination or a procedure performed at room temperature. Abrupt changes of temperatures can be stressful to them. Place them on a warm pad or bag, or work in a ward kept at 80 to 82 degrees Fahrenheit (26-28°C) in order to decrease cold stress. Minimize environmental noises, movements and light to decrease fear in reptiles during procedures. Focus on what is the most important for the animal to reduce handling time and stress. For example, for oral examination, adapt your instrument selection to be appropriate for the animal. For smaller species, a small piece of cardboard is preferred over a standard metal beak opener.

Though reptiles can often be physically restrained for imaging or medical procedures, their level of stress should be taken into consideration. Midazolam and midazolam in combination with alfaxolone or alpha-2 agonists led to a decrease in heart rate and provide sedation and muscle relaxation in many reptilian species (Bisetto, Melo, and Carregaro, 2018; Doss et al., 2017; Larouche et al., 2019). Sedation with midazolam has also been shown to reduce handling-associated acidosis and a faster return to normal behavior after handling in captive estuarine crocodiles (Olsson and Phalen, 2013) There are no scientific reasons to perform procedures under physical restraint in a reptile with no sedation if the same technique would be ethically non-acceptable in a mammal or a bird.

One technique that is used with reptiles but has not been validated in relation to the level of stress is the use of the vasovagal response in some lizard species to induce a temporary immobility. When gentle digital pressure is applied to both orbits (after protecting them with cotton balls for example), many iguanid lizards will enter a state of 'torpor' and remain perfectly immobile until they are 'woken up' by a movement, a noise or a painful stimulus.

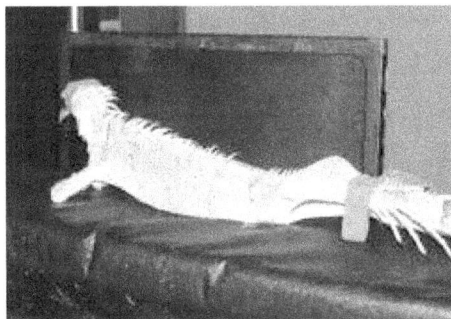

A green iguana immobilized with the vasovagal response to take radiographs.

This response allows taking of radiographs in very flighty reptilian species such as basilisks. As a vagal reflex is induced, heart rate is probably decreased and we can hypothesize that the stress level of the animal is low, but this has not been demonstrated yet. The initial pressure applied may be painful. Therefore, more studies are required before considering this technique to reduce stress in reptiles during procedures.

Training cooperative care
Reptile biomedical training uses the same principles as previously mentioned for small mammals and birds, operant conditioning with positive reinforcement. It can be more challenging to find a good and efficient reinforcer though, especially with large species who may eat only every few weeks. Food items are most commonly used, but

other reinforcers such as scratching can be used in some chelonians. Most companion reptiles can be trained to voluntarily enter a crate, to target and stand still, and walk onto a scale. They can be trained to stand still for nail clipping or ultrasound, and less commonly for venipuncture. Routine handling with positive reinforcement at home is likely to reduce restraint-associated stress in the hospital. A Clik Stik or equivalent is a useful tool to train reptiles and amphibians to follow a target.

Understanding the special bond between small companion animals and their humans

Owner attachment for small companion animals is definitely not related to the animal's size or retail value. Many exotic animal veterinarians can recall owners spending several thousands of dollars on their chicken, dove or bearded dragon. Though attachment might differ in some ways between exotic companions and more traditional ones, the basis of the human-animal relationships remains the same. Attachment is a normal process in social species and is deemed necessary for normal development in multiple species including humans (Fonagy and Target, 1997). Ownership provides humans with social support, no matter the species involved (Serpell, 2003). Animals of all kinds are non-judgmental and provide a listening ear. Many people consider their animal companions to be family members.

Relationships with animals have largely been shown to be beneficial for human physical and emotional health, lowering blood pressure and heart rate, reducing anxiety levels, and improving social skills (Chan and Ricco, 2019; Serpell, 2003; Uchino, 2006). Attachment style has been studied extensively in dogs and only recently in cats and deserves further evaluation in exotic animal companions (Vitale, Behnke, and Udell, 2019).

Small companion mammals

Ferrets are playful and social animals, bringing daily joy to their owners. Many ferret owners are dedicated to the species and share their lives with several individuals. They can take them on a harness and a leash outside like a dog and can cuddle with them like cats.

Rabbits are calm, soft and gentle pets. Many rabbits will spend time on their owner's lap, appearing to enjoy being petted and massaged. Rat owners enjoy the high cognitive function of their companions. Rats can be trained to perform tricks. They are playful, interactive and social animals. They are easy to carry around and can spend a lot of time staying with their owners every day. Unfortunately, rats are a short-lived species, and enduring the repeated loss of their very close companions can be devastating for some rat owners.

Other rodent species can be shyer, but if individuals are trained with positive reinforcement, they can become great companions. Even when hamsters, gerbils and guinea pigs spend most of the time in their cages without being handled, children can develop a very strong attachment to them. They feed and care for them on a daily basis. They observe their behavior and learn to know them very well. Parents may witness the attachment without sharing it, but many adults also develop strong bonds with rodent companions. Chinchillas can live for more than ten years and be associated with various life events that will make them emotionally important for the family.

Companion birds

Acquiring a parrot can be the result of a thorough reflection and research linked to a true interest in developing a relationship with a potential companion, or it can be the consequence of an impulsive act resulting from the attraction to a colorful bird. Some people become rapidly disenchanted if ill-informed about the nature of psittacine birds, and welfare concerns can ensue. However, most parrot owners dedicate a considerable amount of time and resources to their birds and develop a very special bond with them. Species like parrots, with higher cognitive function, can learn to talk, to count, to express their emotions using human words, and will deliberately perform behaviors that increase the depth of interaction they have with their humans.

Most wild psittacine birds live in pairs, and it is not uncommon to see them develop a very special bond with one person in the household. This can become problematic if they start showing aggression towards other people, though aggression around their mate would be normal in the wild. Avian companions are not truly domesticated, but early imprinting causes them to become artificially attached to human beings. Though this is abnormal, and parent-raising should be encouraged to allow birds to develop normal avian behavior and social skills, many people develop very strong relationship with their imprinted birds, who may behave as if humans were their parents at first, then as if they were their mate. Parent-raised parrots trained by humans with positive reinforcement can be excellent pets as well, with more balanced relationships with other birds and humans.

Some species of parrots can live well over 40 years and will share a large part of their owner's lifetime. Some have cognitive skills similar to toddlers. They represent a major financial commitment and time investment. For all these reasons, there is no doubt that many people will develop a unique form of attachment to their companion birds, even beyond what is commonly seen with cats and dogs.

Companion ectotherms

Humans may choose reptiles as companions because of a biological fascination for the species or because of their ornamental value, but many people will develop a close relationship with their ectotherm pet (Wilkinson, 2019). Some reptiles such as tortoises can live as long as humans and may have been transferred through several generations of the same family. It is important to recognize that the emotional attachment someone has for a companion animal is not necessarily related to how reciprocal the attachment is. Always assume some level of emotional attachment when a reptile is brought to the hospital and refrain from any judgment (Wilkinson, 2019). Children especially can develop a very strong bond with their reptile or amphibian, and will often be very knowledgeable about the species, its environment, and request financial support from their parents to provide the best care for their pal.

Conclusions

Small companion mammals, pet birds and ectotherms are integral and well-loved members of many families. By understanding their behavior and needs, adjusting your practice for their welfare, and showing compassion to even the smallest animal of the day, you will make a difference in the lives of your patients and their caretakers, which in turn will be highly rewarding for your teams. All the basic behavior and welfare principles discussed throughout this book also apply to exotic animals. They should not be considered different because they are smaller or behave differently. As with all of our patients, they deserve our compassion and highest standards of care, as they are distinctive beings holding a very special place in their owners' hearts.

Chapter 13
Palliative Care and Euthanasia

By Dr. Cherie T. Buisson, DVM, CHPV, Certified Hospice and
Palliative Care Veterinarian, Certified Silver Low Stress Handling
and Restraint, QPR Suicide Prevention Certified
And Meagan Montmeny, CPDT-KA, Certified Silver Low Stress
Handling and Restraint

"We know that many clients are as neurochemically connected to their pets as they are to their human family members. Facilitating a good-bye that honors that bond is one of the most important things we can do for them." Dr. Patrick Flynn, DVM, MS.

Helping the client to say good-bye

Preparing to say goodbye to our animal companions can lead to confusing emotions ranging from fear and anxiety to guilt and shame and sometimes even relief. While none of these emotions are wrong, they can overwhelm us as we explore palliative care and admit to ourselves and others that euthanasia or death is coming. It is not unusual for people to mourn the loss of an animal companion more deeply than losing a human member of the family (King, 2011; Reisbig, et al., 2017). After all, our animals accompany us through milestones in our lives as an unconditional support system. Throughout this chapter, we will be offering a variety of ways to honor the bond you and your family members share and discussing ways to make your companion's final days a little easier on everyone. First, we will focus on families preparing to say goodbye. Second, we will address the role of veterinary professionals. Third, we will talk about other animal care professionals such as pet sitters, trainers, boarding service providers, and groomers.

The most fear-filled and emotional visit to the vet clinic is likely the last visit - the one where we say goodbye via humane euthanasia. While patients may not perceive it as different from any other visit, the behavior of their owners can transmit a heightened level of stress and fear (Sundman et al., 2019). Our animal companions are highly social animals who enjoy our company. We share a special bond, and studies have shown stress levels in dogs will mirror that of their owners (Sundman, 2019). If you find yourself reading this chapter and knowing that goodbye is coming for a beloved family member, our hearts go out to you. We hope that we can help you on this journey.

Giving them a gentle, peaceful good-bye

A frequent theme reported among home euthanasia veterinarians is that clients love their veterinarians, but the clinic becomes a scary place when they think of bringing companions there to pass. "Cold," "sterile," "stainless steel table," and "noisy" are all words used to describe the place that they once felt comfortable bringing their animal. As the owner's perception of the clinic changes and their stress rises, the stress of the patient may rise as well. Because of their heightened stress, the owner may notice their companion is more stressed. It is a vicious cycle that can result in trauma to both patient and owner even if everything goes as smoothly as possible. We hope to ease the client's fear and at the same time help the patient remain as stress-free as possible during this last part of their life. Euthanasia and death are difficult and sad for everyone, so empathy and compassion are key. You can help your clients understand that the most important aspect of compassion (and the most frequently ignored) is compassion for themselves. Encourage them to treat themselves as they would a friend who is preparing for a loss.

Self-care for your human clients

Anticipatory grief is one of the great thieves of quality time spent with a beloved animal companion at the end of life and interferes with our ability to process grief in a healthy way (Nielsen et al., 2016). We know goodbye is coming, but we don't know exactly when. We may find ourselves crying easily, feeling intense loneliness, or even reacting with anger. It's also easy to find ourselves avoiding the companion so we don't upset them with our grief or so that we don't have to witness their struggles. We may forget to treasure the little moments because we are anticipating when our companion will no longer be with us.

There are support resources available that you can share with clients, not only after a loss but during this early time of turmoil. The Association for Pet Loss and Bereavement (www.aplb.org) has an online anticipatory grief chat once weekly. Day By Day Pet Caregiver Support has a hotline clients can call to talk about their impending loss (484-453-8210). This has a dual benefit - a support system during the rigorous caretaking required at end of life and a built-in, familiar support network once the companion is gone. During this time, it's important for the client to have good self-care and coping mechanisms. Many won't be sleeping due to their animal's nighttime needs or behaviors. Encourage them to ask you to address pain and anxiety in their companion. Lack of sleep is unhealthy for both client and patient and is a serious compromise of everyone's quality of life.

Lack of sleep and special accommodations being made for the patient may put your client at odds with other family members. This can make an already isolating situation markedly worse. Families sometimes gang up on the patient's main caretaker – either demanding the companion be euthanized or demanding that the caretaking continue even when euthanasia is clearly the appropriate and compassionate decision. The latter situation is extraordinarily unfair, especially when other members of the family refuse to take equal responsibility for the patient's needs. The primary (or especially the only) caretaker's opinion should carry the most weight in decision-making unless their devotion to the patient is becoming unhealthy or overlooking the needs of the animal. In this case, a mental health professional should be consulted – although this can be a difficult subject to broach with the client. It is difficult for the caretaker to evaluate their beloved companion's health and wellbeing when they are sleep-deprived, emotional, stressed, bereft and unhealthy.

Helping your client with the euthanasia decision

If you are aware that your client is having difficulties, help them understand that asking for help is a sign of strength and can lead to better choices. Reluctance or desire to euthanize a companion isn't wrong but healing from loss is easier when family members are on the same page. Practicing empathy, actively listening and trying to remain open to your clients' feelings are excellent ways to make sure your patients are receiving the best care possible. In most cases, family members are making decisions out of love, even if fear and anger are hiding the underlying emotion.

Among the many feelings your client may experience is an enormous sense of doubt. "How will I know it's time to say goodbye, and if it is too early - or too late?" The 'perfect time' doesn't exist, and you can help your clients realize the importance of not holding themselves to this impossible standard. There is a zone between 'too early' and 'too late,' and if we can target that zone, then decision making will be less stressful. If we add good palliative care to alleviate discomfort, then the zone becomes wider, sometimes resulting in a peaceful, natural passing. The more animal companions a client has, the more experience they gain in gauging the time that's best for everyone. Even trained professionals look back and think they didn't get it right, so help your clients go easy on themselves. The best thing you can do for your clients is to help them and their beloved animal prepare ahead of time for their final journey together (Nielsen et al., 2016).

Share these questions with your client:

- What do I want this end-of-life journey to look like for my companion?

- Am I willing to say goodbye in the middle of a crisis or emergency situation?

- Am I willing to come home and find my companion deceased (note that there may be obvious signs the animal passed in distress)?

- Do I want to be with my companion at the end?

- Do I want the passing to happen at home or at another chosen spot?

- Do I have other human or non-human family members that should be present?

- Do I want the passing to happen at the vet's office?

- What are my lines in the sand for conditions that will prompt me to euthanize?

- Do I have a palliative care plan (being overseen by a veterinarian) in place to address my companion's discomfort?

Clients often express a wish that their companion would just curl up in bed and pass peacefully on their own. Sometimes this wish prevents them from seeing the pain, anxiety, or other distress being experienced by the animal. Help them realize that a veterinarian should be involved in end-of-life care to help address these issues. Encourage your client to have open and honest conversations with you. It is amazing how talking about fears makes things less intimidating.

You can help ease your client's doubts by supplying science-based explanations for your patient's medical conditions. If your client expresses concern that the patient is uncomfortable, please listen to them and be patient when explaining treatment options. For some reason, many clients perceive that sedation or grogginess from medication is worse than pain. Maybe it's because animals hide their pain so well, but sedation is more obvious. Assure your client that adjustments can be made to medication protocols that are too sedating, and that many medications have fewer sedative side effects once the patient becomes accustomed to them. Please don't let your client deprive their companion of pain medication over fear of sedation. An alert, painful pet in distress is not our goal.

While pain is an important issue, we can also help the client address all areas of the patient's life. Physical, emotional, and psychosocial aspects are all important. Help the client understand that their companion's body, mind, and interaction with the world around them are all important pieces of their quality of life. While no one expects animals to act the same at six months as they do at 16 years of age, comparing the richness of their life in their youth versus how they are now can show the client what has been lost.

Quality of life scales can help simplify an animal companion's complex life into measurable and observable behaviors for your client. However, be cautious of relying on these scales too heavily. It's tempting for the client to give the patient a "grade" and make a particular grade into a boundary for the euthanasia decision. These situations are far more complicated than a quality-of-life scale can assess. We recommend using these scales as a conversation starter to see where the patient currently stands, and to give the client a tool to identify disagreements among family members. Have all caretakers take the quality-of-life survey separately and then compare the answers to see where controversy and agreement lie. The following chart asks owners to rate their companion on a scale of one through ten.

Quality of life evaluation tool

Determine a score of 0 to 10 for each factor. A higher score indicates a better quality of life for each factor.

HURT - Adequate pain control & breathing ability is of top concern. Trouble breathing outweighs all concerns. Is the pet's pain well managed? Can the pet breathe properly? Is oxygen supplementation necessary? Score:

HUNGER - Is the pet eating enough? Does hand feeding help? Does the pet need a feeding tube? Score:

HYDRATION - Is the pet dehydrated? For patients not drinking enough water, use subcutaneous fluids daily or twice daily to supplement fluid intake. Score:

HYGIENE - The pet should be brushed and cleaned, particularly after elimina-tions. Avoid pressure sores with soft bedding and keep all wounds clean. Score:

HAPPINESS - Does the pet express joy and interest? Is the pet responsive to family, toys, etc.? Is the pet depressed, lonely, anxious, bored or afraid? Can the pet's bed be moved to be close to family activities? Score:

MOBILITY - Can the pet get up without assistance? Does the pet need human or mechanical help (e.g., a cart)? Does the pet feel like going for a walk? Is the pet having seizures or stumbling? (Some caregivers feel eutha-nasia is preferable to amputation, but an animal with limited mobility yet still alert, happy and responsive can have a good quality of life as long as caregivers are committed to helping their pet.) Score:

MORE GOOD DAYS THAN BAD - When bad days outnumber good days, quality of life might be too compromised. When a healthy human-animal bond is no longer possible, the caregiver must be made aware that the end is near. The decision for euthanasia needs to be made if the pet is suffering. If death comes peacefully and painlessly at home, that is okay. Score:

A total over 35 points represents an acceptable life quality to continue with pet hospice (Pawspice).
(Villalobos, 2004)

As an alternative, they can use a calendar to mark good days versus bad days or track activities the patient used to enjoy. Help them understand that toward the end, good and bad may break down into hours or even minutes. Visiting www.pethospice.com is another excellent way to get support for evaluating a companion's quality of life.

Encourage your clients to ask themselves, "What would my companion be missing if they weren't here tomorrow?" (Buisson, 2018) and to carefully list both good and bad aspects of the patient's day. Having this conversation with family members and trusted friends can provide another level of support and understanding. If family members and friends are not available or not supportive, your veterinary team and mental health professionals can assist the client.

Clients regularly report that they don't think their companion is in pain because they are not crying. Chronic pain rarely results in whining or crying unless the animal falls down, is lifted in a painful way, or has an acute aggravation of the pain. Most patients with chronic pain will change their behavior to avoid doing things that hurt. This can be so subtle and slow that your client may not even notice. The quality-of-life survey on Dr. Buisson's web page uses a checklist of behaviors to help you help them determine if their four-legged family member is uncomfortable. You can visit www. helpinghandspethospice.com/quality-of-life/ to learn more.

Over-the-counter remedies or single pain medications are rarely enough to make chronic pain bearable in its end stages. Multimodal pain protocols involving various medications, supplements, and procedures (such as laser therapy or acupuncture) are usually necessary. Educate your client that just because their companion isn't com-plaining doesn't mean they are comfortable. Also help them realize that eating, tail wagging, and spending time with the family aren't all that is necessary for a good quality of life. Animal companions need mental stimulation and modified activities to reduce frustration and depression, and to maintain quality of life.

Behavioral Euthanasia

Sadly, medical end-of-life decisions are not the only reasons your clients might need euthanasia services. Behavioral euthanasia is an all-too-common reality in today's world, and it is a critically important service for veterinary practitioners to provide.

You are most likely to see dogs with significant behavioral challenges, often inap-propriately placed in homes by shelters and rescue groups that are trying to "save them all." But you may also have clients who can no longer tolerate the cat who won't reliably use her litter box, birds or other small companion animals whose quality of life is severely compromised by fear, a horse who is putting human life at risk with excessive biting, kicking or bucking, or…

The behavioral euthanasia decision can be an excruciating one for your client. They are making the choice the end the life of their perfectly physically healthy compan-ion animal, and despite the behavioral challenges there is often a strong, emotional bond. Even when they have invested extensive time, energy and resources in trying to resolve the behavior issue, there may still be considerable guilt about making the decision. Maybe there is *something* more they could have done if the were able and willing to spend more time and money.

There is a wonderful resource you can share with your clients as well as fellow animal care professionals who are involved with behavioral euthanasia in any way. It's a Facebook group called "Losing Lulu," and is an exceptionally empathetic support group for those who have had to make or assist with this very difficult decision. You can find it here: https://www.facebook.com/search/top?q=losing%20lulu%20 facebook%20group

It is critically important that you provide your client with reassurances and emotional support. You have probably already given your client suggestions, resources and refer- rals to try to help them. Even if you think they could have done more, you need to accept that they haven't come to this decision lightly, and trying to talk them out of it will only cause them more pain. If you really believe it's a sudden, snap decision, you could gently offer to hold the patient overnight if they want some time to think it over, but if it's a behavioral issue they've been dealing with for some time, that's not likely the case. The same empathy and care you give your client for a medical euthanasia decision is absolutely called for here as well.

Explaining the euthanasia process

If the patient has reached a point where your client believes euthanasia is necessary, it may help them to know what the word actually means. Euthanasia comes from the Greek words meaning "good death" - not in the sense of the death being good for the grieving client, but that their beloved companion passes peacefully, with minimal discomfort. Of course, if a client experiences empathy and support from you, your staff and others, then they may be able to consider the experience in a positive light despite the heartbreak. It may also help them to think of euthanasia as a gift they are giving to their companion. Experiencing grief in order to allow their animal to be free from pain, embarrassing accidents, difficult body functions, and loss of independence and dignity is a worthy sacrifice.

Although many of us say that we would like for our pets to pass away naturally in their sleep, a natural death is not necessarily the best option for all animal companions. You can help your client understand this. To be fair, a true 'natural' death, would involve letting the companion outside, unprotected, where a predator could end their lives quickly, if unpleasantly. Being in a climate-controlled space with food and water provided (or even forced), being carried or assisted to eliminate, and being kept clean, all prolong the death that is inevitable. A natural death may involve distress, or last hours, days or even weeks. A hospice-assisted natural death is a much better option than an untreated natural death that could be prolonged and painful. As long as the patient's comfort and needs are being tended to by a veterinarian, your client may be able to fulfill their wish for a natural death for their companion with minimal suffering. Euthanasia before or when suffering occurs is also a good treatment option for terminal disease.

Perhaps one of the most challenging emotions a client faces when considering the death of their companion is that of relief. One of the authors (Meagan) recalls her own diabetic cat going into kidney failure and her decision to say goodbye. For five years, she'd lived her life around his twice daily insulin injections and careful monitor- ing of his diet and blood sugar. While she was heartbroken at losing him, there was also a feeling of freedom that it was acceptable for her to sleep in a little later or go to visit friends and get home later. It took a while for her to realize that it was fine to feel relieved and that Gus would have thanked her for not allowing him to suffer. She took comfort in the fact that she'd honored her promise to prevent suffering and also given him one final gift of love in the process. In other words, she loved him enough to let him go but also to take on that pain so he wouldn't have to.

As hard as it may be for them, you can help your client try to visualize what they want their companion's final day to look like. Are they able to visit a favorite spot together? Are there friends or family who would like to say goodbye and spend some quiet time together? Are there special foods they might enjoy?

Meagan's diabetic cat was allowed to have cream cheese and cat treats that were normally off-limits, and he enjoyed every minute he got to eat them. It is a bittersweet moment for clients to see their animal companion enjoy something forbidden and know there will be no consequences tomorrow.

Deciding whether to be with a companion at the time of euthanasia is fraught with emotion and controversy for your client. You can help them with this decision by gently explaining how the procedure works, what they are likely to see, and what the patient will experience (Reck, 2012). Encourage them to be present if they think they are able to do so and support their decision not to be there if they realize they can't do it. If they can't or don't want to be present for euthanasia, suggest that they consider staying through the sedation process and then leaving once the patient is asleep. There are studies that show having their trusted human by their side helps to ease fear in companion animals (Villalobos, 2004).

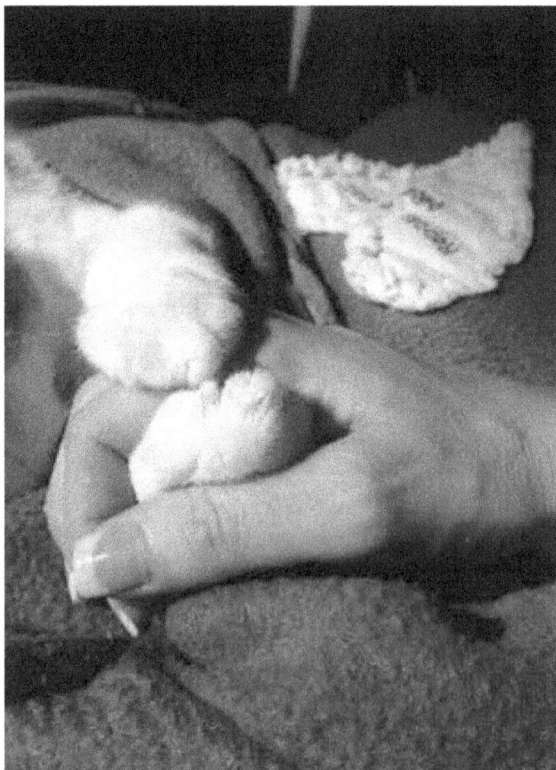

The veterinarian spends a moment holding the paws of a deceased patient.

Different clinics handle the last visit in different ways. Have a standard euthanasia protocol for your clinic that your veterinary team is familiar with so things will go smoothly when the time comes for a patient to leave this world. Here are some questions you can answer to help ease your client's fears:

- Can the client stay with the patient throughout the process? Can the client hold the patient during the process?
- Will the patient be sedated prior to euthanasia?
- Will the patient receive an IV catheter (if so, is this done in the client's presence)?
- How much time will the client have with the patient, both before and after the procedure?
- Will the client receive any memorial items?
- Is there medication that can be given to the patient ahead of time for the ride to the office?

Be prepared to answer any other questions your client might ask, to help them feel more comfortable.

Burial or cremation?

Another decision your client will have to make is how to handle their animal companion after death. Cremation is a common choice. Burial at home (if local ordinances allow), burial in a pet cemetery, and aquamation (water-based cremation) are all options you can offer to your client. Your client may elect to have the patient cremated privately with ashes returned to them, or they may decide they do not want the ashes. Most importantly, there is no right or wrong answer. Help them consider their options ahead of time so they don't have to make a snap decision that might result in regret or family conflict and support whatever decision they may make.

Your client needs to know that processing grief is individual and complicated. There is no straight line to feeling normal again, and no right way to work through the emotions. Support groups and mental health professionals are excellent resources to provide to your client and let them know there are steps they can take that may help ease the pain.

Remind them to be patient and allow themselves to go through the process, taking whatever time they need. If there are children in the family, suggest they avoid phrases like "putting the companion to sleep" or "putting him down." This terminology can be confusing to children and make them fearful of going to sleep at night. It is best to be honest with children that their beloved companion is very ill, and that we have a way to end their suffering in a very gentle way. Please share our references below with your client for book recommendations that help explain death to children.

Books to explain death, coping, and emotions to children:

The Invisible String by Patrice Karst

I Heard Your Dog Died by Bonnie Kreitler

Peaceful Piggy Meditation by Kerry Lee Maclean

Jasper's Day by Marjorie Blain Parker

The Goodbye Book by Todd Parr

When a Pet Dies by Fred Rogers

When I Feel Sad by Cornelia Maude Spelman

Badger's Parting Gifts by Susan Varley

The Day Tiger Rose Said Goodbye by Jane Yolen

Processing grief

Here are some suggestions you can share with clients for tangible ways to process grief:

- Write a letter to your beloved companion - thank them and reminisce.
- Have a funeral.
- Plant a tree or bush.
- Scatter your animal's ashes in a special place (check your local ordinances).
- Have a memorial item (necklace, sculpture, etc.) made from or with your companion's ashes.
- Make a scrapbook- there are lots of internet websites to help.
- Draw or paint your beloved companion or a reflection of your feelings about them.
- Write a memorial of your companion to put online so your family and friends can share your grief and support you.
- Ask friends and family members to make a donation to your favorite animal charity in your beloved animal companion's name.

Educating the veterinary professional

End of life is challenging to navigate. We encourage all veterinary professionals to take some time to learn more about hospice and palliative care through the International Association for Animal Hospice and Palliative Care (www.IAAHPC.org) and the World Veterinary Palliative Medicine Organization (www.WVPMO.org). It is in the best interests of clients and patients to provide care in the space between a terminal/quality of life limiting diagnosis and euthanasia/death. Clients need an enormous amount of support when making decisions for their companion's future. If you feel you can't provide this type of service, please refer your client to someone who does, or consult with a Certified Hospice and Palliative Care Veterinarian and become familiar with this extremely rewarding work (https://learn.iaahpc.org/find-help-now).

As veterinary professionals, the grief we face at losing a patient can be intense. Your team has likely put a great deal of effort into protecting the health of this patient, often throughout her lifetime, and saying goodbye can feel like a failure. While veterinary teams may be accustomed to euthanizing multiple patients in a week or even in a day, each one leaves a wound that takes time to heal. Fitting clients in for a euthanasia on a busy day can leave you feeling guilty and stressed. Consider partnering with a home-based palliative care/euthanasia service or a local mobile veterinarian so you can offer that option to your clients. You can use www.inhomepeteuthanasia.com or www.pethospice.com to locate these services in your area. That way, when your client calls for euthanasia, you are prepared to assist them as compassionately as possible. Coach your receptionists to respond as follows:

- Express sympathy - be sure the words "I am so sorry" are said to every client.

- Offer options - "We can schedule you (today, tomorrow, etc.) or we can give you the phone number of someone who comes to your home to help you say goodbye. Which would you prefer?" Although home euthanasia is becoming more popular, clients often haven't heard of this service. Euthanasia is stressful for staff as well as clients and pets. Sometimes if we move this procedure to the comfort of home, everyone benefits.

- Have prices ready and try not to put clients on hold. Cheerful on-hold music is the last thing a client in this position wants to hear.

- Offer to let clients pay ahead of time if this works for your practice. Otherwise, handle it when you deal with all the other paperwork prior to euthanasia, so they can just leave when they are ready.

- Handling payment in the euthanasia room rather than the lobby can ensure client privacy and keep them with their pet for the entire visit.

Guiding clients through the end-of-life process requires excellent communication skills and empathy. Traumatic memories, like those from an intense grief, are highly volatile, and things we say and do can be remembered very differently by a client compared to what we recall. Remember that listening is the most important aspect of communication. Don't be afraid of silence. It is not necessary or appropriate to continue talking to fill every minute. Allow your client to guide your interaction. Additionally, provide only as much education as your client prefers. Some will want to know every detail (the medication, how it works, what sedative should be used, etc.) while others are happier not knowing. As you are talking with clients, remember that grief can appear as anger, silence, or any other seemingly inappropriate reaction including indifference. At the core of it all is a deep hurt the client may not know how to process or express and a new perception of you and your clinic as being frightening. Barring abuse or violence, client grief behavior shouldn't be taken personally. Most of us wouldn't want to be judged by our behavior on our worst day.

Some clinics have a separate grieving room apart from the clinic with a separate entrance or an outside space which can be a novel and pleasant experience for clients. If the patient has never seen this space before and it is as free as possible from clinical triggers, then they are less likely to associate it with the hospital setting. When decorating the space, aim to create a homey rather than clinical feel, to help make both the client and the patient more comfortable.

Many thrift stores have couches, rugs and small lamps that you can purchase inexpensively to help create a soothing space. Sit in an exam room, tune in to the noises you hear and imagine you are saying goodbye to your beloved companion. Implement noise reduction techniques through architecture, or with fountains or white noise machines to block out some of the less pleasant aspects of the clinic. Develop a protocol to let everyone in the clinic know that a euthanasia is taking place. You can dim lights, place a candle on the counter or create a sign as signals to reduce unpleasant ambient noise such as loud voices.

As discussed in previous chapters, species-specific pheromones may be applied via diffusers or sprayed on objects to help the patient feel more relaxed.

Offer the client the option of remaining with their companion throughout the entire visit by keeping the patient in the room to place a catheter. According to a 2017 study by Csoltova et al., having an owner pet and talk to their dog reduced the patient's heart rate and temperature during a vet visit. This finding highlights the true importance of the human-animal bond, but also helps ease owner fears of something happening out of their sight. For liability reasons, the guardian should generally not be allowed to restrain a patient during a painful or unpleasant procedure (i.e., injection, rectal temperature) unless they are a trained professional. Allow a technician or assistant to hold the patient while the client is nearby or have them offer special treats during handling. In cases where the veterinarian does not have assistance, sedation (oral, transmucosal, injectable, or a combination) in combination with food distraction (if the patient is eating and not nauseated/vomiting) should be used to keep everyone safe. If you feel you must place a catheter, consider giving the patient a pain medication/sedative cocktail first to reduce stress and pain.

The Human-Animal Bond is so important. Proper support during end-of-life helps preserve this Bond and reduce complicated grief.

When working with patients, we recommend Dr. Yin's Low Stress Handling and Restraint Techniques (Yin, 2009). Especially for the euthanasia visit, sedation and anesthesia can reduce or eliminate the need for muzzling or restraint. Having the client give medications at home can greatly reduce stress on all parties involved in the appointment.

If a muzzle must be used, use it only long enough to sedate or anesthetize the patient and then remove it. If the patient is truly a danger to the staff and owner, leaving the muzzle on is acceptable. Frightened cats can either be sedated in their carrier or wrapped in a towel using one of Dr. Yin's techniques. Once they are tucked in using a towel wrap, allow the client to hold their companion. Remember that injectable medications may be administered through the mesh of a soft carrier or the door or holes in a hard carrier. Gravity can guide the cat to the front of the carrier, or a fluffy blanket can be inserted into the front of the carrier to guide the patient to one of the holes at the back of the carrier. The soft carrier can be pushed gently down until the cat is confined in an appropriate spot. Remember that all the rules of handling frightened patients (and people) apply during euthanasia procedures. Soft voices and gentle words should be used, and if you are becoming frustrated, ask a team member to take your place.

Grieving is a process, and it's normal to feel bad for a client who has had to part with their beloved companion. Each time we help a patient pass, we also suffer trauma. Over time, these can accumulate and result in burnout and compassion fatigue. It is critical that we take the time to care for ourselves and to allow ourselves to feel the hurt. Ignoring grief or stifling emotions are temporary fixes that generally result in more damage to our own mental health. Coping skills are vital for veterinary professionals, and sometimes that means seeing a mental health professional to develop strategies to deal with daily trauma.

For stressful feelings that are not a crisis, consider going for a walk, calling a friend, eating a healthy meal, taking a lunch break, drinking water, or sitting and crying until the feeling passes. Maybe take a moment and write a letter to the owner, sharing a memory you have of their companion. Many clients will appreciate receiving a personal letter from you talking about their beloved animal. Please avoid phrases like, "She's in a better place now." While the sentiment is meant to explain the patient being free from pain, it is very easy for a client to hear that the best place for their animal was not with them. You can send the letter to the client or not, depending on how you feel.

It's a lovely gesture to contact the client a few days after they've said goodbye. You can check to see how they're doing and reassure yourself that they are healing. Occasionally, we find clients doing very poorly after a loss. Have resources ready to help those who are grief-stricken or even suicidal. QPR training (Question, Persuade, Refer — www.qprinstitute.com) is recommended for all veterinary professionals, to prepare them to assist their clients and each other in a crisis. Do remember that euthanasia – a good death – is often the last kind service we can provide for our patients.

Some of us are simply unable to process euthanasia in the quantity required in practice. This is not a sign of weakness or a reflection of your abilities. All of us have areas where we shine. Lean into those areas and away from things that dull your finish. It is highly likely that someone in your practice shines in end-of-life situations and would gladly trade with you for a situation where you would excel and find fulfillment. Don't take that person for granted – make sure their emotional needs are also being met! If your job requires an amount of euthanasia that is unhealthy for you and you can't find ways to improve the situation, look for another, healthier path that suits you.

A discussion for other animal care professionals

Training and behavior professionals, groomers, pet sitters, and other animal care professionals are often the first people alerted to a health issue in an animal companion. Animals who are suddenly biting, growling, or hissing should be assessed for disease processes. Those who can't stand up well in the tub or on the grooming table or whose walks are suddenly shorter should also be examined by a veterinarian. Clients are quick to dismiss such things as "just getting old," but age is not a disease. The reason for this decline is often osteoarthritis, which is treatable and can extend the patient's quantity and quality of life. Regardless, there is always an underlying cause for animal companions, especially seniors, to change their behavior enough for humans to notice. Other animal care professionals are our first line of defense against unnecessary suffering. While a veterinarian may examine a patient once or twice a year, animal care professionals interact with them far more frequently, and with enough space in between visits to see changes that an owner who sees them daily may not notice.

Any time you see a client, we recommend asking if there have been any changes in their animal's health. Caretakers may well forget to tell you that Fluffy has heart failure, and that omission could prove dangerous while the patient is in your care. Pet sitters especially need to know a patient's diagnoses and history. If you have a problem and take your client's companion to their usual veterinarian, not knowing the history isn't a big issue. However, if you end up in the emergency room, that knowledge can mean the difference between life and death.

If you are boarding or pet-sitting, you should obtain your client's written consent in advance to provide medical care (including euthanasia if necessary), especially if they won't be reachable while they are gone. Have them provide their veterinarian with a copy of the paperwork, with added verbal instructions to allow you to make decisions for the animal if they cannot be reached. As the companion nears the end of life, regular conversations about quality of life and euthanasia decisions to be made in the owner's absence, if necessary, can prevent confusion, anxiety, and legal issues.

It can be daunting to broach the subject of their animal's health to a client. Express your concerns in a compassionate and nonjudgmental way to open their minds to seeing what you have observed. Inform them of your concerns just as you would a scab or sore on their skin or an observed lameness – with the intention of informing and assisting rather than pointing out a defect in their caretaking.

Clients often seek medical advice when their groomer or pet-sitter refuses to continue working with their pet. Groomers may decline service because the animal is trying to bite or because they fear injuring them. By then, the companion may be so debilitated that a return to anything near normal function is impossible. Some groomers will insist upon a veterinary visit before they will see the animal again. This is reasonable, but hopefully a gentle, honest conversation will result in a vet visit without having to resort to ultimatums. Speaking up early about an animal's health could result in that companion enjoying grooming or walks for many years to come.

The conversation might go something like this:

"Mrs. Smith, have you noticed that Max is tender in the hip area? He was very sensitive today in the tub and that's not like him at all. He also had some trouble standing up for his bath and nipped at me during his shaving. He's a good boy, so I know something must be painful for him to react that way."

If Mrs. Smith dismisses your concerns by saying Max is just getting old, let her know that this behavior tends to get worse rather than better, so addressing it quickly can help Max enjoy his spa day rather than becoming afraid of grooming. If Max is too painful for you to safely groom, be sure to let her know that he's going to need some pain medicine from his veterinarian before another grooming can be scheduled. Listen to your instincts and do not groom an animal who is showing you signs of discomfort or stress.

Pet-sitters may notice that walks are becoming shorter or breathing more labored during a visit. Loss of appetite, difficulty chewing, slow movements, lack of jumping – all of these are signs of disease that warrant a trip to the veterinarian's office. Since animals often have stress-related illnesses, a pet-sitter is unfortunately likely to see changes while owners are away.

If an animal you care for has to be euthanized or passes away naturally, don't be afraid to contact your client and offer your sympathy. Grieving humans may find themselves isolated and lonely because those around them fear the awkwardness that comes with talking to them. Most of us fear not knowing what to say in these situations. "I'm here for you," "I'm so sorry," and any fond memories you can share about their companion will suffice. Avoid phrases that minimize the depth of the loss like telling an owner their companion is in a better place, or they were old, or "only an animal." These phrases, while well-intentioned, can be received entirely differently than they were meant. Feel free to express your grief as well. Knowing that your animal companion is missed by others can be comforting.

Honoring the bond we share with our animal companions, patients and clients takes careful communication, teamwork, and good self-care as we help them transition. Our animals play a variety of roles in our lives from comedian to confidante, snuggle-buddy to running partner, but ensuring their needs are met can be exhausting. When we forget to give ourselves a break from caretaking in order to care for ourselves, our grief can transform into compassion fatigue or caregiver burnout. Here are some symptoms to watch for. Reach out as soon as you notice these behaviors in yourself (or in others) - they are important warning signs:

- Lacking energy
- Fatigue that is overwhelming
- Getting too much or too little sleep
- Gaining or losing weight; changes in eating habits
- Feeling hopeless
- Losing interest in, or withdrawing from, activities you once enjoyed
- Neglecting your own emotional or physical needs
- Feeling your life is being controlled by caregiving

- Becoming unusually irritable, impatient or angry with your animal companion and with others
- Difficulty coping with day-to-day activities
- Stomachaches, headaches and other pains or getting sick easily

(Compassion Fatigue Awareness Project, 2017)

Companion animals who have a team of owners and professionals looking out for them are lucky indeed. If we all remember that we want what is best for the animal and welcome the viewpoints of other team members, we can provide excellent care from the first day to the last. A knowledge of animal behavior is crucial to identify problems and seek solutions early. Knowing what is normal for a patient helps us easily identify when they are acting abnormally. If something a patient is doing makes you say "that's strange" – an investigation is indicated. Animals often tell us everything we need to know if we observe them closely and respond quickly to their calls for help. This understanding is part of our sacred bond with them and must always be respected.

Cited Works

Note: Cited works are listed alphabetically by the first listed author's last name or organization's name.

Ackerman, AE, Lloyd JA. Noise stress in laboratory rodents: Behavioral and endocrine responses of mice, rats, and guinea pigs. *J Acoust Soc Am* 1959; 31:1437–40.

AHLA. Assessing the health and welfare of laboratory animals. In *Practical Animal Handling in Small Mammals* (2019).

Amat, Marta et al. Use of dexmedetomidine hydrochloride oromucosal gel to reduce fear in dogs with noise phobias. Age (years) 2016, no. 3: 1-13.

ASPCA Pro. "Cat Kennel Spot Clean." Accessed on Nov 4, 2019: https://www.aspcapro.org/resource/video-how-spot-clean-cat-kennels. Drawings are downloadable.

American Veterinary Society of Animal Behavior. AVSAB position statement on positive veterinary care. 2016. Accessed Nov 2019: https://avsab.org/wp-content/uploads/2019/01/Positive-Veterinary-Care-Position-Statement-download.pdf.

Anseeuw, Erika, Carolyn Apker, Cheryl Ayscue, Leanne Barker, Don Blair, Jan Brennan, Steve Brooks et al. Handling cats humanely in the veterinary hospital. *Journal of Veterinary Behavior* 1, no. 2 (2006): 84-88.

Appleby D. *The APBC Book of Companion Animal Behaviour*. Souvenir Press; 2016. 320 p.

Araujo, Joseph A., Christina de Rivera, Jennifer L. Ethier, Gary M. Landsberg, Sagi Denenberg, Stephanie Arnold, and Norton W. Milgram. ANXITANE® tablets reduce fear of human beings in a laboratory model of anxiety-related behavior. *Journal of Veterinary Behavior* 5, no. 5 (2010): 268-275.

Arts, JWM. The impact of transportation on physiological and behavioral parameters in Wistar Rats: Implications for acclimatization periods. | *The ILAR Journal* [Internet]. watermark.silverchair.com. 2012 [cited 2019 Oct 2]. pp. 1–17.

ASPCA. "Cat Body Language." (ASPCApro.org,n.d.)

Barlow, N., and D. Goodwin. Efficacy of dog appeasing pheromone (DAP) in reducing stress related responses in rescue shelter dogs. *Proceedings of the Companion Animal Behaviour Therapy Study Group Study Day* (2009).

Bassett, Lois, and Hannah M. Buchanan-Smith. Effects of predictability on the welfare of captive animals. *Applied Animal Behaviour Science* 102, no. 3-4 (2007): 223-245.

Beata, Claude, Edith Beaumont-Graff, Christian Diaz, Muriel Marion, Nicolas Massal, Nathalie Marlois, Gérard Muller, and Catherine Lefranc. Effects of alpha-casozepine (Zylkene) versus selegiline hydrochloride (Selgian, Anipryl) on anxiety disorders in dogs. *Journal of Veterinary Behavior* 2, no. 5 (2007): 175-183.

Beaver, Bonnie V. *Canine Behavior: A Guide for Veterinarians*. WB Saunders, 1999.

Beaver, Bonnie. 2003. *Feline Behavior: A Guide for Veterinarians*. 2nd ed. St. Louis, MO: Saunders.

Beck, A., X. De Jaeger, J. F. Collin, and V. Tynes. Effect of a synthetic feline phero-mone for managing unwanted scratching. *Int J Appl Res Vet Med* 16 (2018): 13-27.

Becker, Marty, Mikkel Becker, and Lisa Radosta. *From Fearful to Free*. Health Com-munications, 2017.

Bednarski, Richard, Kurt Grimm, Ralph Harvey, Victoria M. Lukasik, W. Sean Penn, Brett Sargent, and Kim Spelts. AAHA anesthesia guidelines for dogs and cats. *Journal of the American Animal Hospital Association* 47, no. 6 (2011): 377-385.

Beerda, B., M. B. Schilder, J. A. Van Hooff, H. W. De Vries, and J. A. Mol. Behavioural and hormonal indicators of enduring environmental stress in dogs. *Animal Welfare-Potters Bar-* 9, no. 1 (2000): 49-62.

Belew, A.M., Barlett T., and S.A. Brown. Evaluation of the white-coat effect in cats. *J Vet Intern Med* (1999;13:134–42).

Belkin, Michael, U. Yinon, L. Rose and I. Reisert. 1977. Effect of visual environment on refractive error of cats. *Documenta Ophthalmologica* 42, no. 2 (February): 433-437.

Berger, Jeannine. Feline aggression toward people 911. In *Feline Internal Medicine Volume 7*, Susan Little editor. Elsevier, 2014.

Berns, Gregory S., Andrew M. Brooks, and Mark Spivak. Scent of the familiar: an fMRI study of canine brain responses to familiar and unfamiliar human and dog odors. *Behavioural Processes* 110 (2015): 37-46.

Bhatia, Vikram, and Rakesh K. Tandon. Stress and the gastrointestinal tract. *Journal of Gastroenterology and Hepatology* 20, no. 3 (2005): 332-339.

Bisetto, S.P., Melo, C.F., and A.B. Carregaro. Evaluation of sedative and antinocicep-tive effects of dexmedetomidine, midazolam and dexmedetomidine-midazolam in tegus (Salvator merianae). *Vet Anaesth Analg*. Elsevier Ltd; 2018;45(3):320–328.

Blackwell, Emily J., John WS Bradshaw, and Rachel A. Casey. "Fear responses to noises in domestic dogs: Prevalence, risk factors and co-occurrence with other fear related behaviour." *Applied Animal Behaviour Science* 145, no. 1-2 (2013): 15-25.

Blinks, Jonathan, Sienna Taylor, Alison Wills, and V. Tamara Montrose. 2018 "The behavioural effects of olfactory stimulation on dogs at a rescue shelter." *Applied Animal Behaviour Science* 202, (May): 69-76.

Bloomsmith, Mollie A., Marvin L. Jones, Rebecca J. Snyder, Rebecca A. Singer, Wendy A. Gardner, S. C. Liu, and Terry L. Maple. Positive reinforcement training to elicit voluntary movement of two giant pandas throughout their enclosure. *Zoo Biology*: Published in affiliation with the American Zoo and Aquarium Association 22, no. 4 (2003): 323-334.

Bradbury, A.G., and G.J.E. Dickens. Appropriate handling of pet rabbits: a literature review. *Journal of Small Animal Practice*. 7 ed. 2016;57 (10):503–509.

Bradshaw, John W.S., Rachel A. Casey, and Sarah L. Brown. 2012. *The Behaviour of the Domestic Cat*. 2nd ed. Wallingford, Oxfordshire; Boston, MA: CABI.

Bragg, Ryan F., Jennifer S. Bennett, Annelise Cummings, and Jessica M. Quimby. Evaluation of the effects of hospital visit stress on physiologic variables in dogs. *Journal of the American Veterinary Medical Association* 46, no. 2 (2015): 212-215.

Brayley, Clarissa, and V. Tamara Montrose. The effects of audiobooks on the behaviour of dogs at re-homing kennels. *Applied Animal Behaviour Science* 174 (2016): 111-115.

Brondani JT, Luna SPL, and C.R. Padovani. Refinement and initial validation of a multidimensional composite scale for use in assessing acute postoperative pain in cats. *Am J Vet Res* 2011;72(2):174–83.

Brondani, Juliana T., Khursheed R. Mama, Stelio PL Luna, Bonnie D. Wright, Sirirat Niyom, Jennifer Ambrosio, Pamela R. Vogel, and Carlos R. Padovani. Validation of the English version of the UNESP-Botucatu multidimensional composite pain scale for assessing postoperative pain in cats. *BMC Veterinary Research* 9, no. 1 (2013): 143.

Brown SA. *Small Mammal Training in the Veterinary Practice*. Veterinary Clinics of NA: Exotic Pet. Elsevier Inc; 2012;15(3):469–485.

Bubenik, Loretta J., Giselle L. Hosgood, Don R. Waldron, and Lynne A. Snow. Frequency of urinary tract infection in catheterized dogs and comparison of bacterial culture and susceptibility testing results for catheterized and non-catheterized dogs with urinary tract infections. *Journal of the American Veterinary Medical Association* 231, no. 6 (2007): 893-899.

Buisson, C.T. (December 16, 2018) *The Quality of Life Question We Should All Be Asking*. Retrieved from https://helpinghandspethospice.com/the-quality-of-life-question-we-all-should-be-asking/.

Calvo, G., E. Holden, J. Reid, E. M. Scott, A. Firth, A. Bell, S. Robertson, and A. M. Nolan. Development of a behaviour-based measurement tool with defined intervention level for assessing acute pain in cats. *Journal of Small Animal Practice* 55, no. 12 (2014): 622-629.

Carlstead, Kathy, Janine L. Brown, and William Strawn. Behavioral and physiological correlates of stress in laboratory cats. *Applied Animal Behaviour Science* 38, no. 2 (1993): 143-158.

Carney, Hazel. Nursing care – the art of healing. *Journal of Feline Medicine and Surgery* Vol 14, 5 pp 301-302 (2012).

Catbagan, Davina L., Jessica M. Quimby, Khursheed R. Mama, Jessica K. Rychel, and Patrice M. Mich. Comparison of the efficacy and adverse effects of sustained-release buprenorphine hydrochloride following subcutaneous administration and buprenorphine hydrochloride following oral transmucosal administration in cats undergoing ovariohysterectomy. *American journal of veterinary research* 72, no. 4 (2011): 461-466.

Center for Pet Safety. n.d. *"Center for Pet Safety."* Accessed November 24, 2019. https://www.centerforpetsafety.org.

Center, Sharon A., et al. Fulminant hepatic failure associated with oral administration of diazepam in 11 cats. *Journal of the American Veterinary Medical Association* 209.3 (1996): 618-625.

Chamove, Arnold S. Dogs judge books by their covers. *Anthrozoös* 10.1 (1997): 50-52.

Chan MM and G.T. Rico. The "pet effect" in cancer patients - Risks and benefits of human-pet interaction. *Critical Reviews in Oncology / Hematology*. Elsevier; 2019;143:56–61.

Chávez, Gonzalo, Paulina Pardo, María José Ubilla, and María Paz Marín. Effects on behavioural variables of oral versus transdermal buspirone administration in cats displaying urine marking. Journal of Applied Animal Research 44, no. 1 (2016): 454-457.

Chew, D. J., C. A. Buffington, M. S. Kendall, S. P. DiBartola, and B. E. Woodworth. Amitriptyline treatment for severe recurrent idiopathic cystitis in cats. *Journal of the American Veterinary Medical Association* 213, no. 9 (1998): 1282-1286.

Ciribassi, John, Andrew Luescher, Kirby S. Pasloske, Carol Robertson-Plouch, Alan Zimmerman, and Liane Kaloostian-Whittymore. Comparative bioavailability of fluoxetine after transdermal and oral administration to healthy cats. *American Journal of Veterinary Research* 64, no. 8 (2003): 994-998.

Clark-Price, Stuart. Inadvertent perianesthetic hypothermia in small animal patients. North American Veterinary Clinics of North America: *Small Animal Practice* 45, no. 5 (2015): 983-994.

Coile, D. Caroline, Celia H. Pollitz, and James C. Smith. Behavioral determination of critical flicker fusion in dogs. *Physiology & behavior* 45.6 (1989): 1087-1092.

Coleman, Kristine, Lindsay Pranger, Adriane Maier, Susan P. Lambeth, Jaine E. Perlman, Erica Thiele, and Steven J. Schapiro. Training rhesus macaques for venipuncture using positive reinforcement techniques: a comparison with chimpanzees. *Journal of the American Association for Laboratory Animal Science* 47, no. 1 (2008): 37-41.

The Compassion Fatigue Awareness Project. What is Compassion Fatigue? 2017. Retrieved from http://www.compassionfatigue.org/pages/symptoms.html.

Cook EK. Teaching avian patients and caregivers in the examination room. *Veterinary Clinics of North America Exotic Pet*. Elsevier Inc; 2012;15(3):513–522.

Coppola, Crista L., R. Mark Enns, and Temple Grandin. Noise in the animal shelter environment: building design and the effects of daily noise exposure. *Journal of Applied Animal Welfare Science* 9.1 (2006): 1-7.

Coren, Stanley, Emma Trithart (illustrations). How to read your dog's body language, body language basics. *Modern Dog Magazine* (available online https://moderndogmagazine.com/articles/how-read-your-dogs-body-language/415).

Cotman, Carl W., Elizabeth Head, Bruce A. Muggenburg, S. Zicker, and Norton W. Milgram. Brain aging in the canine: a diet enriched in antioxidants reduces cognitive dysfunction. *Neurobiology of Aging* 23, no. 5 (2002): 809-818.

Crouse, Stephanie J., Edward R. Atwill, Maria Lagana, and Katherine A. Houpt. 1995. SoftSurfaces: A factor in feline psychological well-being. *Contemporary Topics Laboratory Animal Science* 34 (6): 94-7.

Crowell-Davis, Sharon L., Lynne M. Seibert, Wailani Sung, Valli Parthasarathy, and Terry M. Curtis. Use of clomipramine, alprazolam, and behavior modification for treatment of storm phobia in dogs. *Journal of the American Veterinary Medical Association* 222, no. 6 (2003): 744-748.

Crowell-Davis, Sharon L., and Sabrina Poggiagliolmi. Understanding behavior: serotonin syndrome. *Compendium* (Yardley, PA) 30, no. 9 (2008): 490.

Csoltova, Erika, et al. Behavioral and physiological reactions in dogs to a veterinary examination: Owner-dog interactions improve canine well-being. *Physiology & Behavior* 177 (2017): 270-281.

Dalla Costa, Emanuela, Michela Minero, Dirk Lebelt, Diana Stucke, Elisabetta Canali, and Matthew C. Leach. Development of the Horse Grimace Scale (HGS) as a pain assessment tool in horses undergoing routine castration. *PLoS one*, 9, no. 3 (2014): e92281.

Davis, A. and Audubon Zoo. Target training and voluntary blood drawing of the Aldabra Tortoise (Geochelone gigantea). In *Proc. AAZK Conf*, pp. 156-164. 2006.

Dawson, L. C., C. E. Dewey, E. A. Stone, M. T. Guerin, and L. Niel. A survey of animal welfare experts and practicing veterinarians to identify and explore key factors thought to influence canine and feline welfare in relation to veterinary care. *Animal Welfare* 25 (2016): 125-134.

Deabold, Kelly A., Wayne S. Schwark, Lisa Wolf, and Joseph J. Wakshlag. Single-dose pharmacokinetics and preliminary safety assessment with use of CBD-Rich Hemp Nutraceutical in healthy dogs and cats. *Animals* 9, no. 10 (2019): 832.

Deckers, Nynke, Catharina A. Ruigrok, Hans Peter Verhoeve, and Nicky Lourens. Comparison of pain response after subcutaneous injection of two maropitant formulations to beagle dogs. *Veterinary Record* open 5, no. 1 (2018): e000262.

Denenberg, Sagi, and Gary M. Landsberg. Effects of dog-appeasing pheromones on anxiety and fear in puppies during training and on long-term socialization. *Journal of the American Veterinary Medical Association* 233, no. 12 (2008): 1874-1882.

DePorter, Theresa L. 2016. "Use of pheromones in feline practice." In *Feline Behavioral Health and Welfare*, edited by Ilona Rodan and Sarah Heath, 235-244. St. Louis, MO: Elsevier.

DePorter, Theresa L., David L. Bledsoe, Alexandra Beck, and Elodie Ollivier. Evaluation of the efficacy of an appeasing pheromone diffuser product vs placebo for management of feline aggression in multi-cat households: a pilot study. *Journal of Feline Medicine and Surgery* 21, no. 4 (2019): 293-305.

Desmond, Tim, and Gail Laule. Use of positive reinforcement training in the management of species for reproduction. *Zoo Biology* 13, no. 5 (1994): 471-477.

Dijkstra, E., Erik Teske, and Victor Szaatmari. 2018. Respiratory rate of clinically healthy cats measured in veterinary consultation rooms. *Physiology & Behavior* 177: 270-281.

Dodman, N. H., R. Donnelly, L. Shuster, P. Mertens, W. Rand, and K. Miczek. Use of fluoxetine to treat dominance aggression in dogs. *Journal of the American Veterinary Medical Association* 209, no. 9 (1996): 1585-1587.

Dodman, Nicholas H., Elinor K. Karlsson, Alice Moon-Fanelli, Marzena Galdzicka, Michele Perloski, Louis Shuster, Kerstin Lindblad-Toh, and Edward I. Ginns. A canine chromosome 7 locus confers compulsive disorder susceptibility. *Molecular Psychiatry* 15, no. 1 (2010): 8.

Döring, Dorothea, Anita Roscher, Fabian Scheipl, Helmut Küchenhoff, and Michael H. Erhard. Fear-related behaviour of dogs in veterinary practice. *The Veterinary Journal* 182, no. 1 (2009): 38-43.

Doss, G.A., Fink, D.M., Sladky, K.K.. and C. Mans. Comparison of subcutaneous dexmedetomidine-midazolam versus alfaxalone-midazolam sedation in leopard geckos *(Eublepharis macularius)*. *Vet Anaesth Analg*. Elsevier Ltd; 2017;44(5):1175–1183.

Dramard, V., L. Kern, J. Hofmans, C. Halsberghe, and C. A. Rème. Clinical efficacy of L-theanine tablets to reduce anxiety-related emotional disorders in cats: A pilot open-label clinical trial. *Journal of Veterinary Behavior: Clinical Applications and Research* 2, no. 3 (2007): 85-86.

Eichstadt, Lauren R., Lorraine A. Corriveau, George E. Moore, Gregory T. Knipp, Bruce R. Cooper, and Wilson E. Gwin. Absorption of transdermal fluoxetine compounded in a lipoderm base compared to oral fluoxetine in client-owned cats. *International Journal of Pharmaceutical Compounding* 21, no. 3 (2017): 242-246.

Ellis, Sarah L.H. and Deborah L. Wells. 2008. The influence of visual stimulation on the behavior of cats housed in a rescue shelter. *Applied Animal Behaviour Science* 113, no. 1, (September): 116-174.

Ellis, Sarah L.H. and Deborah L. Wells. 2010. The influence of olfactory stimulation on the behavior of cats housed in a rescue shelter. *Applied Animal Behaviour Science* 123, no. 1, (February): 56-62.

Ellis, Sarah LH, Ilona Rodan, Hazel C. Carney, Sarah Heath, Irene Rochlitz, Lorinda D. Shearburn, Eliza Sundahl, and Jodi L. Westropp. AAFP and ISFM feline environmental needs guidelines. *Journal of Feline Medicine and Surgery* 15, no. 3 (2013): 219-230.

Ellis, Sarah et al., 2015. The influence of body region, handler familiarity and order of region handled on the domestic cats measured in veterinary consultation rooms. *The Veterinary Journal* 234: 96-101.

Engler, Whitney J. and Melissa J. Bain. 2014. The effect of different types of classical music at a veterinary hospital on the behavior of pets and owner satisfaction. In *Proceedings of the AVSAB/ACVB Annual Congress*, Denver, CO, USA, July 25, 2014. 27.

Epstein, Mark E., Ilona Rodan, Gregg Griffenhagen, Jamie Kadrlik, Michael C. Petty, Sheilah A. Robertson, and Wendy Simpson. 2015 AAHA/AAFP pain management guidelines for dogs and cats. *Journal of Feline Medicine and Surgery* 17, no. 3 (2015): 251-272.

Estellés, M. Gandia, and D. S. Mills. Signs of travel-related problems in dogs and their response to treatment with dog appeasing pheromones. *Veterinary Record* 159, no. 5 (2006): 143-148.

Ewer, R.F. 1973. *The Carnivores* Ithaca, NY: Cornell University Press.

Fagen, Ariel, Narayan Acharya, and Gretchen E. Kaufman. Positive reinforcement training for a trunk wash in Nepal's working elephants: demonstrating alternatives to traditional elephant training techniques. *Journal of Applied Animal Welfare Science* 17, no. 2 (2014): 83-97.

Fear Free Pets Fear Free Practice Certification Supporting Examples April, 2019 https://fearfreepets.com/wp-content/uploads/delightful-downloads/2019/04/Practice-Certification-Supporting-Examples.pdf.

Fisher, P.G. Standards of care in the 21st century: The rabbit. *Journal of Exotic Pet Medicine*. Elsevier Inc; 2010;19(1):22–35.

Flecknell P. Restraint, anaesthesia and treatment of children's pets. *In Practice*. British Medical Journal Publishing Group; 1983;5(3):85–95.

Fonagy, P. and M. Target. Attachment and reflective function: Their role in self-organization. *Development and Psychopathology*. Cambridge University Press; 1997;9(4):679–700.

Fonken, L.K., M.S. Finy, J.C. Walton, Z.M. Weil, J.L. Workman, J. Ross, and RJ Nelson. Influence of light at night on murine anxiety- and depressive-like responses. *Behavioural Brain Research*. 2009; 205(2):349–354.

Foster, J. A. and K.A.M. Neufeld. (2013). Gut–brain axis: how the microbiome influences anxiety and depression. *Trends in Neurosciences*, 36(5), 305-312.

Fox M. 1969. Ontogeny of prey-killing behavior in Canidae. *Behaviour* 35, 259 – 272.

Frank, D. F., H. N. Erb, and K. A. Houpt. Urine spraying in cats: presence of concurrent disease and effects of a pheromone treatment. *Applied Animal Behaviour Science* 61, no. 3 (1999): 263-272.

Gandia-Estelles, Marta and Daniel S. Mills. 2006. Signs of travel-related problems in dogs and their response to treatment with dog-appeasing pheromone. *The Veterinary Record* 159, no. 5, (July): 143-148.

Gaultier, E., L. Bonnafous, L. Bougrat, C. Lafont, and P. Pageat. Comparison of the efficacy of a synthetic dog-appeasing pheromone with clomipramine for the treatment of separation-related disorders in dogs. *Veterinary Record* 156, no. 17 (2005): 533-538.

Gaultier, E., L. Bonnafous, D. Vienet-Legué, C. Falewee, L. Bougrat, C. Lafont-Lecuelle, and P. Pageat. Efficacy of dog-appeasing pheromone in reducing stress associated with social isolation in newly adopted puppies. *Veterinary Record* 163, no. 3 (2008): 73-80.

Gaultier, E. and P. Pageat. Effect of a feline facial pheromone analogue (Feliway®) on manifestations of stress in cats during transport. In *Proceedings of the 32nd Congress of the International Society for Applied Ethology*, Clermont Ferrand, France, pp198. 1998.

Gazit, Irit and Joseph Terkel. 2003. Domination of olfaction over vision in explosives detection by dogs. *Applied Animal Behaviour Science* 82, no. 1 (June): 65-73.

Giammanco, S, M.A. Paderni, and A. Carollo. 1976. The effect of thermic stress on the somatic reaction of rage and on rapid circling turns, in the cat. *Archives of Physiology and Biochemistry* 84, no. 4, (October): 787–799.

Gibson, Jennifer M., Stephanie A. Scavelli, Chester J. Udell and Monique A. R. Udell. 2014. Domestic dogs (Canis lupus familiaris) are sensitive to the 'human' qualities of vocal commands. *Animal Behavior and Cognition* 1, no. 3, (July): 281-295.

Gilbert-Gregory, Shana E., et al. Effects of trazodone on behavioral signs of stress in hospitalized dogs. *Journal of the American Veterinary Medical Association* 249.11 (2016): 1281-1291.

Girualt, C., et al. Dog behaviors in veterinary consultations: Part 1. Effects of the owner's presence or absence. *The Veterinary Journal*. Volume 280 (2022). Available also online at https://doi.org/10.1016/j.tvjl.2022.105788

Gliner, Jeffrey A. Predictable vs. unpredictable shock: preference behavior and stomach ulceration. *Physiology & Behavior* 9, no. 5 (1972): 693-698.

Gourkow, N., and D. Fraser. The effect of housing and handling practices on the welfare, behaviour and selection of domestic cats (*Felis sylvestris catus*) by adopters in an animal shelter. (2006). *Animal Welfare* 15(4).

Gourkow, Nadine, Sara C. Hamon, and Clive JC Phillips. Effect of gentle stroking and vocalization on behaviour, mucosal immunity and upper respiratory disease in anxious shelter cats. *Preventive Veterinary Medicine* 117, no. 1 (2014): 266-275.

Gourkow, Nadine and Clive JC Phillips. Effect of interactions with humans on behaviour, mucosal immunity and upper respiratory disease of shelter cats rated as contented on arrival. *Preventive Veterinary Medicine* 121, no. 3-4 (2015): 288-296.

Gourkow, Nadine and Clive JC Phillips. Effect of cognitive enrichment on behavior, mucosal immunity and upper respiratory disease of shelter cats rated as frustrated on arrival. *Preventive Veterinary Medicine* 131 (2016): 103-110.

Gouveia K, and J.L. Hurst. Reducing mouse anxiety during handling: effect of experience with handling tunnels. *PLoS One.* 2013;8(6):e66401. Published 2013 Jun 20. doi:10.1371/journal.pone.0066401.

Graham, Lynne, Deborah L. Wells, and Peter G. Hepper. "The influence of olfactory stimulation on the behaviour of dogs housed in a rescue shelter." *Applied Animal Behaviour Science* 91.1-2 (2005): 143-153.

Graham, D., D. S. Mills, and G. Bailey. Evaluation of the effectiveness of synthetic DAP (Dog Appeasing Pheromone) in reducing levels of arousal and improving learning in puppy classes. (2007). In *Companion Animal Therapy Study Day.* Birmingham, UK.

Graham J, and D.R. Mader. Chapter 13. "Rabbits. Basic approach to veterinary care." In: *Ferrets, Rabbits and Rodents. Clinical Medicine and Surgery.* Third Edition. Quesenberry KE, Carpenter JW, editors. Elsevier. 2012; 174-182.

Graham, Lynne, Deborah L. Wells and Peter G. Hepper. 2005. The influence of olfactory stimulation on the behavior of dogs housed in a rescue shelter. *Applied Animal Behavior Science* 91, no. 1, (May): 142-153.

Grandner, Michael A., Lauren Hale, Melisa Moore, and Nirav P. Patel. Mortality associated with short sleep duration: the evidence, the possible mechanisms, and the future. *Sleep Medicine Reviews* 14, no. 3 (2010): 191-203.

Grandner, Michael A., Megan R. Sands-Lincoln, Victoria M. Pak, and Sheila N. Garland. Sleep duration, cardiovascular disease, and proinflammatory biomarkers. *Nature and Science of Sleep* 5 (2013): 93.

Griffith, Cerissa A., Elizabeth S. Steigerwald, and CA Tony Buffington. Effects of a synthetic facial pheromone on behavior of cats. *Journal of the American Veterinary Medical Association* 217.8 (2000): 1154-1156.

Grigg, E. K., and M. Piehler. Influence of dog appeasing pheromone (DAP) on dogs housed in a long-term kennelling facility. *Veterinary Record* open 2, no. 1 (2015): e000098.

Gruen, Margaret E., and Barbara L. Sherman. Use of trazodone as an adjunctive agent in the treatment of canine anxiety disorders: 56 cases (1995–2007). *Journal of the American Veterinary Medical Association* 233, no. 12 (2008): 1902-1907.

263

Gruen, Margaret E., et al. Conditioning laboratory cats to handling and transport. *Lab Animal* 42.10 (2013): 385-389.

Gruen, Margaret E., Simon C. Roe, Emily Griffith, Alexandra Hamilton, and Barbara L. Sherman. Use of trazodone to facilitate postsurgical confinement in dogs. *Journal of the American Veterinary Medical Association* 245, no. 3 (2014): 296-301.

Grzybowski, Andrzej, and Konrad Kupidura-Majewski. What is color and how it is perceived? *Clinics in Dermatology* 37.5 (2019): 392-401.

Guillot, M., P. Rialland, M-È. Nadeau, J. R. E. Del Castillo, D. Gauvin, and E. Troncy. Pain induced by a minor medical procedure (bone marrow aspiration) in dogs: comparison of pain scales in a pilot study. *Journal of Veterinary Internal Medicine* 25, no. 5 (2011): 1050-1056.

Gunn-Moore, D. A. and M. E. Cameron A pilot study using synthetic feline facial pheromone for the management of feline idiopathic cystitis. *Journal of Feline Medicine and Surgery* 6, no. 3 (2004): 133-138.

Gut W, L. Crump, J. Zinsstag, J. Hattendorf, and K. Hediger. The effect of human interaction on guinea pig behavior in animal-assisted therapy. *Journal of Veterinary Behavior.* 2018;25:56–64.

Hart, B. L. Behavioral indications for phenothiazine and benzodiazepine tranquilizers in dogs. *Journal of the American Veterinary Medical Association* 186.11 (1985): 1192-1194.

Hart, B. L., R. A. Eckstein, K. L. Powell, and N. H. Dodman. Effectiveness of buspirone on urine spraying and inappropriate urination in cats. *Journal of the American Veterinary Medical Association* 203, no. 2 (1993): 254-258.

Hart, Benjamin L., Kelly D. Cliff, Valarie V. Tynes, and Laurie Bergman. Control of urine marking by use of long-term treatment with fluoxetine or clomipramine in cats. *Journal of the American Veterinary Medical Association* 226, no. 3 (2005): 378-382.

Heffner, Henry E. 1983. Hearing in large and small dogs: Absolute thresholds and size of the tympanic membrane. *Behavioral Neuroscience* 97, no. 2, (April): 310–18.

Heffner, Rickye S. and Henry E. Heffner. 1985. Hearing range of the domestic cat. *Hearing Research* 19, no. 1, (January): 85-88.

Hemsworth, P. H., J. L. Barnett, and C. Hansen. The influence of inconsistent handling by humans on the behaviour, growth and corticosteroids of young pigs. *Applied Animal Behaviour Science* 17, no. 3-4 (1987): 245-252.

Hepper, Peter G. and Deborah L. Wells. 2006. Perinatal olfactory learning in the domestic dog. *Chemical Senses* 31, no. 3, (March): 207-212.

Hernander, Louise. Factors influencing dogs' stress level in the waiting room at a veterinary clinic. *Biology*, 2009.

Herron, Meghan E., and Traci Shreyer. The pet-friendly veterinary practice: a guide for practitioners. *Veterinary Clinics: Small Animal Practice* 44, no. 3 (2014): 451-481.

Herron, Meghan E., Frances S. Shofer, and Ilana R. Reisner. Retrospective evaluation of the effects of diazepam in dogs with anxiety-related behavior problems. *Journal of the American Veterinary Medical Association* 233.9 (2008): 1420-1424.

Hewson, Caroline. Stress in small animal patients: Why it matters and what to do about it. *Irish Veterinary Journal* 61, no. 4 (2008): 249-254.

Hewson, C. J., U. A. Luescher, J. M. Parent, P. D. Conlon, and R. O. Ball. Efficacy of clomipramine in the treatment of canine compulsive disorder. *Journal of the American Veterinary Medical Association* 213, no. 12 (1998): 1760-1766.

Holden, E., G. Calvo, M. Collins, A. Bell, J. Reid, E. M. Scott, and A. M. Nolan. Evaluation of facial expression in acute pain in cats. *Journal of Small Animal Practice* 55, no. 12 (2014): 615-621.

Houpt, Katherine A. 2018. *Domestic Animal Behavior for Veterinarians & Animal Scientists*. 6th ed. Hoboken, NJ: John Wiley & Sons, Inc.

Howard, Christina J., and Alex O. Holcombe. Unexpected changes in direction of motion attract attention. *Attention, Perception, & Psychophysics* 72.8 (2010): 2087-2095.

Howell, Alicea and Monique Feyrecilde. *Cooperative Veterinary Care*. Wiley Blackwell, 2018.

Ibáñez, Miguel, and Bernadette Anzola. Use of fluoxetine, diazepam, and behavior modification as therapy for treatment of anxiety-related disorders in dogs. *Journal of Veterinary Behavior* 4, no. 6 (2009): 223-229.

iCalmPet. n.d. *Bioacoustic Research & Development (BARD) Canine Research Summary*. Accessed December 21, 2019. https://icalmpet.com/wp-content/uploads/BioAcoustic-Research-and-Development-Executive-Summary.pdf.

iCalmPet. n.d. "Research." Accessed December 21, 2019. https://icalmpet.com/about/music/research.

Irimajiri, Mami, Andrew U. Luescher, Genefer Douglass, Carol Robertson-Plouch, Alan Zimmermann, and Rebecca Hozak. Randomized, controlled clinical trial of the efficacy of fluoxetine for treatment of compulsive disorders in dogs. *Journal of the American Veterinary Medical Association* 235, no. 6 (2009): 705-709.

Ivey E and J. Morrisey. *Ferrets: Examination and Preventive Medicine*. Veterinary Clinics of NA: Exotic Pet. W.B. Saunders Company; 1999; 2(2):471–494.

Jane, John A., Bruce Masterton and Irving T. Diamond. 1965. The function of the tectum for attention to auditory stimuli in the cat. *Journal of Comparative Neurology* 125, no. 2, (October): 165–192.

Jones, Deborah. 2018. *Cooperative Care, Seven Steps to Stress-Free Husbandry*. Self published.

Kato, Maki, Kazuki Miyaji, Nobuyo Ohtani, and Mitsuaki Ohta. Effects of prescription diet on dealing with stressful situations and performance of anxiety-related behaviors in privately owned anxious dogs. *Journal of Veterinary Behavior: Clinical Applications and Research* 7, no. 1 (2012): 21-26.

Keating, Stephanie CJ, Aurelie A. Thomas, Paul A. Flecknell, and Matthew C. Leach. Evaluation of EMLA cream for preventing pain during tattooing of rabbits: changes in physiological, behavioural and facial expression responses. *PloS One* 7, no. 9 (2012):e44437.

Kenshalo, Dan R. 1964. The temperature sensitivity of furred skin of cats. *The Journal of Physiology* 172, no. 3 (August):439–448.

Kenshalo, Dan R., Dennis G. Duncan, and Carolyn Weymark. 1967. Thresholds for thermal stimulation of the inner thigh, footpad, and face of cats. *Journal of Comparative and Physiological Psychology* 63, no. 1, (February):133–138.

Keverne EB (1999). The vomeronasal organ. *Science*. 286 (5440): 716–720.

Kim, Young-Mee, Young-Mee Kim, Jong-Kyung Lee, A.M. Abd el-aty, Sung-Hee Hwang, Jae-Hoon Lee, and Sang-Mok Lee. 2010. Efficacy of dog-appeasing pheromone (DAP) for ameliorating separation-related behavioral signs in hospitalized dogs. *Canadian Veterinary Journal* 51, no. 4, (April): 380-384.

King, J. N., B. S. Simpson, K. L. Overall, et al. Treatment of separation anxiety in dogs with clomipramine: results from a prospective, randomized, double-blind, placebo-controlled, parallel-group, multicenter clinical trial. *Applied Animal Behaviour Science* 67, no. 4 (2000): 255-275.

King, Jonathan N., Jean Steffan, Sarah E. Heath, Barbara S. Simpson, Sharon L. Crowell-Davis, Louise JM Harrington, Alain-Bernard Weiss, and Wolfgang Seewald. Determination of the dosage of clomipramine for the treatment of urine spraying in cats. *Journal of the American Veterinary Medical Association* 225, no. 6 (2004): 881-887.

King, L.C. and P.D. Werner. Attachment, social support, and responses following the death of a companion animal. *Omega* (Westport). 2011-2012;64(2):119-41. PubMed PMID: 22375348.

Kirchoff, Nicole S., Monique AR Udell, and Thomas J. Sharpton. The gut microbiome correlates with conspecific aggression in a small population of rescued dogs (*Canis familiaris*). *PeerJ* 7 (2019): e6103.

Klein, B.G. "Thermoregulation". In *Cunningham's Textbook of Veterinary Physiology*. 5th Edition. 559-566. St. Louis: Elsevier, 2012.

Koch, Colleen S. 2015. "A low-stress handling algorithm: Key to happier visits and healthier pets." Accessed online at *dvm360.com*.

Kogan, Lori R., Regina Schoenfeld-Tacher, and Allen A. Simon. 2012. Behavioral effect of auditory stimulation on kenneled dogs. *Journal of Veterinary Behavior* 7, no. 5, (August): 268-275.

Korpivaara, M., K. Laapas, M. Huhtinen, B. Schöning, and K. Overall. Dexmedetomidine oromucosal gel for noise-associated acute anxiety and fear in dogs—a randomised, double-blind, placebo-controlled clinical study. *Veterinary Record* (2017): vetrec-2016.

Kronen, Peter W., John W. Ludders, Hollis N. Erb, Paula F. Moon, Robin D. Gleed, and Sharon Koski. 2006. A synthetic fraction of feline facial pheromones calms but does not reduce struggling in cats before venous catheterization. *Veterinary Anaesthesia and Analgesia* 33, no. 4, (July): 258-265.

Kruger, John M., Tina S. Conway, John B. Kaneene, Ruby L. Perry, Elizabeth Hagenlocker, Andrea Golombek, and Jennifer Stuhler. Randomized controlled trial of the efficacy of short-term amitriptyline administration for treatment of acute, nonobstructive, idiopathic lower urinary tract disease in cats. *Journal of the American Veterinary Medical Association* 222, no. 6 (2003): 749-758.

Kry, K., and R. Casey. The effect of hiding enrichment on stress levels and behaviour of domestic cats (Felis sylvestris catus) in a shelter setting and the implications for adoption potential. *Animal Welfare* 16, no. 3 (2007): 375-383.

Kuhne, F., J. Hößler, and Rainer Struwe, 2014. Behavioral and cardiac responses by dogs to physical human-dog contact. *Journal of Veterinary Behavior* 9 (3);943-97.

KuKanich, Butch. Outpatient oral analgesics in dogs and cats beyond nonsteroidal anti-inflammatory drugs: an evidence-based approach. *Veterinary Clinics: Small Animal Practice* 43, no. 5 (2013): 1109-1125.

Landsberg, Gary. Therapeutic agents for the treatment of cognitive dysfunction syndrome in senior dogs. *Progress in Neuro-Psychopharmacology and Biological Psychiatry* 29, no. 3 (2005): 471-479.

Landsberg, Gary M., Patrick Melese, Barbara L. Sherman, Jacqueline C. Neilson, Alan Zimmerman, and Terrence P. Clarke. Effectiveness of fluoxetine chewable tablets in the treatment of canine separation anxiety. *Journal of Veterinary Behavior* 3, no. 1 (2008): 12-19.

Landsberg, G., W. Hunthausen and L. Ackerman. *Behavior Problems of the Dog and Cat-E-Book*. Elsevier Health Sciences, 2011.

Landsberg G., Hunthausen, W., and Ackerman, L. *Behaviour Problems of the Dog and Cat*, Third Edition.121, St. Louis: Elsevier, 2013.

Landsberg, Gary, Bill Milgram, Isabelle Mougeot, Stephanie Kelly, and Christina de Rivera. Therapeutic effects of an alpha-casozepine and L-tryptophan supplemented diet on fear and anxiety in the cat. *Journal of Feline Medicine and Surgery* 19, no. 6 (2017): 594-602.

Landsberg, Gary, Y. Pan, Isabelle Mougeot, Stephanie Kelly, Hui Xu, Sandeep Bhatnagar, and Norton W. Milgram. Efficacy of a therapeutic diet on dogs with signs of cognitive dysfunction syndrome. In *Proceedings of the 11th International Veterinary Behaviour Meeting*, vol. 45, p. 114. CABI, 2017.

Langford, Dale J., Andrea L. Bailey, Mona Lisa Chanda, Sarah E. Clarke, Tanya E. Drummond, Stephanie Echols, Sarah Glick et al. Coding of facial expressions of pain in the laboratory mouse. *Nature Methods* 7, no. 6 (2010): 447.

Larouche, C.B., H. Beaufrere, C. Mosley, N. M. Nemeth, C. Dutton. Evaluation of the effects of midazolam and flumazenil in the ball python (Python regius). *Journal Zoo Wildlife Medicine.* 2019;50(3):579–11.

Leach, M. C., S. Allweiler, C. Richardson, J. V. Roughan, R. Narbe, P. A. Flecknell. Behavioural effects of ovariohysterectomy and oral administration of meloxicam in laboratory housed rabbits. *Research in Veterinary Science.* Elsevier Ltd; 2009;87(2):336–347.

Levine, Emily D., Daniela Ramos, and Daniel S. Mills. A prospective study of two self-help CD based desensitization and counter-conditioning programmes with the use of Dog Appeasing Pheromone for the treatment of firework fears in dogs (*Canis familiaris*). *Applied Animal Behaviour Science* 105, no. 4 (2007): 311-329.

Levine, E. D., and D. S. Mills. Long-term follow-up of the efficacy of a behavioural treatment programme for dogs with firework fears. *Applied Animal Behaviour Science* (2008): 657-659.

Ley, Jacqueline M. 2016. Feline communication. In *Feline Behavioral Health and Welfare*, edited by Ilona Rodan and Sarah Heath, 24-33. St. Louis, MO: Elsevier.

Lindsay, S. R. *Handbook of Applied Dog Behavior and Training: Volume 1, Adaptation and Learning.* Ames (IA): Blackwell Publishing Professional (2000).

Lindsay, S. R. *Handbook of Applied Dog Behavior and Training, Volume 3, Procedures and Protocols.* Ames (IA): Blackwell Publishing Professional (2005).

Lloyd, Janice. Minimizing stress for patients in the veterinary hospital: Why it is important and what can be done about it. *Veterinary Sciences* 4, no. 2 (2017): 22.

Lockhart, J., Karri Wilson, and Cindy Lanman, 2013. The effects of operant training on blood collection for domestic cats. *Applied Animal Behaviour Science* 143 (2-4: 128-134.

Loop, Michael and Laura Bruce. 1978. Cat color vision: the effect of stimulus size. *Science*, vol 199, pp 1221-2.

Magnus, E. Behaviour of the pet rabbit: what is normal and why do problems develop? In *Practice.* British Medical Journal Publishing Group; 2005;27(10):531–535.

Mans, C., D. S.-M. Guzman, L. L., Lahner, J., Paul-Murphy, and K. K. Sladky. Sedation and physiologic response to manual restraint after intranasal administration of Mida-zolam in Hispaniolan Amazon Parrots (Amazona ventralis). *Journal of Avian Medical Surgery.* 2012;26(3):130–139.

Marino, C. L., et al. White-coat effect on systemic blood pressure in retired racing Greyhounds. *Journal of Veterinary Internal Medicine* 25.4 (2011): 861-865.

Mariti, Chiara, E. Raspanti, M. Zilocchi, B. Carlone, and Angelo Gazzano. The assessment of dog welfare in the waiting room of a veterinary clinic. *Animal Welfare* 24, no. 3 (2015): 299-305.

Mariti, Chiara, Jonathan E. Bowen, Sonia Campa, Gabriele Grebe, Claudio Sighieri, and Angelo Gazzano. Guardians' perceptions of cats' welfare and behavior regarding visiting veterinary clinics. *Journal of Applied Animal Welfare Science* 19, no. 4 (2016): 375-384.

Mariti, Chiara, et al. Effects of petting before a brief separation from the owner on dog behavior and physiology: A pilot study. *Journal of Veterinary Behavior* 27 (2018): 41-46.

Maros, Katalin, Antal Dóka, and Adám Miklosi. Behavioural correlation of heart rate changes in family dogs. *Applied Animal Behaviour Science* 109, no. 2-4 (2008): 329-341.

Mazur, James. *Learning and Behavior: Seventh Edition*. Routledge. Pub., 2016.

McBride, E.A., S. Day, T. McAdie, A, Meredith, J. Barley, J. Hickman, and L. Lawes. (2006) Trancing rabbits: Relaxed hypnosis or a state of fear? In *Proceedings of the VDWE International Congress on Companion Animal Behaviour and Welfare*. Vlaamse Dierenartsenvereniging v.z.w. pp. 135-137.

McCobb, Emily C., Gary J. Patronek, Amy Marder, Julie D. Dinnage, and Michael S. Stone. Assessment of stress levels among cats in four animal shelters. *Journal of the American Veterinary Medical Association* 226, no. 4 (2005): 548-555.

McDonnell, Sue M., Jaime Miller, and Wendy Vaala. Modestly improved compliance and apparent comfort of horses with aversions to mildly aversive routine health care procedures following short-term alpha-casozepine supplementation. *Journal of Equine Veterinary Science* 34, no. 8 (2014): 1016-1020.

McEwen, B.S. Stress and the individual. Mechanisms leading to disease. *Archives Internal Medicine*. 1993; 153(18):2093-101.

McRee, A. E., T. N., Tully, Jr., J. G. Nevarez, H. Beaufrere, M. Ammersbach, S. D. Gaunt, R. G. Fuller, and L. M. Romero. Effect of routine handling and transportation on blood leukocyte concentrations and plasma corticosterone in captive hispaniolan amazon parrots (Amazona ventralis). *J Zoo Wildlife Medicine*. 2018;49(2):396–403.

Mealey, K. L., K. E. Peck, B. S. Bennett, R. K. Sellon, G. R. Swinney, K. Melzer, S. A. Gokhale, and T. M. Krone. Systemic absorption of amitriptyline and buspirone after oral and transdermal administration to healthy cats. *Journal of Veterinary Internal Medicine* 18, no. 1 (2004): 43-46.

Mertens, Petra A., Sheila Torres, and Carl Jessen. The effects of clomipramine hydrochloride in cats with psychogenic alopecia: a prospective study. *Journal of the American Animal Hospital Association* 42, no. 5 (2006): 336-343.

Michelazzi, Manuela, Greta Berteselli, Michela Minero, and Elena Cavallone. Effectiveness of L-theanine and behavioral therapy in the treatment of noise phobias in dogs. *Journal of Veterinary Behavior* 5, no. 1 (2010): 34-35.

Miklosi, Adam. 2007. *Dog Behavior, Evolution, and Cognition*. New York, NY: Oxford University Press.

Milgram, N. W., S. C. Zicker, E. Head, B. A. Muggenburg, H. Murphey, C. J. Ikeda-Douglas, and C. W. Cotman. Dietary enrichment counteracts age-associated cognitive dysfunction in canines. *Neurobiology of Aging* 23, no. 5 (2002): 737-745.

Miller, Paul E. and Christopher J. Murphy. 1995. Vision in dogs. *Journal of the American Veterinary Medical Association* 207, no. 12 (December): 1623-1634.

Miller, Paul E. and Flickering Lights. Vision in animals. What do dogs and cats see. *The 25th Annual Waltham/OSU Symposium. Small Animal Ophthalmology*. 2001.

Mills, D. S. and J. C. White. Long-term follow up of the effect of a pheromone therapy on feline spraying behaviour. *Veterinary Record* 147, no. 26 (2000): 746-747.

Mills, D. S. and C. B. Mills. Evaluation of a novel method for delivering a synthetic analogue of feline facial pheromone to control urine spraying by cats. *Veterinary Record* 149, no. 7 (2001): 197-199.

Mills, D. S., M. Gandia Estelles, P. H. Coleshaw, and C. Shorthouse. Retrospective analysis of the treatment of firework fears in dogs. *Veterinary Record* (2003): 561-562.

Mills, Daniel, Daniela Ramos, Marta Gandia-Estelles, and Claire Hargrave. 2006. A triple blind placebo-controlled investigation into the assessment of the effect of Dog Appeasing Pheromone (DAP) on anxiety related behavior problems of dogs in the veterinary clinic. *Applied Animal Behavior Science* 98, no. 1, (June): 114-126.

Mills, Daniel S. and Jeremy N. Marchant-Forde, eds. *The Encyclopedia of Applied Animal Behaviour and Welfare*. CABI, 2010.

Mills, Daniel, Maya Braem Dube, and Helen Zulch. 2013. *Stress and Pheromonatherapy in Small Animal Clinical Behaviour*. Chichester, West Sussex: Wiley-Blackwell.

S. Mineka, and K. A. Kelly, The relationship between anxiety, lack of control and loss of control. In *Stress, Personal Control, and Health*, edited by Steptoe, A., and Appels, E. (Eds.), 163-191. Oxford: Oxford University Press, 1989.

Mitsui, Shohei, Mariko Yamamoto, Miho Nagasawa, Kazutaka Mogi, Takefumi Kiku-sui, Nobuyo Ohtani, and Mitsuaki Ohta. Urinary oxytocin as a noninvasive biomarker of positive emotion in dogs. *Hormones and Behavior* 60, no. 3 (2011): 239-243.

Moberg, Gary P. "Biological response to stress: implications for animal welfare." In *The Biology of Animal Stress: Basic Principles and Implications for Animal Welfare* (New York: CABI Publishing, 2000), 1-6.

Moffat, Kelly. 2008. *Addressing Canine and Feline Aggression in the Veterinary Clinic*. North American Veterinary Clinics: Small Animal Practice.

Mondo, Elisabetta, Monica Barone, Matteo Soverini, Federica D'Amico, Giovanna Marliani, Massimo Cocchi, Michela Mattioli, Marco Candela, and P. E. Accorsi. Gut microbiome structure and adrenocortical activity in dogs with aggressive and phobic behavioral disorders. *BioRx* iv (2019): 573865.

Moody, Carly M., et al. Can you handle it? Validating negative responses to restrain in cats. *Applied Animal Behavior Science*, 204: 94-100. 2018.

Moon-Fanelli, Alice A., and N. H. Dodman. Description and development of compulsive tail chasing in terriers and response to clomipramine treatment. *Journal of the American Veterinary Medical Association* 212, no. 8 (1998): 1252-1257.

Morgan, Kathleen N. and Chris T. Tromborg. Sources of stress in captivity. *Applied Animal Behaviour Science* 102, no. 3-4 (2007): 262-302.

Mormède, Pierre, Stéphane Andanson, Benoit Aupérin, Bonne Beerda, Daniel Guémené, Jens Malmkvist, Xavier Manteca, et al. Exploration of the hypothalamic–pituitary–adrenal function as a tool to evaluate animal welfare. *Physiology & Behavior* 92, no. 3 (2007): 317-339.

Moura, L. N., M. L. Silva, M. M. F. Garotti, A. L. F. Rodrigues, A. C. Santos, I. F. Ribeiro. Gestural communication in a new world parrot. *Behavioural Processes*. Elsevier B.V; 2014;105:46–48.

Nakabayashi, Miyabi, Ryohei Yamaoka, and Yoshihiro Nakashima. 2012. Do faecal odours enable domestic cats (Felis catus) to distinguish familiarity of the donors? *Journal of Ethology* 30, no. 2, (January): 325–329.

Narishetty, Sunil Thomas, Betsy Galvan, Eileen Coscarelli, Michelle Aleo, Tim Fleck, William Humphrey, and Robert B. McCall. Effect of refrigeration of the antiemetic Cerenia (maropitant) on pain on injection. *Veterinary Therapeutics* 10, no. 3 (2009): 93.

National Research Council. *Nutrient Requirements of Dogs and Cats*. National Academy Press, 2006.

National Research Council. *Guide for the Care and Use of Laboratory Animals*. Washington, DC: National Academy Press, 2013.

Neff, William D. and Joseph E. Hind. 1955. Auditory thresholds of the cat. *The Journal of the Acoustical Society of America* 27, no. 3, (April): 480–483.

Nibblett, Belle Marie, Jennifer K. Ketzis, and Emma K. Grigg. Comparison of stress exhibited by cats examined in a clinic versus a home setting. *Applied Animal Behaviour Science* 173 (2015): 68-75.

Niedfeldt, Rebecca L. and Sheilah A. Robertson. Postanesthetic hyperthermia in cats: a retrospective comparison between hydromorphone and buprenorphine. *Veterinary Anaesthesia and Analgesia* 33, no. 6 (2006): 381-389.

Nielsen, M. K., M. A. Neergaard, A. B. Jensen, et al. Do we need to change our understanding of anticipatory grief in caregivers? *Clinical Psychological Review*. 2016 Mar;44:75-93.

Ogata, Niwako and Yukari Takeuchi. Clinical trial of a feline pheromone analogue for feline urine marking. *Journal of Veterinary Medical Science* 63, no. 2 (2001): 157-161.

Ogata, Niwako, Takefumi Kikusui, Yukari Takeuchi, and Yuji Mori. Objective measurement of fear-associated learning in dogs. *Journal of Veterinary Behavio*r 1, no. 2 (2006): 55-61.

Ogata, Niwako and Nicholas H. Dodman. The use of clonidine in the treatment of fear-based behavior problems in dogs: an open trial. *Journal of Veterinary Behavior: Clinical Applications and Research* 6, no. 2 (2011): 130-137.

Olsson, A. and D. Phalen. Comparison of biochemical stress indicators in juvenile captive estuarine crocodiles (Crocodylus porosus) following physical restraint or chemical restraint by midazolam injection. *J Wildl Dis*. 2013 Jul;49(3):560-7. doi: 10.7589/2012-06-160.

Orlando, Jillian M., Beth C. Case, Andrea E. Thomson, Emily Griffith, and Barbara L. Sherman. Use of oral trazodone for sedation in cats: a pilot study. *Journal of Feline Medicine and Surgery* 18, no. 6 (2016): 476-482.

Osella, M. C., L. Bergamasco, and F. Costa. Use of a synthetic analogue of a dog appeasing pheromone in sheltered dogs after adoption. In *Current Issues and Research in Veterinary Behavioral Medicine*, ed. D. Mills et al., (2005). 270-273.

Overall, Karen L. Medical differentials with potential behavioral manifestations. The Veterinary Clinics of North America. *Small Animal Practice* 33, no. 2 (2003): 213-229.

Overall, Karen. *Manual of Clinical Behavioral Medicine for Dogs and Cats*. Elsevier Health Sciences, 2013.

Pachtinger, G.E. How I treat - feline hepatic lipidosis. *Clinician's Brief*, October 2016, https://files.brief.vet/migration/article/31101/hit_feline-hepatic-lipidosis_0-31101-article.pdf.

Pageat, P. Functions and use of the facial pheromones in the treatment of urine marking in the cat: interest of a structural analogue. In *Proceedings and Abstracts of the XXI Congress of the World Small Animal Veterinary*. Associaiton., pp. 197-198. 1996.

Pageat, P. Usefulness of the F3 synthetic pheromone, Feliway, in preventing behavior problems of cats during holidays. In *Proceedings of the First International Conference on Veterinary Behavioural Medicine.*, pp 231.1997.

Pageat, Patrick and Emmanuel Gaultier. 2003. Current research in canine and feline pheromones. The Veterinary Clinics of North America *Small Animal Practice* 33, no. 2, (March): 187-211.

Palestrini, Clara, Michela Minero, Simona Cannas, Greta Berteselli, Elisabetta Scaglia, Sara Barbieri, Elena Cavallone, Maria Puricelli, Francesco Servida, and Paola Dall'Ara. Efficacy of a diet containing caseinate hydrolysate on signs of stress in dogs. *Journal of Veterinary Behavior: Clinical Applications and Research* 5, no. 6 (2010): 309-317.

Pan, Yuanlong, Brian Larson, Joseph A. Araujo, Winnie Lau, Christina De Rivera, Ruben Santana, Asa Gore, and Norton W. Milgram. Dietary supplementation with medium-chain TAG has long-lasting cognition-enhancing effects in aged dogs. *British Journal of Nutrition* 103, no. 12 (2010): 1746-1754.

Pankratz, Katherine E., et al. Use of single-dose oral gabapentin to attenuate fear responses in cage-trap confined community cats: a double-blind, placebo-controlled field trial. *Journal of Feline Medicine and Surgery* 20.6 (2018): 535-543.

Pantages E and C. Dulac. (2000). A novel family of candidate pheromone receptors in mammals. *Neuron* 28 (3): 835–845.

Part, C. E., J. L. Kiddie, William A. Hayes, D. S. Mills, Rachel F. Neville, D. B. Morton, and L. M. Collins. Physiological, physical and behavioural changes in dogs (Canis familiaris) when kennelled: testing the validity of stress parameters. *Physiology & Behavior* 133 (2014): 260-271.

Pekkin, Anne-Maria, Laura Hänninen, Katriina Tiira, Aija Koskela, Merja Pöytäkangas, Hannes Lohi, and Anna Valros. The effect of a pressure vest on the behaviour, salivary cortisol and urine oxytocin of noise phobic dogs in a controlled test. *Applied Animal Behaviour Science* 185 (2016): 86-94.

Pereira, Joana Soares, Sara Fragoso, Alexandra Beck, Stephane Lavigne, Artur Severo Varejao, and Goncalo da Graca Pereira. 2016. Improving the feline veterinary consultation: the usefulness of Feliway spray in reducing cats' stress. *Journal of Feline Medicine and Surgery* 18, no. 12, (December): 959-964.

Pike, Amy L., Debra F. Horwitz, and Heidi Lobprise. An open-label prospective study of the use of l-theanine (Anxitane) in storm-sensitive client-owned dogs. *Journal of Veterinary Behavior* 10, no. 4 (2015): 324-331.

Pike A, A. Learn, C. S. Nicolas, V. A. Chala. A dental chew containing L-theanine (VEGGIEDENT® Zen) can help relax dogs when given before a stressful event: a double-blinded, cross-over study. *Proceedings of the 6th International Conference on Depression, Anxiety and Stress Management*, London, UK. *Journal Depression Anxiety* no. 8 (2019): 39.

Pineda, S., B. Anzola, A. Olivares, and M. Ibanez. Fluoxetine combined with clorazepate dipotassium and behaviour modification for treatment of anxiety-related disorders in dogs. *The Veterinary Journal* 199, no. 3 (2014): 387-391.

Polgár, Zita, Emily J. Blackwell, and Nicola J. Rooney. Assessing the welfare of kennelled dogs-A review of animal-based measures. *Applied Animal Behaviour Science* (2019).

Poole T. and P. English. *The UFAW Handbook on the Care and Management of Laboratory Animals*. 1999. Blackwell Science Oxford. Volume 1. 1030 p.

Pratsch, Lydia, Natalia Mohr, Rupert Palme, Jennifer Rost, Josef Troxler, and Christine Arhant. Carrier training cats reduces stress on transport to a veterinary practice. *Applied Animal Behaviour Science* 206 (2018): 64-74.

Protopopova, Alexandra. Effects of sheltering on physiology, immune function, behavior, and the welfare of dogs. *Physiology & Behavior* 159 (2016): 95-103.

Pryor, Patricia A., Benjamin L. Hart, Kelly D. Cliff, and Melissa J. Bain. Effects of a selective serotonin reuptake inhibitor on urine spraying behavior in cats. *Journal of the American Veterinary Medical Association* 219, no. 11 (2001): 1557-1561.

Pugh, Cassandra M., Joseph T. Sweeney, Christopher P. Bloch, Justine A. Lee, Justine A. Johnson, and Lynn R. Hovda. Selective serotonin reuptake inhibitor (SSRI) toxicosis in cats: 33 cases (2004–2010). *Journal of Veterinary Emergency and Critical Care* 23, no. 5 (2013): 565-570.

Puttonen, Sampsa, Mikko Härmä, and Christer Hublin. Shift work and cardiovascular disease—pathways from circadian stress to morbidity. *Scandinavian Journal of Work, Environment & Health* (2010): 96-108.

Pypendop, B.H. "Anesthesia and perioperative care." In: *The Cat: Clinical Medicine and Management*, ed. S. E. Little (St. Louis: Elsevier, 2012), 112-127.

Quesenberry, K. E., T. M. Donnelly, and C. Mans Chapter 22. Biology, husbandry and clinical techniques of Guinea pigs and Chinchillas. In: *Ferrets, Rabbits and Rodents. Clinical Medicine and Surgery*. Third Edition. Quesenberry KE, Carpenter JW, editors. Elsevier. 2012; 279-294.

Quesenberry K. E., and C. Orcutt. Chapter 2. Ferrets. Basic approach to veterinary care. In: *Ferrets, Rabbits and Rodents. Clinical Medicine and Surgery*. Third Edition. Quesenberry KE, Carpenter JW, editors. Elsevier. 2012; 13-26.

Quimby, Jessica M., Melissa L. Smith, and Katharine F. Lunn. Evaluation of the effects of hospital visit stress on physiologic parameters in the cat. *Journal of Feline Medicine and Surgery* 13, no. 10 (2011): 733-737.

Quimby, Jessica, and Katharine Lunn. *Mirtazapine as an Appetite Stimulant for Cats*. U.S. Patent Application 13/486,278, filed October 17, 2013.

Ramirez, K. (2013). *Husbandry Training in Zookeeping: An Introduction to the Science and Technology*, eds.: M.D. Irwin, J.B. Stone, and A.M. Cobaugh. University of Chicago Press.

Reck, Julie. *Facing Farewell*. Dogwise Publishing (2012).

Reid, J., A. M. Nolan, J. M. L. Hughes, D. Lascelles, P. Pawson, and E. M. Scott. Development of the short-form Glasgow Composite Measure Pain Scale (CMPS-SF) and derivation of an analgesic intervention score. Animal Welfare. Wheathampsted- 16 (2007): 97.

Reid, J., E. M. Scott, G. Calvo, and A. M. Nolan. Definitive Glasgow acute pain scale for cats: validation and intervention level. *Veterinary Record* 108, no. 18 (2017).

Reid, Pamela J. Adapting to the human world: dogs' responsiveness to our social cues. *Behavioural Processes* 80.3 (2009): 325-333.

Reinhardt V. Comfortable quarters for laboratory animals. *Animal Welfare Institute* 2002. 114 p.

Reisbig, A.M.J., M. Hafen, A. A. Siqueira Drake, D. Girard, and Z. B. Breunig. (2017). Companion Animal Death: A Qualitative Analysis of Relationship Quality, Loss, and Coping. OMEGA - *Journal of Death and Dying*, 75(2), 124–150.

Reisner, Ilana. Dog as a second language. Today's *Veterinary Practice* January/February: 57-59, 79 2013.

Reynolds, Luke, James Beckmann, and Andrea Kurz. Perioperative complications of hypothermia. Best Practice & Research *Clinical Anaesthesiology* 22, no. 4 (2008): 645-657.

Reynolds R.P., W. L. Kinard, J. J. Degraff, N. Leverage, J. N. Norton. Noise in a laboratory animal facility from the human and mouse perspectives. *Journal of the American Association of Lab Animal Science*. 2010 Sep; 49(5): 592–597.

Rigterink, A., G. E. Moore, and N. Ogata. (2018). Pilot study evaluating surface temperature in dogs with or without fear-based aggression. *Journal of Veterinary Behavior*, 28, 11-16.

Robertson, Sheilah A., Susan M. Gogolski, Peter Pascoe, Heidi L. Shafford, Jennifer Sager, and Gregg M. Griffenhagen. AAFP feline anesthesia guidelines. *Journal of Feline Medicine and Surgery* 20, no. 7 (2018): 602-634.

Rochlitz, I., A. L. Podberscek, and D. M. Broom. Welfare of cats in a quarantine cattery. *Veterinary Record* 143, no. 2 (1998): 35-39.

Rochlitz, I. Recommendations for the housing of cats in the home, in catteries and animal shelters, in laboratories and in veterinary surgeries. *Journal of Feline Medicine and Surgery* 1, no. 3 (1999): 181-191.

Rochlitz, Irene. A review of the housing requirements of domestic cats (Felis silvestris catus) kept in the home. *Applied Animal Behaviour Science* 93, no. 1-2 (2005): 97-109.

Rooney, N.J., E. J. Blackwell, S. M. Mullan, R. Saunders, P. E. Baker, J. M. Hill, C. E. Sealey, M. J. Turner and S. D. Held. The current state of welfare, housing and husbandry of the English pet rabbit population. BMC Res Notes. *BioMed Central*; 2014;7(1):1–13.

Rodan, Ilona et al. AAFP and ISFM feline-friendly handling guidelines. *Journal of Feline Medicine and Surgery*. 2011.

Rooney, N. J., C. A. Corinna, and Rachel A. Casey. Minimizing fear and anxiety in working dogs: a review. *Journal of Veterinary Behavior* 16 (2016): 53-64.

Ryan, Linda. *Better Veterinary Visits – Working Towards a Patient-Friendly Practice*. 2018.

Russell, P.A. Fear-evoking stimuli. In *Fear in Animals and Man* (New York: Van Nostrand Reinhold, 1979), 86-124.

Sadegh, A.B. Comparison of intranasal administration of xylazine, diazepam, and midazolam in budgerigars (*Melopsittacus undulatus*): clinical evaluation. *Journal of Zoo Wildlife Medicine*. 2013;44(2):241–244.

Sales, G.D., K. J. Wilson, K. E. Spencer, S. R. Milligan. Environmental ultrasound in laboratories and animal houses: a possible cause for concern in the welfare and use of laboratory animals. *Lab Animals*. 1988;22(4):369-375. doi:10.1258/002367788780746188.

Samara, Emil, Meir Bialer, and Raphael Mechoulam. Pharmacokinetics of cannabidiol in dogs. *Drug metabolism and disposition* 16, no. 3 (1988): 469-472.

Sattar, Syed A., V. Susan Springthorpe, and Michael Rochon. A product based on accelerated and stabilized hydrogen peroxide: evidence for broad-spectrum germicidal activity. *Canadian Journal of Infection Control* 13, no. 4 (1998): 123-130.

Savvas, Ioannis, Dimitrios Raptopoulos, and Timoleon Rallis. A "light meal" three hours preoperatively decreases the incidence of gastro-esophageal reflux in dogs. *Journal of the American Animal Hospital Association* 52, no. 6 (2016): 357-363.

Schaffer, D. P. H., N. L. L. C. de Araújo, A. C. S. Raposo, E. F. M. Filho, J. V. R. Vieira, and A. P. Oriá. Sedative effects of intranasal midazolam administration in wild caught blue-fronted amazon (amazona aestiva) and orange-winged amazon (amazona amazonica) parrots. *Journal of Avian Med Surgery* 2017;31(3):213–218.

Schepers, F., P. Koene, and B. Beerda. (2009) Welfare assessment in pet rabbits. *Animal Welfare* 18, 477–485.

Scherk, Margie A., et al. (2013). 2013 AAFP Feline Vaccination Advisory Panel Report. *Journal of Feline Medicine and Surgery* 14 (9): 785-808.

Schroll, S., J. Dehasses, and R. Palme. "The use of the DAP collar to reduce stress during training of police dogs (*Canis familiaris*): A preliminary study." In *Current Issues and Research in Veterinary Behavioral Medicine*, Purdue Univ Press (2005): 31-34.

Seksel, K. and M.J. Lindeman. Use of clomipramine in the treatment of anxiety-related and obsessive-compulsive disorders in cats. *Australian Veterinary Journal* 76, no. 5 (1998): 317-321.

Seksel, K., and M.J. Lindeman. Use of clomipramine in treatment of obsessive-compulsive disorder, separation anxiety and noise phobia in dogs: a preliminary, clinical study. *Australian Veterinary Journal* 79, no. 4 (2001): 252-256.

Seligman, Martin E.P., Steven F. Maier, and James Geer. "Alleviation of learned helplessness in the dog." In *Origins of Madness*, pp. 401-409. Pergamon, 1979.

Serpell J. Anthropomorphism and anthropomorphic selection—beyond the "cute response." *Social Animals*. Brill; 2003;11(1):83–100.

Sheppard, G. and D.S. Mills. Evaluation of dog-appeasing pheromone as a potential treatment for dogs fearful of fireworks. *Veterinary Record* 152, no. 14 (2003): 432-436.

Shepherd, Kendal. Behavioural medicine as an integral part of veterinary practice. In *BSAVA Manual of Canine and Feline Behavioural Medicine*, pp. 10-23. BSAVA Library, 2009.

Shryock, Jennifer. *Family Paws Parent Education* Website https://www.familypaws.com/kiss-to-dismiss-not-all-licks-are-the-same/.

Simpson, Barbara Sherman. Canine communication. Veterinary Clinics of North America: *Small Animal Practice* 27, no. 3 (1997): 445-464.

Siracusa, Carlo, Xavier Manteca, Rafaela Cuenca, Maria del Mar Alcala, Aurora Alba, Santiago Lavin, and Josep Pastor. 2010. Effect of a synthetic appeasing pheromone on behavioral, neuroendocrine, immune, and acute-phase perioperative stress responses in dogs. *Journal of the American Veterinary Medical Association* 237, no. 6, (September): 673-681.

Snowdon, Charles T., David Teie, and Megan Savage. Cats prefer species-appropriate music. *Applied Animal Behaviour Science* 166 (2015): 106-111.

Sotocinal, Susana G., Robert E. Sorge, Austin Zaloum, Alexander H. Tuttle, Loren J. Martin, Jeffrey S. Wieskopf, Josiane C.S. Mapplebeck, et al. The Rat Grimace Scale: A partially automated method for quantifying pain in the laboratory rat via facial expressions. *Molecular Pain* 7 (2011): 1744-8069.

Steimer, Thierry. The biology of fear-and anxiety-related behaviors. *Dialogues in Clinical Neuroscience* 4, no. 3 (2002): 231.

Steagall, Paulo, V., and Beatriz P. Monteiro. Acute pain in cats: recent advances in clinical assessment. *Journal of Feline Medicine and Surgery* 21, 25–34 (2019).

Stella, Judi L., Linda K. Lord, and C.A. Tony Buffington. Sickness behaviors in response to unusual external events in healthy cats and cats with feline interstitial cystitis. *Journal of the American Veterinary Medical Association* 238, no. 1 (2011): 67-73.

Stella, Judi, Candace Croney, and Tony Buffington. Effects of stressors on the behavior and physiology of domestic cats. *Applied Animal Behaviour Science* 143.2-4 (2013): 157-163.

Stella, Judi, Candace Croney, and Tony Buffington. Environmental factors that affect the behavior and welfare of domestic cats (Felis silvestris catus) housed in cages. *Applied Animal Behaviour Science* 160 (2014): 94-105.

Stella, Judith L. and Candace C. Croney. Environmental aspects of domestic cat care and management: implications for cat welfare. *The Scientific World Journal* (2016).

Stellato, Anastasia, Sarah Jajou, Cate E. Dewey, Tina M. Widowski, and Lee Niel. Effect of a standardized four-week desensitization and counter-conditioning training program on pre-existing veterinary fear in companion dogs. *Animals* 9, no. 10 (2019): 767.

Stemkens-Sevens S., K. van Berkel, I. de Greeuw, B. Snoeijer, and K. Kramer. The use of radiotelemetry to assess the time needed to acclimatize guinea pigs following several hours of ground transport. *Laboratory Animals*. 2009;43(1):78–84.

Stephen, Jacqueline M. and Rebecca A. Ledger. "An audit of behavioral indicators of poor welfare in kenneled dogs in the United Kingdom. *Journal of Applied Animal Welfare Science* 8, no. 2 (2005): 79-95.

Sundman, A.S, E. Van Poucke, A. C. Svennson Holm, A. Faresjo, E. Theodorsson E., P. Jensen, and L. Roth. (June 6, 2019) Long-term stress levels are synchronized in dogs and their owners. Retrieved from https://www.ncbi.nlm.nih.gov/pmc/articles/PMC6554395/.

Swallow, J., D. Anderson, A. C. Buckwell, et al. Guidance on the transport of laboratory animals. *Labratory Animals*. 2005;39(1):1-39. doi:10.1258/0023677052886493.

Takahashi, L.K., B. R. Nakashima, and H. C. Hong. The smell of danger: a behavioral and neural analysis of predator odor-induced fear. *Neuroscience Biobehavioral Review* 2005;29: 1157–67.

Tan, R.H.H., A.J. Dart, and B.A. Dowling. Catheters: a review of the selection, utilization and complications of catheters for peripheral venous access. *Australian Veterinary Journal* 81, no. 3 (2003): 136-139.

Tanaka, Aki, Denae C. Wagner, Philip H. Kass, and Kate F. Hurley. Associations among weight loss, stress, and upper respiratory tract infection in shelter cats. *Journal of the American Veterinary Medical Association* 240, no. 5 (2012): 570-576.

Tasaki, T., M. Kojima, Y. Suzuki, Y. Tatemats, and H. Sasaki. Creating a stable short-term housing environment for rabbits in a cargo van. *Journal of the American Association of Lab Animal Science*. 2019;58(4):456–461.

Taylor, Katy, and Daniel S. Mills. A placebo-controlled study to investigate the effect of Dog Appeasing Pheromone and other environmental and management factors on the reports of disturbance and house soiling during the night in recently adopted puppies (*Canis familiaris*). *Applied Animal Behaviour Science* 105, no. 4 (2007): 358-368.

Tod, Elaine, Donna Brander, and Natalie Waran. Efficacy of dog appeasing pheromone in reducing stress and fear related behaviour in shelter dogs. *Applied Animal Behaviour Science* 93, no. 3-4 (2005): 295-308.

Travain, Tiziano, Elisa Silvia Colombo, Eugenio Heinzl, Danilo Bellucci, Emanuela Prato Previde, and Paola Valsecchi. Hot dogs: thermography in the assessment of stress in dogs (Canis familiaris)—a pilot study. *Journal of Veterinary Behavior* 10, no. 1 (2015): 17-23.

Trudelle-Schwarz McGowan, R. Tapping into those 'gut feelings': impact of BL999 (Bifidobacterium longum) on anxiety in dogs. *ACVB Symposium* 2018.

Tucker, Arthur O. and Sharon S. Tucker. 1988. Catnip and the catnip response. *Economic Botany* 42, no.2, (April): 214–231.

Tynes, Valarie. The physiologic effects of fear. DVM 360, Aug 2014.

Uchino, B.N. Social support and health: A review of physiological processes potentially underlying links to disease outcomes. *Journal of Behavioral Medicine*. 5 ed. Springer US; 2006;29(4):377–387.

Valtolina, Chiara et al. Clinical evaluation of the efficacy and safety of a constant rate infusion of dexmedetomidine for postoperative pain management in dogs. *Veterinary Anaesthesia and Analgesia* 36.4 (2009): 369-383.

Van Haaften, Karen A., et al. Effects of a single pre-appointment dose of gabapentin on signs of stress in cats during transportation and veterinary examination. *Journal of the American Veterinary Medical Association* 251.10 (2017): 1175-1181.

van Zeeland, Y.R.A., S. G. Friedman, and L. Bergman. Chapter 5. Behavior. In: *Current Therapy in Avian Medicine and Surgery*. Edited by Speer BL. Saunders. 2015; 177-251.

Varga, M. *Textbook of Rabbit Medicine*. Elsevier Health Sciences; 2013. 512 p.

Villalobos, Dr. A., (2004) Canine and Feline Geriatric Oncology: Honoring the Human-Animal Bond. Hoboken, NJ: Blackwell Publishing. Retrieved from https://www.aplb.org/resources/quality-of-life_scale.html.

Vinke, C. M., L. M. Godijn, and W. J. R. Van der Leij. "Will a hiding box provide stress reduction for shelter cats?" *Applied Animal Behaviour Science* 160 (2014): 86-93.

Virga, V., Katherine A. Houpt, and J.M. Scarlett. Efficacy of amitriptyline as a pharmacological adjunct to behavioral modification in the management of aggressive behaviors in dogs. *Journal of the American Animal Hospital Association* 37, no. 4 (2001): 325-330.

Vitale, K.R., L. R. Mehrkam, and M. A. R. Udell. Social interaction, food, scent or toys? A formal assessment of domestic pet and shelter cat (*Felis silvestris catus*) preferences. *Behavioral Processes* 2017; 141: 322–328.

Vitale, K.R,. A. C. Behnke, and M. A. R. Udell. Attachment bonds between domestic cats and humans. *Current Biology*. Elsevier; 2019;29(18): R864–R865.

Volk, John O., Karen E. Felsted, James G. Thomas, and Colin W. Siren. Executive summary of the Bayer veterinary care usage study. *Journal of the American Veterinary Medical Association* 238, no. 10 (2011): 1275-1282.

Volk, John O., James G. Thomas, Elizabeth J. Colleran, and Colin W. Siren. Executive summary of phase 3 of the Bayer veterinary care usage study. *Journal of the American Veterinary Medical Association* 244, no. 7 (2014): 799-802.

Von Borell, Eberhard, Jan Langbein, Gérard Després, Sven Hansen, Christine Leterrier, Jeremy Marchant-Forde, Ruth Marchant-Forde, et al. Heart rate variability as a measure of autonomic regulation of cardiac activity for assessing stress and welfare in farm animals—a review. *Physiology & Behavior* 92, no. 3 (2007): 293-316.

Wagner, Denae, Kate Hurley, and Jenny Stavisky. Shelter housing for cats: Practical aspects of design and construction, and adaptation of existing accommodation. *Journal of Feline Medicine and Surgery* 20, no. 7 (2018): 643-652.

Waiblinger, S., C. Menke, J. Korff, and A. Bucher. Effects of different persons on the behaviour and heart rate of dairy cows during a veterinary procedure. *KTBL SCHRIFT* (2001): 54-62.

Wakshlag, Joseph J., Christopher Frye, Lauri Jo Gamble, Jordyn Boesch, Wayne S. Schwark, Holly Brown, Lisa Wolfe, Sabine Mann, and Erin S. Berthelsen. Pharmacokinetics, safety, and clinical efficacy of cannabidiol treatment in osteoarthritic dogs. *Frontiers in Veterinary Science* 5 (2018): 165.

Warwick, Clifford et al. Exotic pet suitability: Understanding some problems and using a labeling system to aid animal welfare, environment, and consumer protection. *Journal of Veterinary Behavior* 26 (2018): 17-26.

Wauben, Ine and Patricia E. Wainwright. The influence of neonatal nutrition on behavioral development: a critical appraisal. *Nutrition Reviews* 57, no. 2 (1999): 35-44.

Wells, Deborah L., Lynne Graham, and Peter G. Hepper. 2002. The influence of auditory stimulation on the behaviour of dogs housed in a rescue shelter. *Animal Welfare* 11, no. 4, (November): 385-393.

Wells, D. L. and P. G. Hepper. The influence of olfactory stimulation on the behavior of dogs housed in a rescue shelter. *Applied Animal Behavioral Science* 2005;91:143–53.

Wells, Deborah L. 2006. Aromatherapy for travel-induced excitement in dogs. *Journal of the American Veterinary Medical Association* 229, no. 6, (September): 964-967.

Westropp, Jodi L., Philip H. Kass, and C. A. T. Buffington. Evaluation of the effects of stress in cats with idiopathic cystitis. *American Journal of Veterinary Research* 67, no. 4 (2006): 731-736.

White, J.C, and D.S. Mills. Efficacy of synthetic feline facial pheromone (F3) analogue (Feliway) for the treatment of chronic non-sexual urine spraying by the domestic cat. *Biology* (1997).

White, Marilyn M., Jacqueline C. Neilson, B. L. Hart and Kelly D. Cliff. Effects of clomipramine hydrochloride on dominance-related aggression in dogs. *Journal of the American Veterinary Medical Association* 215, no. 9 (1999): 1288-1291.

Wilkinson, S.L. Chapter 3. Understanding the human-herp relationship. In: *Mader's Reptile and Amphibian Medicine and Surgery*. Edited by Divers SJ, Stahl SJ. Elsevier. 2019; 11-15.

Yeon, S. The vocal communication of canines. *Journal of Veterinary Behavior Clinical Applications and Research*. 2(4), 2007.

Yin, Sophia A. *Low Stress Handling, Restraint and Behavior Modification of Dogs & Cats*. CattleDog Pub., 2009.

Zoran, Debra L. Pancreatitis in cats: diagnosis and management of a challenging disease. *Journal of the American Animal Hospital Association* 42, no. 1 (2006): 1-9.

Index

About the Contributors

Pat Miller, CBCC-KA, CPDT-KA. Ms. Miller owns and operates Peaceable Paws LLC in Fairplay, MD where she offers group training classes, private behavior consultations, and dog trainer academies. She is a pioneer in the force-free, positive reinforment training movement, Training Editor for *The Whole Dog Journal,* the author of numerous books including *The Power of Positive Dog Training, Do Over Dogs* and *Beware of the Dog,* and also presents seminars worldwide.

Dr. Leslie Sinn, CPDT-KA, DVM, DACVB. Dr. Sinn owns and operates Behavior Solutions LLC in Ashburn VA focusing on helping clients address behavioral problems in all species. She has presented nationally and internationally in person and online as well as written numerous blog posts, articles and chapters on behavior.

Dr. Lynn Honeckman, DVM. Dr. Honeckman founded Veterinary Behavior Solutions, in Orlando, Florida. She is a member of the Fear-Free Advocacy Committee and has earned Elite status. Dr. Honeckman is also the committee chairperson for AVSAB position statements, including the recent Positive Veterinary Care and Humane Training documents. She is dedicated to helping veterinarians and pet guardians understand behavior disorders.

Dr. Deb Bryant, DVM, DACVB. Dr. Bryant operates Veterinary Behavior Serices of Minnesota focusing on dogs, cats and horses.

Dr. Fiia Jokela, DVM, DABVP (canine/feline). Dr. Jokela is the owner of Chicagoland Veterinary Behavior Consultants. She is also a behavior consultant for Chicago's Anti-Cruelty Society and provides post-adoption consultations for PAWS Chicago. Dr. Jokela is a resident with the American College of Veterinary Behaviorists.

Dr. Jessica Hekman, DVM, PhD. Jessica Hekman is a veterinary geneticist who has studied the behavioral genetics of dogs. She is the founder of the Functional Dog Collaborative and teaches at Virginia Tech.

Dr. Andrea Y. Tu, DVM. Dr. Tu is the Medical Director for Behavior Vets NYC and serves as the veterinary consultant for the outreach group PAWS NY. Dr. Tu, who is fluent in Chinese, has lectured nationally and internationally, published numerous research articles in both veterinary and human medicine, and is a contributing author in several books. She has been interviewed by various print and video media, and is working towards becoming a board-certified veterinary behaviorist with the American College of Veterinary Behaviorists.

Dr. Ashley L. Elzerman, DVM, DACVB, ECAWBM (BM). Dr. Elzerman is a board-certified veterinary behaviorist and heads the behavior department at Zoetis, Inc.

Katelin Thomas, CDBC, CPDT-KA. Ms. Thomas is a certified behavior consultant and proud owner of K9 Turbo Training, a force-free training company out of Detroit, MI. Katelin is fear free certified with special interests in cooperative care, consent, community education, and shelter behavior. She is a nationally recognized speaker, trainer, and professional consultant with a passion for empowering and teaching others using science and empathy.

Dr. Ariel Fagen, DVM, DACVB. Dr. Fagen is the chief medical officer at the Veterinary Behavior Center in Boulder, Colorado.

Dr. E'Lise Christensen, DVM, DACVB. Dr. Christensen is Chief Medical Officer at Behavior Vets NYC, one of the largest companies in the country providing veterinary behavior and animal training resources for families and animal behavior professionals. She is an experienced media personality, international speaker, and author.

Jolanta Benal, PMCT2, CPDT_KA, CBCC-KA. Ms. Benal is based in Brooklyn, NY and is the author of *The Dog Trainer's Complete Guide to a Happy, Well-Behaved Pet - (Quick & Dirty Tips)*. Now retired from dog training, in the past she provided an educational and entertaining podcast for dog lovers as well as an online dog training courses for professional dog trainers.

Dr. Amy L. Pike, DVM, DACVB. Dr. Pike is a board-certified veterinary behaviorist and owner of the Animal Behavior Wellness Center with locations in Fairfax and Richmond Virginia. Dr. Pike speaks all over the world about veterinary behavior medicine, has been published in various veterinary journals, has conducted, co-authored and published three scientific research studies, and is a contributing author in numerous clinical textbooks. In addition, she mentors clinical behavior residents at ABWC, the first private practice to be approved by the American College of Veterinary Behaviorists as an institutional residency location.

Dr. Karen van Haaften, DVM, DACVB. Dr. Van Haaften is a board-certified veterinary behaviourist and the Senior Manager of Behaviour and Welfare at the British Columbia SPCA. In her shelter behaviour medicine role, she supports 36 networked shelter with their behaviour caseloads, and she also consults on cruelty investigation cases and provincial animal welfare policy. Her research interests include psychopharmacology, behaviour modification for under-socialized cats, and humane training methods.

Dr. Marion Desmarchelier, DMV, IPSAV, DES, MSc, Diplomate ACZM, DACVB. Dr. Desmarchelier graduated from college in Lyon, France in 2003. She worked in a mixed practice for a year before starting a zoological medicine internship at the University of Montreal in Québec. Then she worked in a referral hospital in France with small animal and exotics for a year before starting a residency program in zoo medicine in Montreal, in collaboration with the Granby Zoo and the Quebec Aquarium. Marion did her master's work in clinical sciences studying pain in a facture model in pigeons. She worked as a professor in zoological medicine at the Atlantic Veterinary College in Prince Edward Island for four years before going back to Québec. Marion became a diplomate of the American College of Veterinary Behaviorists in 2018. Marion is currently an associate professor in Clinical Sciences at the Faculté de Médecine Vétérinaire at the University of Montreal.

Dr. Cherie T. Buisson, DVM, CHPV. Dr. Buisson is a Certified Hospice and Palliative Care Veterinarian with certifications in Low Stress Handling and Restraint and in QPR Suicide Prevention. She is the owner of Helping Hands Pet Hospice & Home Euthanasia Service in Seminole, FL.

Meagan Montmeny, CPDT-KA, MS. Ms. Meagan Montmeny has enjoyed a sixteen-year career in animal welfare. During that time, she developed and implemented a variety of behavioral interventions to ease shelter stress on each pet. Meagan holds certifications in Low-Stress Handling and Restraint, Fear Free, and as a Certified Professional Dog Trainer. In her career, she has worked collaboratively with veterinarians across the country and is grateful for their mentorship and partnership.

www.ingramcontent.com/pod-product-compliance
Lightning Source LLC
Chambersburg PA
CBHW080606270326
41928CB00016B/2943